D1454268

Steve Sturdy

Wellcome Unit for the
History of Medicine
Manchester University
July 1990.

War is Good for Babies and Other Young Children

War is Good for Babies and Other Young Children

A History of the
Infant and Child Welfare Movement
in England
1898–1918

Deborah Dwork

Tavistock Publications
London and New York

First published in 1987 by
Tavistock Publications Ltd
11 New Fetter Lane, London EC4P 4EE

Published in the USA by
Tavistock Publications
in association with Methuen, Inc.
29 West 35th Street, New York, NY 10001

© 1987 Deborah Dwork

Photoset by M C Typeset Limited, Chatham, Kent
Printed in Great Britain at the
University Press, Cambridge

All rights reserved. No part of this book may be printed or reproduced, or
utilized in any form or by any electronic, mechanical or other means, now
known or hereafter invented, including photocopying and recording, or in any
information storage or retrieval system, without permission in writing from the
publishers.

British Library Cataloguing in Publication Data

Dwork, Deborah
  War is good for babies and other young children: a history of the infant and
  child welfare movement in England 1898–1918
  1. Child welfare—England—History—20th century
  I. Title
  362.7′95′0942   HV751.A6

  ISBN 0–422–60660–X

Library of Congress Cataloging-in-Publication Data

Dwork, Deborah.
  War is good for babies and other young children.

  Bibliography: p.
  Includes indexes.
  1. Maternal and infant welfare—Great Britain—History—20th century.
  2. Child welfare—Great Britain—History—20th century. 3. Public welfare
  —Great Britain—History—20th century. I. Title.
  HV700.G7D86   1987   362.7′95′0941   86–14571

  ISBN 0–422–60660–X

Contents

Figures

Tables

Plates

Acknowledgements

One of the pleasures of finishing this study is that it provides the opportunity to thank the many people who have helped me. I am extremely grateful to William Bynum for his kind but incisive criticism, pithy remarks, and general moral and intellectual support. The members of the Wellcome Institute community have graciously facilitated and assisted this work, and I am appreciative of their individual and collective efforts. From the Wellcome Trust I have received financial support which extended beyond anyone's expectations, and for this I am truly grateful. I also wish to extend thanks to Christine Alexander and Janet Rose whose stunningly efficient typing and invariably pleasant response were most welcome. My most special thanks go to three people. Robert Jan van Pelt read and criticized this work page by page, shared the solitude of research and writing, and aided and abetted me in the task I had set myself. Ken Marek did not read a word but, as Barbara Rosenkrantz has said, 'any woman who has the support from her family which enables her to take on serious study is fortunate indeed', and Ken approved, sustained, and believed. Finally, this work is dedicated to George Rosen who first introduced the history of medicine to me and introduced me to the history of medicine.

For permission to reproduce copyright material, the author and publisher would like to thank:

The Wellcome Institute Library, London for *Plates 1, 2, 3, 4, 5, 6, 7, 8, 9, 13*, and *Figure 6*.
The Greater London Photographic Library for *Plates 10, 11, and 12*.

Part One
The Problems Perceived

I

Infant mortality
and the future of the race

Queen Victoria's Diamond Jubilee took place during the brilliant summer of 1897. The leaders and representatives of all the nations subject to the British crown had assembled in London to pay homage to their frail and ageing Queen. Their number and diversity were a visible symbol of her vast and great Empire. It was a magnificent display of Imperial splendour, strength, and unity.

In the photographs and films which record the Jubilee celebrations, however, one can see that these leaders and representatives, and above all the Queen herself, had grown old. Reflection upon past achievements led to the contemplation of new possibilities. These old people had made history, it was now up to the young to create the future. That future, as perceived by those then in power, needed large numbers of healthy Britons to continue to administer, soldier, and settle the vast Dominions. And here there was reason for concern. The annual reports and summaries of the Registrar-General indicated that while the general mortality rate was decreasing, the infant mortality rate was increasing. To make matters worse, the birth rate was also declining. This was clearly of concern to politicians, physicians, and the public. The rhetoric of both the contemporary popular and professional press emphasized the national importance of these trends. The graphic representation of the annually diminishing net population gains was an omen of inevitable Imperial decline.

The office of the Registrar-General of England was established in 1836, and registration of births and deaths was begun on 1 July 1837. Although registration of deaths was compulsory from that time, it was the Births and Deaths Registration Act of 1874 which made it mandatory to report a birth within forty-two days.* By the turn of the

* Registration of stillbirths was not compulsory for another forty years. From 1

twentieth century failure to register* was negligible,[1] and the data thus collected made precise calculations of vital statistics possible. Between 1876, when the first returns under the compulsory law were collected, and 1897, the year of the Diamond Jubilee, the crude birth rate per 1,000 population dropped from 35.5 to 30.5, a decrease of 14.1 per cent,[2] (*Figure 1*). Although the birth rate in other European countries showed a similar decline, this was little cause for solace given contemporary notions of imperial responsibility, and given the fact that, except for France, the percentage decrease in England and Wales was the largest.[3] *Figure 2* illustrates the declining birth rates of several European nations, and the relative place held by England and Wales.

Figure 1 Crude birth rate per 1,000 population in England and Wales, 1876–1897

(*Source*: Arthur Newsholme (1899) *The Elements of Vital Statistics*, 3rd edn, p. 78.)

During the same period, 1876 to 1897, the general mortality rate decreased while the infant mortality rate actually showed a slight increase. In 1876 the death rate per 1,000 population was 21.0, by 1897 this had dropped to 17.4, or a net reduction of 17.1 per cent.[4] The

---

September 1915 all stillbirths occurring after twenty-eight weeks of pregnancy were made compulsorily notifiable. At that time it was estimated that stillbirths amounted to 3 per cent of total live births (G.B., P.P., 45th Annual Report of the LGB, *Supplement* containing a Report on Child Mortality, Cd 8496, 1916, p. 7).

* Prior to that, failure to register was estimated at approximately 5 per cent (Arthur Newsholme, *The Elements of Vital Statistics*, London, Swan Sonnenschein, 1899, p. 73.

Figure 2 Crude birth rate per 1,000 population in Austria-Hungary, Germany, England and Wales, and France, 1876–1897

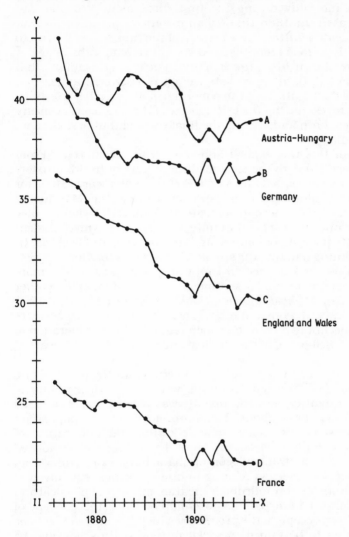

(*Source*: Arthur Newsholme (1899) *The Elements of Vital Statistics*, 3rd edn, p. 78.)

infant mortality rate, by contrast, was 146 per 1,000 live births in 1876 and rose to 156 twenty-one years later. This was an increase of 6.8 per cent.[5] It was recognized, as Arthur Newsholme (then Medical Officer of Health (MOH) for Brighton) stressed in an article on the statistical study of infant mortality from a public health standpoint, 'that *this stationary infantile mortality has been associated with a great decline in the general death-rate of the community*'.[6] Even more startling was the revelation that mortality during the first three months of life had definitely increased. In 1888 the Registrar-General began to publish data on infant deaths during three periods of the first year of life: up to three months, three to six months, and six to twelve months of age.*[7] The returns are shown in *Figure 3*. They indicate, for example, that between 1888 and 1901 there was an average 6.8 per cent increase in infant mortality during the first three months of life. In other words, in terms of percentages, during the last quarter of the nineteenth century fewer babies were born and, during the final years of that period, more of those born, died.

Concern about this was explicit and came from all quarters. From Whitehall to Fleet Street to the local medical officers of health, anxiety and uneasiness were expressed. As Dr Frederick McCleary (MOH for Battersea) wrote, alluding to the speciousness of the Malthusian position in the face of the need to populate the Empire, 'England is now regarded as the nucleus of a great Empire, with colonies which, though vast in extent are poor in population, and the fact must be faced that in view of our declining natality, the stream of emigrants that formerly left our shores cannot be expected to continue.'[8] This was only a more grandiloquent version of similar sentiments expressed in, among other places, the *British Medical Journal* (*BMJ*). An editorial of May 1901 noted simply, but with consternation, 'There has been for some years past a steadily declining birth-rate, which requires the consideration of all who have the well-being of the country and of the empire at heart.'[9]

At the turn of the century there was concern about the physical and mental condition of future generations as well as about their numbers. Not only was quantity needed, quality was wanted as well. Late nineteenth-century ideas about the improvement of the population stemmed from scientific discussions following the publication of Charles Darwin's *Origin of Species* in 1859. The theory of evolution led to questions about the transmission of characteristics or traits from one generation to another. As relating to human beings, this involved the incredibly complex conundrum of the transmission of physical and intellectual qualities from parents to children. Once the concept of evolution had been accepted, the process by which it occurred had to be understood so as to be tamed to social purposes; thus it would be possible to control the quality of progeny.

Biological arguments were reflected in, and provided a structure for, sociological models, reformer programmes, and political platforms.

---

* No explanation for this innovation was given. The *Annual Report* merely stated: 'It will be noticed that in the Report the deaths of infants in the first year of life have for the first time been sub-divided and shown for shorter sub-periods' (G.B., Registrar-General's Office, 51st *Annual Report*, 1888, C. 5846, London, HMSO, 1889, p.ix).

Figure 3 Age distribution of infant mortality per 1,000 registered births, England and Wales, 1888–1920

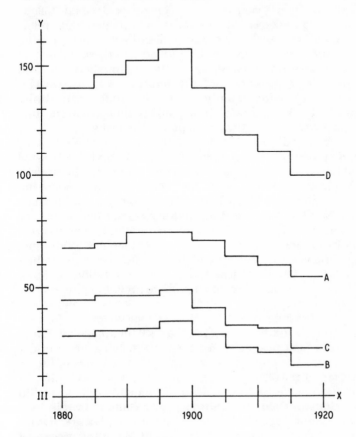

Legend
A = Infants 0–3   months
B = Infants 3–6   months
C = Infants 6–12 months
D = Infants 0–12 months

(*Source*: Janet M. Campbell (1927) The Protection of Motherhood. *Reports on Public Health and Medical Subjects*, no. 48, p. 7.)

Social Darwinists, environmentalist reformers, and the Fabian-Liberal Imperialists used the theory of evolution as a paradigm. English social Darwinism, as espoused by Herbert Spencer,[10] borrowed much from J.B. Lamarck's (1744–1829) theory of the heredity of acquired traits. Those most able to adapt to their environment would survive and prosper, while those less able would falter and die. The elimination of the unfit would be achieved by *laissez-faire* politics; political inaction

7

would allow the proper performance of natural laws. According to Spencer, inevitable progress as a result of constant improvement of the species, passed on from generation to generation, would follow. Lamarckianism also influenced the so-called 'environmentalist' reformers, who adapted the biologist's ideas about the effect of the environment on the development of the individual. These reformers believed that the poor physical condition of the urban labouring class was directly due to the conditions under which they lived – the urban slum. Amelioration of slum conditions would result in healthier individuals who would then pass on these gains to their children; thus future generations were reached through present reforms.

The theory of heredity proposed by August Weismann (1834–1914) in the late 1880s disputed Lamarck's doctrine.[11] Weismann hypothesized that the germ cells (idioplasm) are insulated from the body cells (trophoplasm). Consequently, conditions of life or environmental factors which may indeed affect the body cannot change the germ cells. Heredity is therefore not influenced by environmental exacerbation or amelioration. Weismann believed that people cannot purposively direct mutations and variations by creating appropriate external conditions. Such natural phenomena were, he thought, fortuitous and unpredictable. Mendel's (1822–84) botanical breeding investigations (1865), rediscovered in 1899, were quickly understood to provide a possible key for planned propagation.

These scientific developments[12] provided people such as Francis Galton (1822–1911), Karl Pearson (1857–1936), and Arnold White (1848–1925) with a biological basis for their 'study of agencies under social control that may improve or impair the racial qualities of future generations either physically or mentally'.[13] This was, according to Galton, the definition of 'eugenics', a word he coined and first used in Inquiries into Human Faculty (1883). Francis Galton, by his own account, was profoundly influenced by his first cousin Charles Darwin's Origin of Species.[14] Galton was interested in controlling the process of selection in order to improve the human breed. To do so he had to develop a way of quantifying variations of evolutionary change so as to measure the effects of his principles in action. He devised a system of applying statistical methods and techniques to biological phenomena, thus reducing observations to quantitative terms admitting direct comparison. To control racial progress, Galton developed the concepts of positive eugenics, encouragement of reproduction by 'desirable' couples, and negative eugenics, discouragement of reproduction by the 'undesirables'.[15] Karl Pearson, Professor of Applied Mathematics and Mechanics at University College, London, from 1884, was Galton's colleague, collaborator and, later, biographer. Pearson's interests were much the same: he played a leading role in creating the new science of biometrics and, from his analyses, he developed a similar philosophy of the role and function of eugenics.[16] For both Galton and Pearson, and in contrast to the environmentalist reformers, racial progress was entirely due to nature, not nurture. Pearson was only peripherally interested in the *number* of progeny: his concern was primarily the quality of the coming generation. 'Society', he asserted, 'will have in some fashion to interfere and to restrict the anti-social in the matter of child-bearing.'[17] 'Anti-social' for Pearson meant 'the propagators of inefficient and unnecessary human beings.'[18]

Pearson's call for 'efficiency' was not unique; indeed, eugenics itself developed within a particular social, economic, and political framework which revolved around the concept of efficiency. The 'quest' for national efficiency, as the historian G.R. Searle has called it, began in the 1880s,[19] primarily as a response to fears about the decline of Britain as a military and commercial power. The progress of Germany from undeveloped division to modernized unification was a major catalyst in arousing anxiety about the erosion of Britain's position as a great power. Bismarck's mergence of Germany (1866–71), and her subsequent military and industrial growth and colonial expansion, were factors with which British politicians had to reckon.

Military doubts were not limited to a fear of German competition alone. Between 1875 and 1885 the European states, one after another, adopted conscription, while Britain relied on a small volunteer army. In *The Present Position of European Politics* (1887), Sir Charles Dilke, then one of the promising younger leaders of the Liberal Party, analysed the strength of Britain's forces in the field in comparison with the other European nations. According to Dilke, Britain did not even maintain a second-rate standard; the British, he believed, 'could place in the field in Europe a force about equal to that of Servia or Belgium, this is, a force far inferior in numbers to the Roumanian army, and while certainly superior to the Servians in efficiency, not certainly superior to the Roumanians'.[20] Similarly, the Dual Alliance between France and Russia emphasized the potential weakness of Britain's traditional strength: her naval power. As R.C.K. Ensor has explained in *England, 1870–1914*, Lord Salisbury, then Prime Minister and Foreign Secretary

'regarded France and Russia as the two aggressive Powers. France had since 1879 pursued a policy of violent and unscrupulous expansion overseas; since 1882 she had everywhere edged her knife against England; during 1887–9 she underwent the strange fever of Chauvinism evoked by General Boulanger. Russia's restless ambitions had been broadcast by Penjdeh at the beginning of 1885 and by her threats to Sofia at the end of it.'[21]

The partnership of Britain's two most formidable naval competitors was therefore seen as all the more threatening to the Empire.

G.R. Searle has correlated the weakening of Britain's sea power with the deterioration of her economic position by noting that the 'relative decline of the British Navy was one of the many indications that Britain had lost her old monopolistic position as an industrial state'.[22] This loss was another factor in the call for 'national efficiency' at the close of the nineteenth century. Contemporary anxiety about the competence of British industry to maintain its position in the world market was openly expressed. The highly active and influential biologist T.H. Huxley (1825–95) used a Darwinist superstructure (reflected in the title, 'The Struggle for Existence: A Programme'), to outline a 'programme of industrial development'. He wrote of fighting 'the battle of competition', and winning 'the race of industries'. Huxley elucidated the dilemma in which the country found itself with regard to the rest of Europe: 'we are in reality engaged in an internecine struggle for existence with our . . . neighbours.' In order to 'hold our own in the war of industry', 'our goods should be preferred to those of our rivals . . . our customers must find them better at the price.' This could be accomplished, 'safe industrial development' could be achieved, with 'a stable society made up of healthy, vigorous, instructed [i.e. efficient] people'[23] and an enlarged and enriched educational system, focusing particularly on technical instruction.

The preoccupation with Britain's position in the world production tables was based on fact. Germany was indeed becoming a formidable industrial competitor, and Britain was failing to develop, particularly in the new science-based industries.[24] As production in France, Germany, Italy, and the United States increased, the importance of Britain as a commercial power declined. In 1870 Britain's international trade exceeded that of the combined total of the first three countries named; by 1900 her supremacy was lost for ever.[25] The Liberal Imperialists, or the 'party of national efficiency',[26] a faction of the Liberal Party led by Lord Rosebery, were very well aware of this. The solution for many contemporary observers, including the Liberal Imperialists and, as we have seen, as proposed by Huxley, lay in an efficient industrial population, an efficient educational system, and in the maintenance and preservation of the Empire, Britain's natural, and captive, market.

Given these contemporary perceptions of Britain's (slipping) place in the world, it is not surprising that the call for national efficiency and for support of the Empire was heard by many. The Liberal Imperialists' version of Liberalism included a devotion to the Empire and a concomitant domestic reform policy, influenced by the Fabian leadership, and having as its goal the supremacy of Britain achieved by the encouragement of national efficiency through improved housing and education, and through temperance reform.[27] The Fabians, like the Liberal Imperialists and the Eugenists, perceived the problems of Britain within the context of 'the struggle for existence between nations'.[28] As socialists, the Fabians were dedicated to 'the emancipation of Land and Industrial Capital from individual and class ownership, and the vesting of them in the community for the general benefit',[29] but the Fabian concept of collectivism was designed to serve the whole (British) nation, not the (international) working class. In the Fabian Tract no. 69, *The Difficulties of Individualism*, Sidney Webb analysed the primary problem of individualism and the virtues of socialism: 'Perhaps the most serious difficulty presented by the present concentration of energy upon personal gain is its effect upon the position of the community in the race struggle.' According to Webb, 'This "difficulty" of Individualism can be met . . . only by the application of . . . Socialist principles.'[30]

The solutions of the Eugenists, the Liberal Imperialists, and the Fabians were radically different from each other, but they had a shared objective: the improvement of the quality of the race. Their common goal arose from a common fear: the trepidation that, due to physical and moral ill-health, racial inferiority, inadequacy, and deficiency, Britain would fail, or be found wanting, in the struggle for national existence. It seemed as if their fears came true all too soon.

The reverses suffered by the British army during the Boer War (1889–1902) crystallized and emphasized the, until then, relatively latent fears of national inefficiency and race degeneration. The Imperial splendour of the Diamond Jubilee seemed as nought through the gloom of Black Week. The brilliant summer had dissolved in the bleak December. The campaign in South Africa suggested that the army, which excelled at ceremonial displays, was ineffective as an instrument of Imperialist policy. While the news from South Africa of military failures reflected the incompetence, amateurishness, and deficient education of the officers, the news at home of eager but unfit recruits reflected the physical debility and ill-health of the would-be soldiers. If the graph of a dropping birth rate was perceived as an omen of an expected (future) Imperial decline, the recruitment statistics were a statement of immediate national poverty. This was a problem of the here and now, and reaction to the statistics reverberated throughout the country. Shortly after the war, at the height of the national deterioration discussions, even the *BMJ*, which was generally sceptical of the alarmist announcements declared:

'Now, more than at any other time in the history of the British people, do we require stalwart sons to people the colonies and to uphold the prestige of the nation, and we trust that the searching inquiry* which the Duke of Devonshire's speech seems to foreshadow if it does not dispel the fears engendered by the memorandum of the Director-General [sic Inspector-General] may, at any rate, be a means of arresting the physical decline of the nation.'[31]

The following year, Aimée Watt Smyth's influential book *Physical*

* On 2 September 1903, six weeks after the article was published, the Inter-Departmental Committee on Physical Deterioration was appointed.

11

Deterioration: Its Causes and the Cure, was published. Smyth prefaced her book with the explanation, 'In the following pages I have brought together the main facts concerning the causes of physical deterioration . . . to which recent recruiting statistics have called public attention.'[32] She continued with a discussion of the 'facts with regard to recruiting':

> 'So self-satisfied were we, that nothing short of a great national peril could have saved us from drowning in that river of Lethe in which we were plunged. The facts which came to light during the South African War revealed to us our true position, and the public which had rejoiced vicariously in the triumphs of heroes of the football field and the cycle track, were dismayed to learn that of those who wished to serve their country in her day of trial, a startling number were found physically unfit to carry a rifle, and that even of those who passed the recruiting officer a large proportion were deficient in the physical stamina and the moral qualities which go to make a soldier.'[33]

The number of articles on the subject was so overwhelming that, by 1905, Arthur Newsholme remarked in exasperation, 'The statement that our national physique is degenerating has been so frequently made and so vigorously repeated that if one doubts this fundamental point it is against the weight of public statements made in nearly every journal with confidence and assurance.'[34]

Arnold White, a journalist with jingoist and racist predilections and eugenic interests, may have been the first to write incendiary, alarmist reports focusing on the recruitment statistics. In his article in *The Weekly Sun* of 28 July 1900, White emphasized a fact which he and others reiterated endlessly thereafter. In Manchester, between October 1899 and July 1900, three out of every five men who had offered to enlist had been rejected as physically unfit.[35] White expanded on, and extrapolated from this in his diatribe, *Efficiency and Empire*, which was published in 1901. In the introduction White posed the question, 'In South Africa we have a lesson. Shall we profit by it sufficiently to reconsider our ways?' His thesis was that 'Our species is being propagated and continued increasingly from undersized, street-bred people.' It was within this context that he subsequently interpreted the recruitment rejection figures; for White the problem was not poverty and its related hardships, but the reproduction of and by the unfit.

The facts, according to White, were clear and unequivocal. In 1898, the medical department of the army inspected 66,501 recruits and 23,287 were rejected. However, the situation was worse than these figures indicated, as out of every one hundred soldiers in India (in other words, men who had passed the necessary medical examinations and basic training course), sixty-seven were found to have contracted one or another contagious disease; in short, they were constitutionally prone to illness.[36] The Manchester figures were even more startling and consequently that much more ominous.

'In the Manchester district 11,000 men offered themselves for war service between the outbreak of hostilities in October 1899 and July 1900. Of this number 8,000 were found to be physically unfit to carry a rifle and stand the fatigues of discipline. Of the 3,000 who were accepted only 1,200 attained the moderate standard of muscular power and chest measurement required by the military authorities. In other words two out of every three men willing to bear arms in the Manchester district are virtually invalids.'[37]

Furthermore, there was no reason to believe that the townspeople of Lancashire were physically inferior to those in other cities in the United Kingdom. 'On the contrary, the population of London includes a larger proportion of incapables per thousand than the population of Manchester or Liverpool.' Certain conditions of town life, such as bad drink, improper food, contaminated air, and overcrowding led to a deterioration of health, but White's solution was not the amelioration of these complaints. Since 'Britain's population is replenished not wholly but increasingly from its least desirable specimens' (unlike in Germany, France, Russia, and the United States), the solution was 'to awake the nation to its own peril'[38] and prevent this class from endangering the Empire by precluding their procreation. Within this frame of reference, the decline of the birth rate was, obviously, not a misfortune. For White, the decline in the French birth rate was a healthy phenomenon, and the goal in Britain was to replicate that among the urban working class while increasing the number of births in the suburban middle and professional classes.

The Eugenist Karl Pearson naturally enough responded to the Boer War news in a similar fashion to Arnold White. Although less vicious than the vitriolic White, Pearson shared the journalist's alarm. In an address delivered to the Literary and Philosophical Society of Newcastle in November 1900, Pearson explained that the South African conflict betokened more than an 'immediate national danger'. For him it was simply one aspect of 'the struggle for existence among nations', and the British losses to the Boers were an ominous indication of a possible future trend. The issue facing the nation was, for Pearson as for White, 'the all-important question of parentage'. The problem was that it was 'the feckless and improvident who have the largest families' while 'the professional classes, the trading classes, the substantial and provident working classes – shortly, the capable elements of the community with a certain standard of life – have been marrying late, and have been having small families.' In Pearson's judgement 'this is at the expense of the nation's future . . . we cannot recruit the nation from its inferior stocks without deteriorating our national character.'[39]

While Eugenists like Karl Pearson and Francis Galton[40] exploited the mood of the moment to popularize their cause, the Fabians took the opportunity to present a programme of domestic policy for Rosebery's

Liberal Imperialists. Although both groups agreed on the necessity for increased national effiency, the means by which this was to be achieved differed radically. The Eugenists pursued a positive parentage programme, the Fabians comprehensive domestic reform. In 'Lord Rosebery's Escape from Houndsditch',* which appeared in the September 1901 issue of *The Nineteenth Century*, Sidney Webb outlined the action the national efficiency party should take to ameliorate social conditions. What was required, Webb said, was a '"National Minimum"' standard of life below which no employee in 'any trade in any part of the kingdom shall be allowed to descend'. This standard, as Webb envisioned it, included an improved educational system for an intellectually healthy race. To ensure a physically healthy race, pure water supplies, proper drainage systems, healthy housing, and municipal services such as paving, street-cleaning, and hospital accommodation were needed. In short, 'to it [the National Minimum] is committed the great trust of seeing that no single family in the land is denied the indispensable conditions of healthy life.' That such a standard had not yet been achieved was proved by the fact that there were 'not fewer than eight millions of persons, one-fifth of the whole population, existing under conditions represented by a family income of less than a pound a week, and constituting not merely a disgrace, but a positive danger to our civilization'.[41]

B. Seebohm Rowntree's investigations, begun in 1899 and published in 1901, confirmed this diagnosis. One of the earliest of a growing body of social surveys, Rowntree's remarkable book *Poverty: A Study of Town Life* set many precedents. In this systematic enquiry into the living and working conditions of the York working class, an objective definition of poverty was set for the first time, based on the income required 'to obtain the minimum necessaries for the maintenance of merely physical efficiency'.[42] Food, rent and rates, and sundries such as clothing, light, fuel, and soap were included. Rowntree's food standard was based on his study of the recent nutritional researches of Atwater, Dunlop, and Paton which correlated specific quantities of foodstuffs with physical health; his resultant dietary was 'even less generous than that allowed to able-bodied paupers in the York Workhouse'.[43] The rents actually paid and the lowest prices possibly obtainable for sundries were used in the household budget calculations. Employing a team of

* Houndsditch was the centre of the tailoring trade. In the first few paragraphs Webb elucidated the metaphor, explaining that 'Mr Gladstone [spent] the last twenty years of his life . . . "patching up old clothes" [and] Sir Henry Campbell-Bannerman pieces together the Gladstonian rags and remnants, with Sir William Harcourt holding the scissors and Mr John Morley the thread. Mr Asquith and Sir Edward Grey are sufficiently up to date resolutely to refuse even to try on the repatched garment, . . . Lord Rosebery is the only person who has turned his back on Houndsditch and called for a complete new outfit' (Sidney Webb, 'Lord Rosebery's Escape from Houndsditch', *The Nineteenth Century*, September 1901, p. 366).

investigators to canvas each of 11,560 families living in 388 streets (and comprising a population of 46,754 or almost exactly two-thirds of the city's inhabitants), Rowntree collected information as to occupation, wages, housing conditions, number of inhabitants, and assessments of social conditions.[44] Rowntree estimated that approximately 28 per cent of the total population of the city was living in poverty with incomes of less than 30s per week.[45] This demarcation of £1 10s was based, he emphasized repeatedly, on the proviso that 'no allowance is made for any expenditure other than that absolutely required for the maintenance of merely physical efficiency.' This meant, Rowntree hastened to add, not a single penny spent for a railway ticket or bus fare, no newspapers purchased or letters posted, and no charitable contributions, insurance policies, or savings plans were possible.[46]

Rowntree directly correlated poor health and stunted stature with the living conditions which arose out of penury. That over a quarter of the population lived in such impecunious circumstances, ill-housed, ill-clothed, ill-fed, that physical efficiency was *not* maintained, was reflected in the recruitment statistics. The medical examination of 3,600 recruits who applied for enlistment at York, Leeds, and Sheffield between 1897 and 1901 proved that nearly half the men who came forward were unfit to pass; 950 (26.5 per cent) were rejected outright and 760 (21 per cent) were provisionally accepted as 'specials'. The reasons for rejection were under-development (31.1 per cent), disease (30.6 per cent), defective vision (15.7 per cent), and decayed teeth (10.5 per cent).[47] Rowntree, like Webb, was adamant about the long-term national importance of this, as well as its immediate impact on individuals.

'Even if we set aside considerations of physical and mental suffering, and regard the question only in its strictly economic and national aspect, there can be no doubt that the facts set forth . . . indicate a condition of things the serious import of which can hardly be overstated.'[48]

While it is clear that the publication of *Poverty* did elicit a response from certain sectors of the population,[49] concern about the physical condition of recruits was not a national issue until the publication of an article concerned specifically with that subject a few months later. 'Where to Get Men' in the January 1902 issue of *Contemporary Review* by Major-General Sir John Frederick Maurice under the pseudonym 'Miles' attracted national attention.* For Maurice, the issue of the physical condition of the men offering to enlist in the army arose out of

* There are a number of possible reasons why it was Maurice's article which stimulated such public concern. *The Contemporary Review* was a more polished publication than *The Weekly Sun*, but less costly than a book. Then, too, while White's article covered just two columns and Rowntree's recruitment statistics discussion only five out of 300-plus page book, Maurice's piece ran to a concise eight

his personal experience and within the context of contemporary discussion about the possible adoption of universal conscription on the Continental model. From this starting point, Maurice confronted the question of what these figures implied about the state of the nation's health. He based his argument upon his observations while making monthly visits to the Herbert Hospital in Woolwich to sanction the discharge from the army of men who had been brought forward by a medical board as no longer fit for service. The Major-General began his essay by pointing out that there was no need to increase 'the supply of numbers for our armed forces . . . if we could only obtain as effective soldiers all those who are anxious to enlist in the Regular Army we should have more than we require.' The figures he adduced to support his contention were, he admitted, estimates. Nevertheless, the numbers themselves were given such prominence, and repeated throughout the course of the article so frequently, that the impression of fact rather than hypothesis was conveyed. According to Sir Frederick Maurice, if 'we add up [the] various percentages . . . taking into account those whom the recruitment officers do not think it worth while to bring before the doctors [10 per cent], those whom the doctors reject [35 per cent] and those who are rejected after trial in the Army [15 per cent], sixty per cent, are rejected, and that, to put it in its simplest terms, out of every five men who are willing to enlist only two are fit to become effective soldiers.' The two most common causes for rejection from the army or failure to complete two years of active duty were the poor condition of the teeth and flat feet. Defective teeth, Maurice explained, were due to improper nutrition 'during the period of life when teeth are forming. In other words the baby or young child must have its proper supply of milk if the young man by the time that he is of virile age is to have his proper complement of sound teeth.' Flat feet were 'due entirely to the ignorance of mothers in the care of their infants',[50] but this was not clarified.

Thus the statistics themselves constituted an issue of imperial importance and, furthermore, they reflected social conditions which were of national significance as well. 'What I want to insist upon is, that a state of things in which two out of five of the population below a standard of life are fit to bear arms is a national danger which cannot be met by any mere schemes of enlistment, and that true patriotism requires that that danger be recognised.' Developing this implication of consequences extending beyond the realm of the army, Maurice stated his concern explicitly. 'We have actually more men offering than we should require if only the conditions of life were such as are necessary for a healthy nation whether in arms or not.' And, he concluded, 'till we can develop a population out of which more than two in five of those

---

pages. Finally, Maurice's army reputation lent a specific validity to his concern which far outweighed that of White (especially among serious readers) or even of Rowntree.

who wish to enlist are fit to become soldiers, we are in face of a far more deadly peril than any that was presented by the most anxious period of the South African War.'[51]

Although 'Where to Get Men' was published under a pseudonym, it is clear that Sir Frederick Maurice did not maintain his anonymity very long. He himself explained that he had not intended to pursue the problem, but his 'article excited so much interest that [he] was asked by the Civic Society of Glasgow to give them a lecture on the subject'.[52] Consequently, Maurice undertook a more comprehensive study and published his results, 'National Health: A Soldier's Study', in the January 1903 issue of *The Contemporary Review*.This article was signed by him. Twice the length of the first report, the later study was basically an amplification of the former. Extending his list of the immediate causes of the poor physical state of the men, Maurice included heart weakness, pneumonic troubles, and rheumatism. He focused on 'the generally low anaemic condition of the whole body'[53] which was too often found. The bulk of the article was devoted to discussing the possible aetiology of this condition, and entreating the public to support a national enquiry into the subject. 'We want the truth. . . . By whatever means it be done we need an exhaustive investigation of the question.'[54]

The publication of the Report of the Royal Commission on Physical Training in March 1903 provided an additional impetus to the organization of just such an investigation. The Commission had been appointed one year earlier 'to inquire into the opportunities for physical training in the State-aided schools and other educational institutions of Scotland; and to suggest means by which such training may be made to conduce to the welfare of the pupils; . . . and thus to contribute towards the sources of national strength'. Presenting their findings and recommendations, the Commission deliberately declined to address the issue of the progressive deterioration of the population. 'It is enough', they concluded, 'that . . . whatever may be the case with the population as a whole, there exists in Scotland an undeniable degeneration of individuals of the classes where food and environment are defective, which calls for attention and amelioration in obvious ways, one of which is a well-regulated system of physical training.'[55]

A few weeks later (2 April), Surgeon-General Sir William Taylor, Director-General of the Army Medical Service, issued a memorandum addressing the questions of 'whether [the] impeachment of the national health has a solid foundation in fact, and . . . whether the condition is true of the population as a whole, or only of a certain section of it'.[56] Taylor began with a direct reference to the enormous response to Maurice's articles.

'A deep interest has been aroused, both in the lay and medical press, by the writings of Sir Frederick Maurice . . . pointing to the fact that there is an alarming proportion of the young men of this country, more especially among the urban population, who are unfit for military service on account of defective physique.'[57]

He noted indications that this was a problem found in the labouring class only, and he associated this with poverty-related social conditions, quoting the studies of Charles Booth and B. Seebohm Rowntree. Taylor questioned Maurice's evidence, but agreed that the rejection percentage was alarming and he called for a commission to conduct an enquiry into the causes of and remedies for physical deficiency, appealing to the Secretary of State to obtain the advice of the Colleges of Physicians and Surgeons as to the necessity for, composition, and scope of, such a commission.

It took three months for the Home Secretary to take up this suggestion, and in early July both Colleges, upon his request, considered the questions.[58] They agreed that such a commission would be useful and thus, on 2 September 1903, the Inter-Departmental Committee on Physical Deterioration was appointed to report on the scope and nature of the enquiry which a Royal Commission might conduct on the subject. In the event, the Inter-Departmental Committee's terms of reference were subsequently enlarged to permit it to make a report of essentially Royal Commission status. It is noteworthy that although this Committee was appointed to enquire into conditions of, and relating to, health, only one member (Dr J.F.W. Tatham) was a physician, and he was more involved with the statistics of public health than with practical work in the field. By contrast, fully half of the members were involved in one or another capacity with the educational system.*

The Committee examined witnesses and took evidence, but did not conduct original investigations. Sitting for less than a year, its report was signed on 20 July 1904. As we shall examine various aspects of the proceedings in detail later on in our story, only a very brief summary will be given here. Similar to other studies of social conditions, the Committee enquired into the concomitants of urbanization: overcrowding, pollution, the poor conditions of employment. And, like Booth and Rowntree, the Committee discovered the concomitants of poverty: malnutrition, disease, deprivation. It is striking, however, that while the discussions of the ill-effects of urbanization in addition to those regarding reproduction rates and recruitment statistics in total occupy

---

* The Committee comprised Mr Almeric W. Fitz Roy (Chairman), Clerk of the Council; Colonel G.M. Fox, Inspector of Physical Training under the Board of Education; Mr J.G. Legge, Inspector of Reformatory and Industrial Schools; Mr H.M. Lindsell, Principal Assistant Secretary to the Board of Education; Colonel G.T. Onslow, Inspector of Marine Recruiting; Mr John Struthers, Assistant Secretary to the Scottish Education Department; and Dr J.F.W. Tatham of the General Register Office, with Mr Ernest H. Pooley, barrister, as secretary.

the first half of the report, the second is devoted entirely to a consideration of the conditions attending the life of the juvenile population. Starting with an examination of the physical condition of grown men, in the end the Committee turned to the next generation. The genesis of the enquiry had been the recruitment rejection figures, but the culmination of the evidence was a series of recommendations pertaining to the improvement of child health. These included more stringent execution of public health statutes (to protect the purity of the milk supply, for example), and a large number of educational measures, which perhaps reflected the composition of the Committee. It was also an indication of what was then considered possible or practicable. It was easier to teach cookery, hygiene, and domestic economy to women and girls, to advise physical exercise for children of both sexes; it was even easier to provide health visiting of infants and sterilized milk for them, than to address radically the causes which made all of this necessary: to improve wages, housing, and the terms of employment.

In conclusion the Committee reported that no evidence existed of inherited racial physical decline; contrary to the Eugenists' belief that progressive evolution had become degeneration, the Committee felt that education and environmental conditions were the key factors in creating and consequently ameliorating 'those evils, the existence of which is admitted'. Speaking rather plainly to the Eugenists, they wrote:

'The Committee hope that the facts and opinions they have collected will have some effect in allaying the apprehensions of those who, . . . on insufficient grounds, have made up their minds that progressive deterioration is to be found among the people generally. . . . The Committee have recognised what can be done [immediately], and are confident that if their recommendations are adopted a considerable distance will have been traversed towards an amendment of the conditions they have described.'[59]

The response to the report was, predictably, mixed. Eugenists such as Karl Pearson and Francis Galton, unconvinced by the evidence the Committee presented to support its conclusion, and confident of their own accuracy (both in terms of statistics and logic), continued to advocate their programme of positive and negative parenting. Sidney Webb, speaking for the Fabian-Liberal Imperialists, held similar views with a socialist twist. Given a state-controlled national minimum standard of living, he argued, those who were limiting their families would no longer be forced to do so. This would balance the population increase of the less desirable and fit, and thereby prevent racial deterioration. Webb suggested a financial endowment of motherhood to encourage the self-controlled and foreseeing members of each class to have children.[60]

Physicians concerned with public health had been working on the practical problems addressed by the Committee for a number of years, and they were delighted with the report. As a group they were not very Eugenist in approach or philosophy and, like the Committee, they looked to amelioration of environmental conditions and the educational system to solve the too-often found problems of poor physical health. The medical press, particularly *Public Health*, the journal of the Society of Medical Officers of Health, and the *British Medical Journal*, the organ of the British Medical Association, had begun to cover the national degeneration issue extensively with the 1902 recruitment revelations. Indeed, between 21 November 1903 and 6 February 1904 (while the Committee was sitting) the *BMJ* ran a series entitled, very simply, *Physical Degeneration.** An editorial, published with the last of the articles, clearly stated the *BMJ* party line, five-and-a-half months prior to the publication of the report:

'That there is unfitness is beyond all doubt, but progressive deterioration cannot be proved in the absence of data. . . . The most impressive conclusion arrived at, after carefully considering all the different sides of this inquiry into the question of the national physique is that at the root of the unfitness which undoubtedly exists in the ranks from which our soldiers are drawn, is the question of proper infant feeding. It cannot too often be repeated that a child wisely fed for the first two or three years of its life has every chance of growing up into a strong man or woman; a child rendered rickety and puny by ignorant feeding will in all probability never make up the ground it has lost. A great number of infants, especially in towns, have from one cause or another to be fed artificially. The natural substitute for the mother's milk is cow's milk. At present cow's milk is too often, when it reaches the houses of the poor, in a state which renders it dangerous to life. Can any reasonable mind be surprised at the great infant mortality and at the unfitness of the majority of the survivors? Without clean milk there will be continued death and unfitness; without statistics there will be no certain data to prove physical deterioration; the moral is that every effort should be made to get clean milk, and to obtain the weighing, measuring, and medical supervision of school children. Then, and then only, will this great national problem be satisfactorily solved.'[61]

The philosophy of Eugenics, the policy of national efficiency, and the reaction to the Boer War did not create the infant and child welfare movement, but they did focus attention on and provide a stimulus for it; they brought this particular branch of public health into the national newspapers. Furthermore, concern about national degeneration

---

* These articles were later expanded into the book by Aimée Watt Smyth, *Physical Deterioration*.

provided a justification and a rhetoric for this aspect of health care. It validated infant and child welfare work and it validated an enlarged role for the physician to play in this issue of national importance. 'It is not only the right but the duty of the State to watch over the development of its future citizens,' the *BMJ* maintained. 'But it is a duty which it persistently neglects. The future of the race, therefore, rests largely with the medical profession.'[62] As we shall see, this justification and this rhetoric were used repeatedly to convince the public (particularly the opposition) of the national, Imperial importance of such seemingly unheroic, mundane matters as milk, meals, and routine medical examinations.

II

The nature and extent of the waste

During the nineteenth century, the medical profession was only one of the many actors who brought the tragedy of the decreasing birth rate and increasing infant mortality rate on to the stage of imperial policy. This changed at the turn of the twentieth century. It was then that physicians began to claim the leading role in this drama, allowing only bit parts to the Eugenists and the Fabian-Liberal Imperialists. This perception by the profession of its primary position was reflected in the *BMJ* assertion that 'the future of the race . . . rests largely with the medical profession'.[1] It is not difficult to understand this stance. There may not have been too much they could do to increase the birth rate, but neither could anyone else. It was the physicians, however (and they believed only they), who had the skills, the professional expertise, to address the issue of the prevention of infant death. As Reginald Dudfield, the Medical Officer of Health of the Borough of Paddington put it, 'No influence external to the individual can raise the birth-rate to its former height, but we [physicians] ought to be able to do something to stop the leakage due to the high infantile mortality.'[2]

By the turn of the twentieth century it was well recognized that such action was necessary, as can be seen in the 1904 *Report* of the Inter-Departmental Committee on Physical Deterioration. Chapter VII of this document dealt wth 'conditions attending the life of the juvenile population', and began with a discussion of 'the nature and extent of the waste that goes on under the name of "infant mortality"'. The Committee specifically associated the declivity of the birth rate with the increased importance of diminishing the number of infant deaths. Physicians as well as such non-medical official bodies as the Committee stressed the social significance of this issue. In his serious and sober study of infantile mortality, for example, Arthur Newsholme emphasized 'rousing the community to a sense of its importance, especially in

22

relation to the serious decline of our national birth-rate'.[3] In short, Newsholme asserted, 'the lowered birth-rate in this country makes the saving of infantile life a matter of Imperial importance.'[4]

This interest in decreasing the infant mortality rate cannot be dismissed as a cultural crisis of the capital. The tiny print passages at the back of each issue of the *BMJ* provide ample evidence of the prevalence of this concern. An example from 1901 is illustrative.

'Dr Marsh, the Medical Officer of Health [for] East Macclesfield, . . . in a recent report, asserts that the infant death rate can, "without any exaggeration, be described as simply appalling, and demands the most serious and earnest consideration of all interested in the health and well-being of the community." In view of this statement, the *Macclesfield Courier and Herald* remarks: "It behoves the Council to look facts fairly in the face, and see what can be done to bring about a better state of things. If it does not . . . then it is incurring a grave responsibility, especially in face of Dr Marsh's straightforward statement that "the causes of this terribly high death-rate amongst infants are largely preventable ones".'[5]

Was Dr Marsh's assertion true? Were the causes of infant death largely preventable? What, in fact, were the constituents which caused the ascending line in the graph of infant mortality? 'There are at the present time five main pathological conditions . . . which prove more fatal than any other diseases within the first twelve months of life', George Newman, the MOH for Finsbury, and an expert on infant mortality, explained in 1906. He listed these as: epidemic diarrhoea; respiratory diseases (including bronchitis and pneumonia); prematurity and congenital defects; atrophy and debility; and meningitis and convulsions.[6] To facilitate comparison from year to year, and between localities, these five causes of infant mortality were often reduced to three by combining prematurity, congenital defects, atrophy, and debility under the single designation 'wasting disease', and by dropping meningitis and convulsions which, as a group, was relatively far less important than the other three.

Figure 4 illustrates the relative importance of the primary causes of infant death at the beginning of the twentieth century. The preponderance of the three major categories of wasting, diarrhoeal disease, and respiratory disease is at once evident. Furthermore, it was well recognized at the time that these causes were actually more lethal at the turn of the century than they had been twenty-five years previously. *Table 1* is an adaptation from one prepared for the Inter-Departmental Committee on Physical Deterioration, under Dr Tatham's direction, from the official returns to the General Register Office.[7] Tatham noted that while there had been, over the past quarter of a century, a decrease in the mortality rate of several causes of infant death, fatalities from prematurity and congenital defects, diarrhoeal diseases, and pneumo-

Figure 4 Rate per 1,000 registered births of infant deaths due to major causes of infant mortality, England and Wales, quinquennial 1901–1905

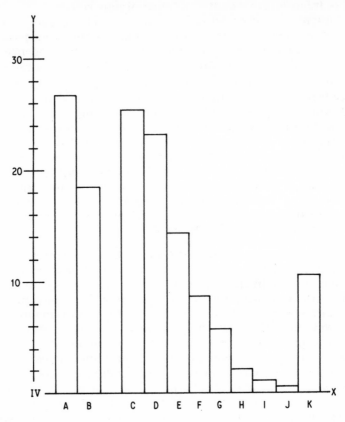

(*Source*: David Forsyth (1909) *Children in Health and Disease*, p. 229.)

Table 1 *Number of infant deaths in England and Wales in total and from various diseases in a group of urban and a group of rural counties in the quinquennia 1873–1877 and 1898–1902*

| | Urban counties | | Rural counties | |
	1873–1877	1898–1902	1873–1877	1898–1902
Total births	2,352,794	2,639,402	653,734	548,653
	(100%)	(112.2%)	(100%)	(83.9%)
Total deaths	378,743	435,103	80,714	68,651
(1–12 months)	(100%)	(114.9%)	(100%)	(85.1%)
Diarrhoeal diseases	48,248	91,262	6,697	9,148
	(100%)	(189.2%)	(100%)	(136.5%)
Respiratory diseases	20,572	32,533	4,057	4,489
	(100%)	(158.1%)	(100%)	(110.6%)
Wasting diseases	34,831	65,577	8,574	12,547
	(100%)	(188.3%)	(100%)	(146.3%)

(*Source*: G.B., P.P. (1904) *Report of the Inter-Departmental Committee on Physical Deterioration.* Vol. 1: *Report*, Cd 2175, p. 131.)

nia unfortunately compensated all too well for the reduction. The increase in pneumonia mortality was, he observed, simply a reflection of an increase in the death rate among the whole population from that disease, and in any case this particular factor was relatively negligible in altering the aggregate figures. As Tatham explained:

'With diarrhoeal diseases and with premature birth and congenital defects the case is far different, the increased mortality from these causes being very marked. Taking together diarrhoeal diseases and diseases of the stomach and liver, the recent five years show an increase of more than 70 per cent in the urban, and of nearly 70 per cent in the rural counties. From premature birth and congenital defects the increase, though numerically smaller, was proportionally even greater than that from diarrhoeal diseases.'[8]

Deaths due to prematurity and congenital defects were, by and large, considered to be non-preventable. 'These children are simply born in such poor physical condition that they are unfit to live, and find a few hours or days of extra-uterine life too much for them. They are not so much diseased as merely unfit, and either not ready or not equipped for a separate existence', Newman wrote.[9] He then, however, devoted a full thirty pages to a discussion of ante-natal influences on infant mortality. Indeed, as we shall see in Chapter V, there were enough medical researchers and medical care providers interested in reducing infant mortality through the prevention of prematurity and congenital debility to generate specific schemes devoted to this end. John Ballantyne's book, *Ante-Natal Pathology and Hygiene*,[10] for example, provided an impetus to the study of ante-natal hygiene generally. The investigations of D. Noel Paton at the Research Laboratory of the Royal College of Physicians, Edinburgh, into the influence of diet during pregnancy on the weight of the offspring, led to the conclusion that the malnutrition of indigent women was one cause of the high mortality rate of their infants.[11] This was translated into practical terms, as we shall see later, with various (albeit limited) programmes to provide an enriched diet for pregnant women. Nevertheless, at the beginning of the twentieth century, as George McCleary, MOH for Battersea remarked, 'The causes of infantile mortality are . . . classified as (1) preventable, and (2) non-preventable, the latter group consisting of conditions of definite antenatal origin, such as premature birth and congenital defects.' Although McCleary urged, 'We must get rid of the expression "non-preventable" in relation to infantile mortality, and set ourselves to investigate the antenatal factors, and to bring them within the scope of our administrative measures',[12] it was beyond the range of most general practitioners and the majority of medical officers of health to do so. For the time being, therefore, the principle impetus to reduce infant mortality was channelled towards combating the single most obvious, dramatic – and 'preventable'– cause: infant diarrhoea.

Infant diarrhoea, or cholera infantum, was a very different sort of pathological condition than prematurity or the 'wasting' disorders. Whereas the latter appeared to be a general debility, not assignable to any specific cause, which made it impossible for the infant to thrive, infant diarrhoea was clearly a specific pathological entity. The disease process was visible: healthy children suddenly sickened violently and all too frequently died. It was precisely because cholera infantum attacked healthy children, because the onset was so unexpected and abrupt, that it made immediate demands on the healing skills of medical practitioners. It is thus understandable that they focused on this cause of infant mortality; their participation in the discussion about the potential of prevention and possible methods of treatment was reflected in letters and short communications to the professional journals. For instance, a letter to the *Lancet* from Thomas Dutton, a London practitioner, urged the necessity of recommending 'that all milk used as food for infants should be first boiled or sterilised'.[13] Similar letters from practitioners all over the country stressed the virtues of sterilization as a means of preventing disease – specifically epidemic diarrhoea. The question of appropriate treatment was of even greater interest. Thus W. Cecil Bosanquet, physician to out-patients at the Victoria Hospital for Children, noted that there was 'the greatest diversity of opinion' on the subject, and that 'an immense number of drugs and remedial measures have been recommended'.[14] The briefest perusal of the journals provides abundant evidence of interest in preventing and treating 'summer diarrhoea or gastro-enteritis',[15] 'zymotic enteritis and diarrhoea',[16] 'gastro-intestinal disorders',[17] and 'infantile diarrhoea'[18] — terms used synonymously.

One problem in collating information about this pathological condition was the sheer multiplicity of its names. In an effort to resolve this issue of nomenclature, the Royal College of Physicians appointed a Committee on 27 July 1899 'to deal with the whole question' of terminology, the ambiguity of which had prevented clear and accurate statistical analysis.[19] The following January, the Committee presented a report recommending that the College 'authorise the use of the term "epidemic enteritis" (or, . . . "zymotic enteritis") as a synonym for epidemic diarrhoea', and that it 'should urge the entire disuse . . . of such terms as "gastro-enteritis", "muco-enteritis", or "gastric catarrh"'.[20] The College adopted the recommendation, and practitioners were duly exhorted not to forget to use the prefix 'epidemic' when the cause of death was what was commonly known as 'epidemic diarrhoea'.[21]

In view of these qualifications, we shall discuss diarrhoeal mortality rates in the aggregate. *Figure 5* illustrates the course of total infant mortality, and of that part due to diarrhoeal diseases. *Table 2* gives the percentage increase or decrease of infant mortality due to diarrhoea and to all other causes of infant mortality in quinquennial periods. These two figures illustrate the situation in which physicians found themselves at the turn of the twentieth century. During the past twenty years infant mortality due to diarrhoeal diseases had gone up dramatically and without remission. The question was, why?

The first step towards answering this question was to ascertain precisely who was at risk from the disease. The returns of the local medical officers of health indicated a great variability of the death rate between geographical locations and from one season to the next. For example, in 1897 and 1898 the infant mortality rate from diarrhoeal diseases in the rural part of West Sussex was 10.1 per 1,000 births, as compared with 19.1 in the urban area of the same administrative county.[22] According to George Newman, the discrepancy in the number of infant deaths from diarrhoea in rural districts and towns was even greater; indeed, he wrote, it 'may be as much as seven or eight times as great in the towns as in the country'.[23] Similarly, the seasonal incidence of the disease was equally marked. The common name 'summer diarrhoea' reflected the dramatic increase of the number of deaths at this time of year. 'During the summer of 1899 the epidemic of infantile diarrhoea spread all over England, and the death-rate everywhere rose; for example, in 67 large towns from 156 to 179 (or *plus* 23) per 1,000.'[24] In short, diarrhoea was primarily a disease of urban areas with a predominantly summer incidence.

It was not until the early years of the twentieth century that several large-scale epidemiological studies were undertaken in order to

Figure 5 Total infant mortality and infant mortality due to diarrhoeal diseases, per 1,000 births in England and Wales, 1880–1920

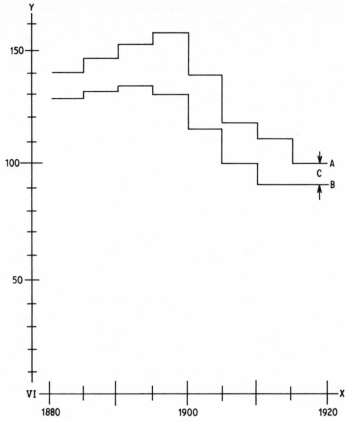

Legend
A = Total infant mortality
B = Infant mortality less diarrhoeal diseases
C = Infant diarrhoeal mortality

(*Source*: Arthur Newsholme (1923) *The Elements of Vital Statistics*, 4th edn, p. 425; (1903) *BMJ*, 30 May, p. 1267.)

determine the conditions under which urban infants contracted the disease each summer. What factors influenced the course of the epidemic; which were favourable and which preventive? Precisely who, among the town babies, was more likely to contract the disease, and why?

The first risk factor of primary importance to emerge was the influence of the method of feeding. E.W. Hope, the Medical Officer of Health for Liverpool, was one of the earliest investigators to correlate food source with fatality. In an article published in July 1899, Hope stated his conclusions succinctly.

28

Table 2   *Percentage increase or decrease of infant mortality due to diarrhoea and to all other causes of infant mortality in quinquennial periods, England and Wales, 1876–1920*

Period	Decrease or increase per cent	
	Diarrhoeal infant mortality	All other causes of infant mortality
1876–1880 to 1881–1885	−12	−3
1881–1885 to 1886–1890	+22	+3
1886–1890 to 1891–1895	+18	+3
1891–1895 to 1896–1900	+55	−4
1896–1900 to 1901–1905	−26	−8
1901–1905 to 1906–1910	−21	−14
1906–1910 to 1911–1915	+6	−8
1911–1915 to 1916–1920	−52	−10

(*Source*: Arthur Newsholme (1923) *The Elements of Vital Statistics*, 4th edn, p. 425.)

'Out of 233 deaths [from diarrhoea], of infants under three months of age, into which I made personal inquiry, only 16 of the infants had been fed upon the breast alone; the remaining 217 received other food as well as, or instead of, breast-milk, administered either out of a bottle or in some other way. It is abundantly plain, therefore, that the infants who suffer most are those which are artificially fed.'[25]

The following year H. Meredith Richards, Medical Officer of Health for Croydon, began to investigate all deaths under one year of age. Using the services of health visitors to make personal enquiries, he found that 'during the first six months of life the death rate from diarrhoea was . . . in round numbers: 5 per 1,000 among the entirely breast-fed, 35 per 1,000 in those fed on condensed milk, [and] 38 per 1,000 in those fed on cows' milk.' Like Hope, Richards concluded that

'there can therefore be no reasonable doubt that hand-feeding is a common antecedent of fatal diarrhoea in infants, and that those who are hand-fed are much more likely to suffer from diarrhoea than are those who receive the food which nature intended for them.'[26]

Corroborative evidence was offered by Arthur Newsholme, John Robertson, and William J. Howarth. Newsholme investigated the feeding methods of the 226 fatal cases of infant diarrhoea which had occurred in Brighton during the three-year period, 1900–1902. Information was obtained regarding 191 infants. Of these, 18 or 9.4 per cent were breast-fed, 84 or 44 per cent were fed on condensed milk, and 89 or 46.6 per cent were fed on cows' milk.[27] Robertson, the Medical Officer of Health for Birmingham, did a similar study of a representative 236 of the 3,647 infants who died of diarrhoea between 1899 and 1903 in his district. Of the sample infants (all aged under six months) 10 per cent had been breast-fed only, 10 per cent were fed by breast and bottle, and 80 per cent were bottle-fed. At the same time, Robertson conducted a survey of the feeding habits of 1,200 healthy babies and found the percentages to be quite different, with 56.0 per cent fed by breast, 28.7 per cent mixed and 14.4 per cent bottle-fed only.[28]

Howarth, the Medical Officer of Health for Derby, arranged in 1900 to receive weekly lists of the births registered during the past seven days from the local registrar. From November of that year until November 1903 women inspectors enquired into the feeding method of each registered child by personally visiting the mother and infant at home. These findings were analysed in 1904, and the results were published one year later. Out of a total of 8,343 infants, 5,278 (63.3 per cent) were breast-fed, 1,439 (17.3 per cent) were partly breast- and partly bottle-fed from a very early stage, and 1,626 (19.5 per cent) were entirely bottle-fed. The mortality rates from 'diarrhoea and epidemic enteritis' in addition to those from 'gastritis and gastro-enteritis' were as expected: 52, or 10 per 1,000 of the breast-fed, 36 or 25.1 per 1,000 of the mixed-fed, and 94 or 57.9 per 1,000 of the bottle-fed babies died. In other words the mortality rate of the bottle-fed infants was nearly six times greater than that of the breast-fed babies. Howarth also discovered that the mortality rate from all causes was higher among artificially than naturally fed babies. 'In not one single instance does the death-rate in any class of disease among hand-fed children even approximate that recorded among children who are breast-fed; the rate is invariably higher.'[29]

The high mortality rate from condensed as well as cows' milk was another important point elucidated by these early epidemiological investigations. Richards's enquiries revealed that of the 191 infants aged one week to six months who died of diarrhoeal diseases, 60 or 33 per cent had been fed condensed milk and 88 or 48 per cent cow's milk.[30] Similarly, Newsholme, investigating 191 fatal cases of infant diarrhoea in Brighton found, as we have seen, that 44 per cent were fed condensed milk and 46.6 per cent cows' milk.[31] Howarth also conducted an enquiry 'to ascertain the mortality [from all causes] among hand-fed children in relation to the kind of food on which they have been reared'. His results showed that 158 of the 895 infants fed on only milk and water died (or 177 per 1,000), 38 of the 149 infants fed on condensed milk (255 per 1,000), 40 of the 159 fed on 'mixed foods', i.e. bread, rusks, oatmeal, sago, tapioca, etc. (252 per 1,000), and 85 of the 422 fed on a variety of patent foods (202 per 1,000).[32]

The investigations of Hope, Richards, Newsholme, and Howarth were seminal in many ways. They provided a stimulus, and a formula, for further epidemiological surveys by other medical officers of health. This can be seen in individual reports, such as that of 1907 by Alfred Harris, Medical Officer of Health for Islington, on the prevention of infantile mortality. Harris had found that, between 1896 and 1905, diarrhoea and enteritis was the primary cause of infant death in his area, being responsible for 17.9 per cent of the total infant mortality. During the summer months of 1905 and 1906 he conducted an enquiry into the feeding methods of those infants – 220 – who died during that period. His results were predictable, given that 'it is now a well recognized fact that in infants fed on the breast diarrhoea is infinitely less fatal' than for those artificially fed: 22 of the 220 (10 per cent) were breast-fed, and 198 (90 per cent) were bottle-fed, either with cows' milk (39 per cent), condensed milk (18 per cent), or mixed sources.[33] The influence of the early investigations can clearly be seen in Newsholme's concise compendium of later research studies in his *Second Report on Infant and Child Mortality* for the Local Government Board in 1913. This survey of the literature showed that later works had refined, but not substantially altered, the conclusions of the earlier investigations.[34]

The early studies were also seminal in that they asked key questions which increasingly demanded recognition and answers. They noted, for example, the relationship between the use of condensed milk and high infant mortality from diarrhoea, and hypothesized why this was so. The discussion this stimulated finally led to a government enquiry on the subject.   In 1911 Dr F.J.H. Coutts presented a report to the Local Government Board regarding condensed milks, with special reference to their use as infant food. Coutts observed that while the use of full cream condensed milk had decreased in recent years, that of the skimmed variety had considerably and steadily increased. This was, he explained, dangerous for several reasons. First, condensed milk was not found to be a bacteriologically sterile substance as had been believed previously. Then too, there was an enormous disproportion between the amount of carbohydrate found in human milk and in sweetened condensed milk, due to the quantity of sugar the latter contained. Machine-skiming exacerbated the differences between the milks, as it virtually deprived the condensed form of fat. 'There is universal agreement in medical opinion as to the dangers arising from feeding infants on skimmed milk, either fresh or condensed,' Coutts asserted. 'The injurious results . . . are malnutrition (as indicated by emaciation and atrophy), rickets, scurvy. Infants so fed show lowered vitality, with consequent lessened resistance to all disease, and with increased liability to certain diseases such as diarrhoea.' Coutts went on to associate the effects of a condensed milk diet with the problem of national deterioration. He used the rhetoric of efficiency to emphasize his conclusion.

'A considerable proportion [of babies fed on condensed machine-skimmed milk] die during the first year of life, thus swelling the statistics of infantile mortality; those which survive are apt to be stunted, ill-developed, of poor physique, and physically and mentally of a less efficient type.'[35]

Three years later, in 1914, Coutts presented a report to the Local Government Board on the use of proprietary foods for infant feeding, another topic addressed, as we have seen, by the early investigators.* Having analysed 106 different brands of proprietary foods Coutts found that the vast majority had too high a carbohydrate and too low a fat content to be nutritionally sound for infants. He concluded that 'many proprietary foods are not in fact suitable for the feeding of infants under 7 or 8 months of age [indeed] they may cause serious injury.'[36] This was most notably, as in the case of infants fed machine-skimmed condensed milk, diarrhoea, scurvy, and rickets.

Were diarrhoeal deaths due to the type of food the infant received? Or, as other investigators claimed from their epidemiological studies, were factors such as housing or maternal employment the determinants of mortality?

Studies of the bearing of different types of housing upon the mortality rate of the population at all ages led to a consideration of this problem as it affected infants and children in particular. As early as 1893, Herbert Jones, the Medical Officer of Health for Crewe, reported an investigation he had undertaken to compare the mortality rates found in back-to-back as contrasted with through houses.** This was not the first such study; Jones himself referred to Dr Tatham's work in Manchester (1888) and Dr Bell's in Bradford (1891). 'But,' Jones explained,

> 'as the deductions drawn from these two . . . are distinctly at variance, and as there are in both of them many vulnerable points, before I began . . . I laid down certain conditions which it seems to me must exist or must be approached as nearly as possible if we wish to obtain accurate and precise results.'[37]

Jones's requirements reflect his attempt to compare like with like. Two representative areas were chosen, each containing few, if any, of the opposite type of house. All the houses had identical sanitary conveniences, were built with the same material, and were supplied with the same water. Furthermore, the tenants of both types of houses were of the same socio-economic group, earning similar wages and engaged in similar work. Finally, Jones recognized the value of aggregate figures and trends: a large number of houses was required to be considered

---

* Indeed, Coutts referred directly to several of these studies, and specifically discussed Howarth's and Robertson's research (G.B., Ministry of Health, *Reports to the Local Government Board on Public Health and Medical Subjects*, N.S. no. 80, Food Reports, no. 20, pp. 24–5).

** The principal difference between a 'through' and 'back-to-back' house is that in the former both the front and back walls belong exclusively to the dwelling, while in the latter the back wall is a common wall with another dwelling at the rear. Thus the two dwellings are contiguous (or 'back-to-back'), which makes it impossible for either to have windows in that wall. This precludes cross ventilation or access to direct sunlight in the rear rooms.

representative of the type, and he examined the statistics over the six-year period 1887–92.

The results of his investigation showed that the average annual death rate per 1,000 population in the through houses was 15.6, and 21.1 in the back-to-back community. With regard to diarrhoea mortality among the entire population, Jones said, 'we have so few deaths . . . that little can be learned from its death-rate, though we find the back-to-back houses have nearly twice as many deaths as occur in the through houses', or an annual average of 0.40 as compared with 0.22 per 1,000 population.[38] One of the problems with these statistics is that we do not know the proportion of infants to the general population in these two communities. Thus, although we know that, in general, it was the infant population which bore the brunt of diarrhoeal deaths, we do not know (nor can we determine) whether these particular figures reflect a high infant mortality rate from this disease. In any case, this problem was not of interest to Jones.

Contemporaries focused on the second part of Jones's statement, and the conviction that back-to-back housing was a determinant of diarrhoeal mortality persisted, giving rise to similar studies. For example, in 1896 Arnold Evans, the Medical Officer of Health for Bradford, reported the results of his own investigation. Evans divided the wards of Bradford into two groups, one with more than 60 per cent of back-to-back houses, and the other with less than 60 per cent. He then analysed the vital statistics for the three years 1890–92 according to this division. The mortality rate from all causes was 20 per cent higher in the back-to-back group than in the other. Like Jones, however, Evans remarked that 'in reference to the diarrhoeal diseases, the figures are so small that I do not attach much importance to them.'[39] Nevertheless, he went on to discuss diarrhoeal mortality in some detail and concluded the article with figures for only two specific diseases, phthisis and diarrhoea. The mean death rate per 1,000 population during the years 1890–92 from phthisis was 1.93 in the back-to-back and 1.71 in the through group; the figures for diarrhoea were 0.83 and 0.36 per 1,000 respectively.[40] This summation emphasized the seeming correlation between back-to-back housing and diarrhoeal mortality – despite Evans's caveat, the figures told their own story of a higher death rate from diarrhoea among the inhabitants of back-to-back than among those of through houses.*

* That this investigation was later interpreted as evidence linking back-to-back housing with a higher diarrhoeal mortality rate is reflected in the fact that Dr L.W. Darra Mair, in his *Report on Back-to-Back Houses* to the Local Government Board, went so far as to calculate precisely the percentage increase of the diarrhoeal death rates. 'Dr Evans . . . found that the . . . death-rates for phthisis and diarrhoea were 13 per cent and 131 per cent higher respectively.' Darra Mair went on to criticize Evans's study: 'The statistics of this investigation are open, however, to the same objection as those of previous investigations, namely, that correction for differences

John F.J. Sykes, Medical Officer of Health for St Pancras, in 1901 showed a similar rise of the infantile death rate from diarrhoea in stable dwellings. In a series of lectures on 'The Influence of the Dwelling upon Health', Sykes presented statistics for the same three-year period (1890–92), comparing the inhabitants of stable dwellings* in St Pancras with the whole of St Pancras and the whole of London. The diarrhoea death rate per 1,000 population was over three times as high in the stable dwellings (1.66) as in St Pancras generally (0.53) and more than two-and-a-half times as high as in the whole of London (0.62).[41] Sykes concluded that this high mortality 'is not due to poverty . . . the probability appears that . . . the construction of the homes of the infants in stable dwellings [is the] prominent factor in the causes of mortality'.[42]

The diarrhoeal death rate of Birmingham in 1904 varied so greatly according to house size that Dr Robertson, the Medical Officer of Health, commented,

'for practical purposes all the deaths occurred in small houses occupied by the artisan classes, that is to say, this enormous mortality among infants is limited to the working classes. . . . For one reason or another, the middle and better classes are able to prevent their infants from contracting this fatal disease, whether the children be breast-fed or bottle fed. . . . 98½ per cent of the deaths . . . occurred in houses of five rooms or under, and only 1½ per cent in houses of over five rooms.'[43]

However, Howarth's study, which we have already discussed, came to a very different conclusion. Howarth ascribed 'the very striking differences in the aggregate death rates of breast-fed and hand-fed children' to a '"lessened power of resistance" or "diminished vitality"' in the latter. He went on to say 'that these conditions are not the result of marked differences in social position is shown from . . . particulars relating to the house accommodation of 100 children fed naturally and by hand and taken in consecutive order from the register.' As 60 of the 100 breast-fed, and 82 of the 100 hand-fed infants lived in houses with five or more rooms, the latter were, as a group, better housed and thus 'perhaps it is justifiable to assume they are of at least equal social position'. Therefore, Howarth reasoned, 'it is more probable that these enfeebled constitutions are the direct result of improper feeding.'[44]

In 1908 Dr L.W. Darra Mair was requested by the Local Government Board to investigate the effect on health of living in back-to-back houses. The largest and most meticulous study of its kind to that date,

---

* 'Stable' dwellings were nothing more than the dwellings above stables.

in age and sex distribution could not be made, and, in addition, the period covered by them was short' (G.B., Ministry of Health, *Report on Back-to-Back Houses*, by Dr L.W. Darra Mair, Cd 5314, London, HMSO, 1910, p. 7).

Darra Mair was assiduous in his efforts for statistical accuracy. First of all, he was much more comprehensive in approach than previous investigators; he studied thirteen industrial towns in the West Riding of Yorkshire and examined the vital statistics for a ten-year period (1898–1907). Furthermore, Darra Mair only compared houses of both types which were in good structural condition and in similar neighbourhoods, so as to limit the issue to the questions of ventilation and sunlight. And finally he, unlike previous investigators, corrected the death rates for variations in the age and sex constitution of the populations he studied. His results showed a mean annual death rate from diarrhoea of 8.1 per 1,000 children under five years of age in through houses, 8.5 per 1,000 under five in back-to-back houses, and 8.0 in back-to-back houses excluding those having side ventilation. Thus housing as a risk factor for diarrhoeal disease finally came to be recognized as probably irrelevant, possibly ancillary, and certainly not of central importance.[45]

At the same time other investigations correlated maternal employment with infantile diarrhoeal deaths. The most obdurate advocate of this determinant was George Reid, the Medical Officer of Health for the Staffordshire County Council. Reid began to associate a high infant mortality rate with the employment of married women in the early 1890s. His reasoning was, unfortunately, as clear as mud, but his contention was that mothers 'sometimes from necessity, but more frequently from inclination, neglect their home duties and go to work in factories'. Not only did they fail to breast-feed, but they also failed to pay proper attention to bottle-feeding; consequently their infants suffered from a higher diarrhoeal mortality rate than did the infants of non-working mothers. Reid based his argument upon his interpretation of the vital statistics of his area. 'When I first had occasion to inquire into the mortality returns of the County of Stafford, I was greatly impressed at finding a very marked difference in the infant mortality-rate of the northern and southern towns,' Reid informed the Section of State Medicine at the annual meeting of the British Medical Association in 1901. He went on to explain that these towns 'differ in one important respect – while in the former [northern] the trade is chiefly potting, in which large numbers of married women are engaged, in the latter [southern] the population is mainly employed in coal mines and iron works, industries which do not admit of the employment of women'.[46]

Reid reiterated his conclusions repeatedly. In a paper read before the National Conference on Infantile Mortality in 1906,[47] for example, he presented the same argument and figures, but made even greater claims regarding the evil effects of working mothers on infants. By this time, however, an extensive body of information regarding infant mortality rates from all causes, including specifically diarrhoeal diseases, had been accumulated. Careful analysis of this material, as the *Lancet* pointed out referring directly to Reid's paper, disproved his deductions. In an editorial on 'Infantile Mortality and the Employment of Married Women in Factories' the *Lancet* examined the Registrar-General's returns in various Lancashire towns, as they related to this issue. The editorial noted that the evidence was not consistent with Reid's hypothesis, and concluded that 'the proportion of such employment cannot be held to be a controlling factor of infantile mortality'.[48] This assessment was fairly well accepted by those involved in the infant welfare movement. By the end of the first decade of the twentieth century, maternal employment was understood to be, at best, tangentially related both to infantile mortality in general, and diarrhoeal deaths in particular.

We have seen that clearly it was artificially fed infants who were at risk from diarrhoeal disease. While factors such as housing and maternal employment were found to be only erratically correlated with diarrhoeal mortality rates, infant feeding, the nature of the food the infant received, was increasingly seen as the primary determinant for this disease. Thus it was understood that breast- versus bottle-feeding could be, and was, consistently related to a differential in the diarrhoeal mortality rates. Although this was indisputable, the precise reason for it was absolutely unclear. What was the aetiology of epidemic diarrhoea? And how did cow's milk fit into the pattern of the development of this disease?

Epidemic diarrhoea was one of the last diseases to be explained by the theories of humours and miasmata. Edward Ballard's classic *Report on Diarrhoea* which, through an extensive demonstration of pathology and symptomology, identified the specific nature of the disease, nevertheless emphasized the great importance of 'emanations' from the ground. At the request of the Local Government Board, Ballard began this enquiry in 1880 and, after eight years of investigation, presented his results in December 1888. It is noteworthy that this period was in the midst of the 'golden age' of bacteriology. Louis Pasteur's (1822–95) research on fermentation and the diseases of silkworms had been completed in the 1860s, while Joseph Lister (1827–1917) developed, implemented, and announced his 'antiseptic principle'. In 1876 Robert Koch (1843–1910) had demonstrated the causal role of the anthrax bacillus and in 1879 Neisser isolated the gonococcus. Between 1880 and 1888, precisely the period of Ballard's investigation, Pasteur was working on the development of vaccines through the modification of the virulence of pathogenic micro-organisms, Koch discovered the tubercle bacillus (1882) and the cause of cholera (1883), and several other scientists were successful in identifying the aetiologic agents of a number of diseases (Loeffler and Shutz, glanders; Fehleisen, the erysipelas streptococcus; Klebs and Loeffler, the diphtheria bacillus, etc.).

It is clear that Ballard himself believed in the germ theory of disease. Still, his analyses and recommendations betrayed an intellectual ambivalence and an ambiguity with regard to practical applications. In his report, Ballard noted the long-observed correspondence between the prevalence of diarrhoea and meteorological conditions; and he postulated the dominant influences of the deep (four-foot) earth temperature. In conjunction with this, the quality of the soil was an important factor. 'I think I am in a position to say', Ballard wrote,

'that the influence of soil is a decided one; . . . it is observable most distinctly in relation to [diarrhoea]. Where the dwelling-houses of a place have as their foundation *solid rock* . . . the diarrhoeal mortality is, notwithstanding many other unfavourable conditions and surroundings, low, and indeed may be almost altogether unnoticeable. . . . On the other hand, *a loose soil*, permeable more or less freely by water and by air, is a soil on which diarrhoeal mortality is apt to be high.'

Ballard's hypothetical explanation of the diarrhoeal disease cycle was a rather confused combination of the germ and miasmatic theories of disease. He believed 'that the essential cause of diarrhoea resides ordinarily in the superficial layers of the earth, where it is intimately associated with the life processes of some micro-organism not yet detected, captured, or isolated'. Upon occasion this 'micro-organism is capable of getting abroad from its primary habitat, the earth, and having become air-borne obtains opportunity for fastening on non-living organic material' such as food. 'In food [this] micro-organism finds . . . nidus and pabulum convenient for its development, multiplication, or evolution, [and] from food [this] micro-organism can manufacture . . . a substance which is a *virulent chemical poison*. . . . This chemical substance is, in the human body, the material cause of epidemic diarrhoea.' Emanations were the means by which 'the essential cause' of diarrhoea 'got abroad'.

'Sewer or cesspool emanations, especially in the concentrated form, and suddenly let loose, may occasion attacks of fatal diarrhoea; emanations of this sort . . . are of themselves capable of occasioning a diarrhoeal epidemic even in a non-diarrhoeal season of the year.'[49]

Consequently, Ballard advised the protection of the daily environment from 'telluric emanations'. He recommended that 'the whole surface of the earth beneath houses should be so effectually and uniformly sealed with impervious material . . . as to prevent any chance of emanations rising into them from the soil.' As milk was 'the staple article of food of artificially fed infants', it was a primary vehicle of infection for this micro-organism once it had escaped from the earth. 'Special care should be taken for the protection of milk,' Ballard warned. Like the house, the cow-shed and 'the dairy should be similarly protected from the rise of ground air'. Within the home 'the practice . . . of storing milk on the ground floor . . . or in some underground cellar should be altogether discouraged. . . . Pantries [must be] protected against the rise of ground air.'[50]

Ballard's study was enormously influential. Although the discoveries and developments in bacteriology and the aetiology of infectious disease established a framework for more precise investigation of the contaminant which caused infant diarrhoea, subsequent researchers felt obliged to consider the influence of the four-foot earth temperature and the soil conditions in their investigations. Like Ballard, Arthur Newsholme (especially in his earlier papers) stressed the meteorological and geological conditions which gave rise to epidemic diarrhoea. Newsholme's theoretical understanding was, like Ballard's, a curious composite of the miasmic and germ theories of disease. A sentence discussing such causes as 'effluvia . . . air and soil' was followed by another accepting 'the rigid logical definition of cause as the "unconditional invariable antecedent"' which, in the case 'of epidemic diarrhoea is the hypothetical micro-organism'. Combining these two schools of thought, Newsholme contended, 'But even this "invariable antecedent" can scarcely claim to be the "unconditional" cause. . . . For the occurrence of epidemic diarrhoea certain conditions of temperature and rainfall and soil . . . are required.'[51] Newsholme concluded that the aetiology of the disease is *an unclean soil, the particular poison from which infects the air, and is swallowed, most commonly with food, especially milk*.[52] In other words, faecal filth contained, or harboured, the responsible micro-organism which, airborne, settled on aliments to be ingested. Within the context of this theory Newsholme's geological and meteorological concerns were understandable. Impervious and rocky soils were not conducive to diarrhoea 'probably because polluting faecal and other organic impurities do not cling to or soak into such soils'.[53] Increased rainfall was preventive because it was 'the natural scavenger. . . . Frequent rains mean frequent removal of infective material.'[54] Newsholme delimited the role of milk precisely. It was 'not the actual cause of diarrhoea' but simply 'a vehicle of infection . . . to which this contagium [of diarrhoea] gains access'. There were, he explained, four possible points of exposure to this 'particular poison': on the farm, in transit to town, during delivery to the home or in the shop, and in the home of the consumer; he himself believed that 'domestic infection is the most common source of diarrhoea.'[55]

As bacteriological studies of the aetiology of epidemic diarrhoea began to appear in increasing numbers in the professional journals, Newsholme too started to adduce experimental evidence to support his argument, even though his expertise was in epidemiology and statistical analyses. In a paper specifically entitled 'Domestic Infection in Relation to Epidemic Diarrhoea' (1906), he presented the results of experiments regarding the bacteria content of cows' and condensed milks (which were undertaken at his request at the Brighton Municipal Laboratory) as well as the data from his extensive epidemiological investigations concerning feeding methods and diarrhoeal deaths (1,380 babies were canvassed throughout the three years, 1903–5). Observing that condensed milk was, due to its mode of manufacture, bacteriologically relatively pure and, furthermore, transported in sealed, impermeable tins, Newsholme argued that the 'calamitous results' of feeding with this type of milk was additional proof for his contention that the home of the consumer was the most common point of infection. He reasoned that 'if the infection of summer diarrhoea were chiefly derived from the farm or from contamination during transit diarrhoea should be more fatal among babies fed on fresh cow's milk than among babies fed on condensed milk.' However, his statistics showed that the probability of death from diarrhoea was half as great among the former as compared with the latter group. Although Newsholme noted that 'it is possible that condensed milks may have formed a pre-condition of diarrhoea by causing defective nutrition, by producing a semi-scorbutic condition, or by setting up preliminary catarrhs of the digestive tract',* he did not consider this to be of sufficient importance to affect his study, or the logic of his results. Thus he concluded, 'I have no hesitation in adhering to the opinion . . . that diarrhoea is mainly due to domestic infection.'[56]

Sheridan Delépine (1855–1921), Procter Professor of Pathology and Director of the Public Health Laboratory at Owens College, Manchester, perceived epidemic diarrhoea as a variety of food poisoning and, like Newsholme, believed milk to be the most common vehicle of infection among infants. Unlike Newsholme however, Delépine was convinced that milk was infected at the farm or in transit, *not* in the home of the consumer. Inspection of dairy farms, and microscopical and bacteriological examination of nearly 2,500 milk samples taken directly from a single cow, mixed from a number of cows, or obtained from railway depots upon arrival from the country, convinced him that milk was well and truly infected prior to arrival in the home.

This was only one of several points Delépine made in a paper read before the Epidemiological Society of London on 12 December 1902. He presented both experimental and investigative evidence to support his position. Noting that 'general evidence seems to show that the most common forms of food poisoning give rise to symptoms resembling closely those of epidemic diarrhoea', Delépine surmised that the latter 'is generally the result of a more *widely disseminated, and less massive form of bacterial infection of food* than is the case with regard to the more definite outbreaks of food poisoning'. During the eight-year period

---

* As we have seen, this line of thought was taken up, and found to be of importance, in Dr F.J.H. Coutts's *Report to the LGB on an Inquiry as to Condensed Milks*. In short, condensed milk was found to be, quite simply, of far less nutritional value to infants than fresh cows' milk.

1895–1902, Delépine had studied outbreaks of infection due to milk as well as to solid foods such as cheese, pork-pies, and tinned salmon. He also, from 1896 to 1901, had investigated the effect of inoculation with over 2,000 samples of milk upon guinea pigs. Comparison of the bacilli isolated from those milk specimens found to be pathogenic with bacilli obtained from infective food revealed that these micro-organisms, 'with few exceptions, belonged to the colon group of bacilli'.[57] In other words, Delépine concluded that faecal pollution of cows' milk was responsible, by and large, for the epidemic diarrhoea from which infants suffered.

Newsholme and Delépine agreed that the transmission of summer diarrhoea was through the oral–faecal route, and that food (most often milk) was the vehicle of infection. They differed primarily as to the point of contamination, the former believing it to be in the home of the consumer and the latter either on the farm or in transit. The relation between faecal filth and epidemic diarrhoea had, in fact, been noted before. For example, in 1893 J. Spottiswoode Cameron, the Medical Officer of Health for Leeds, reported the results of action taken by the Leeds Sanitary Authority to reduce the high mortality from diarrhoea in that area. Cameron explained that, in response to a special study on diarrhoea that he had submitted to the Sanitary Committee in 1892, it had been decided 'to use certain special cleansing measures on the approach of summer' in one district, which comprised nearly a tenth of the town. The results were remarkable: 'only in one district in Leeds did the rate not exceed that of 1892, and that was the one specially scavenged. . . . In [this] district the death-rate [from diarrhoea] actually decreased.'[58]

E.W. Hope, MOH for Liverpool, similarly correlated faecal filth with diarrhoeal mortality, and he too looked to scavenging as a means of prevention. Writing in March 1899, Hope maintained that 'the dust, or particles, of faecal filth are the most potent in causing those changes in food which give rise to fatal inflammatory diseases of the stomach and bowels.' Consequently, simple instructions 'widely distributed amongst the poorer classes at the commencement of summer' specifically advised that 'the water-closets should be repeatedly and thoroughly flushed, and sinks and drains kept clean by frequent flushing each day. A free and unstinted use of water is far better than any disinfectant.'[59] Hope referred specifically to horse manure as a source of faecal filth – a common nuisance in turn of the century cities with which modern urbanites are unfamiliar. Whereas Newsholme, in his theory of domestic infection, pointed primarily to contamination with human waste, and Delépine, in his theory of infection at the farm or in transit to cow dung, Hope looked both to humans and to horses as sources of infective waste.[60] F.J. Waldo, Medical Officer of Health to the parish of St George-the-Martyr in Southwark, developed this line of thought in the Milroy Lectures which he was invited to give in 1900. Waldo's theory was that 'both the organic material and the offending micro-organisms that act as the *causa causans* of summer diarrhoea are to be found in the horse-dung that is daily deposited in vast quantities upon our highways.'[61]

Although all the theories regarding the aetiology of epidemic diarrhoea which we have examined were reasonable working hypotheses based on the germ theory of disease, they each ultimately depended upon bacteriological evidence to be proven correct. Conclusive confirmation could only be obtained from the one source which was beyond the expertise of the medical officers of health: the pathology of the afflicted infant. As a matter of fact, bacteriologists, working quite independently of the theories we have discussed, had already begun to search for clues or evidence from the discharges of the patients themselves. This was made abundantly clear in an article by M.H. Gordon on 'The Bacteriology of Epidemic Diarrhoea' which, as Sheridan Delépine remarked, 'gives a fairly complete account of our present knowledge'[62] of the subject. Gordon began by pointing out that:

'the investigation of the bacteriology of epidemic diarrhoea is beset practically with considerable difficulties owing to the necessity of seeking the *contagium vivum* in the intestinal contents. The fact that in health the faeces contain many million living micro-organisms per gramme, and that these micro-organisms comprise several different species, renders the task of isolating the particular organism presumably concerned in the production of the disease in question far from an easy one. In this respect there is obviously a marked contrast to a disease [in] which tissues normally sterile are found to be teeming with a microbe of one particular kind. In the case of epidemic diarrhoea . . . the chances of error are far greater.'[63]

The article continued with what was basically a review of the already substantial body of literature. Although at that time only seventeen years old, the corpus was so extensive precisely because, unlike epidemiological investigations which have only a limited applicability from one culture to another, bacteriological results were universal. By their very nature, the studies could be (and were) repeated and tested in laboratories everywhere. Thus, a large proportion of the research discussed by Gordon, and by other writers in their literature review sections, had been done abroad, particularly in Germany and America.

The bacteriology of infantile diarrhoea can be said to have begun in Germany in 1885 when Escherich published the results of his seminal study of the bacteriological flora of the infant intestine. According to Escherich the intestine of the neonate was sterile, but was quickly colonized. This took as few as four to as many as eighteen hours depending upon the dust and temperature conditions in which the infant lived.[64] Escherich also found that B. *lactis aerogenes* was the only species present in the upper part of the small intestine of a healthy milk-fed baby. Descending down the intestine, the variety as well as the size of bacteria increased, with the bacillus *coli communis* greatly predominating over all the other species of micro-organisms.[65] In a monograph on the same subject published the following year (1886), Escherich observed that a much greater variety of bacteria was found in the intestines and stool of the diseased as compared with the healthy infant.[66] At that point, however, he was not prepared to offer an explanation for this phenomenon or to identify one particular organism as the responsible pathogenic agent.

The American, William D. Booker, began research to follow up on 'the fundamental work of Escherich upon the bacteria in the healthy intestine of sucklings'.[67] Working out of the Johns Hopkins Hospital, Baltimore, and the Thomas Wilson Sanatorium for Sick Children (a richly endowed hospital ten miles from Baltimore devoted exclusively to the treatment of summer diarrhoea, to which 350 to 400 infants were sent each summer – the only season the Sanatorium was open), Booker conducted a bacteriological investigation of the faeces of infants affected with diarrhoea. He presented his work in 1887 at the International Medical Congress in Washington, DC. The first researcher to attempt an intensive investigation into this problem on a relatively large scale (seventeen infants were examined, sixteen of whom were ill and one, a control, healthy), he was nevertheless unsuccessful in isolating one specific responsible organism. Booker, like Escherich, found that the number of organisms in the faeces of the ill and healthy child was equal, but that the variety was greater in the former case.[68]

Throughout the 1890s Booker continued his research, examining in total over thirty strains of bacteria discovered in the stools of 123 infants suffering from the disease and in the organs of 33 infants who had died of it. In a paper published in 1897 Booker made some general remarks, based upon the evidence he had obtained during the past ten years, regarding the bacteriological differences found in diseased as compared with healthy infants. He observed that

'in infants affected with summer diarrhoea the inconstant varieties [i.e. all varieties other than the so-called "constant" or "obligatory" bacteria of the healthy milk faeces: bacillus *coli communis* and bacillus *lactis aerogenes*] of bacteria are much more prominent and frequently appear in immense numbers in the small intestine, and their whole number often exceeds by far that of the two constant varieties in the colon. Bacillus *coli communis* and bacillus *lactis aerogenes* appear more uniformly distributed through the intestine than is wont to be the case under normal conditions. Bacillus *coli communis* is more abundant in the duodenum than bacillus *lactis aerogenes*. . . . In the colon bacillus *lactus aerogenes* appears in much greater abundance than in the healthy intestine.'

Furthermore, Booker specified that the constant bacteria of the healthy milk faeces did not disappear in the diseased state. Turning from the general conditions found in the diseased state to a consideration of the particular responsible organism, Booker could not be very precise. 'No single micro-organism is found to be the specific exciter of the summer diarrhoea of infants,' he concluded.

> 'The affection is generally to be attributed to the result of the activity of a number of varieties of bacteria, some of which belong to well known species and are of ordinary occurrence and wide distribution, the most important being the streptococcus and the *proteus vulgaris*.'[69]

Shiga's isolation of B. *dysenteriae* from the stools and intestines of dysentery patients the following year, 1898,[70] led to questions as to whether Booker's cases may have been associated with bacilli of the dysentery group. Later evidence seemed to indicate that this may well have been the case. In a paper on 'The Etiology of Summer Diarrhoea in Infants' (1904), Charles W. Duval and Victor H. Bassett of the Thomas Wilson Sanatorium concluded that the dysentery bacillus 'is an important, if not the most important, cause of the summer diarrhoeas of children'.[71]

The cause of summer diarrhoea was one of the first lines of investigation to be undertaken by the scientists associated with the newly founded Rockefeller Institute for Medical Research in New York City. Simon Flexner co-ordinated the research of twelve bacteriologists working independently from Boston to Baltimore; L. Emmett Holt reviewed the clinical observations of the various physicians associated with the project. In order to delimit the problem, attention was confined to the dysentery bacillus. Although it was well understood that demonstrating the presence of this organism did not prove a causal relationship with epidemic diarrhoea, it was felt that the most logical way to proceed was to select one possible factor and investigate it thoroughly. A report of their results was published in 1904.[72] It was found that the relation between infection with the dysentery bacillus and infantile diarrhoeal disease generally was not clear. The range of clinical presentation was extensive. Severe cases characterized by much mucus and some blood in the stools seemed to be more clearly correlated with the presence of either the Flexner-Harris or the Shiga type of bacillus, than were more mild cases with mucus, but no blood.

The detailed clinical descriptions in this report led physicians in Britain to question whether the 'cholera infantum' in America was the same disease as the summer diarrhoea found at home. This issue had not really been raised before as the only earlier similarly extensive investigation was that of Booker, and his cases did not present blood or mucus in the stools and thus were comparable to the British clinical picture. H. de R. Morgan of the Bacteriological Department of the Lister Institute of Preventive Medicine in London became increasingly aware of this problem in the course of his own work on the aetiology of epidemic diarrhoea. Writing in 1906, he noted that 'it remains to be determined how far the summer diarrhoeas of other countries conform in type to those of the United States.' During the previous summer, Morgan had examined stool and blood samples and intestinal scrapings from fifty-eight infants admitted with diarrhoea to the Victoria Hospital for Sick Children in Chelsea and the Hospital for Sick Children in Great Ormond Street. As a control, he also examined the stools of twenty healthy children under two years old. Morgan's results differed distinctly from the Rockefeller group: 'None of the bacteria found by me in infantile diarrhoea correspond with those of known pathogenic bacteria.' He identified the bacilli he found by numbering them, and he came to the tentative conclusion that his 'bacillus No. 1 . . . may possibly be a factor, or one of the factors, in the disease'.[73]

Morgan continued his research during the summer of 1906, investigating the bacteriology of the stools, small and large intestines, spleens, and mesenteric glands of fifty-four infants on the special diarrhoea ward at the Hospital for Sick Children, Great Ormond Street. As before, he observed that 'the type of summer diarrhoea of infants in America appears to be clinically and bacteriologically different from that which occurs in this country.' And again the evidence led him to put forward bacillus No. 1 (which Morgan later named after himself) as a, by now probable, causative agent. This micro-organism, he claimed, had never been isolated in any other pathological condition, nor in water, milk, sewage, or healthy human faeces, but it had been found in the majority of diarrhoeal cases studied by him. Furthermore, 'it is pathogenic for animals, producing diarrhoea and death in young rabbits, rats, and monkeys, when these animals are experimentally fed on cultures.'[74] By February 1909, when Morgan presented his research to the epidemiological section of the Royal Society of Medicine, he was convinced that 'the association of Morgan's bacillus with summer diarrhoea has . . . been abundantly established' and must 'be considered an important aetiological factor in summer diarrhoea'.[75] Given the importance of bottle-feeding as a risk factor for this disease, it is noteworthy that Morgan's bacillus was not isolated in milk. However, it was found in house flies which, during the past few years, had increasingly been seen as a possible vehicle, or conveyance, of infection.

The concept of the animal vector was not new, and the spectacular discoveries in the 1890s had highlighted this aspect of the germ theory of disease. Theobald Smith's (1859–1934) report (1893) on the role of ticks in the transmission of Texas cattle fever riveted scientific attention, and the notion of an intermediate animal carrier was firmly established. In 1894–95 David Bruce (1855–1931) demonstrated the role of the tsetse fly in the transmission of nagana, a disease of cattle and horses in Zululand. And in 1897, Ronald Ross (1857–1932) conclusively proved the carrier function of mosquitoes in malaria, which was confirmed by the Italian zoologist G.B. Grassi (1854–1925) and his colleagues Bignami and Bastianelli the following year. The influence of this research was explicitly affirmed by George H.F. Nuttall, Demonstrator (and later Quick Professor of Biology) of Bacteriology at Cambridge, in his monograph of 1899, *The Part Played by Insects, Arachnids, and Myriapods in the Propagation of Infective Diseases in Man and Animals.*

'The facts which have been established by the brilliant researches of Ross, Grassi, Bignami, and Bastianelli . . . have at last aroused more general attention to the part which insects may play in the propagation of disease, and it is probable that the new impetus given by these investigations will lead to fruitful researches in other directions. . . . It is certain that insects may under certain conditions play a most important part – both active and passive – in the propagation of bacterial diseases. . . . *Musca domestica* [the common house-fly] and allied species are chiefly to blame [as passive carriers]. Such flies are incapable of "biting" but may, from the nature of the food which they seek, carry pathogenic bacteria about on their bodies or within their alimentary tract, and deposit them on lesions of the mucous membranes or skin or on food.'[76]

J.T.C. Nash, the Medical Officer of Health for Southend-on-Sea, was one of the earliest proponents in Britain of flies as a vehicle for the transmission of epidemic diarrhoea. At a conference of Essex medical officers of health to discuss infant mortality in that region (November 1901), Nash presented his experience of diarrhoea during the previous summer. He noted that while in July and August 1901 twenty-three infants had died of diarrhoea, there had not been a single such case during the same months of 1902. Although the cool and wet weather of that year may have been influential, Nash believed that '*the most remarkable phenomenon of these months . . . was the almost complete absence of Musca domestica.*' The next month (September 1902) the fly appeared and diarrhoeal deaths ensued. Nash concluded that 'where refuse and midden heaps are in the proximity of cowsheds and dairies they are . . . a source of great danger . . . partly, and to a [large] degree, by the risk of flies carrying contamination direct from the refuse heap to milk or to the udders of the cow or the hands of the milker.' He therefore particularly advocated such preventive measures as 'the daily removal of all forms of refuse from the proximity of all cowsheds and dairies, *and the covering over of all standing milk so as to exclude all dust and flies*'.[77]

These ideas were presented to a wider audience through Nash's contibution to Sheridan Delépine's paper on the aetiology of epidemic diarrhoea at the Epidemiological Society meeting in January 1903.[78] Arthur Newsholme, who had introduced the discussion of Delépine's paper with his own 'Remarks on the Causation of Epidemic Diarrhoea', also noted the probability that flies were a common vehicle for the transmission of faecal filth to milk. His belief that this contamination occurred in the home rather than, as Delépine contended, the farm, was in his view supported by evidence that flies were carriers of pathogenic micro-organisms.

> 'The sugar used in sweetening the baby's milk is often black with flies, which have come from a neighbouring privy or manure-heap, or even from the liquid stools of a diarrhoeal patient in a neighbouring house. Flies have to be picked out of the half-empty can of condensed milk, before its remaining contents can be used for the next meal of the infant.'

And he recommended 'a crusade against the domestic fly, which . . . probably plays a large part . . . in spreading infection'.[79]

Newsholme used the theory of flies as a vehicle of infection to interpret the statistics regarding the disproportionately high diarrhoeal mortality rate among infants fed on a diet of condensed milk and, incidentally, to strengthen his hypothesis of domestic infection. Newsholme noted (as we have already discussed) that 'the probability of death from diarrhoea was twice as great among infants fed on condensed milk as among infants fed on fresh cow's milk.' This could not be explained by 'a simple bacterial count, nor a statement of the presence or absence of . . . kinds of bacteria' especially since, he stressed, *the original bacterial contents* [of fresh cows' milk] *are much reduced in condensed milk'*. The pathogenicity of condensed milk could, however, perhaps be explained in part, Newsholme thought, by his observation that 'there can be no doubt that a tin of condensed milk when opened is, during the three or four days which elapse before it is emptied, very attractive to flies and receives apart from the visits of flies a considerable amount of domestic infection in the form of dust.'[80] He concluded that this, in conjunction with the nutritionally defective diet condensed milk afforded, were the probable causes of the excess of diarrhoea among infants fed this food.

An article by J.E. Sandilands (MOH for Kensington) published in the same journal earlier that year on 'Epidemic Diarrhoea and the Bacterial Content of Food' supported Newsholme's theories regarding the pathogenicity of condensed milk for infants.[81] Sandilands, like Newsholme, noted the disproportionate diarrhoeal mortality among infants fed on a diet of condensed milk. Referring to 'the existence of a wide-spread belief in a more or less intimate relationship between the high bacterial content of milk sold in large towns and the prevalence of diarrhoea amongst those who consume it', he decided to investigate the multiplication of bacteria in one particular brand of the condensed product, Nestlé's milk. Sandilands exposed the condensed milk to air for twenty-four hours and then incubated diluted and undiluted samples at various temperatures for a number of days. His results showed that 'compared with that of cow's milk the bacterial content of contaminated Nestlé's milk is remarkably low, and remains low for a week or more at the ordinary summer temperature of 70 degrees F. . . . If we may judge by laboratory experiment, . . . even in a hot summer the contents of a tin will have been consumed before large numbers of bacteria have developed and before decomposition has set in.' As Sandilands did not perceive condensed milk to be, *per se*, so pathogenic as to cause such a disproportion of diarrhoeal deaths, he turned his attention to Newsholme's theory of domestic infection. Noting in particular a passage in the latter's *Report on the Health of Brighton for 1903* regarding the role of flies in transmitting faecal matter to foodstuffs, Sandilands went on to allege, 'There is no substance more attractive to flies than human excrement, and no one who has depended on Nestlé's milk in a tropical country will forget the revolting sight presented by an open tin to which flies had gained access.' Sandilands agreed with Newsholme that 'it is to the greater attraction for flies presented by sweetened milk compared with cow's milk, that . . . the greater prevalence of diarrhoea among infants fed on Nestlé's milk' is due. And he concluded, 'I can find no feature in the history of a normal epidemic of summer diarrhoea which cannot be adequately explained by the double supposition that diarrhoea stools are infectious and are frequently conveyed to the food of the healthy by flies.'[82]

The role of the common house-fly as a vehicle of infection commanded so much interest by 1907 that the Public Health Committee of the London County Council decided to investigate this aspect of the epidemic diarrhoea problem. The results of this research were published by Dr Hamer, Medical Officer to the Council, in two reports in 1908.[83] Hamer found, for example, that an increased number of flies did not signify a rise in the diarrhoeal mortality rate, nor did a stationary quantity prevent such a rise. The Local Government Board took up the matter where Hamer left off. In 1908 John Burns, the President of the LGB, authorized an investigation into the possible carriage of infection by flies. Under the auspices of this study a great deal of research was carried out regarding the natural history of various house-flies (particularly the common *Musca domestica*) and their behaviour in relation to a number of diseases. The numerous reports to the Local Government Board on flies elucidated many aspects of their life-cycle, flight habits, and so on.[84]

By 1909 several investigators were conducting studies to establish the precise role of flies as carriers of the colon bacilli. J.T.C. Nash, for example, had moved from observation to experimentation, and in 1909 he published a paper reporting the results of his investigations during the past few years. Nash had devised a simple experiment to ascertain the extent to which flies pollute milk. He did nothing more than put two 'ordinarily clean saucers' filled with milk 'from the ordinary morning supply' on his kitchen table; one was covered with a 'clean' plate, the other was not. Five hours later, two flies were found in the uncovered saucer and bacteriological examination of both milks revealed 'that there were more than twice as many bacteria in the milk which had been polluted by flies as in the other which had been kept covered and protected from flies'.[85]

J.E. Sandilands also continued to be interested in the link between flies and epidemic diarrhoea and, like Nash, he too changed his approach to the problem. Whereas his early work concentrated on deductive reasoning from personal experience and bacteriological examination of condensed milk, by 1909 he decided to conduct a prospective epidemiological investigation to assess the communicability of diarrhoea from the sick to the healthy. Sandilands found that 'with the aid of the house fly' his observations could, 'without any undue strain, be fully explained on the assumption that the effective cause of fatal summer diarrhoea is conveyed to the healthy in the freshly-passed excrement of the sick, and is not acquired from any other source'.[86]

Sandilands's paper raised more questions than it answered. While he did begin to examine the question of morbidity as well as mortality, he collected his data over the very limited time period of four months. And although he depended upon the agency of flies as a conveyance for infection, he did not undertake fly counts or bacteriological examinations. James Niven (the Medical Officer of Health for Manchester) attempted to address these issues. A much more ambitious undertaking than Sandilands's investigation, Niven designed an extensive epidemiological study to investigate the relationship between fly prevalence and diarrhoea incidence. After a preliminary trial in 1903,* Niven selected a number of householders whom he thought 'could be relied upon to carry out continuous and careful counts day by day of the number of flies caught'. Thus, beginning in July 1904, Niven collected detailed data recording daily individual enumerations of captured flies for the entire diarrhoeal season of July to November in 1904, 1905, 1906, 1908, and 1909. He correlated this with an annual curve of the number of diarrhoeal fatalities reported each week during the same period and found that 'that correspondence is close and intimate'.[87]

While Niven attempted to elucidate the aetiology of epidemic diarrhoea by examining its mode of transmission, O.H. Peters contributed to the research in this field by designing an intensive as well as extensive epidemiological study of the disease incidence, which included morbidity and mortality at all ages. In a paper entitled 'Observations upon the Natural History of Epidemic Diarrhoea', Peters described his painstaking method of house-to-house visitation to obtain accurate data, his complicated statistical analyses to ensure

---

* This is noteworthy, as it is one of the first epidemiological pre-trials to be mentioned in the diarrhoea literature.

precision, and the reasons for his tentative conclusions. Peters took a number of factors into account: age, family relationships, socio-economic conditions, sanitary facilities, food, and the clinical and epidemiological features of diarrhoea. His results were remarkable: the investigation elucidated much which had not been previously either known or studied. For example, Peters determined that the age incidence of diarrhoeal mortality and morbidity differed greatly. Infants sustained nearly the entire mortality, but morbidity from the disease could affect as many as 10 per cent of the entire population with a hundred times as many cases as fatalities.[88] While occupation and school attendance appeared to have little effect upon the incidence, the sharing of yards in common and dirtiness of the household had a marked influence, in both cases probably due to the handling of and proximity to faecal matter.[89] Referring to the argument that the provision of water-closets, good drains, refuse receptacles, and yard paving would reduce the incidence of diarrhoea because it would promote the proper disposal of waste, Peters asserted that they were to 'no avail' or 'only of minor importance; faecal infection having most to do with pollution of the interior of the household by young children not old enough to use the w.c., or by involuntary passage of stools in children of more mature years'.[90] Proceeding to the role of food in the transmission of the disease, Peters claimed that boiling cow's milk 'gave no protection whatever' and that 'the milk supply apparently plays no part . . . in introducing diarrhoea into the home'.[91] His own conclusion was that 'it appeared not improbable that the phenomena of diarrhoea prevalence are almost wholly concerned with the local evolution of various infective foci, and a piled-up mass of evidence has been presented as to the bulk of infection being derived by transmission from person to person.'[92] However, 'the correspondences of the diarrhoea and fly curves are such as to be quite compatible with the theory of fly infection' and 'a great deal of evidence was for, and none against' this mode of transmission as well.[93] According to Peters more research in this regard was needed.

Peters was right. That much more research was in fact needed before the aetiology of summer diarrhoea was clarified, was reflected in contemporary paediatrics and bacteriology textbooks. A perusal of the 'Inflammatory or Zymotic Diarrhoea; Cholera Infantum' sections in six editions of Ashby and Wright's *The Diseases of Children* running from 1889 to 1922 illustrates the general trends we have seen in this chapter. Written specifically for medical practitioners, the discussion of the aetiology of epidemic diarrhoea was limited in comparison with the attention paid to symptomology, sequelae, prognosis, and especially treatment. All the editions note the relation between disease incidence and temperature, and the far greater risk of bottle- versus breast-feeding. The 1889 version paid particular attention to the role of heat, contending that 'the hot weather [favours] the development of some form of organism which, entering the system, gives rise to the disease'. Various causes were adduced as possibly responsible: 'the use of sour milk, unripe fruit, inhalation of sewer gas, emanations from the soil, etc.'. Focusing on the first of these, the authors argued that 'while it is doubtful if sour or contaminated milk can be the constant cause, yet it seems probable that the milk supply has in some epidemics been at fault.'[94]

Three years later (1892), Ashby and Wright were more assertive in this regard. 'There is the strong probability that milk often is the vehicle by means of which certain micro-organisms or poisons enter the system', they claimed.[95] The specific role of heat was no longer mentioned. By 1899 the authors declared:

'There can be little doubt that the immediate cause of infantile diarrhoea is an infection of the alimentary canal by various toxine-producing bacteria, contained in milk or other forms of food. No specific organism has been detected, but the investigations of Booker and others point to the streptococci and *Proteus vulgaris* as being among the chief performers. Some however believe that the normal bacteria of the alimentary canal, such as B. *coli communis* and B. *lactis aerogenes* . . . will, under certain circumstances, take on a condition of virulency and produce toxines.'[96]

The last two editions accepted that the immediate cause of epidemic diarrhoea was a bacterial infection of the alimentary canal, most commonly from contaminated milk, and the attempts of various researchers to isolate the specific micro-organism were cited. These versions also paid increasing attention to the role of flies; indeed by 1922 the authors (no longer Henry Ashby and George Wright but Hugh Ashby and Charles Roberts) contended that 'the common house-fly is usually the means by which the infection is carried.'[97]

An examination of Topley and Wilson's classic text, *Principles of Bacteriology and Immunity* reveals that not only the first but even the second edition (1936) contains an entire chapter devoted to 'Summer Diarrhoea', with little more information than that which we have examined here, and emphasizing 'our ignorance of the exact aetiology of summer diarrhoea'.[98] It was not until 1945 that Dr John S.B. Bray, working at the Hillingdon Hospital, Middlesex, published his discovery of the role of pathogenic *Escherichia coli (E. coli* 0111–B4) in infantile gastro-enteritis, and confirmed the theory that flies can, and do, act as vehicles of transmission.[99] But this is beyond the scope of our story. During the period which we consider, no conclusive answer had been found. However, in the mist of partly complementary and partly conflicting theories, certain vague contours of landmarks became increasingly visible. Throughout the first decade of the twentieth century it gradually became clearer that the aetiology of the disease was to be found in the faecal organism, and that this could be transmitted from the sick to the healthy by common house-flies. Breast- versus bottle-feeding was the compass which oriented the researchers from point to point. While the expedition into the unknown had been stimulated by concern regarding the future of the Empire in the face of a decreasing birth rate and increasing infant mortality rate, this scientific journey had developed its own momentum. Within the context of the concurrent development of bacteriology and epidemiology, and their relation to the practice and provision of medical care, such a scientific enquiry was fully justified.

The original question of why the infant mortality rate increased during the last quarter of the nineteenth century had become obsolete, and in fact was never answered. The focus of the question had shifted to an attempt to understand, and thus control, the second greatest cause of infant death: epidemic diarrhoea. For many historians of science this episode, with no significant successes nor dramatic failures, no exceptional personalities to rival the stature of a Koch or Pasteur and, in the last analysis, no clear results, is naturally of only limited interest. But for historians of medicine, particularly historians of public health, it is fascinating. The indistinctly seen landmarks of flies and faecal infection, and the compass of breast- versus bottle-feeding indicated a route of immediately applicable possibilities. In short, they suggested a course of action.

III

Milk or 'pus as a beverage'

The basic inescapable fact that bottle-fed babies definitely did die from epidemic diarrhoea in far greater numbers than breast-fed infants was a useful compass for general practitioners, politicians, and concerned citizens, as well as for epidemiologists, bacteriologists, and specialized medical officers of health. Attempting to isolate and identify the precise aetiologic agent and mode of transmission of epidemic diarrhoea, the latter three inculpated milk as a vehicle of infection. The former were not so nice in their distinctions, and in an imprecise way generally correlated dirty milk with a high infant mortality rate. They incriminated milk as the responsible agent, and turned their attention to the standard of the milk supply and the conditions under which it was produced, transported, and delivered, in addition to the prevention and treatment of epidemic diarrhoea. The medical journals of turn-of-the-century England were replete with examples of these concerns. Such illustrations ranged from the practitioner's deduction (1899) from his 'own experience that diarrhoea, vomiting, and the concomitant symptoms in infants were frequently produced by ordinary dairy milk',[1] to simple expressions (1901) of 'the opinion that a great part of the excessive infant mortality was due to defective milk supply',[2] to the straightforward assertion (1904) that 'in close relation with infant mortality is the *Milk Question*'.[3]

William Hallock Park addressed this issue of the milk question in an article on 'The Great Bacterial Contamination of the Milk of Cities', which was endlessly cited later. 'From a careful study of the question,' Park informed his readers,

> 'I think that the milk now consumed is unnecessarily contaminated and unwholesome, and that this is largely due to the present almost complete ignorance of persons, commercially interested, who do not appreciate the fact that bacteria arising from contamination by stable and barnyard dirt are capable . . . of an enormous development which may render good milk utterly unfit for food.'[4]

Park was the Assistant Director of the Research Laboratory of the Department of Health of New York City, and the evidence he presented in this paper (published in England in the *Journal of Hygiene*) was primarily based on his experience in that city but, as both the editors and readers of the *Journal* knew, his remarks were pertinent to the English situation as well. Two years previously, in 1899, G. Leslie Eastes had presented his 'results of the examination of 186 samples of milk by microscopical and bacteriological methods'[5] to the Section of Pathology of the BMA. Eastes explained that the samples of milk were obtained from all parts of the kingdom, from medical officers of health, public institutions, and from private sources. He found tubercle bacilli, pus, muco-pus, blood, and streptococci in an overwhelming percentage of the samples. In conclusion Eastes asserted that

> 'milk which contains pus or muco-pus and streptococci is unfit for human consumption, but unfortunately, according to my figures, this would entail condemning 80 per cent of the samples I have examined. No farmer, however, dreams of allowing a cow with an inflamed udder to suckle a calf. Why then should he be permitted to sell such contaminated milk for human consumption?'[6]

Speaking before the Society of Medical Officers of Health a few months later, Walter Pakes, Demonstrator of Sanitary Science and Bacteriology at Guy's Hospital, confirmed Eastes's condemnatory results. Pakes's investigation of London milk led him to claim that it usually contained the 'very unfortunate' average of 3,000,000 to 4,000,000 bacteria per cubic centimetre,[7] and that some samples were 'totally unfit for consumption, especially by children'.[8]

Although (as we have seen in Chapter II) bacteriological investigations failed to identify the precise micro-organism responsible for infant diarrhoea, this method of examination, newly added to the sanitarian's armoury, had revealed that milk was not only subject to adulteration, but also to gross contamination. By the early years of the twentieth century it was well understood, albeit in a general way, that this pollution was harmful to the public health, particularly to the infant portion of the population. The question then arose as to where, when, and how milk was contaminated, and why the industry was not more strictly controlled. Articles extensively detailing the points of con-tamination in milk production and distribution began to appear in greater numbers in the medical journals after the turn of the twentieth century. 'Some Points on the Hygiene of the Udder, and the Conditions of Milk Production in Rural Districts' by F.T. Harvey, a Fellow of the Royal College of Veterinary Surgeons, is an example of these early discussions. Harvey specified particular aspects of milk production which could be ameliorated relatively easily but were all too often ignored. He remarked, for example, that 'the existence of an impervious floor is very needful in a cowshed, but one very rarely sees anything of the kind put in. In one form or another it is not very expensive, and anything like thorough cleansing is very difficult without it.'[9]

The quantity of literature on the milk question increased enormously in 1903. Two of the most influential books on the subject published that year were Edward F. Willoughby's *Milk, Its Production and Uses*[10] and Harold Swithinbank and George Newman's *The Bacteriology of Milk*.[11] Willoughby, a physician and an inspector of farms and general adviser on scientific matters to Welford and Sons, the largest of the metropolitan dairy companies, concentrated on the generally poor conditions of milk production and the inadequate legal regulation of the industry. His arguments were corroborated by Swithinbank and Newman, who approached the subject slightly differently. A full three-quarters of their 600-page book was devoted to a discussion of milk bacteriology: techniques, results of investigations, and a review of the relevant European and American literature. The remainder, a critical analysis of the legal control of the milk supply, identified four major aspects of milk production: the milk-herds, the housing of the herds, milkers and milking, and the after-treatment of milk and conditions of sale. Both of these books were reviewed in the medical journals, and were cited and quoted repeatedly.

The same subject was taken up in a series of articles run by the *BMJ* between 21 March and 2 May 1903, entitled 'A Report on the Milk Supply of Large Towns'.[12] This seven-part account was so popular, and generated so much discussion, that it was collated and published as a pamphlet 'to be obtained through any bookseller. Price 6d.'[13] The series concentrated on the 'defects and their remedy' of the milk supply, more or less on the macroscopic level; 'it would be foreign to our present purpose to go at any length into the subject of the bacteriology of milk,' the author, Aimée Watt Smyth, explained. Rather, the point of the report was to discern and clarify various problematic aspects of the milk industry, the effect of dirty milk on the (especially infant) population, and to propose possible reform or improvements. 'Milk is a delicate and unstable fluid, yet it is the only animal product which is habitually taken raw,' Watt Smyth remarked to begin the series. She then proceeded to the issues of central concern.

'No one will seriously propose that milk should be taken for human consumption from other than healthy cows.

'But, granted that this condition be observed, there are still dangers connected with the use of milk as it is now commonly distributed by the trade and consumed in large towns. A large proportion of the fatal cases of summer diarrhoea are with good reason attributed to the consumption of milk in an infective state.

'These dangers are well known, but owing to the supineness of the public are permitted to continue.

'Milk may be deliberately adulterated* by dishonest traders, . . .

54

milk may be "faked". . . . But apart from dishonesty and the application of "trade secrets", milk from a country farm, though not adulterated, may by the time it reaches the consumer's table or the infant's bottle be a highly dangerous liquid.'[14]

The explanation was not hard to find:

'This is due to want of ordinary cleanliness, and to the carelessness with which any and every operation, from the milking of the cow to the delivery of the milk, is too often carried out. The cow's udders are soiled and the milker's hands are dirty, but neither are washed. The milk pail and churn are insufficiently cleansed. The milk is insufficiently cooled or not cooled at all at the farm. The churns are perhaps left at a roadside station on the platform for hours in the sun. The cans are often not securely closed so that dust can enter, and are commonly not sealed, so that they may be tampered with by dishonest or careless persons. They may be opened at the railway terminus in a careless way to allow their contents to be measured. Further opportunities for contamination occur during the manipulation of the wholesale dealer and the small retailer. It is not wonderful that the milk finally delivered swarms with bacteria indicating for the most part excrementitious pollution.'[15]

Four points of contamination, in addition to a diseased cow, were specified in the article. As alluded to in the quotation above, they are synonymous with those identified by previous writers: '(1) milking and treatment in the dairy, (2) transit to the city, (3) collection, manipulation, storage and distribution by the wholesale and retail dealers, (4) storage in the house of the purchaser.'[16] The remainder of the report was, for a large part, devoted to an examination of each of these points, and to practical remedies for the problems they posed. A horrifying description of an ordinary farm, calculated to elicit a condemnatory response from the reader, was followed by a detailed discussion of several types of model farms found both in the United Kingdom and abroad, thus offering immediately operant alternatives. The net result was to help stimulate a movement, supported by the medical profession generally, to ameliorate the milk supply.

There were two other major factors which added force to the impetus for the improvement of milk quality besides the disgrace of filth and the widely accepted correspondence between dirty milk and high infant mortality from epidemic diarrhoea. The first of these was the question of morbidity with the potential sequela of ill-health especially in relation

---

* 'Adulteration' was distinguished from 'contamination'. The former referred to the illegal practice of altering the defined constituents of milk through the addition of water, chalk, or most dangerously, chemical preservatives. 'Contamination' referred to the usually inadvertent bacteriological pollution of milk.

to the physical deterioration of the race. As public anxiety regarding the possibility of national degeneration escalated following the debacle of the Boer War, concern about milk as a potential factor in that deterioration increased concomitantly. And just as Sir Frederick Maurice's articles on the physical condition of recruitment volunteers aroused massive interest in this issue, similarly Aimée Watt Smyth's series on the hygienic state of the milk supply focused concern on that piece of the imperial problem. The correlation was clear: poor milk led to poor health. Thus it was not surprising that Maurice referred to the young child's need for 'its proper supply of milk' in order to develop a 'proper complement of sound teeth' – the lack of which was 'one of the most common causes which tend to unfit men for the rough work of active service'. He explained further that it was 'the universal belief of the most scientific students of the building up of the human frame that primarily the soundness of the teeth depends on the supply to the child of the food that is suited to the period of life when teeth are forming' (i.e. milk).[17] An abundant supply of good milk would help ensure the proper development of teeth, a poor supply could prevent it. Similarly, Watt Smyth alluded to the potentially poor physical condition of infant survivors of epidemic diarrhoea, caused by contaminated milk, in her 'Report on the Milk Supply'. She contended that 'an attack of acute diarrhoea often leaves behind a condition of general debility and impaired nutrition.'[18]

By the time the Inter-Departmental Committee on Physical Deterioration was appointed (2 September 1903) and had begun to meet, the correlation between the milk supply and the future health of the nation had become an oft-repeated commonplace. Edmund Cautley, for example, of the Belgrave Hospital for Children and author of the influential text *The Natural and Artificial Methods of Feeding Infants and Young Children*[19] (which was in such great demand that it was reprinted that year), expounded on this theme in a paper he delivered before the council of the Charity Organization Society in November 1903. 'There is not,' he declared,

'the shadow of a doubt that on the methods of feeding and rearing infants during the early stages of existence depend the health and strength of the children, and, in fact, the strength and physique of the nation. One is almost justified in asserting that the physique of the nation varies directly as its food supply during infancy and early childhood.'[20]

Not surprisingly, Watt Smyth agreed. Her series of articles on the milk supply of large towns was followed by another on physical degeneration which, as we have seen in Chapter I, formed the basis for an expanded book on this theme. The third in this latter series, subtitled 'The Food Factor in Deterioration', expressed the same sentiments Cautley had professed.

'The root of the national deterioration is in the health of the mothers during pregnancy and the feeding of the infants during their earliest years. . . . Until there is a plentiful supply of pure clean milk available for infants . . . and also for small children . . . they will grow into puny, sickly, rickety human beings who will never recover their false start in life.'[21]

As the Inter-Departmental Committee on Physical Deterioration sat throughout the winter and spring of 1903–4, both the popular and professional press thoroughly discussed the issue of national degeneration in general, and the role of the milk supply as a primary contributory factor in particular. *The Pall Mall Gazette*, for instance, ran a front page article entitled 'Milk and Men' on 12 April 1904, in which it was concluded that 'undoubtedly bad milk in infancy is responsible for a vast amount of the unfitness in the class from which recruits are drawn.'[22] A few months later *The Daily Chronicle* ran a seven-part series on 'Milk and Disease'. The 'expert' who wrote these articles contended that 'London milk is contaminated from start to finish, from its source to the consumer; that this contamination is a serious and constant menace to the health of the community, and that it is in a very large measure responsible for the ghastly wastage of infant life in the poorer parts of the Metropolis; and that there is practically no machinery in existing legislation, so far as London is concerned, to put a term to the evil.' Emphasizing the importance of these matters to the general public the author concluded part one of the series:

'In view of these facts, in view of a falling birth-rate, and the ghastly figures of infant mortality, and in view of a general awakening to the dangers of our physical deterioration as a nation, a layman may plead some excuse if he trenches on matters that more properly belong to the medical profession. A safeguarding against the contamination of our London milk supply is not held up as a short cut to the millenium, but to bring up a race of scrofulous, anaemic, and ricketty [sic] children is assuredly not the way to breed the heirs proper to an imperial race.'[23]

In the subsequent articles the author discussed the sources of contamination,[24] the impotence of existing legal regulations in England either to control or ameliorate the situation,[25] and solutions which had been implemented abroad.[26] His basic theme, however, was that the high infant mortality due to epidemic diarrhoea and the 'rickety or physically deteriorated' condition of the survivors was most definitely due to the poor quality of the milk supply, and not to 'the ignorance of the mother'.[27] Pressing for action, the author concluded that 'the terrible wastage of infant life' caused by the milk supply was 'a matter of national concern. 150,000 infant lives a year is a higher price than any nation can, with a falling birth-rate, afford to pay.'[28]

The medical press was (sometimes literally) written with the same pen. The *BMJ*, for example, was no more derelict in its duty to condemn the quality of the milk supply than *The Pall Mall Gazette* or *The Daily Chronicle* had been and, using the rhetoric of physical degeneration, advocated reform of the conditions of milk manufacture. In an article stridently entitled 'Pus as a Beverage' the editors announced the alarming results of an enquiry they had sent to the medical officers of counties and of combined districts to ascertain 'what steps their authorities have taken to protect the milk supply'. They concluded, in short, that 'the conditions under which milk is obtained and dispatched to towns are exceedingly unsatisfactory. . . . The report affords a striking and indisputable proof, plain for any man or woman, medical or lay, . . . that milk may be drawn and distributed in a condition which must be disgusting.' That this was a serious matter with potentially grave consequences was rather turgidly expressed.

> 'The evil effects caused by the consumption of this miserable liquid are as yet imperfectly realized by the public and even by the profession. They do not end with the murderous epidemics which sweep through the poorer quarters of large towns in warm weather. They lie at the root of much of the chronic ill-health of infancy and childhood, and find expression at last in puny men and women, and in undergrown lads whom recruiting sergeants dare not submit to the examination of the army medical officers.'[29]

Successive articles stressed the primary importance of contaminated milk in causing poor health. Abandoning the rhetoric of and allusions to progressive physical deterioration, the editors focused on the related notion of the future poor health of the nation due to childhood illnesses of milk origin.

Given this persistent insistence upon the primary importance of a proper milk supply in order to protect the public health and the national interest, it is not surprising that the *BMJ* analysed the *Report* of the Committee on Physical Deterioration from this point of view. In an article on the *Report* the editors noted with gratification,

> 'As has been over and over again set forth in these columns, no radical improvements will be attained until the health of infants and young children is first looked to, in order that they may be in a proper healthy condition to benefit by education when their time comes to spend nine of the growing years of their lives cramped up on school benches. It is therefore with deep satisfaction that we see that the Committee has understood this point, almost universally passed by, even by the most intelligent reformers. It has, as we have before them, struck at the root of the question – a clean milk supply.'[30]

In fact, although the Committee by no means ignored this issue (they took much evidence, and their report upon the 'defective supply' comprised five of the total eighty-four pages devoted to describing their findings), they certainly did not perceive the provision of pure milk as the primary route to radical improvement. They very clearly, and equally persistently, emphasized the importance of education at many levels. 'The real remedy,' they wrote in a section on the 'defective milk supply', 'is to be sought in that social education . . . by means of which at first in the school and afterwards in continuation classes, and finally by the fostering care of philanthropic and municipal agencies, the foundations of maternal competence may be laid.' Nevertheless, the Committee agreed that, in the immediate future, 'the crux of the question lies in the steps that should be taken to bring an adequate supply of pure milk within the reach of the poorer classes.'[31] Like the *BMJ*, the Committee found that although progressive physical deterioration did not exist, it was imperative that steps be taken to protect infant and child life in order to ensure a future healthy population. While a poor physical constitution was not necessarily inherited, it could certainly be acquired, and the wretched contemporary conditions of life of the urban labouring class left little room for healthy development. Thus, in conclusion, the Committee reiterated once again that they were 'impressed with the enormous sacrifice of infant life due to insufficient or improper feeding. The ultimate remedy', they repeated, 'lies in . . . social education.' In the meantime, however, 'the purity of the supply of milk to the community' had to be ensured, and a number of practical measures were recommended.[32]

In addition to the generally accepted correspondence between filthy milk and high infant mortality from epidemic diarrhoea, and the connection between such milk and morbidity, possibly producing permanently weakened physical constitutions (with potentially all too obvious national consequences), there was a third major factor which added force to the impetus for an improved milk supply: the relation between contaminated milk and the spread of communicable diseases, particularly tuberculosis. The development of the germ theory of disease had led to the rapid recognition during the second half of the nineteenth century of the role of milk in the communication of such diseases as typhoid or enteric fever, scarlet fever, diphtheria, and septic sore throat. Outbreaks of the first three diseases were clearly visible and, consequently, epidemiologically identifiable. As early as 1857 Dr Michael Taylor of Penrith demonstrated the conveyance of typhoid fever by means of milk and, ten years later (1867), he showed that scarlet fever could also be traced to an infected supply. William Power (later Sir William Power, Chief Medical Officer of the Local Government Board) in 1878 adduced evidence to prove that an outbreak of diphtheria in Kilburn and St John's Wood had been spread by milk. Power's position as a prominent medical officer of health helped to focus wider attention on the potential danger to the community of an infected milk supply.

This was supported further by Ernest Hart, the editor of the *British Medical Journal*. At the International Medical Congress in London in 1881, Hart gave a paper in which he cited fifty epidemics of typhoid fever, fifteen of scarlet fever, and four of diphtheria which had been conveyed through contaminated milk.[33] By the early years of the twentieth century this principle was widely recognized and well accepted; the body of evidence was convincing. For example, during the half century since Taylor had first inculpated milk, 200 epidemics of typhoid fever in England had been traced to an infected supply and it was estimated that 17 per cent of all enteric outbreaks were caused by milk infection.[34]

By 1880 it was understood that the common channels of contamination were from a human source and, in the case of typhoid, also through washing milk vessels with infected water, or contact with dried excreta dust. The law took cognizance of the fact that milk was a special food, peculiarly liable to such contamination and particularly in need of special regulations for its protection and preservation, in Articles 9 and 15 of the Dairies, Cowsheds, and Milkshops Order of 1885, which were mandatory, and in Section 4 of the Infectious Diseases (Prevention) Act of 1890, which was merely adoptive. Section 4 allowed a medical officer of health to prohibit the supply of milk which was causing infectious disease to his district, whether such milk was derived from sources within or without his own district. The legal machinery to activate cessation of distribution was, however, cumbersome and consequently slow moving. Furthermore, even when milk was shown to be the vehicle of contagion in one district, the finding was not applicable for another area. It was not permissible to prevent distribution of the implicated supply until the identical procedure of a report by a veterinary surgeon followed by an order of a local justice and notice served on the dairyman had been completed in the new district.

Article 9 of the Dairies, Cowsheds, and Milkshops Order prohibited any person suffering from a 'dangerous infectious disorder, or having recently been in contact with a person so suffering' to continue to work in 'the production, distribution, or storage of milk . . . until in each case all danger therefrom of the communication of infection to the milk or of its contamination has ceased'.[35] As every cow-keeper, dairyman, or purveyor of milk was required to be registered with the local authority, and as it was also mandatory to report the existence of any contagious or infectious disease among them or their families, this article should have been adequate. Unfortunately, however, there were no inspectors to enforce execution, so it was not as effective as it might have been. Article 15 was even more problematic. This clause ordered that the milk from a cow suffering from a disease might not be mixed with other milk, or sold or used for human food in any way, nor might it be given, without being previously boiled, to other animals. 'Disease' was defined by the Contagious Diseases of Animals Act, and tuberculosis was not included in its provisions.*[36]

Tuberculosis was the primary cause of death among adults, and was responsible for slightly more than half of all deaths between the ages of fifteen and forty during the last decades of the nineteenth and first decade of the twentieth centuries. The discovery of the tubercle bacillus by Robert Koch in 1882 was therefore a momentous achievement, not only in terms of the development of bacteriology, but also because of the enormous consequences it had in the campaign against the disease. Although it did not alter the medical management of consumptives for more than half a century (a specific antibiotic was not found until 1944), the isolation of the responsible aetiologic agent laid the foundation for the ultimate battle with tuberculosis. It demonstrated incontrovertibly that tuberculosis was an infectious illness and not a hereditary disorder as had been believed. As such it could be prevented, and anti-tuberculosis leagues, societies, and associations were established to help implement and popularize preventive measures. The medical and social dimensions of tuberculosis can be compared to those of cancer in the 1980s. Scientific research to find a cure for tuberculosis was supported and encouraged then, just as for cancer a century later. The anti-spitting campaigns of the turn of the century were very much like the anti-smoking crusade of the 1970s and 1980s. Full use was made of the available media to reach the public to teach the principles of prophylaxis. Indeed, the connection is literally continuous; the anti-tuberculosis societies of the early 1900s evolved into the anti-cancer associations.**

Tuberculosis was not nearly so lethal among infants as it was among adults in the prime of life. In his book on *Infant Mortality*, George Newman listed tuberculous diseases seventh among the causes of infant mortality in 1903, and claimed that they were responsible for 4.6 per cent of all infant deaths.[37] Nevertheless, the energy and attention which were brought to bear on tuberculosis as a major public health problem of the turn of the century in a number of ways supported efforts to reduce infant death also. First, within the context of the struggle against tuberculosis, mortality from this disease among infants and young children was by no means a negligible factor. Between 1901 and 1910 in England and Wales, 18.8 per cent of total male deaths at all ages from tuberculosis occurred before the age of five, primarily during the first year of life.[38] In other words, although anti-tuberculosis measures were directed principally towards protecting people aged fifteen to forty who were most at risk, they had ramifications among the infant

* The only diseases of cattle which barred their milk from sale were cattle plague, pleuro-pneumonia, and foot-and-mouth disease.
** Note, for example, the evolution of the National Association for the Study and Prevention of Tuberculosis originally chartered in the United States in 1904. As this society developed it acquired various names: The National Tuberculosis Association (1919), The National Tuberculosis and Respiratory Disease Association (1968), and finally The American Lung Association (1973).

population as well. More importantly for the infant population in general, the anti-tuberculosis campaign and the drive to reduce infant mortality from all causes intersected at one particular point: the milk supply.

Koch had isolated the tubercle bacillus both in animals and human beings, and he noted that although the macroscopic condition of tuberculous organs in both cases differed, the structure of the tubercle itself was identical. On the basis of this identity, and from the preliminary results of feeding experiments, he proposed that the milk from tuberculous animals may give rise to infection of human beings. This put tuberculosis in the same category as other diseases of the cow (such as foot-and-mouth disease, for example) which were transmissible to people. Unlike milk-borne scarlet fever, typhoid fever, or diphtheria, which were due to either direct or indirect contamination from a human source, tuberculosis was communicable to people through the contaminated milk or meat of an infected animal. In 1888, therefore, a departmental committee recommended that the Contagious Diseases (Animals) Act be extended to include this disease. The proposal was not adopted due to difficulties of diagnosing tuberculosis in animals and to the protests of owners of pedigree cattle.[39]

The question was, how great a danger did tuberculosis-contaminated milk pose to the public health? What percentage of milch cows were infected, and how important was bovine infection as a cause of disease? That same year (1888), German Sims Woodhead, then Sanitary Research Scholar and Superintendent of the Royal College of Physicians Laboratory in Edinburgh, endeavoured to answer these issues. In an important series of lectures he delivered before the Honourable the Grocers' Company in the University of London, which provided a basis for much work by later investigators, Woodhead presented a synthesis of the research he had conducted for the past two years on pulmonary tuberculosis and tabes mesenterica. He explained that in order better to understand the focus of invasion of the tubercle bacillus in the body he had examined 127 cases of tuberculous children post-mortem. The ages of the children ranged from under one year to fifteen; sixty-two were aged one to five-and-a-half years. Woodhead found that only forty-three cases (of which twenty-four were aged one to five-and-a-half, and one was less than a year old) presented tubercular ulceration of the intestine. Nevertheless, he noted that 'although the intestines [were] directly affected by the tubercle in such a small proportion of cases, the mesenteric glands [were] found to be in some stage or other of tubercular degeneration in no less than 100 instances or 79 per cent of the whole.' All sixty-two of those aged one to five-and-a-half presented such lesions. In fourteen cases (nine aged one to five-and-a-half) the mesenteric glands alone were affected; no tubercle was found in any other part of the body.[40] As further proof of his conclusion that tabes mesenterica was a more common and, consequently, a more important disease than had been recognized previously, Woodhead adduced the figures for phthisis, tabes mesenterica, and scrofula deaths given in the Registrar-General's supplement of 1871–80. These showed that between 1851 and 1880 the death rate from phthisis had decreased from 1,305 to 767 per million children living, aged 0 to 5 years, while the mortality from tabes and scrofula had increased from 1,920 to 2,550 per million children of the same age group.[41]

Woodhead emphasized 'that the maximum affection by mesenteric tubercle is attained between one and five years' and he hypothesized that 'this fact, taken in connexion with the very large percentage of all tubercular cases (in children) in which mesenteric disease is developed points very decidedly to the supposition that in these tubercular glands is the primary lesion of the body.' The question Woodhead then posed was how to explain the causation of mesenteric tubercle in children at these ages, and the answer he gave was simple and straightforward.

'In the class from which the patients [he examined post-mortem] are drawn, the infants are during the first year of life, and sometimes longer, suckled at the breast, but afterwards the diet is extremely mixed, . . . of course it is almost invariably partially composed of milk. It is after this first year that there is such a rapid rise in the number of cases in which the mesenteric glands are affected.'[42]

It seemed that the milk supply was implicated, and this turned out to be the case. Systematic and painstaking examination of over 600 cows in the Edinburgh dairies which Woodhead, together with John McFadyean (Professor of Comparative Pathology at the Royal Veterinary College), had carried out revealed that at least six (1 per cent) suffered from tubercular mammitis yielding enormous numbers of bacilli in their milk.

In Woodhead's opinion this meant that milk was 'a source of tubercular infection, especially in children'. Referring to feeding experiments undertaken by other investigators which proved that ingestion of tuberculous milk could give rise to the disease in animals,* he stressed that it was 'of course impossible to bring direct experimental proof to bear in the case of the human subject'. Nevertheless, he concluded,

'the indirect evidence recently adduced by various continental observers and the examination of series of cases such as those [here]

---

* Discussions of the cause and effect relationship between tuberculous milk and meat and disease in human beings were necessarily based on circumstantial or statistical evidence. In addition, an enormous body of experimental literature accrued, especially from France, Germany, Denmark, and the US, proving the pathogenicity of milk and meat from tubercular cows for all kinds of animals. See, inter alia, the work of Nocard, Chauveau, Viseur, Calmette, Gerlach, Harmz, Gunther, Klebs, Johne, Bang, Ravenel, and Smith.

brought forward, should be very strong evidence indeed that in children, especially in those who are subject to the wretched hygienic treatment and bad feeding to which unfortunately so many of our poorer-class children are exposed, tuberculosis may be contracted as the result of the ingestion of milk from tuberculous udders.'[43]

By 1890 the question of the pathogenicity of bovine tuberculosis had become so urgent that a Royal Commission was appointed to study the effects upon human beings of food from tuberculous animals. While the Commission was sitting, research continued along the lines Woodhead had set out. Walter S. Colman, then pathologist to the Hospital for Sick Children, Great Ormond Street, presented a paper on 'The Distribution of Tubercle in Abdominal Tuberculosis' to the Section of Diseases of Children at the annual meeting of the BMA in 1893. In general, Colman's series of fifty-nine post-mortem examinations of cases of tuberculosis at Great Ormond Street corroborated Woodhead's findings. But while Colman accepted that the ingestion of tuberculous milk could give rise to the disease, he did not find this mode of infection to be so prevalent as Woodhead claimed it to be. J. Walter Carr, assistant physician to the Royal Free Hospital, 'endorsed absolutely' Colman's conclusions in a paper he gave before the Medical Society of London in May 1894. Carr had studied the post-mortem records of 120 necropsies made at the Victoria Hospital, Chelsea, upon children suffering from tuberculous lesions in order 'to ascertain as accurately as possible in each where the disease actually started'. Carr explained that it was 'a matter of the greatest importance, from the point of view of prophylaxis, to ascertain in what way the bacilli usually obtain entrance, and in what part is usually situated the primary focus [of] infection'. He noted particularly that 'if primary tuberculosis of the intestines or mesenteric glands be set up at all by direct infection, it is undoubtedly mainly by the agency of milk.' Like Woodhead and Colman, Carr found that infants and young children were at greater risk than older children, but the proportion of primary site infection that he determined agreed with those of the latter and not the former investigator. Consequently he concluded, as had Colman, 'that milk containing tubercle bacilli is highly infective', but 'that this does not seem to be by any means a frequent mode of infection as compared with that through the lungs'.[44]

Less than six months later, in October 1894, Woodhead (by then Director of the Laboratories of the Royal College of Physicians of London and Surgeons of England) delivered a lecture at the opening meeting of the North London Medico-Chirugical Society. Speaking on 'The Channels of Infection in Tuberculosis' Woodhead reiterated, and clarified, his position. He did not on this occasion specifically adduce new data, but presented his general conclusions based on the sum total of his and other investigators' experimental research. Woodhead pressed rather eloquently for greater recognition of the importance of alimentary infection, but at the same time clarified that he had no wish to decry the importance of infection by inhalation.

'In the face of facts and statistics it is impossible to overrate these, but I am leaving this part of the subject to take care of itself, for the reason that in most cases our attention is so forcibly drawn to the subject, and it is dinned into us so continually, that there is little fear that we shall lose sight of or even attach too little value to it; whilst on the other hand, there appears to be even now too little attention paid to the question of infection commencing in the alimentary tract. We speak glibly of infection by tuberculous meat and milk, we think of a few cases that have come under our observation, in which one or other of these agents (especially milk) was thought to have played a causal *role*, but that ingesta of various kinds are daily adding to our numbers of cases of tuberculosis is not yet, I am sure, fully realised in this country.'[45]

Sheridan Delépine, by then Professor of Pathology at Owens College, agreed with Woodhead. In a paper on 'Tuberculous Infection Through the Alimentary Canal' published the following year (1895), he expressed his unequivocal support of Woodhead's tenets. Delépine began the article by remarking, with some exasperation, that

'when a truth, whether scientific or other, goes against the interests of a large and powerful class of the community, it is generally ignored or resisted till a more powerful class enforces its recognition. For the last 30 years farmers and butchers have been roughly disturbed by mere scientists, medical observers and veterinary surgeons, who have come to the conclusion that it is not safe for man or beast to feed on tuberculous products.'

Reiterating the basic fact that 'the identity of bovine and human tuberculosis is a thing to be accepted as a fundamental proposition', Delépine turned his attention to the incidence of this disease in children. Like Woodhead, Colman, and Carr, Delépine noted that infants 'begin to be liable to tuberculosis after they have reached the age of six months (i.e. after most of them have begun to be fed on cow's milk, or foods other than the maternal milk)'.[46]

The divergence between Colman and Carr on the one hand, and Woodhead and Delépine on the other, was essentially a question of the different perceptions both parties had of the degree to which tuberculous milk posed a serious risk to infant and child health. Colman and Carr agreed that contaminated milk was a risk factor, but they did not think it played a major role in producing tuberculous disease in children. Woodhead and Delépine thought differently. 'While there is ample evidence to prove that among the channels of infection the air passages are most important,' Delépine wrote, 'a large number of children must, however, become infected through their alimentary canal.' He cited Woodhead's post-mortem examination results of 1888, and said that the evidence he himself had obtained from a series of over a hundred experiments corroborated Woodhead: affliction of the mesenteric glands was, he found, practically synonymous with primary infection through the alimentary canal.[47] Thus he concluded that the ingestion of tuberculous milk was indeed a serious danger to child health.

Soon after Delépine's article was published, the Royal Commission which had been appointed in 1890 to enquire into the effect of food derived from tuberculous animals on human health issued its *Report*. In the course of their charge the Commissioners had initially taken evidence but, not finding it sufficiently uniform, they decided to institute original experimental research. These investigations were conducted by outside experts: John McFadyean, Sidney Martin (Professor of Pathology at University College, London), and Sims Woodhead.[48] Not surprisingly, their conclusions were in accordance with the position Woodhead and Delépine had maintained for some time. The experimental results were straightforward: a certain proportion of animals fed tuberculous material developed the disease, while control animals kept under similar conditions did not become ill. On the basis of both the evidence brought before the Commission and the laboratory research carried out at its behest, the Commissioners were prepared to commit themselves positively. 'As regards man, we must believe – and here we find ourselves agreeing with the majority of those who gave evidence before us – that any person who takes tuberculous matter into the body as food, incurs some risk of acquiring tuberculous disease.' Furthermore, they said, 'We find the present to be a convenient occasion for stating explicitly that we regard the disease as being the same disease in man and in the food-animals.' While human beings could be infected by ingesting tuberculous meat, 'the milk of cows with tuberculosis of the udder possesses a virulence which can only be described as extraordinary' the Commissioners claimed. And they concluded, 'No doubt the largest part of the tuberculosis which man obtains through his food is by means of milk containing tuberculous matter', children naturally being more particularly at risk. Although there was little information on this point, the Commissioners conjectured that 'probably the proportion of tuberculous persons contracting their disease through food is larger among children than among their seniors'.[49]

The Commissioners noted that their charge did 'not extend to enquiry or report on administrative procedures available for reducing the amount of tuberculous material in the food supplied by animals to man' and they regarded 'such questions as beyond [their] province'.[50] By that time Koch had already announced (4 August 1890) his discovery of tuberculin, a concentrated filtrate of tubercle bacilli grown in a glycerol-containing medium which he believed could be used as a preventive and curative vaccine. Despite great initial enthusiasm and endorsements from such eminent bacteriologists as Paul Ehrlich and Joseph Lister, subsequent evidence (particularly post-mortem demonstrations of intense local inflammatory reactions and revelations that Koch had misrepresented the technique of preparation, failed to perform autopsies on his experimental animals, and explained the agent's curative action in terms of its necrotizing rather than allergenic properties) indicated that tuberculin was positively harmful when used in this capacity. However, the contrasting response of healthy and tuberculous animals to tuberculin injections (the latter producing a marked local reaction) was quickly recognized as of specific diagnostic value, and the serum was then used as a tool to detect the presence of tuberculosis in cattle. This made control of the disease among cattle-herds feasible; tuberculin made it relatively easy to identify afflicted animals which then could be either isolated from the rest of the herd or slaughtered. Several countries, such as the United States, Germany, Belgium, and Denmark, had begun to take steps along these lines in an attempt to eliminate bovine tuberculosis in the long run and, more immediately, to reduce the amount of tuberculous food offered for sale in the market place. Neither this issue, nor the legal problems associated with it, was addressed by the Royal Commissioners in 1895 as they deemed it outside their reference, and a second Royal Commission was appointed the following year to enquire into administrative procedures to control the danger to the population from the use of tuberculous meat and milk as food.

The controversy regarding the specific importance of tuberculous milk as a risk factor for children nevertheless continued unabated. As we have seen above, the statistics of the Registrar-General seemed to support those who were more seriously concerned about the dangers of contracting tuberculosis through ingestion. Unfortunately, as in the case of epidemic diarrhoea, the statistics for tabes mesenterica were subject to the vagaries of disease classification. This was pointed out by Carr in 'A Protest Against the Use of the Term "Consumptive Bowels" in the Wasting Diseases of Infants'. He noted that the term was 'still in common use, both amongst the laity and medical men, in marasmic conditions of young children', and expostulated against it because it was imprecise and very often inaccurate.[51] However, John Tatham, Superintendent of Statistics at the Registrar-General's Office, who was well known and well respected for accuracy, contended in his evidence given before the Second Royal Commission on 20 January 1897 that although tabes mesenterica was an 'indefinite term' including illnesses other than tuberculosis it was, nevertheless, 'time-honoured', and he believed that the statistics he adduced were useful to compare one year with another. Furthermore, even though 'tabes mesenterica' often meant simply a disease accompanied by wasting or, more particularly, diarrhoea, mortality statistics were not recorded at a loss or gain of one or the other. To the contrary: the rates from diarrhoeal and tabes mesenterica deaths increased and decreased simultaneously. Analysing the changes in mortality between the quinquennial periods 1881–85 and 1886–90, at the separate ages of infancy, Tatham found that an actual increase had occurred in the three to six month age period. He noted the coincidence of this age with the introduction of cow's milk, but did not claim that this explained the rise.[52]

Tatham's statistical analysis was much publicized by Sir Richard Thorne-Thorne, Medical Officer of the Local Government Board and one of the Royal Commissioners appointed in 1896, in the Harben Lectures he gave in 1898. In fact, nearly all the later writers who referred to this matter cited Sir Richard, and not Dr Tatham's testimony. Thorne-Thorne contended that

'there was abundant statistical evidence, at any rate since 1857 [sic 1837] when civil registration of deaths was instituted, of a general and progressive reduction in the mortality from all forms of tuberculosis, and at all ages, with one very important exception. . . . While the mortality of tabes mesenterica had been reduced by 8.5 per cent at all ages, and 3 per cent between those of one and ten, there had been an increase of 21.7 in the mortality among infants under one year.'[53]

In explanation of this phenomenon he reasoned that 'the reduction in the mortality from all forms of tuberculosis had been mainly determined by that of phthisis as the predominant form, and that this in its turn had resulted partly from . . . better social conditions [such as] the construction of sewers and drains . . . paving, damp-proof courses, concrete foundations, etc. The influence of such sanitary improvements was felt especially among children whose lives were passed at home.' Tabes mesenterica, however, was due to the ingestion of the tubercle bacillus, 'the two possible vehicles . . . being meat and milk',[54] neither of which was affected by the sanitary improvements which had been instituted.

Sheridan Delépine also cited the statistics of the Registrar-General to help prove his contention that milk was an important vehicle of infection in young children. In a public lecture on 'Tuberculosis and the Milk-Supply, with some General Remarks on the Dangers of Bad Milk' delivered on 15 September 1898, Delépine repeated the evidence, conclusions, and opinions he had presented on previous occasions. 'The difficulty of dealing with tuberculosis is further increased by the general ignorance of the public,' he declared. 'The danger which they incur from a contaminated milk-supply is appalling in its magnitude, yet because this danger is of an insidious nature and its effects are often so gradual that it is difficult to trace their onset they prefer to have their quietude not disturbed.' Delépine maintained that not only was infection through the intestine a frequent occurrence in children but also the tubercle bacillus occurred sufficiently frequently in milk to justify 'serious fears in connexion with the use of this article of diet'.[55]

The use of Tatham's statistics regarding the rise in the mortality rate from tabes mesenterica catalysed a stream of debate challenging the accuracy of such figures. Carr opened the discussion with a letter entitled 'What is Tabes Mesenterica in Infants?' published in the *Lancet* on 17 December 1898. Directly disputing Thorne-Thorne's claimed increase (Tatham was nowhere mentioned), Carr repeated the conviction that he held together with Ashby and Wright: '"mesenteric disease was much more frequently diagnosed than discovered post-mortem."' He also reiterated his own belief 'that milk may and frequently does convey tuberculosis', but he argued that such 'genuine tuberculous diseases' have little to do with 'so-called tabes mesenterica' which was nothing other than 'gastro-intestinal catarrh'. Improving the milk supply would not, therefore, reduce the tabes mesenterica figures.[56] Leonard G. Guthrie, physician and pathologist to the Children's Hospital, Paddington-Green, explained in an article on 'The Distribution and Origin of Tuberculosis in Children' that Carr's remarks on Thorne-Thorne's statements had stimulated him to look into the matter himself. His results corroborated Carr's conclusions and contentions: thoracic tuberculosis was found to be more common than abdominal in the proportion of three to two and, more importantly with regard to the statistics, 'tabes mesenterica as a cause of death [was] practically unknown'.[57] Thus Guthrie, again like Carr, had little faith that purification of the milk supply would ameliorate the incidence of tuberculosis in children.

Sir Richard Douglas Powell, physician in ordinary to the Queen and physician to the Middlesex Hospital, further confused the situation when he gave the address in medicine at the annual meeting of the BMA in Portsmouth in August 1899. 'Pulmonary consumption', Powell asserted, 'is comparatively rare before puberty, infantile mortality being almost exclusively from bowel consumption through milk infection.'[58] At the same meeting, in the Section of Diseases of Children, George Still presented the results of his post-mortem examinations as pathologist to the Hospital for Sick Children, Great Ormond Street. Out of 769 consecutive necropsies on children under twelve years of age, 269 were found to have had tuberculosis, and 117 of these (43.4 per cent) were among children less than two years old – the period during which milk was the staple diet. Nevertheless, Still found that the lung appeared to be the primary channel of infection in 138, and the intestine in 63, of the 269 cases. The figures for the 117 youngest children were 63 in the first instance and 20 in the second. (The remainder of the cases were of uncertain origin or through the ears, bones, or joints.) He concluded that

'the special frequency of tuberculosis in infancy and in early childhood seems therefore . . . not to be due to the milk diet to which it has been attributed, though there can . . . be little doubt that this is responsible for a certain proportion of cases of tuberculosis at this age, about 17 per cent of the cases during the first three years of life being intestinal in origin.'[59]

Carr seized upon both papers, and wrote a lively letter to the *BMJ* complaining that 'traditional beliefs die hard in medicine . . . and it is a deeply-rooted belief that in young children tuberculous infection is more common through the intestine than through the lungs.' Carr cited Thorne-Thorne and Powell specifically and remarked reprovingly (if plaintively) that 'statements . . . from the leaders of the profession are naturally accepted almost without question, and protests from juniors pass unheeded.' He went on to say that he nevertheless hoped that 'Dr Still's valuable paper . . . will materially help in the growth of more accurate views on the subject'.[60] Not surprisingly, this letter stimulated an irritated response in 'defence of the average obsolescent seniors'. A letter by Dr H.B. Donkin of Harley Street, for example, claimed that the 'deeply-rooted belief' of which Carr spoke had been dead so long that it 'by this time scarcely stinks'.[61]

This sort of sparring continued intermittently for the next few years until Still, among others, attempted to clarify the facts of the situation constructively. In a paper on 'Tuberculosis in Childhood' published in July 1901, Still took great pains to disentangle those points which had become confused. He explained that the statistics of the Registrar-General were 'rendered valueless by the lack of post-mortem verification in the majority of cases'. Even when necropsies had been undertaken, interpretation required care: the relative frequency of tuberculous lesions in the various glands (the mesenteric, for instance) was not so important as the apparent duration of the process at those sites in determining the route of primary infection. Most importantly, Still was more interested in identifying the major risk factors in childhood tuberculosis than in proving that thoracic infection occurred more frequently than abdominal. Thus, he clearly stated that 'the view that milk infection is chiefly responsible for the heavy incidence of tuberculosis on childhood is untenable', but he did not leave the matter there. 'Whilst fresh, pure air is the first and by far the most important requisite in the prevention of tuberculosis in children, and especially in infants,' Still declared, 'the danger of tuberculous milk is a very real one, and calls for the most stringent precautions. On my own showing, nearly one-fourth of the mortality from tuberculosis in infancy is due to intestinal infection; and much of this is probably due to milk-conveyed tubercle bacilli.' This was much more than the previous polite bows by the champions of thoracic infection to acknowledge the existence of a real danger from tuberculous milk. Indeed, Still pursued the matter further. 'There can be little doubt that properly regulated inspection of cows and cowsheds would do much to abolish milk-infection altogether,' he asserted, and he concluded with the practical suggestion that 'until this ideal is attained milk should be rendered innocuous by pasteurisation or by heating just to the boiling-point, and then at once rapidly cooling.'[62]

Interest in such matters as the 'properly regulated inspection of cows and cowsheds', to which Still had referred, had increased with the publication in 1898 of the *Report* of the second Royal Commission on Tuberculosis. In the course of their enquiry into 'what administrative procedures are available and would be desirable for controlling the danger to man through the use as food of the meat and milk of tuberculous animals', the Commissioners took much evidence and personally conducted inspections. A number of them, accompanied by John McFadyean, travelled to Belgium, Germany, and Denmark to compare continental with English practices. They found that 'nothing that has come before us . . . has raised any doubt in our minds as to the accuracy' of the first Commission's statement that any person who takes tuberculous matter into the body as food incurs some risk of acquiring tuberculous disease. 'At the same time', the Commissioners continued, 'we think there has been a tendency in some minds to exaggerate the extent of the risk arising from meat.' They had no such reservations with regard to tuberculous milk, however. 'Whatever danger may be incurred by the consumption of the flesh of tuberculous animals . . . there can be little doubt that the corresponding danger in respect of milk supply is a far greater one.'[63]

The Commissioners' recommendations reflected this perception as well as their understanding that the extant legislative regulations to protect the public from tuberculous products were a dead letter in many places.[64] As they believed that only cows suffering from tuberculosis of the udder yielded contaminated milk* the Commissioners advised the compulsory notification under penalty to the local authority of all diseases of the udder, and proposed legislating power for carrying out inspections and investigating the source of any particular supply regardless of the district in which it was situated. An emasculated

---

* The findings of both the first and second Royal Commissions on Tuberculosis were in accordance with contemporary bacteriology texts. In R.T. Hewlett's first edition of his *Manual of Bacteriology*, for example, he noted, 'It is generally acknowledged now that tubercle bacilli do not find their way into milk, even from an extensively diseased cow, unless the udder is affected. When this is the case the bacilli may be met with more or less numerously, and are apparently extremely virulent, more so than is usual. As guinea-pigs and rabbits fed on tubercular milk readily become infected there must be, to say the least, considerable risk to young children who might consume such milk. To avoid risk, all milk intended for the food of infants and young children should be pasteurised by heating to a temperature of 68 to 70°C for twenty minutes, or sterilised by boiling' (R.T. Hewlett, *Manual of Bacteriology*, 1898, pp. 204–05).

version of this recommendation was incorporated into Article 15 of the Dairies, Cowsheds, and Milkshops Order as the Amendment Order of 1899 which enlarged the regulation of the use of milk from diseased cows to include 'such disease of the udder as shall be certified by a veterinary surgeon to be tubercular'. This legislation was decidedly weak, as notification of udder disease in general was not compulsory, so tuberculosis could easily escape unnoticed. Furthermore, of course, pus due to other non-tubercular infection could get into the milk and, even if notified, was not restricted or forbidden from sale as human food.

Many of the other recommendations of the second Royal Commission were not translated into legislation at all. They recommended, for example, that meat inspectors should be required to pass an approved examination and, perhaps most importantly, that the Board of Agriculture should supply tuberculin and the services of a veterinary surgeon free of charge to farmers wishing to eliminate tuberculosis from their herds.[65] Frustrated by the inadequate and ineffective national legislation, a number of local authorities obtained special powers to control the trade of tuberculous milk by private Acts. In Delépine's September 1898 lecture he presented the work he had done with his colleague James Niven (MOH for Manchester) to ascertain the pathogenicity of milk samples, and the usefulness and practicability of introducing supervision of the supply. During the previous four years Delépine had examined 208 samples, 7 from cows not known to be tuberculous, 22 from cows in an advanced state of tuberculosis, 54 from town dairies, and 125 'from country farmers being collected by sanitary inspectors at the railway stations immediately on arrival of the cans from the country'. He found that 'the milk of non-tuberculous cows does not produce tuberculosis [and that] the milk of at least 1 out of every 4 cows much affected with tuberculosis is capable of communicating tuberculosis'. With regard to the efficacy of control, Delépine found that

> 'the milk coming from country farms which are not under the constant supervision of the health authorities is capable of communicating tuberculosis in 17.6 per cent of the cases examined [while] in towns, . . . where cowsheds are under constant supervision, the number of cases in which the milk proved to be infectious was considerably less, being reduced to 5.55 per cent.'[66]

Niven used these results to present a trenchant case for independent control of the milk supply to the Congress of the Sanitary Institute which took place in Birmingham the same September. He emphasized that 'these samples . . . were taken without selection. It thus appears that a great stream of infective milk is flowing into our cities, which could scarce fail to cause much of the actual tabes mesenterica and tubercular meningitis which we observe.' He explained that 'it appeared to the Sanitary Committee of the City of Manchester that if we are to deal with this matter by actual administration, we must be armed with proof that such administration is practicable.' Following a trial procedure, the Committee found that 'if we can take samples, and have them bacteriologically examined, and if, further, we can go and investigate and deal with the condition of cows from which tuberculous milk is derived, we know that, beyond a doubt, we can do a vast amount of useful administrative work.' In short, Niven argued that 'every district should have the right to protect itself against the importation of tuberculous milk. For that reason every district should have the right to investigate the condition of those cowsheds and cows from which its milk supplies are derived.' Regarding the recommendations of the Royal Commission, Niven declared that while 'they do not go so far as some of us would wish' they nevertheless 'suggest a welcome instalment [sic] of legislation'.[67]

Given the working partnership of Professor Delépine and Dr Niven,* it is hardly surprising that when even the conservative suggestions put forward by the Commissioners in 1898 were not made law, it was The Manchester Corporation (General Powers) Act, 1899 which was the first to be passed, and which was a model for other municipalities. The Manchester Milk Clauses provided for increased powers of inspection extended to all localities purveying milk to the city, prohibition of the sale of tuberculous milk within the city, isolation of cattle suffering from tuberculosis of the udder, and compulsory notification of all suspected cases of this form of the disease.[68] During the next few years a number of other boroughs and urban districts adopted similar legislation, some of which, such as Croydon, Liverpool, Birmingham, Sheffield, Leeds, and Sunderland, pursued enforcement rather vigorously. Sims Woodhead, by then Professor of Pathology at Cambridge University, struck the key note at a conference on the prevention of tuberculosis held at Leeds on 10 March 1899, under the auspices of the Sanitary Committee of the West Riding County Council and numbering 800 representatives. 'We are a very practical people,' Woodhead asserted, 'and when we see a thing is necessary, we don't wait for the Government to help us, but in our own interests we do it for ourselves.'[69]

* In England, at that time, the co-operation between Delépine and Niven was matched only by that of Dr Hope and Professor Boyce in Liverpool, and was, consequently, noteworthy. A *Lancet* editorial of 1 October 1898 commented favourably, urging the establishment of similar alliances. 'In Manchester Professor Delépine, working in conjunction with Dr Niven, has organized in the Owens college a system of laboratory investigation which promises to effect a complete transformation in the character of the work of the Health Department in the Manchester district. . . . In this matter Manchester [has] followed the lead of such cities as Paris, Berlin, and Lille, where there appears to be a definite arrangement between the municipal authorities and the great pathological and bacteriological institutes by which the former obtain the benefit of the use of the laboratories and workers in the institutes and the latter receive substantial subsidies through the aid of which they are enabled to become vastly more efficient than they could otherwise hope to be,' (*Lancet*, 1 October 1898, p. 883).

Whatever steps the government may have eventually been tempted or persuaded to take were effectively baulked by no less a person than Robert Koch himself. On 23 July 1901 Koch astounded the public in general and the scientific world in particular with his announcement at the British Congress on Tuberculosis that

'human tuberculosis differs from bovine, and cannot be transmitted to cattle. . . . Though the important question whether man is susceptible to bovine tuberculosis at all is not yet absolutely decided, and will not admit of absolute decision to-day or to-morrow, one is nevertheless already at liberty to say that, if such susceptibility really exists, the infection of human beings is but a very rare occurrence. I should estimate the extent of the infection by the milk and flesh of tuberculous cattle, as hardly greater than that of hereditary transmission ["though . . . not absolutely non-existent, it is nevertheless extremely rare"], and I therefore do not deem it advisable to take any measures against it.'[70]

Lord Lister, who chaired the session, expressed the general reaction when he emphasized that 'what had chiefly riveted their attention had been the startling thesis that bovine tubercle could not develop in the human body. This was', he stressed, 'a matter of enormous practical importance, because, if this conclusion were sound, it would greatly simplify their preventive measures; but it would be a very serious and grievous thing if the rules now in force for securing purity of milk supply should be relaxed and it should turn out after all that the conclusion was erroneous.' In Lister's opinion the evidence adduced by Koch to show 'that bovine tubercle could not be transmitted to man did not seem at all conclusive. It consisted in the alleged rarity of primary tuberculo-intestinal lesions in children, in spite of the multitudes of tubercle bacilli swallowed by them in milk.' However, Lister pointed out, 'even if it were admitted that primary tuberculous intestinal lesions were as rare in children as Koch's statistics indicated, it was certainly true that tabes mesenterica existed in a considerable percentage of children who died of tuberculous disease without tubercle being found in any other part of the body.'[71] Nocard of France and Bang from Denmark, speaking after Lister, flatly disagreed with Koch.[72] Woodhead spoke last. 'Personally', he said, he 'held the view that bovine tuberculosis played some part in the genesis of the disease in man'. He suggested that the Congress appeal to the Minister of Agriculture to institute a commission of enquiry, and that until the question had been settled the present precautions should be continued.[73]

Given the weight of clinical and bacteriological evidence confirming the identity of human and bovine tubercle bacilli and the transmissibility of bovine tuberculosis to human beings through the alimentary canal, which had been presented both prior to and indeed at the Congress itself, the reaction of the participants and the press was to be

74

expected. An editorial on 'Professor Koch and Tuberculous Milk and Meat', published four days after Koch's address, may perhaps have described the situation best. Beginning with Koch's concluding remarks on the subject (quoted above) the editors went on to expostulate, 'Already, before these memorable words of Professor Koch could be published in *The Lancet*, they had carried solace or given rise to astonishment, and even incredulity, in most parts of the civilised world. . . . Accustomed as we are to accept the researches of Professor *Koch* almost without demur, we feel, nevertheless, a little staggered by the directness and conclusiveness of [his] statement.' With some pique the editors noted that 'it would have been difficult for our most distinguished and honoured guest to have chosen a more fitting or a more dramatic occasion for his remarkable announcement, seeing that not a little of the labours of the State Section of the Congress is concerned with the control of our milk and meat supplies.' They pointed out further that if we can 'consume bovine tubercle with impunity it is clear that much meat and milk have been wasted', that in Britain alone 'there have recently been two Royal Commissions upon the question of tuberculosis', and finally that while it was easy to urge continuation of present precautions 'on all sides our medical officers of health will be met' with Koch's pronouncements, 'putting back reform in our milk and meat traffic [as] those who are familiar with the excuses of sanitary authorities for a policy of inactivity'[74] could well imagine. In other words, the editors did not believe a word Koch said, and they lamented the potential and all too probable damage his conclusions would cause.

It must be remembered that by the time Koch startled the scientific world in general, and stymied public health officers in particular, with his announcement at the Congress, bacteriologists, pathologists, and practising physicians, in addition to the two Royal Commissions, had convincingly argued the case for the transmissibility of bovine tuberculosis to human beings, especially children, through the alimentary canal and, consequently, for protection against a contaminated milk supply. As we have seen, statistical studies based on the reports of the Registrar-General, children's hospital records, and post-mortem examinations, as well as animal feeding experiments, provided sufficient circumstantial and practical evidence to persuade both the profession and the public of the pathogenicity of contaminated milk. Indeed, by the turn of the century the correlation between tuberculous milk and intestinal and abdominal infection had become a commonplace. Furthermore, tuberculin testing in relatively small sample herds had revealed that it was probable that a large percentage of British cows were tuberculous. According to Woodhead, for example,

'it had been calculated — and the calculation was based on a considerable number of observations — that something like 49 per cent of the cattle in this country react to the tuberculin test, and

75

allowing an error of 5 per cent, this would still leave over 40 per cent of tuberculous cattle in our dairies.'[75]

It was estimated that a substantial proportion of these suffered specifically from tuberculosis of the udder. This was reflected in the milk supply of large towns. The annual reports of the medical officers of health of those areas which had adopted and subsequently vigorously enforced Milk Clauses routinely included information regarding the microscopical and bacteriological inspection of milk samples destined for human consumption. Delépine, for instance, recorded that the percentage of tubercle-infected milk samples arriving in Manchester from the country was 13.3 in 1897, 20.0 in 1898 and, after passage of the Milk Clauses in 1899, 11.1 in 1900.[76]

In short, scientists and physicians were convinced that bovine tuberculosis transmitted through the milk supply was a real and present danger for human beings, and they were not willing to reject their own results or conclusions, or abandon their plans for amelioration. Nor, however, were British scientists, in the main, ready to reject Koch's results and conclusions. Consequently, at the close of the Congress on Tuberculosis the participants passed a resolution requesting the government to appoint another Commission to investigate Koch's assertion, as Sims Woodhead had recommended. On 31 August 1901, the third Royal Commission on Tuberculosis was authorized to determine whether the human and bovine forms of the disease were identical and reciprocally infective. The Commission conducted its own research in addition to taking evidence; it sat from 1901 until 1912 and issued four reports, the last dated 1911.

There is no doubt that Koch's pronouncement proved obstructive. Time, money, and effort were spent to confirm what had already been accepted as proven. For the next decade medical and scientific research on tuberculosis focused primarily on proving the communicability of the bovine form to human beings, and delineating the conditions under which this occurred, and only secondarily on the need for specific legislative powers or reforms. Although several urban and county authorities passed Milk Clauses, no national legislation which would control the trade was carried. Koch's announcement meant that a clean milk supply could not be achieved immediately through the argument, or demanded upon the basis, of tuberculosis prevention. Proof had to be forthcoming first.

Marshalling the evidence to construct this proof began, despite Koch, at the Congress itself, as John McFadyean pointed out in the address he gave on 'Tubercle Bacilli in Cow's Milk as a Possible Source of Tuberculous Disease in Man'. 'As recently as a few days ago,' McFadyean began,

'I was under the impression that it would not be necessary to formally

76

prove that the term "tuberculosis" as it is now employed by medical men and veterinary surgeons relates to one and the same disease. . . . To-day, however, the position of anyone who undertakes to discuss the inter-communicability of human and bovine tuberculosis is very different from what it would have been a week ago, for in the interval the greatest living authority on tuberculosis – the world-renowned discoverer of the tubercle bacillus and the man to whom we are mainly indebted for our knowledge of the cause of tuberculosis – has declared his conviction that human and bovine tuberculosis are practically two distinct diseases.'

Yet, McFadyean reminded his audience, the research of hundreds of workers during the past eighteen years supported 'the conclusion that human and bovine tuberculosis were identical diseases [with] the possibility and probability of reciprocal infection', and he challenged Koch's main assertion that cases of primary abdominal tuberculosis were extremely rare.[77]

McFadyean recapitulated the basic argument against Koch's recommendation that no measures be taken to prevent the transmission of tuberculosis from animals to man.

'What has been said with regard to the extent of the danger to which the public are exposed through the sale of milk containing tubercle bacilli may be summed up as follows. The danger cannot be defined by stating how many persons are thus infected annually, or what fraction the persons thus infected form of the total number who contract tuberculosis in the course of a year. At the same time, it is impossible to doubt that the danger is a real one, since at the present time milk is a vehicle by which tubercle bacilli are often introduced into the bodies of human beings.'[78]

Experimental evidence in contradiction of Koch's pronouncements was also presented at the Congress. The most important was Mazÿck P. Ravenel's (then Bacteriologist of the State Live Stock Sanitary Board of Pennsylvania and Lecturer on Bacteriology at the University of Pennsylvania), comprehensive paper describing the meticulous work he had done for the past two years to study the comparative virulence of the tubercle bacillus from human and bovine sources. Ravenel had discerned that the bovine bacillus was far more pathogenic than the human for all species of experimental animals tested, except pigs. This was, he felt, a salient point of central significance. Whereas Koch argued that since the human bacillus was not pathogenic for cattle (or only very feebly so) the reverse must also be true, Ravenel approached the problem from a different angle. He stressed the 'considerably greater pathogenic power' of the bovine tubercle bacillus in comparison with the human strain. The question he then asked was, 'How should we interpret this in regard to man? Is it fair to conclude that this increase of virulence will hold good for man also?' His answer was reasonable and prudent. 'Until the contrary is proven, or until good reason for believing the contrary is shown, it is, in my judgment, right that this conclusion be held, at least as a working hypothesis.'[79]

Naturally enough, in addition to the appointment of a third Royal Commission on Tuberculosis, research designed specifically to investigate the points Koch had raised began immediately the Congress closed. As the *BMJ* reported, 'On the morning after Professor Koch made his announcement . . . the Americans had commenced experiments with the view of testing the soundness of his observations.' The article went on proudly, 'Following their example Professor Delépine has not allowed any grass to grow under his feet, and [has conducted] a series of experiments designed to test some of Professor Koch's statements in regard to the communicability of human tuberculosis to cattle. These experiments are specially interesting from the fact that they were carried out after – though so soon after – Professor Koch's pronouncement had been made, and that they were arranged with the special object of testing one of the most important points raised'[80] – his denial of the pathogenicity of human tubercle bacilli for cattle. Delépine published a preliminary communication regarding his results in the same issue. 'The cost of the experiment,' he explained, 'which I took upon myself to avoid delays, prevented my using more than four calves.' Delépine inoculated three and fed one of the experimental animals with human tuberculous sputa. Of the four *only two survived long enough to allow definite results to be obtained, and these two calves had contracted tuberculosis as the result of ingestion of or peritoneal infection with human tuberculous sputa.*[81]

In the course of an address on 'The Relationship of Human and Bovine Tuberculosis' delivered before the Section of Pathology at the annual meeting of the British Medical Association the following year (1902), D.J. Hamilton, Professor of Pathology at the University of Aberdeen, remarked on the sheer number of researchers who had successfully inoculated a variety of animals with human tuberculosis. In addition to the extensive, meticulous work of the French scientist Arloing, who had presented a report of his investigations to the Academy of Medicine in Paris in December 1901 after three series of experiments on calves, sheep, goats, rabbits, and guinea-pigs, 'positive results have been obtained by Bollinger, Klebs, Rievel, Crookshank, Sidney Martin, Thomassen, Nocard, de Jong, Ravenel, and Behring, and . . . perhaps I may be allowed to say, by myself.' Hamilton finished his paper with the rather mild statement that 'the general inclination, at the present time, in spite of what Koch has asserted to the contrary, is to regard bovine tuberculosis as equally virulent for man.'[82] Delépine, the President of the Section and the first to speak after Hamilton's address, was much more assertive. 'Koch's statements', he said, 'were so obviously in contradiction with a number of observations that from the first several workers [Delépine himself included] could not allow the great weight of his opinion to overcome the conclusion which they had come to on the basis of repeated observations.'[83]

While scientists and concerned members of the medical profession appear to have been convinced or reassured of the fallaciousness of Koch's argument relatively quickly, it is clear from an article in the *BMJ* announcing the publication of the second interim report of the Royal Commission (1907) that many people either did not, or chose not to believe that Koch had been wrong. With obvious relief, the editorial began,

> 'In their . . . report the members of the Royal Commission on Tuberculosis have . . . dealt the death blow to a doctrine which, during the last few years, has exercised a mischievous influence upon the interests of public health. . . . After investigating the subject with a thoroughness which justifies us in saying that they have pro- nounced the final word, the Tuberculosis Commissioners have decided that the bovine tubercle bacillus undoubtedly is a danger to man, and is a serious danger.'

They concluded, rather hopefully, that it would 'no longer be possible for those concerned with the provision of human food to seek relief from their responsibilities by appealing to a scientific hypothesis which has now been proved to be untrue' and that it was 'imperative that cow's milk intended for human food should be free from bovine tubercle bacilli'.[84]

The Royal Commissioners had indeed conducted exhaustive resear- ches,* and their results were cited endlessly not only in Britain but in the European and American literature as well. Bacilli isolated from cases of tuberculosis occurring spontaneously in bovines were studied, and the results of their introduction into a number of different animals by feeding and inoculation recorded. Bacilli isolated from sixty cases of the disease in human beings were also studied. The Commissioners found that in fourteen cases (one obtained from sputum, three from

* The five members of this Royal Commission were particularly well suited to their task of original research, rather than the hearing of evidence. The list of their names reads like a roll-call of honour in the history of science. Sir Michael Foster, who died while the Commission was still engaged in its studies, was a Fellow of the Royal Society and Professor of Physiology at Cambridge. Foster was succeeded by William H. Power, also FRS, and Medical Officer to the Local Government Board. Rupert William Boyce was Professor of Pathology of University College, Liverpool. German Sims Woodhead, Professor of Pathology at Cambridge, Sidney Harris Cox Martin, Professor of Pathology at University College, London, and John McFadyean, Principal and Professor of Comparative Pathology and Bacteriology at the Royal Veterinary College, had all worked extensively on the subject prior to the appointment of this Commission (1901), and they were the three external experts requested by the first Royal Commission on Tuberculosis (1890) to undertake experimental research under its terms of reference.

tuberculous cervical lesions, and ten from the mesenteric glands of primary abdominal tuberculosis in children) results of experimentation revealed the characteristic features of bacilli of bovine origin. They therefore resolved that 'there can be no doubt but that a certain number of cases of tuberculosis occurring in the human subject, especially in children, is the direct result of the introduction into the body of the bacillus of bovine tuberculosis.'[85]

The question of the inter-transmissibility of human and bovine tuberculosis finally had been answered, but the problem of the extent to which this posed a risk to the public health remained. That is to say, the proportion of human tuberculosis which was of bovine origin was not clear. From the beginning of the 'bovine debates', Koch's statement that the percentage was practically nil aroused interest in and focused attention upon this aspect of the issue, and as it was a clinical question medical practitioners became involved in this controversy to a far greater extent than in that of transmissibility. Letters, articles, and short communications from physicians discussing the incidence of tuberculous peritonitis or tabes mesenterica began to appear in numbers in the professional journals within a fortnight of Koch's address. The consensus which had been achieved prior to the Congress had been shattered by the pronouncements of the great scientist, stimulating a recrudescence of the former confusion and inciting a return to the old factions. As with verifying once again the identity and inter-transmissibility of human and bovine tuberculosis, re-establishing the infective nature of tuberculous milk, confirmed by the fact that approximately one-quarter of cases of tuberculosis in children examined post-mortem were abdominal or intestinal, was a waste of time, effort, and energy. However, unlike the former case, in which prior to Koch's announcement (and indeed, subsequently as well) there had been a marked uniformity in professional opinion, the latter issue had been vigorously disputed until just before the Congress.

On 10 August 1901 two letters exemplifying the opposing positions regarding the pathogenicity of tuberculous milk were published in the *BMJ*. The first was from J. Alfred Coutts, a physician at the East London Hospital for Children, and the other was from Alfred Hillier, Secretary to the National Association for the Prevention of Consumption (London) and author of the aptly entitled book, *Tuberculosis*.[86] Coutts had no doubt but that Koch was correct in 'his estimate of the infrequency with which tuberculosis is primarily incurred in the intestines through the agency of infected food' — an estimate with which, Coutts claimed, 'many clinical observers in this country will cordially agree'. (No names were given.) Therefore, he said, he had no 'sympathy or support' for 'certain wild schemes involving the wholesale destruction of cattle presenting any evidence of tuberculosis or reacting to the tuberculin test' and he expressed a 'regret that too much stress had been laid upon the frequency of infection through the agency of food by some authorities actuated by a laudable desire to check and control the disease'.[87]

Hillier, on the other hand, had no doubt that Koch was wrong. He described Koch's statement as 'astounding' and argued that 'Professor Koch had so far adduced no direct evidence whatever' in support of his contention. Hillier emphasized that 'the incidence of tabes mesenterica in relation to milk consumption was remarkable' and quoted statistics to this effect, including those given by Thorne-Thorne in the Harben Lectures of 1898, showing that between 1851 and 1895 there had been a 27.7 per cent increase in deaths from this cause among infants. Hillier concluded that 'these statistics, taken in conjunction with the established virulence of tuberculous milk for other animals, while they do not demonstrate, undoubtedly strongly suggest a danger to infants from its consumption . . . in the shape of tabes mesenterica.'[88]

As we have seen, the accuracy of these official statistics had been questioned several times before, and as this argument once again arose repeatedly throughout the latter half of 1901 and early 1902,[89] the *BMJ* decided to address the issue. In an article entitled 'Tuberculosis in Infancy and Childhood' the editors referred to the Carr–Donkin debate of 1899 and said that, despite Donkin's protests to the contrary, 'it appears to be true that the belief that tuberculosis is a common disease in childhood and frequently fatal is very general.' They surmised that

'the belief probably rests not on the statement of textbooks but on the statistics of tabes mesenterica published by the Registrar-General. The late Sir Richard Thorne-Thorne whose name was almost synonymous with accuracy, by appearing to adopt these figures as proof of the prevalence of abdominal tuberculosis, gave them a wider currency than they could otherwise have attained. But it is probable that in this instance he placed too much reliance on the official statistics; it is at least certain that medical men who have had much experience at children's hospitals have never been able to accept the conclusion that intestinal tuberculosis or indeed tuberculous infection of any of the abdominal organs is a common disorder in children, or anything but very rare in infants.'[90]

In his second book on tuberculosis, which was published the following year (1903), Alfred Hillier also addressed this issue. He explained that 'as Sir Richard Thorne-Thorne's statements were based on statistics furnished by Dr Tatham of the Registrar-General's Department' he, Hillier, wrote to Tatham 'to inquire whether in his opinion the returns upon which these statistics were based were of a reliable character'.[91] Tatham's reply was reprinted in full in Hillier's book.

'I am strongly of the opinion that the indefinite term "tabes mesenterica" is frequently held to comprise other forms of disease than those which are due to tubercle. . . . I have done my best to prevent the further use of the term, and to substitute for it "tuberculous peritonitis". Personally I adhere strongly to the idea that very much of the mortality which is returned as due to "tabes mesenterica", ought really to be classed under the head of "epidemic diarrhoea".'[92]

Tatham's assertion indicated a nexus of issues with which we are by now familiar: first, the terminology and classification of infant deaths, and second, the basic fact that whether milk was the vehicle of infection for tabes mesenterica (or 'tuberculous peritonitis') or epidemic diarrhoea, the underlying precipitating cause for the infant mortality in either case was contaminated milk.

Despite these qualifications and explanations, Thorne-Thorne's statistics continued to be quoted for the next few years, and the issue of their accuracy was discussed both in the medical journals and at medical meetings.[93] At the same time, new investigations such as that of L. Kingsford (1904), Newsholme's deputy Medical Officer of Health in Brighton, proved that while Thorne-Thorne's statistics were probably exaggerated, the risk of infected milk to infant and child health was serious nevertheless. Kingsford 'analysed the post-mortem records of 339 cases of tuberculosis in children of all ages up to 14 years, taken from the East London Hospital for Children'. He found that 162 (48 per cent) occurred during the first two and 270 (80 per cent) during the first five years. Of the 339, sixty-four (18.8 per cent) were abdominal cases; a figure which, as Kingsford noted, was very close to those adduced by other investigators in Great Britain,* but quite a bit larger than had been found in America, France, or Germany. In Kingsford's opinion there was no 'satisfactory explanation' for this phenomenon but he felt one factor which may have tended 'to diminish the frequency of abdominal tubercle [was] the much larger scale on which sterilised milk [was] prepared and sold there as compared with . . . this country'.[94]

The second interim report of the Royal Commission on Tuberculosis (1907) confirmed Kingsford's results and his reasoning, as well as those of the early investigators in this field. As we have seen, the Commissioners found that 'there can be no doubt that in a certain number of cases the tuberculosis occurring in the human subject, especially in children, is the direct result of the introduction into the body of the bacillus of bovine tuberculosis.' They maintained, moreover, that 'there also can be no doubt that in the majority at least of these cases the bacillus is introduced through cow's milk.' The Commissioners were absolutely decided as to the role of milk as a vehicle of tubercular infection, and as

* Kingsford specifically cited Still, Shennan, Guthrie, Carr, Ashby, and Batten. In the aggregate, these studies revealed 214 primary abdominal out of a total of 1,119 cases of tuberculosis, or 19.1 per cent. In America the figure was considerably lower at 3 per cent, and in France and Germany 2.5 per cent.

to the need for more effective public health powers to delimit this health risk. Their results, they emphasized, 'point clearly to the necessity of measures more stringent than those at present enforced being taken to prevent the sale or consumption of such milk.'[95]

The second interim report conclusively clarified what had come to be understood prior to the British Congress on Tuberculosis in 1901 and subsequently had been obscured and confused by Koch's pronouncements: milk was a factor, but not the chief factor, in the causation of tuberculosis, and abdominal infection was a form, but not the principal form, of the disease in infants and young children. Studies to refine and clarify particular aspects of the Royal Commission investigations were of course undertaken, but the basic conclusions reported in 1907 were not challenged. The most important of these was the 1912 Local Government Board sponsored investigation to determine the frequency of tuberculous infection, latent or manifest, in childhood, the distribution of this disease within the body, and the relative incidence of the bovine and human types of the bacillus.[96] The enquiry was undertaken by Arthur Eastwood and Fred Griffith in the Board's Pathological Laboratory (London), and 'in view of the importance of the subject it was arranged that a parallel investigation should be undertaken at Cambridge by Dr A. Stanley Griffith'.[97] Arthur Newsholme (then Medical Officer to the Board), in a prefatory note to the studies, and the authors themselves were careful to explain that their studies were 'to supplement the work of that Commission, because they are based on material from an unselected series of deaths, whereas . . . the material investigated for the Commission was selected, special attention being devoted to cases where the portal of entry of the bacillus was presumably alimentary'.[98]

A total of 195 children aged two to ten years dying from all causes were examined, 150 in London and 45 in Cambridge. In an attempt to avoid selection bias, every case which came to the post-mortem rooms of the hospitals participating in the study (none of which was specially devoted to the treatment of tuberculous patients) between 4 June 1912 and 3 February 1913 was included. Evidence of tuberculous infection was found in 118 of the 195 children; in 92 (47.2 per cent of the total or 78 per cent of the tuberculous group) tuberculous lesions were present and living bacilli were obtained in culture, in 6 (3.1 per cent of the total and 5.1 per cent of the tuberculous) living bacilli were obtained, although no lesions were present, and in 20 (10.3 and 16.9 per cent respectively) lesions were found, but the bacilli were apparently dead. In sum, 98 of the 195 children yielded cultures of live tubercle bacilli, 81 (82.7 per cent) of the human and 18 (18.4 per cent) of the bovine type. Although these statistics could not be extrapolated to the general juvenile population, they did indicate how very prevalent the disease was, both as a cause of morbidity as well as mortality among children. Furthermore, 'these figures while showing the greater importance of infection of human source, illustrate also the danger of cow's milk as a source of tuberculosis in childhood, and corroborate the conclusions upon this subject which were arrived at by the recent Royal Commission.'[99] As this was an 'unselected' series, it was perceived as even more revealing than the Royal Commission's *Report* as to the serious risk to which children were exposed through pathogenic milk.

The percentage of the milk supply infected with tubercle bacilli had been a matter of concern since the late 1890s, especially in those areas which had passed Milk Clauses. In addition to the annual reports of those localities, many other studies were conducted to determine the local percentage. Then too, popular press articles dealing with the milk supply focused specifically on this aspect of the problem. One of the most important of the local studies was George Newman's 'Report on the Milk Supply of Finsbury' in 1903. Published the same year as a monograph, this work was reviewed in the medical press and presented as a forty-page abstract with an accompanying editorial in *Public Health*. The enquiry was an in-depth local study of the problems he had examined in his book, *The Bacteriology of Milk* (1902). Every conceivable aspect of the issue was addressed, including the source of Finsbury's milk; where and how, from cow to consumer, it could be (and was) contaminated; the condition of the milk, including an examination for adulteration with preservatives and the bacteriological content; the relation between milk and disease, especially epidemic diarrhoea; the present control of the milk supply, and possibilities for improvement. With regard to tuberculosis, Newman found that not one of twenty-five samples of milk obtained in Finsbury and subjected to examination was infected with the bacillus. Nevertheless, he had no doubt that some percentage 'of the milk coming into Finsbury actually contains the germs of this disease'.[100] In support of his conviction Newman noted the figures found in other localities. In Liverpool, he said, about 2 per cent of the town-produced and 9 per cent of the country-produced milk was found to be tuberculous, and 22 per cent of the milk examined on one occasion in Hackney also proved to be contaminated. Furthermore, during 1901 in 6 per cent of the milk tested in Croydon and 7 per cent of that in London as a whole the tubercle bacillus was detected. In 1902, 10 per cent of the milk examined in Woolwich, 11 per cent in Camberwell, and 14 per cent in Islington were tuberculous-infected.[101]

The Daily Chronicle series on 'Our Milk Supply' emphasized this last figure. The headline of the first article ran: 'Contamination Leads to Widespread Disease and Many Deaths; A Great Evil and How to Cure It; Fourteen per Cent. of London Milk Contains Tubercle Germs.' The author explained:

'It is . . . a fact, ascertained by careful scientific investigation, and vouched for by official documents, that in one of the Metropolitan Boroughs of London 14.3 per cent of the milks examined from 200 samples taken at random from the local milk-shops and churns at the railway stations was definitely tuberculous (i.e. contained the bacilli of tuberculosis); 15.1 was found after experiment to be "suspicious", giving a total of 29.4 per cent of milks that were of "a dangerous character". There is no reason for believing the milk supply of this particular district was either better or worse than that of any other part of London. The 200 samples examined in all probability fairly represented the general London milk supply.'[102]

The figures presented in this article were probably too high, but there is no doubt that a significant percentage of the milk supply was infected with the tubercle bacillus. At the request of William Collingridge, Medical Officer of Health for the City of London, Klein analysed a number of milk samples representing the supply from various counties to London. In 1904, 7.7 per cent were found to be tuberculous; the figure for 1905 was 9.1, for 1906, 8.0, and 1907, 8.3 per cent.[103] The number of samples Klein examined each year was relatively small, never exceeding a hundred. His results, therefore, were not completely trustworthy. Sheridan Delépine, by contrast, had in the course of his work tested literally thousands of samples. In 1908 he was asked by the Local Government Board 'to present the result of [his] investigations on the prevalence and sources of tubercle bacilli in cows' milk'. In summary Delépine noted that

'between the years 1896 and 1908, 5,320 samples of mixed milk coming from 12 different counties have been tested bacteriologically at the [Public Health] Laboratory, and 474 of these samples have produced tuberculosis in experimental animals. In other words, 8.9 per cent of the mixed milk (i.e. milk as supplied to consumers) contained a sufficient number of tubercule bacilli to produce tuberculous infection.'[104]

As we have seen, existing legislation was not sufficient to protect the purity of the milk supply prior to Koch's spectacular announcement at the 1901 Congress on Tuberculosis, and the effect of the statement was such that no new national legislation was passed until the third Royal Commission on Tuberculosis had presented its results. In the meantime, many authorities did not even implement the legislation which was available on an adoptive basis. Much of the strength and operation of the Dairies, Cowsheds, and Milkshops Orders was the responsibility of the local authorities. It was up to them to enforce the Order and also, under Article 13, to frame regulations for controlling the conditions under which milk was produced and sold within their several districts. (These regulations were circumscribed by the spirit of the Order generally, which was more interested in the structural environment than preventive hygienics.) Stringency in the form, or efficiency in the application of these regulations depended upon the position taken by the local authority. And as George Newman tartly remarked, the local authorities, in general, were either too intimately or too little interested in the milk trade to adopt these regulations in any other than an academic spirit.

In 1903 the *BMJ* addressed 'a set of questions to the medical officers of counties and the medical officers of health of combined districts, asking them what steps their authorities have taken [under the Dairy, Cowsheds, and Milkshops Order] to protect the milk supply'. Fifteen of the twenty-six medical officers of county councils and twelve of the thirty-one officers of combined districts replied by the end of the year. In the opinion of the editors these men, a self-selective group, must be from those authorities 'in which most zeal is displayed in combating insanitary conditions'. The editors, in analysis, said that 'judging from the general tenor of the replies . . . we think that it is quite safe to conclude that throughout England and Wales the conditions under which milk is obtained and dispatched to towns are exceedingly unsatisfactory, and that law and regulations are alike, to a very large extent, dead letters.'[105] Five years later, in the Presidential Address delivered to the West of England and South Wales Branch of the Society of Medical Officers of Health, L.M. Bowen-Jones (MOH, Carmarthen Urban and Rural Districts) cited this study as still relevant. Speaking on 'The Control of the Milk Supply', Bowen-Jones noted that 'some 30 per cent of the sanitary authorities had made no regulations under the Dairies and Cowsheds and Milkshops Order, 1885. . . . Very few of those who had made regulations had provided efficient means for the supervision which is necessary to ensure that they are carried out.'[106]

By contrast some authorities, as we have seen, were sufficiently interested in the problem of the milk supply to pass special protective legislation. Unfortunately, in operation these Model Milk Clauses were not found to be ideal either. In Manchester, for example, the penalty for contravening the regulations could not exceed forty shillings. Thus it could be more lucrative for a dairyman to attempt to circumvent the regulations, even paying the fine if need be, rather than cease to sell milk from a tuberculous cow or inform the medical officer of health of the disease among his herd. Furthermore, although more efficient (and infinitely more precise in application) than the mandatory articles of the Dairies, Cowsheds, and Milkshops Order (1885) or the adoptive Infectious Disease (Prevention) Act (1890) the tuberculosis control regulations were more dilatory than was desirable.

H. Meredith Richards, MOH for Croydon, described some of the difficulties he had encountered trying to enforce the local Act which had been passed in 1900 in an article on the control of the milk trade. 'Local experience of the practical working of the model tuberculous clauses has not been satisfactory,' Richards admitted ruefully.

'Considerable loss of time (usually five or six weeks) is entailed by the preliminary animal inoculation. Should the result prove the milk to be tuberculous, the consequent proceedings are fairly easy if the cowshed in question is within the borough. When, however the milk is obtained from a distance much time is taken up in visiting the farm, and the search for the diseased cow is not infrequently fruitless, as the herd may have changed since the initial sample was taken. Lastly, even if the tuberculous udder is detected, there is no guarantee that the farmer will withdraw the diseased animal from his milking stock.'[107]

Milk from such a cow, rejected or excluded from one area, was not necessarily destroyed; it could be (and was) sent to another place where there were no powers to prevent its sale. As Sir James Crichton-Browne stated succinctly, 'London . . . receives and swallows milk that has been declared unfit for sale in Manchester and Liverpool.'[108] This was echoed in the popular press. 'London Receives Supplies which Other Towns have Condemned'[109] ran one headline in *The Daily Chronicle* series.

For this as well as other reasons, even the most enthusiastic supporters of the Clauses eventually developed reservations regarding their operation and results. In his report to the Local Government Board (1908) on the work he had done in Manchester, Sheridan Delépine noted that while the Sanitary Authority of Manchester had been able, through skilful administration of the Clauses, to obtain 'a considerable improvement in the milk supply, . . . some farmers who supplied tuberculous milk to Manchester [had], after this had been discovered, ceased sending their milk to the town, and now send it elsewhere'. Regulation in one district was clearly not sufficient to protect the public health. Occurrences of this kind indicated 'the necessity of strict control of the milk supply of *every district*'. Delépine also pointed out various defects in the operation of the Clauses, emphasizing the considerable time, effort, and energy needed by the Authority. Commitment to the goal of a pure milk supply was essential as 'measures having for object the control of milk supplies, to be efficient must be carried out uninterruptedly year after year, very systematically and over fairly *extensive continuous areas*'.[110]

William G. Savage (County MOH for Somerset and Lecturer on Bacteriology at University College, Cardiff and London) discussed the Model Milk Clauses at considerable length in his book *Milk and the Public Health* (1912). 'In considering the value of these special powers', he concluded

'it must always be remembered that their sole object is the protection of the particular city for which they were obtained. . . . Their effect on the amount of bovine tuberculosis in the country as a whole is, for practical purposes, *nil* as long as they are only locally applied. Their *national* as distinct from their *local* value is negligible.

87

As regards their effectiveness to protect the community . . . against the dangers of bovine tuberculosis spread by milk, the figures . . . show that . . . only a moderate measure of success has been attained. The writer, from a careful study of the results obtained, is of the opinion that these clauses, confined in their powers as they are by restrictions and limitations, have not effected results commensurate with the cost of working them.'[111]

Most importantly, Savage pointed out, the clauses were based upon the assumption 'that the presence of tubercle bacilli in milk is due to the herd supplying the milk containing one or more cows affected with clinically recognisable udder tuberculosis'.[112] The findings of the third Royal Commission on Tuberculosis, as well as other researchers, had proved conclusively that this was false; tubercle bacilli had been detected in the milk of cows not noticeably suffering from the disease but which the tuberculin test had revealed to be afflicted.

The final Report of the Commission was published in 1911, and the recommendations it contained were incorporated into the Milk and Dairies Act of 1914 and the Milk and Dairies (Consolidation) Act of 1915. The former prohibited the sale of tuberculous milk or the milk of a cow suffering from emaciation. It also gave the local authorities considerable powers: to obtain a sample of milk from any cow, or from any particular teat of a cow, to prohibit the sale of milk believed to be tuberculous, and to appoint a veterinary surgeon to be responsible for the inspections required under the Act. The Tuberculosis Orders of 1913 and 1914 of the Ministry of Agriculture were designed to work in conjunction with the Milk and Dairies Act. These Orders required the slaughter, with compensation to the dairyman, of every cow suffering from tuberculosis of the udder, or tuberculosis with emaciation, or giving tuberculous milk. Furthermore, any person with such a cow in his possession was required to give notice to the authority. The Milk and Dairies (Consolidation) Act was even more comprehensive in the power it gave to the local authorities and the Local Government Board. This legislation provided for the registration of dairymen as well as of premises, the supervision of the inside of dairies, and the handling, cooling, and conveyance of milk. The 1915 Act also authorized the use of the designation 'certified milk' in the sale of milk, and the term was defined to specify that the milk was produced and distributed under particular conditions, and met a set bacteriological standard. Unfortunately, Britain soon felt the financial effects of the First World War and the lack of manpower, both of which were essential to the implementation of the Act. In the event its operation was postponed for another decade.[113]

Scientific knowledge with regard to tuberculosis was reflected in the 1913–15 Acts and Orders which were passed but not implemented. Yet, as we have seen, the definitive conclusions which formed the basis of this national legislation had been established, albeit in a more general way, at the turn of the century. Statistical studies by that time had shown a direct correlation between bottle-feeding with cows' milk which contained an enormously high number of bacteria and epidemic diarrhoea. Examination of milk samples revealed that this sort of gross contamination was all too common. Scientific research had indicated that communicable disease in general, and tuberculosis in particular, were transmissible through contaminated milk. It was estimated that approximately 10 per cent of the milk supplied to large towns was tuberculous. Furthermore, at this early date anxiety about national deterioration, triggered by the Boer War, focused attention on the milk supply as a factor in degeneration.

At the turn of the century, however, no decisive national action was taken; improvement of the milk supply rested with local initiative. And as we have noted, the passage of Model Milk Clauses was only of limited success. It is true that the infant mortality rate from abdominal tuberculosis and diarrhoeal diseases decreased during the period of our study, but it is doubtful that this was due in any significant way to these local acts. Although some contemporaries believed this to be the case (Nathan Raw, for instance, observed the 'remarkable diminution' in non-pulmonary tuberculosis among Liverpool children which, he said, 'I attribute entirely to the energetic measures which have been adopted by the health authority towards safeguarding the milk supply'[114]), most made no such claims. The cause and effect relationship was too obscure or indistinct; there were too many uncontrollable variables. Consequently, people interested in preserving infant life looked to different methods to diminish disease and death. The experience of other countries facing similar problems was helpful and, as we shall see, the French milk depot system appeared to be a reasonable, practicable way to effect immediate change. The statistics of their results were inspiring – they seemed to demonstrate a direct relationship between control of the *infant* milk supply and the health of the children thus fed.

When at long last the 1913–15 Acts and Orders were passed the situation was much clearer than it had been in 1899 when the Manchester Milk Clauses were enacted. Much research had been done and more was known, facts had been verified and hypotheses proven. Thus Hugh Ashby, writing in 1915, explained very simply and without reservation that non-pulmonary tuberculosis was 'more common in England than in other countries . . . because so much raw milk is used [here]. In America, where the milk supply is much more satisfactory, I was impressed by the small amount of tuberculosis in children compared with what one sees in England.' With regard to the newly passed legislation to control contamination, he said, 'It is satisfactory to know that the government of this country is at last becoming alive to the fact that bovine tuberculosis is a real source of danger.'[115] It was by this time the first year of the Great War, and no longer as in 1899 a question of the spectre of national deterioration but the reality of the necessity for national survival.

Part Two
The Solutions Undertaken

PART TWO

The Social and Environmental

IV

From goutte de lait to infant milk depot

At the turn of the century there was a great deal of concern, both public and professional, that the milk supply was a source and disseminator of several evils. Its immediate victims were infants and young children (i.e. those who were the greatest consumers), but it was easy to presage that this meant the ultimate casualty would be the Empire. Epidemiological studies had shown that milk was the vehicle of infection for communicable diseases such as enteric fever, scarlet fever, and diphtheria; the latter two most commonly diseases of childhood. The first Royal Commission on Tuberculosis (1890–95), as well as other researchers, had concluded that milk, passing through the alimentary canal, was a mode of transmission of this disease to children, inducing tabes mesenterica. And finally, although a specific aetiologic agent for epidemic diarrhoea had not been isolated, it was commonly accepted that bottle-feeding with impure milk was the major risk factor for this disease.

The significance of these facts and favoured hypotheses was perceived by many contemporary observers to indicate national danger. Contaminated milk not only killed potential Empire-builders, it could also permanently weaken those infants who had sickened but not died, causing them to grow up frail, infirm, and feeble. Contamination meant loss of nutritional value; such milk hindered the proper growth of infants who never specifically became ill but also never flourished. In short, the pus (as the *BMJ* called the milk supply) drinkers of today would be the rejected recruits of tomorrow. For contemporary physicians the facts and hypotheses provided a clue to the possible diminution of the morbidity and mortality of infants and young children. While physicians did not, as a professional group, believe in progressive national degeneration – due to contaminated milk or anything else – they clearly saw that such milk was responsible for

93

disease and death. In practical terms, improvement of the milk supply was a means to promote health.

Nevertheless, at the turn of the century the scientific and statistical evidence proving or indicating a causal link between an infected supply and specific diseases, and the fear-mongering rhetoric of national deterioration, were not forceful or powerful enough to catalyse action to improve the purity of the milk supply on a national level; they were, however, sufficient to effect local change. The Model Milk Clauses enacted by some authorities were one such local response to the problem of the milk supply. These regulations, focusing primarily on the prohibition of tuberculous milk in a specific district, affected the general milk supply to that area. Other authorities concentrated on activities to improve the infant milk supply. They made it their business to introduce systems for the provision of clean milk for infants and young children only.

These two forms of local initiative were parallel developments in response to a common problem. They were born, matured, and died more or less simultaneously during the first decade of the twentieth century. The very same year (1899) the Manchester Sanitary Authority secured the passage of the Milk Clauses, the Health Committee of the St Helens Corporation opened the first milk depot in England. And just as much of the inspiration for administrative measures to control the danger to human beings from tuberculous food came from foreign examples, especially Denmark, Germany, and the United States, similarly the concept of the milk depot was also imported from abroad, in this case specifically from France.

In France the problem of national depopulation had become a matter of concern a generation earlier than in England. The French birth rate had decreased sooner and more sharply than the English and their infant mortality rate was higher. In France the birth rate was already as low as 26.2 per 1,000 in 1860. From 1877 onwards a further slow decline began and by the turn of the century it had fallen to approximately 22 births per 1,000 population.Their infant mortality rates exacerbated the already slow population growth. Between 1877 and 1886, 226 per 1,000 infants died while in England the corresponding figure was 167 per 1,000.[1]

The profoundly demoralizing debacle of the Franco-Prussian War gave rise to the fearful spectre of present and future French national impotence (just as the Boer War reverses would do in England thirty years later), and the French began to pay increased attention to their population problems from this point. But naturally the war did not change the trend of the relevant vital statistics. During the last three decades of the nineteenth century France had a lower birth rate and a higher infant mortality rate than every other continental nation. The net result of this situation was that France had, in comparison with all other European nations, by far the smallest proportion of children per 1,000 inhabitants at all ages.[2]

The significance of this state of affairs was not lost on contemporary politicians or physicians. The French were not anxious about their slow population growth for internal reasons; like the British several years later, they were concerned that France would be left behind in the race for cultural and military supremacy. 'Dépopulation', the catchword of the time, did not actually mean a decreasing population, it signified 'que l'augmentation de la population est inferieure en France à celle des autre pays d'Europe'.[3] The rhetoric of the time reverberated through the popular and professional press: this 'natalité pathologique' would have political, economic, military, and cultural consequences. In short, France would become a second- or even third-rate nation.

The single greatest cause of infant mortality in France was epidemic diarrhoea. Balestre and Gilletta de Saint-Joseph, for example, analysed the statistics 'sur la mortalité de la première enfance dans la population urbaine de la France de 1892 à 1897'. They found that 'sur 1.000 décès d'enfants 0 à 1 an: 385 sont dus à la gastro-entérite'; 147 to pulmonary affections, 171 to congenital debility, 25 to tuberculosis, and all other causes combined totalled 272 per 1,000. As in England, it was clear that bottle-fed babies suffered disproportionately. *Figure 6* illustrates the discrepancy between the death rate from diarrhoea among breast- and bottle-fed infants in Paris in 1898. (This graphic representation was so successful that it was reproduced in numerous books and journals outside France and provided the basis for a number of posters to remind mothers of the dangers of summer diarrhoea. The original diagram was used for the next twenty years at least, as can be seen in *Plate 1*: an affiche issued by the Babies of the Empire Society in 1918.) As Balestre and Gilletta reported, 'Ce sont surtout les enfants élevés artificiellement qui succombent', especially during the summer.[4]

French bacteriologists, investigating the flora of the normal intestine as well as the specific pathological conditions found in infants suffering from epidemic diarrhoea, had no more luck in identifying or isolating the responsible aetiologic agent of this malady than their colleagues elsewhere.[5] It is not surprising that, analogous to the situation in England a decade later, French physicians turned to pragmatic solutions in the hope of immediate results. The first of these organized attempts to reduce infant mortality was the establishment in 1890 of L'Oeuvre de la Maternité at Nancy by Professor François-Joseph Herrgott (1814–1907). The object of this charitable society was to educate and aid the mothers delivered at his clinic in the maternity hospital, and to encourage them to breast-feed. A gift of money was offered to each mother who both nursed and brought her infant back to the clinic to be weighed and examined one month after birth; the sum depended upon the manner in which the baby had been cared for and

Figure 6 Death rate from diarrhoea among infants, Paris, 1898

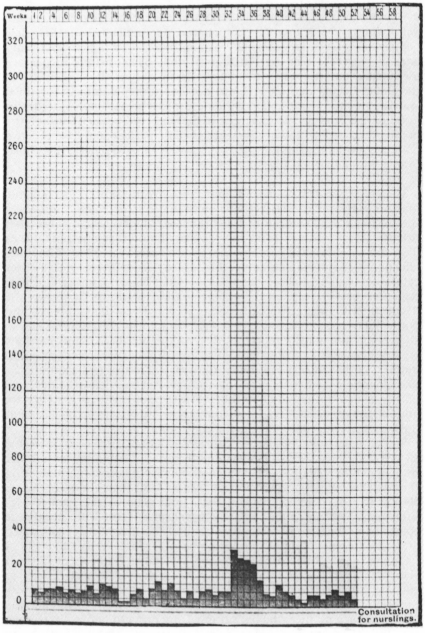

Light grey   =   'Eiffel Tower' of mortality among bottle-fed infants
Grey/black   =   Mortality among breast-fed infants
Base-line   =   Nil mortality among Consultation infants
(*Source*: Pierre Budin (1907) *The Nursling*.)

Plate 1 'Save the Babies' poster issued by the Babies of the Empire Society in 1918 to warn against the dangers of summer diarrhoea

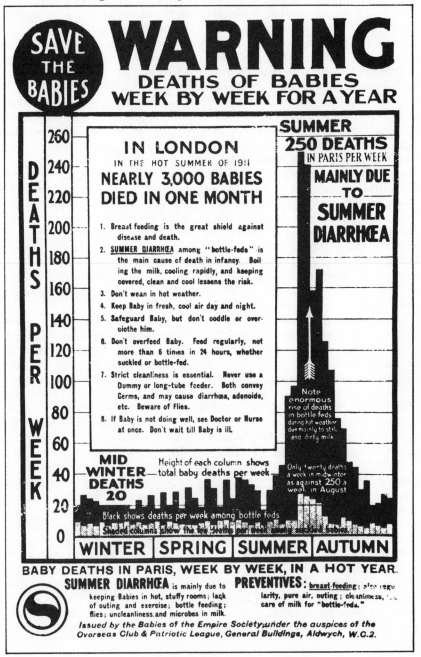

(*Source: Maternity and Child Welfare* (1918), vol. 2, p. 278.)

the needs of the family. Between 1890 and 1900, 23,382 francs were distributed according to this plan among 2,052 mothers.[6]

Much more influential, however, was the infant welfare scheme of Pierre Budin which he began when he was Chef de Service at the Charité Hospital in Paris. In 1892 Budin, with the authorization of Dr Peyron, the Director-General of the Assistance Publique of Paris, organized the first formally structured consultation de nourrissons (suckling infant clinic). The women who were delivered at La Charité* (where they were admitted free of charge) were requested to attend an out-patient clinic, the consultation, established specifically for their infants every Friday morning. There the child was weighed and examined. Records were kept of this information and particulars such as teething, illness, method of feeding and quantity of milk, and general observations regarding growth and development were noted.[7] This was not obtained solely for the physician's use; it was shared with the mothers. The principle was to interest the women in the health and growth of their infants while at the same time inducing them to observe strictly all the physician's directions. Budin believed that although the mothers were 'ignorant and poor' they were 'eager to fulfil their obligations to their children'. It was, he submitted, his 'duty to supervise, direct, and help them to the best of [his] ability', and he quoted his student Henri de Rothschild to the effect that the consultations were really schools for mothers.[8]

Budin's primary tenet of infant care was the establishment of and perseverance with breast-feeding.[9] When it was absolutely impossible to raise the child solely on breast milk, or if the mother had no milk at all, the baby was given sterilized cows' milk which was, in general, undiluted. Budin obtained commercially pasteurized milk 'to preserve it during transit'. Upon arrival at the hospital this milk was measured into 'small graduated bottles, which each contain enough for one feed', and sterilized in a bain-marie at 100°C. The daily milk supply for all the infants receiving cows' milk was provided each morning at the clinic where it was collected by a member of the child's family.[10]

Budin's second principle of successful infant care was his insistence upon maternal acquiescence to and compliance with his instructions. 'You must not infer that my task is always easy,' he told his students somewhat ruefully. When he began the consultation, he admitted, women who were successfully nursing their infants ceased after a time to attend the clinic, and only those who were receiving the sterilized milk for their babies continued to come. Within a decade, however, he was able to claim that 'nowadays mothers are beginning to appreciate the benefits of medical supervision, and many who give their children nothing but the breast now attend with unfailing regularity.'[11]

The reason for this maternal loyalty was manifest; Budin's results

* In Paris at this time there were twelve services d'accouchement (maternity services).

were truly wonderful. His achievement, throughout the 1890s, in slashing the morbidity and mortality rates among the infants atteⁿding his consultation, especially when compared with the statistics which obtained among the general infant population in the city of Paris, were astonishing and inspiring.[12] Indeed, the system straightaway promised so well that the following year (1893) Gaston Variot opened a consultation supported by private charity at the Belleville Dispensary, which was located in one of the poorest districts of Paris. The situation Variot faced was different in several ways from that with which Budin had to contend, most of which stemmed from the fact that the Dispensary was not, in contrast to La Charité, a maternity hospital. Variot did not have prenatal contact with the mothers, nor did he see the infants immediately or even shortly after birth. Infants who were failing to thrive, who were weak and ill, were brought to his consultation, often already 'deficient in weight by one-third and sometimes one-half of the normal'. These babies were 'of the lowest and poorest classes . . . almost invariably fed artificially and rarely if ever breast-fed by their mothers, who are . . . obliged to work in the manufactories or in the workshops'. Unlike Budin, Variot could not insist upon or as much as encourage breast-feeding. 'It is utterly impossible to resort to suckling to combat infantile mortality,' he declared, 'the mothers have no longer any milk.'[13]

Variot therefore organized a system of milk distribution accompanied by medical examination of the infants. He obtained commercially sterilized milk* which was distributed either gratuitously or at a reduced price to the mothers each day in litre or half-litre bottles. The babies attending Variot's consultation were weighed and examined, as at the Charité, and the results of both physicians were remarkable.

In addition to being an eminent paediatrician, Variot was also an effective writer, and he established and edited the journal *La Clinique Infantile* which publicized the work of the various infant welfare systems. He was so successful in this that his consultation attracted a variety of visitors: philanthropists, physicians, and even the artist Jean Geoffroy who painted 'The Philanthropic Society of the Goutte de Lait de Belleville' (*Plate 2*). This picture, exhibited in the Salon of 1903 and subsequently acquired by the municipality of Paris, depicts the three major functions of the clinic. The left panel illustrates a physician and mother weighing her infant, the central panel the medical consultation regarding the health and development of the child in relation to the recorded growth, and the right panel the mother collecting her baby's milk.

The number of consultations de nourrissons increased rapidly throughout the 1890s. By 1898, four of the twelve services d'accouchement in the city had established consultations de nourrissons. In

---

* Commercially sterilized milk was kept at 110–120°C for ten to fifteen minutes.

Plate 2
'L'Œuvre de la Goutte de Lait' by Jean Geoffroy (Dr Variot's Consultation at the Belleville Dispensary, Paris)

(*Source:* G.F. McCleary (1905b) *Infantile Mortality and Infant Milk Depôts*, frontispiece.)

addition to those which were maternity hospital based, a number of physicians followed Dr Variot's example and opened similar services at dispensaries and general hospitals. Due to the ardent advocacy of Paul Strauss, a politician (a member of the Senate) philanthropist, and a friend of Budin, the Conseil Général de la Seine resolved to organize similar services in the municipal dispensaries and charities throughout Paris. The first such city consultation was opened in 1895 at the Maison de Secours in the eleventh arrondissement.[14] By 1903 there were twenty-five consultations de nourrissons in Paris, twelve funded by private charity and thirteen through municipal monies.[15]

Infant welfare work in the provinces was equally as energetic – and at least as influential – as that undertaken in the capital. The earliest, and that of greatest consequence, was the system developed by Dr Léon Dufour at Fécamp in Normandy. Unaware of Budin's work in Paris, Dufour in 1894 opened an independent baby welfare clinic, unattached to any hospital or dispensary, and supported by private subscriptions. Dufour named his establishment the 'Goutte de Lait', a term which became popular and was commonly used. Despite the differences in name and with regard to the particulars of the patient population, the principles of Dufour's Goutte de Lait and Budin's consultation de nourrissons were essentially identical. The mother was encouraged to breast-feed if she could, and as much as possible; even if she could not provide the complete dietary, she was urged not to abandon nursing altogether but only to supplement her own supply with cows' milk. The responsibility of the Goutte de Lait was to provide what the mother lacked. And here there were some differences between Budin and Dufour; the latter appeared to be like Variot, much more conscious that it could be, and often was, impossible for the mother to suckle her baby. Dufour had a pragmatic approach to the issue. The ideal situation, he felt, was maternal nursing, at least to the extent to which she was able. However, the function of the Goutte de Lait was to help infants. 'Le but de l'œuvre,' Dufour emphasized, 'dès sa fondation, a été celui-ci; lutter contre la mortalité des enfants en bas âge.'[16]

Dufour welcomed any and every infant. He seems to have asked no questions concerning legitimacy or the occupation of the mother, although he was interested in discerning the social class of the family as the Goutte de Lait was 'principalement dirigée sur la classe pauvre, celle où les difficultés de l'alimentation artificielle sont les plus grandes'. Dufour accordingly classified the infants into three categories: '(a) Section gratuite, la première, la base de l'opération. (b) Section demi-payante. (c) Section payante.'[17] The daily charges ranged from ten centimes (one penny) among the poor who could afford to pay something to as much as one franc. In case there was any doubt or suspicion that the children were not treated equally, Dufour explicitly dispelled the notion, declaring that 'les enfants de ces trois sections reçoivent le même lait, préparé de la même manière, et distribué dans un matériel semblable.'[18]

The practical organization of the Fécamp Goutte de Lait was as efficient as it was uncomplicated. Each child was issued a double set of baskets and bottles for his sole use. Every day the mother received one basket with as many bottles of modified ('humanized') sterilized milk as the child required for a twenty-four-hour period; the bottles were filled proportionally. Upon the return of the basket-and-bottle set the following day, the mother was given the alternate kit.[19] Medical examination of the infants and hygiene instruction for their mothers were integral parts of Dufour's Goutte de Lait, just as they were of the consultation de nourrissons. Thus the three primary principles of the two institutions were identical: to encourage and aid breast-feeding, to supply good quality sterilized milk for those infants who required it, and to provide continuous (weekly) medical care and supervision of the infants during their first one to two years of life.[20]

The results of both types of infant welfare programmes fully justified their existence − and their expense. The results Budin obtained specifically with regard to the reduction in infant mortality from epidemic diarrhoea were simply splendid. *Figure 6* illustrates the diarrhoeal death rate among breast- and bottle-fed infants (to obtain the total mortality from the disease both curves must be added together) in Paris through 1898. At that time, fifty-three infants were regularly attending Budin's consultation at the Clinique Tarnier, nineteen breast-fed and thirty-four bottle-fed. The mortality rate among these infants, represented by the horizontal base-line in the figure, was zero.

Dufour's results were almost as spectacular, even though the majority of the infants brought to his Goutte de Lait had already been weaned. The mortality from diarrhoea throughout the year 1895–96 was 6.80 per cent among the infants attending the Goutte de Lait, while it was 18.18 per cent among the entire infant population in the town of Fécamp. During 1896–97 the figures were 3.97 and 9.51 per cent respectively, in 1897–98, 2.26 and 12.00, and in 1898–99, 1.28 and 9.67 per cent.[21]

It is not surprising that, with results such as these, the Gouttes de Lait, like the consultations de nourrissons, quickly became popular throughout the country, nor is it any wonder that the number of infants in attendance increased each year. In 1898 only 174 babies regularly attended the Consultations of the Assistance Publiques de Paris, but that number quickly rose to 539 in 1899, 721 in 1900, and 1,438 in 1901.[22] In a town like Fécamp such an increase encompassed a significant proportion of the total infant population of the municipality; four years after the clinic was established more than one-third of the babies born in that town were brought to Dufour's clinic by their mothers.[23]

It is no wonder either that when English physicians in general, and medical officers of health in particular, were casting about for a way to prevent infant death they turned to the examples provided by Budin, Variot, Dufour, and their colleagues. A leader article in *The Journal of State Medicine*[24] of December 1898 briefly but enthusiastically describing Dufour's Goutte de Lait at Fécamp caught, and held, the attention of F. Drew Harris, the Medical Officer of Health for St Helens. 'So impressed was I with its possibilities for reducing infant mortality', he told the Section of State Medicine at the 1900 annual meeting of the BMA, 'that, acting on the advice of the Chairman of the Health Committee, I at once put myself in communication with Dr Dufour.' Harris wrote a report to his Committee with the information Dufour sent him 'which resulted in the immediate appointment of a small subcommittee to visit and further investigate the subject'.[25] Upon their return, the subcommittee (which included Harris) wrote another report successfully urging the Health Committee to commence work along the lines and according to the principles of the Fécamp Goutte de Lait.

The St Helens milk depot was opened on 8 August 1899 and although it was evidently based on the French model, the dissimilitude between the two establishments was clear: it was the difference between a baguette and stick bread. They had the same name and looked alike physically, but there the resemblance ended. First, Harris did not once mention breast-feeding in his account of his work. The title of his talk, 'The Supply of Sterilised Humanised Milk for the Use of Infants in St Helens' indicated his primary objective. There was absolutely no discussion of any effort to encourage mothers to nurse. Second, Harris's system was rather unsuccessful in its attempt to provide medical care for the infant. The mothers were requested to bring their babies once a week to be inspected and weighed but, he confessed, 'I regret that it has not been possible to insist on this.' In Dufour's clinic, by contrast, repeated failure to bring the infant to be examined threatened forfeiture of the milk until the child was presented. Last, while in France

'the charge of the milk is graduated according to the ability of the parents to pay, being gratuitous to the very poor and increasing gradually . . . the Council at St Helens . . . felt that it was impossible to follow this plan, and that one uniform rate must be charged. The price was fixed at 2d per day's supply, as it was found that this sum rather more than covered the cost of materials and of fuel.'[26]

This was twice the price Dufour charged the paying poor of Fécamp. In other words, whereas the consultations de nourrissons and Gouttes de Lait were designed to provide (possibly gratuitous) medical care for infants during the first two years of their lives, which included a proper milk supply if necessary, the St Helens depot undertook only the latter function. This, however, was done very much according to Dufour's theories. Harris, like his French mentor, added water, cream, sugar, and salt to fresh milk*, which was sterilized at the depot and pumped directly into sterile stoppered bottles.

The depot was popular, at least initially; within 'a very short time' of its opening 80 children were on the books. One year later that figure had increased to 140. Despite his 'fragmentary' records, Harris claimed a reasonable success. The figures he adduced showed a death rate of 103 per 1,000 among the 232 depot infants who had received the milk for any period of time exceeding one week in comparison with '157 per 1,000 births, taking the borough as a whole'. In the main, he appeared to have had the co-operation of the medical practitioners in the district who, he said, 'have in many instances recommended the use of the milk to their patients with results which have in many cases been most beneficial'.[27] He certainly received a positive response from the Section of State Medicine, and perhaps he inspired them. The following year (1901) no less than three municipalities established milk depots: Ashton-under-Lyne, Dukinfield, and Liverpool.

The English milk depots which were opened during the first few years of the twentieth century were more alike than they were different. In general they provided clean milk to infants of varying ages but undertook little, if any, medical supervision. None the less, each depot was distinctive in its own way, reflecting the enthusiasms and energies of their individual founders. For example, E.W. Hope, the Medical Officer of Health for Liverpool, was interested in reaching as many infants as possible. Unlike in St Helens, the medical officers in Liverpool seemed to make more of an effort to maintain contact with the infants to whom they dispensed milk. Mothers were encouraged to bring their babies to be weighed at least once a fortnight. The Liverpool Health Committee also appointed lady inspectors 'to teach mothers the proper method of feeding infants'[28] and to look in on depot infants at home; an average of three to five visits were made to each child while in receipt of the milk.

In these two ways records were kept on the majority of infants who were fed in this fashion. In a paper on 'Infantile Mortality and the Supply of Sterilised Milk' delivered at the Liverpool Medical Institution on 17 March 1904, Dr Hope presented a review of the milk depot activities and their results. By this time there were four corporation milk stations, and arrangements had been made with over forty dairies situated in various parts of Liverpool to keep a stock of municipal sterilized milk. During nearly two years of operation, from the opening of the first depot in early 1901 until 31 December 1903, '6,295 infants had been fed upon this milk. . . . Careful records relating to 4,453 of the total whom it had been more easy to keep under observation than the

---

* It is noteworthy that the French physicians, as we have seen, used commercially pasteurized or even commercially sterilized milk. Neither was available at this time in England.

remainder who had been supplied through dairies, showed a mortality-rate of 78 per 1,000'.[29] This compared favourably with that of the entire infant population of the city: 159 per 1,000 births (the lowest ever recorded) in 1903 and an average of 178 per 1,000 over the three-year period 1900–1902.[30] Hope pointed out that 'the large number of infants thus supplied had rendered almost impossible so close a medical observation as that, for example, referred to by Professor Budin at the Clinique Tarnier in Paris' through which the infant mortality rate was reduced to 36.5 per 1,000. Still, he believed that the Liverpool system saved many lives and that 'the educational value of the method was also considerable.'[31]

The first milk depot in London was established by the Battersea Borough Council and opened on 5 June 1902. A year previously, the indefatigable infant welfare worker and writer George Frederick McCleary had been appointed Medical Officer of Health for the borough, and it was on his recommendation that the council decided to take this action. At this time John Burns, the prominent and very popular Socialist worker and labour leader, who was born in Battersea in 1858 and had lived there nearly all his life, represented the borough on the London County Council (first elected 1889) and in Parliament (first elected in 1892). Battersea, because of Burns, was much in the public eye. It was thus thanks to Burns and McCleary that Battersea became the most well-publicized, well-known, and well-documented of the English stations (with the possible exception of Finsbury, which will be discussed presently). Burns himself was interested in child welfare (among other things; his work at this time was primarily in trade unionism and his own career). And McCleary was certainly an active and energetic Medical Officer of Health. He presented papers at international as well as national meetings and congresses and published reports of his work, specifically in the area of infant health programmes, in numerous periodicals. Whereas Hope excelled in reaching a large number of infants in Liverpool, McCleary was very successful in promoting the philosophy and function of the infant welfare movement in general and the role of milk depots in particular.[32]

The practical working of the Battersea depot was more or less identical to that of St Helens. As in the latter city there was, initially, a uniform charge for the milk but McCleary soon found that the 1s 6d per child per week was too low a sum to cover the costs of older infants. He introduced a graduated scale in relation to the amount of milk consumed, which depended upon the age of the child. The cost for infants of less than six months remained at the original rate of 1s 6d; it then increased to 2s for those aged six to twelve months, and the charge for children above one year was 2s 6d. An additional 9d per week was assessed to each rate for children who lived outside the borough.[33]

There were several points upon which McCleary was very particular. From the outset he felt that 'one of the most important considerations to be borne in mind in establishing a Milk Depot is the control of the source of the milk supply.' Therefore, he explained, 'the milk is obtained from a specially selected [by McCleary himself] farm.'[34] McCleary was careful to include a number of clauses relating to the health of the cows in the contract. For example, all the cows on the farm had to have a negative reaction to the tuberculin test as certified by a veterinary surgeon, and they were inspected periodically by a council-appointed veterinarian.

Although McCleary had no doubt as to the advantages of breast-feeding and deplored its decline in popularity and practicability he did not, at least initially, harass mothers on this point. Nor were they forced, or even pressed, to bring their infants to the depot to be weighed and examined. Aimée Watt Smyth remarked upon this non-invasive approach with some dismay in her description of a visit to the Battersea depot, published as part of the series on 'The Milk Supply of Large Towns' in the *BMJ* (1903). 'It seems to [me] that the merit in . . . institutions supplying humanized milk is the effort to do good. But to sell humanized milk without careful advice to each mother, medical inspection of the infant, and weekly weighing, involves some waste of energy.' She advocated closer adherence to the French models with their encouragement of breast-feeding and continuous medical care of the infants.[35]

Watt Smyth's criticism of the Battersea depot was published in April 1903, nearly a year after it had opened. McCleary evidently agreed with the points she raised. He too held the French systems in high esteem and he decided to emulate them to as great a degree as possible. His description of the working of the depot in an article of October 1905 on 'The Municipal Feeding of Infants' included an element which had not been mentioned in previous accounts, and which reflected this resolve.

'At the Battersea depot, special precautions are taken to ensure that the milk shall not be used to the detriment of breast-feeding. The milk is not supplied unless the applicant can produce a written recommendation from a medical practitioner, and every opportunity is taken to impress upon the mothers that the milk, like all artificial foods, is but an imperfect substitute for mother's milk, and that it should never be used in preference to mother's milk.'[36]

This probably proved to be more of an impediment, preventing mothers from obtaining clean milk for their infants, than an encouragement to nurse, although it was certainly not McCleary's intention to construct a system which would work to the disadvantage of the infants.

The following month (November 1905) McCleary took additional action to bring his depot closer to the Goutte de Lait model, and he began to hold a consultation for the babies fed on the municipal milk.[37] By that time it had become clear that despite the fact that mothers were 'urged to bring the child once a week to be weighed it [had] been found impossible to insist on this'. McCleary therefore relied upon the efforts of lady sanitary inspectors who visited the depot children at home and endeavoured 'to secure that the instructions are properly carried out'. He recognized that, as he wrote in 1904, 'the most important difference . . . between the English . . . and the French Gouttes de Lait is in the supervision of the children.'[38] At that time McCleary was still rather anxious not to antagonize the local general practitioners, and he was careful to defuse criticism on this score. 'Any steps in this direction should be taken with the cordial co-operation of the local medical practitioners; otherwise success will certainly not attend the depot.'[39]

McCleary never explained precisely why he opened the consultation service, nor was there any attendant fanfare. In contrast to his numerous descriptions of the depot, he never published an account of his consultation methods, observations, or results. In his paper on 'The Public Supply of Pure or Specially Prepared Milk for the Feeding of Infants' which he delivered before the first National Conference on Infantile Mortality in 1906, he did not mention his consultation once, although he argued the necessity for 'periodical medical supervision' of depot infants.[40] Perhaps McCleary failed to discuss the consultation because it was a failure. It is also possible that he simply wished to be discreet; his previous statements indicated that he knew this was potentially an explosive issue. He may not have wanted to call attention to his consultation work, although he had reason to believe that he himself could proceed (with caution) in Battersea. In February 1904 McCleary had 'addressed a circular letter to the medical practitioners in the district and to the visiting physicians of certain children's hospitals to which Battersea children are taken, asking for an expression of opinion as to the value of the milk'. He never specified how many letters he sent out, but by July he had received forty-five replies. Three physicians claimed they did not have sufficient data to form an opinion, one practitioner was disappointed with the results obtained, and the remaining forty-one were favourably impressed.[41] In any case, the following year (1906) McCleary left Battersea to take up the position of Medical Officer of Health for Hampstead.* His replacement, G. Quin Lennane, continued to operate the depot, which by that time supplied over 600 children with milk each year. There is no evidence that he continued the consultation service. To the contrary: reports of his work noted the educational function and value of the lady home visitors, but did not mention mothers and infants attending a weekly clinic.[42]

As at St Helens, Liverpool, and Battersea, the depots which were subsequently established in England made provision, unsuccessfully, for baby weighing and medical supervision. The mothers simply did not

* Somewhat surprisingly, McCleary did not establish a depot in Hampstead, although he remained active in the infant welfare movement both nationally and internationally.

bring their infants to the depot to be examined and consequently lady visitors were sent to the homes of the infants to check on them and the care they received from their mothers. The one exception to this general pattern was in Finsbury where a depot was established which more than any other in England followed the French Goutte de Lait model. By the time this depot opened on 23 November 1904, numerous articles on both the French and English institutions had appeared in the popular as well as the medical press. As in the case of reports on the milk supply and national physical deterioration, the quantity of literature on this subject also greatly increased in 1903. Periodic short reports had, as a matter of course, appeared previously, particularly in the 'Special Correspondence: Paris' sections of the *BMJ*. These accounts ordinarily included a very brief précis of the Académie de Médecine proceedings, which in turn often involved a paper on these paediatric programmes.[43]

The first serious discussion of infant milk depots as a topic worthy of attention on its own (following the initial catalyst in the *Journal of State Medicine*), was published (as we have seen) as part of the 'Report on the Milk Supply of Large Towns'. 'Up to the present the only attempt made in England to combat infant mortality from diarrhoea, and to assist the poor in their infants, has been the establishing of depots for humanized or sterilized milk,' Watt Smyth began. Frankly admiring the infant welfare systems developed by the French, Watt Smyth reported on them in considerable detail.[44] The same day that Watt Smyth's article was published in the *BMJ*, the *Lancet* also ran a short editorial on 'Municipal Infant Milk Depots', which briefly recounted the work of Dufour at Fécamp and the experiences of the similar programmes at St Helens, Liverpool, and Battersea. The editors expressed their opinion as to the value of these depots concisely and unequivocally. 'There is no doubt that if the excellent system of providing municipal depôts for the supply of wholesome milk and milk of standard composition for the use of babies were universally adopted infant mortality would be enormously reduced,' they declared, urging other municipalities to follow 'such a good example'.[45]

Not surprisingly, the subject of infant milk depots was discussed at the 1903 Congress of the Royal Sanitary Institute and at the annual meeting of the British Medical Association. In the former instance McCleary presented a paper on the Battersea depot system, its function, and the results obtained. At the latter meeting T.D. Lister, Assistant Physician at the Royal Hospital for Children and Women, presented a paper 'On the Utilization of Infants' Milk Depots' before the Section of Diseases of Children. Lister argued that the 'rapid and widespread . . . movement in the direction of the general establishment of milk depots for infant feeding [was] a matter of direct interest to those who have to practise among the children for whom the depots are primarily intended'. He recommended 'the co-operation of practising members of the profession', claiming that 'this would be both to their advantage as well as the best way to solve the problem.'[46]

The role of the municipality in the provision of modified milk for infants, and the function of practising physicians in such public health projects increasingly attracted attention. It had become clear that the development of these infant welfare schemes in England differed from the original French models, and some doubt arose as to the wisdom of this course. In September 1903 a brief synopsis of papers describing organized efforts to reduce infantile mortality in France and Belgium, which had been delivered before the Sixth Section of the Eleventh International Congress on Hygiene and Demography in Brussels, was published in the *BMJ*.[47] This review was accompanied by an editorial elucidating certain salient aspects of the French and Belgium programmes as compared with those found in England. In the opinion of the editors co-operation and co-ordination between the depot officials and local general practitioners had to be secured: 'efforts should be made to overcome the difficulties in the way of weekly medical examination in connexion with the supply of sterilized milk.'[48]

That many physicians agreed was made clear by the formation of the Infants' Health Society, which grew out of the Infants' Hospital at Hampstead. The hospital was a rather singular institution; it was founded in March 1903 at the initiative of Ralph Vincent, who became the Senior Physician to the Hospital, and through the munificence of Mr (later Sir) Robert Mond. Vincent was a raw milk and 'percentage feeding' enthusiast; his experience in private practice had led him to believe that infant mortality was primarily due to feeding disorders. He arranged for milk to be supplied to the hospital from a model farm at Sudbury in Middlesex, and he ensured that every detail was under medical supervision in order to provide a clean, constant, and reliable milk supply.[49] Feeding was of central concern to the hospital's operation. As a letter to the *Manchester Guardian* (30 June 1903) entitled 'National Physique and the Feeding of Infants' explained, the hospital endeavoured to cure, primarily through proper feeding practices, those diseases which arose from mismanagement or poor nutrition.[50]

On 11 February 1904, the Infants' Health Society was formed, and the Hospital was merged into the Society on the principle that prevention was more important than treating. Many of the cases which had come into the hospital had resulted from malnutrition, and the staff physicians decided that their energies would be better spent organizing milk depots in conjunction with medical supervision. The Infants' Health Society perceived the establishment of medically supervised milk depots to be a project of imperial importance. In an open letter to *The Times* to solicit support, the organizers of the Society declared:

'It is impossible to exaggerate the importance of thus combating at the very fountainhead the present terrible waste of infant life and the physical degeneracy of so many of the survivors, evils which have occupied the attention of the public recently from the point of view of the general welfare of the community and of Army recruiting.'[51]

It is noteworthy that both Frederick Maurice and Henry Ashby were among the signatories; it is another example of the conjunction between anxiety with regard to physical deterioration as seen from the military perspective (personified by Maurice) and concern about the health of children from the point of view of the medical profession (Ashby). Delineating the steps which needed to be taken to solve the problem, the Society called for the establishment of milk depots or out-patient departments 'where babies can be seen regularly by a doctor and provided with milk', and for the employment of trained nurses, resident in various districts, to visit homes and 'bring to light any neglect'.[52]

George Carpenter, editor of the recently established *British Journal of Children's Diseases*, had similar ideas, which he expressed in several consecutive editorials in 1904.[53] Carpenter elaborated upon the role the medical profession should play in the immediate provision of pure milk for infants. First, he advocated the establishment of milk dispensaries at children's hospitals. In an editorial on 'La Goutte de Lait' he developed his plan for hospital milk dispensaries. Like the Infants' Health Society, Carpenter believed that milk distribution had to be accompanied by medical supervision. Children's hospitals were 'the suitable authorities in whose charge such undertakings could well be placed, seeing that their physicians are trained experts in the treatment of infantile disorders and in the ordering of infantile dietaries'. Naturally, where there were 'but few children's hospitals milk dispensaries would be a necessity, and even in London, with its various children's hospitals as adjuncts, additional milk dispensaries would have to be provided to meet the demand and cover the ground'. The single most important factor, Carpenter stressed, was medical superintendence. It was for this reason that 'the municipal milk dole *divorced from medical guidance*, as is now being tried in Battersea and Liverpool, is not a system which can be recommended.' In conclusion, Carpenter referred to the imperial importance of the scheme he recommended.

> 'The adoption of the French system of the Goutte de Lait in this country under expert medical guidance, coupled with the distribution of milk of approved cleanliness, would prove of immense service to our infantile population and to our future national physique.'[54]

The importance of milk depots under medical supervision both to save infant life and to improve the national physique was noted in the articles on the milk supply published in *The Pall Mall Gazette* and *The Daily Chronicle* in 1904 which we discussed in Chapter III. 'Milk and

Men', which appeared in the former newspaper on 12 April, and was almost certainly written by Aimée Watt Smyth, spoke to these issues directly. Describing the way the consultations de nourrissons and Gouttes de Lait were run, Watt Smyth particularly (and positively) remarked upon the medical supervision of the infants and the control exercised by these organizations over the source of their milk supply. 'In England, unfortunately, the importance of these factors has not been properly grasped,' she lamented. Like George Carpenter, Watt Smyth approved of the idea of milk depots opened in conjunction with children's hospitals, and she praised the establishment of such a centre 'managed on the wisest and best methods' at the Shadwell Hospital for Children. Looking forward to the successful multiplication of depots 'under efficient medical control' and urging the public to support 'such a splendid scheme', she declared that it was 'sincerely to be hoped that the day is not far distant when clean fresh milk may be within the reach of every labouring woman in Great Britain who seeks to bring up healthy sons and daughters for the Empire'.[55]

The 'Milk and Disease' series run by *The Daily Chronicle* in July 1904 also struck the imperial note (as we saw in Chapter III).[56] The author of the articles suggested a number of remedies based on 'lessons from abroad', including the establishment of depots for 'the distribution of sterilised milk together with regular medical supervision of the infants . . . at stated intervals' modelled after the French Goutte de Lait system. Arguing 'that some similar scheme, introduced in connection with the out-patients' department of our children's hospitals, would . . . be a very fruitful field for philanthropic work', he cited the examples of the Infants' Hospital in Hampstead and the milk dispensary opened by the East London Hospital for Children in Shadwell.[57]

The question of milk depots also was taken up by the Inter-Departmental Committee on Physical Deterioration, and they heard much evidence from various witnesses on this issue.[58] In their report (20 July 1904) the Committee did not explicitly discuss the role of physicians, or of medical supervision generally, in a milk distribution system. They emphasized the need 'to bring an adequate supply of pure milk within the reach of the poorer classes', and recommended the establishment of depots in every town. In this as in all matters, however, the Committee predominantly relied upon education to solve the problem. 'The principal hope for future generations', they believed, was training 'to raise the standard of domestic competence'. But, in the short run, 'with the formation of a sufficient number of milk depots', they argued, 'the machinery of [birth] registration and of municipal health visitors could be utilized to bring to the knowledge of mothers of young children where supplies of milk could be obtained.' The part the medical profession should play was left extremely vague. The Committee merely remarked that 'to the spread of this knowledge hospitals and infirmaries in the district could contribute their share.'[59]

The Finsbury Infant Milk Depot was opened on 23 November 1904 and, unlike the earlier municipal milk distribution systems established in St Helens, Liverpool, and Battersea, emphasized the province of the physician and the function of education. The depot was established under the auspices of the Finsbury Social Workers' Association and the staff reflected the perceived requirements of medical supervision and education through health visiting. 'The work entailed was undertaken by a voluntary committee of medical men, assisted by some lady visitors,' George Newman (then the Medical Officer of Health for Finsbury) explained in *A Special Report on an Infants' Milk Depot* (1905). The Finsbury depot was run on a small scale, and was designed to provide high quality milk and constant care to a limited number of infants only. The Medical Committee had absolute control over the milk they supplied, they supervised the management of the enterprise as well as the infants using the milk, and they systematically studied its effects on the children. The Committee was also particular as to who received the milk and only 'infants who could not be breast-fed' were enrolled.[60]

In Finsbury, as at Battersea, it was believed that 'the first essential in the establishment of an Infants' Milk Depôt is *a pure milk*,' and arrangements were made with a farm to provide the required milk according to certain regulations and specifications.[61] All the cows were tested once a year with the tuberculin test, and reactors were eliminated from the herd. The milk was modified according to the medical committee's prescription, and pasteurized in winter and sterilized in summer.[62]

The depot was planned to be both a remedy and a school, but was not intended as the prophylactic measure attempted elsewhere. Infants who needed the milk were introduced by medical practitioners (33 per cent of the cases), hospitals (23 per cent), sanitary inspectors (37 per cent), nurses, and birth registrars. (In 1905, 75 per cent of the infants who were admitted were already ill, and some were dying.) A medical and sociological record of each child was kept including information pertaining to the child's legitimacy, the name, occupation, and wages of the parents, the physical and sanitary conditions of the home, and the feeding and physical history of the infant. Medical supervision was taken seriously. The parents, or guardians, were required to bring their child to the depot once a fortnight to be weighed and examined; as in France, the milk was only supplied on this condition. This seems to have been more for the benefit of the physicians' studies than for the child, however, as no medicines were prescribed or provided, nor was advice given. If the child were ill the mother was simply instructed to consult her general practitioner or go to a hospital.[63] The milk was dispensed as it was elsewhere, and a sliding scale of charges according to the age of the infant was also used in Finsbury. The cost for a week's supply ranged from 1s 6d for babies under six months old, to 1s 9d for those aged six to nine months, to 2s for older infants.[64]

The educational function was also considered to be of primary importance. 'Each child fed on the depôt milk is visited in its own home once a week, and in some cases more frequently,' Newman reported. 'In this way a direct personal influence is brought to bear on the mother, and homely advice is given and precautions taken as to the management of the infant.'[65] It was found that the printed instructions given to the parents at the depot were often misunderstood, while actual demonstration was a more effective pedagogical device. Then too, it was in this way that information regarding the sanitary conditions of the child was obtained.

In his book on *Infant Mortality* (1906), Newman discussed the Finsbury depot in considerable detail. He presented a variety of statistics to prove that depot infants 'suffer much less from epidemic diarrhoea than other artificially fed children' and that 'they have a much lower fatality, even when they are attacked' with that disease. The decisive difference between depot infants (who were, after all, entirely bottle-fed and 'of the poorest classes') and their cohorts was, he declared, that the former '*were receiving pure milk and proper supervision*'. In conclusion Newman claimed that although an Infants' Milk Depot was only a palliative measure, the results of the Finsbury enterprise showed that such establishments were 'of substantial value in the reduction of infant death rates among a certain class'. Furthermore, the evidence indicated that the depot also fulfilled the educational function originally intended. It was found to be 'an important training school of infant management'. In sum, Newman asserted that 'on the whole, the results show an exceptional measure of success, and such as justify the establishment of similar depôts elsewhere.'[66]

It is ironic that three years after Newman endorsed the efficacy of infant milk depots and urged their multiplication throughout the country, Finsbury was the first borough to shut down its programme. Although a contradictory outcome, the closure was not so bizarre as would initially appear. During the intervening years, the attitude towards milk depots within the medical and social work community had changed considerably. This development can be seen in the establishment of alternative forms of infant welfare work (which will be discussed in the next chapter), and was reflected in the proceedings of those newly organized institutions which provided a forum for professional opinion, the national congresses on infantile mortality.

The initiative for the first National Conference on Infantile Mortality was taken in a railway carriage betwen Le Havre and Fécamp on 23 October 1905 by Bailie W.F. Anderson, Chairman of the Health Committee of the Glasgow Corporation; Archibald K. Chalmers, Medical Officer of Health for Glasgow; Alderman Broadbent, Mayor of Huddersfield; Samson G. Moore, Medical Officer of Health for Huddersfield, and

George F. McCleary of Battersea. These five men were on their way to visit Dr Dufour's Goutte de Lait at Fécamp after attending the first Congrès International des Gouttes de Lait which had been held in Paris on 20 and 21 October. Although twenty-two countries sent delegates to the Congress, including the whole of continental Europe, the British government did not, and was represented by envoys from the three local authorities of Glasgow, Huddersfield, and Battersea. Impressed by the enthusiasm, energy, and efficiency with which the French approached infant welfare work, especially when compared with its relatively embryonic state in Britain, Anderson, Chalmers, Broadbent, Moore, and McCleary, while on their journey, discussed ways of stimulating similar activity at home. 'It occurred to us,' McCleary wrote nearly thirty years later, 'that the most effective method of bringing about an extensive development of the [infant welfare] movement in Great Britain would be to hold a national conference on infant mortality in the following year.'[67]

On 13 and 14 June 1906, the first National Conference on Infantile Mortality met in the Caxton Hall, Westminster, under the patronage of King Edward VII and Queen Alexandra. The President was John Burns who opened the sessions with an address ostensibly on the causes of infant mortality for which, he claimed, 'in equal parts the mother, society, and industry were mutually and jointly responsible.' In fact, Burns did nothing more than fulminate against modern women while praising his mother. He inveighed specifically against 'married women at work' who failed to provide 'a mother's influence and restraining care' for their children, failed also to prepare food properly for their families ('no kindly figure in a white apron', no 'amenities of a well-ordered dinner table'), but 'disproportionately and stupidly' spent wages on alcoholic drink. In other words, Burns said, 'I believe at the bottom of infant mortality, high or low, is good or bad motherhood.' His remedies were consistent. 'We have got to restrict married women's labour as often and as soon as we can,' he declared, and he suggested educating women in the art of maternity. His famous conclusion, endlessly reiterated by others was, 'First, concentrate on the mother. What the mother is the children are. The stream is no purer than the source. Let us glorify, dignify, and purify motherhood by every means in our power.'[68]

Burns was a herald of the future. At the first National Conference on Infantile Mortality seventeen papers were given, nine of which dealt with various aspects of maternity as they affected, or could be brought to bear on children. These included a discussion of such health problems in childbirth as premature delivery and alcoholism as well as the value of maternal education programmes and health visiting systems in combating infant mortality. The milk question was of interest to only two speakers.[69] Clearly, the pedagogical function was paramount. Maternal instruction by municipal officials was now the primary objective; the route to the child was through the mother.

The second National Conference on Infantile Mortality was held on 23–25 March 1908. This time not one of the nine papers discussed the milk supply, milk depots, or the medical supervision of infants, and nearly all of them concentrated on ways in which the child could be reached through the mother. The first paper presented at the Conference struck the key-note. An address on 'The Human Mother' by the Eugenist physician Caleb W. Saleeby, it crystallized and emphasized the trend Burns had indicated, towards a focus on the mother as the primary object of direct attention rather than the infant, and on maternal education as the means by which the infant mortality figures could be improved. Saleeby advanced his construct of maternity within a 'biological' context. He argued that while human beings, unlike animals, have lost their instinct, mothers have maintained 'the maternal instinct in essence. The human mother is habitually ignored,' Saleeby continued, 'it being assumed that the mother, as a mother knows what is best for her child. But experience [shows] that the human mother, just because she is human, intelligent and not instinctive, does not know.' Therefore, he contended, 'From my point of view as a student of general biology the crèche and the milk depôt *must be* inferior to the school for mothers, meals for expectant and nursing mothers, and the like, whatever the statistical result in particular cases.'[70] In conclusion he formulated the theme of the conference, and of infant welfare work by this date and for the future:

> 'I ask you to accept the principles of maternalism [I have] laid down as cardinal, permanent, unalterable. There is no State womb, there are no State breasts, there is no real substitute for the beautiful reality of individual motherhood. . . . We must remember the cardinal peculiarity of human motherhood, its dependence . . . upon education . . . needed by the human mother in every particular, small and great, since she relies upon intelligence alone, which is only a potentiality and a possibility until it be educated.'[71]

Saleeby certainly had a way with words. Persuasive as he may have been, it is doubtful that milk depots suffered a decline in popularity due to his particular maternalism construct, or even to more general biological ideas regarding the unique nature of the human mother as the only animal not ruled by instinct and peculiarly educable. Nevertheless, it was true that the milk depot movement was already subsiding; a station opened in York in 1903 (a voluntary endeavour run by the York Health and Housing Association under the direction of Seebohm Rowntree)[72] closed two years later, and the Finsbury establishment shut down in 1909, one year after the second National Conference. In his 'Second Report on Infant and Child Mortality' to the Local Government Board, Arthur Newsholme noted that by 1913 only thirteen depots in England and Wales had been opened, of which three had

Plate 3 Infants' Milk Depot, York, 1903

(*Source*: W.S. Craig (1946) *Child and Adolescent Life in Health and Disease*, p. 19.)

already closed.[73] The infant milk depot idea, so accepted and successful in France where it flourished for many years, never really got off the ground in England. As Janet Lane-Claypon, Lecturer on Hygiene at King's College for Women, University of London, described the situation in 1913, 'As a whole, it may be said that the star of the milk depot never rose far above the horizon in England, and is now waning.'[74]

As early as 1904 rumbles of difficulties could be discerned from a number of the accounts of milk depots in the professional press.[75] For instance, in an analysis of the annual report of F. Drew Harris which appeared in the *Lancet* in October 1904 the editors noted that 'the result of last year's [depot] work is not altogether satisfactory.' The depot evidently was not very popular. In 1900, 332 children were registered on the books, but by 1903 that number had dropped to 183. 'The medical officer of health is unable to understand the apathy of the public "in neglecting what, on the face of it, is a most useful institution",'[76] the editors remarked, citing Harris. One tentative explanation was that the depot was too distant for many who needed it, and Harris suggested establishing additional branches in various parts of the town. The problem may have been, of course, as was found in Salford in 1905, that there simply were not that many artificially fed infants. Interested in beginning to provide sterilized milk if necessary, the Health Committee of Salford instituted an enquiry into the feeding practices of 1,595 infants and found that only 156 (9.8 per cent) were bottle-fed.[77]

Another weakness of the system was that the value of the depot was very hard to measure. The usual practice was to compare the infant mortality in the community at large with that of the depot babies. But such statistics, as medical officers of health well knew, were meaningless. They admitted as much, but presented the figures as they did not have a more accurate method to assess the effect of the milk supplied. Lacking anything much more substantive, reports on the stations' results also commonly included statements to the effect that the medical practitioners in the area were pleased with the system. Sidney Davies (MOH, Woolwich) elucidated the problematic nature of infants' milk depot statistics in an article on that subject. Davies explained that the infant mortality rate was the number of children dying less than one year old to 1,000 born. The depot population, however, was not so uniform nor so stable, as 'their age distribution differs from that of the population under one [and] the numbers under one month are very few, and fewer still under one week.' In addition, depot children were often ill when admitted to the programme and they took the milk for varying periods. Davies pointed out further that one-sixth of the total deaths under one year occurred during the first week of life 'mainly due to premature birth and ante-natal and parturient conditions [which] are very little affected by feeding'. Hence these deaths should be excluded 'from all statistics as to different methods of feeding infants' which would further complicate accurate calculations. In conclusion Davies contended that it was possible to compute the statistics properly, but he did not appear hopeful as he said it 'would involve much labour'.[78]

In a paper on 'Phases in the Development of the Infant Welfare Movement in England' Lane-Claypon maintained that the milk depot idea had failed and analysed why this was so. 'In the first place,' she said, 'the expense involved is very heavy, varying roughly from just under to just over £1 ($5) per head per child on the books.' Furthermore, 'this expense is incurred on behalf of a comparatively small number of infants, since it touches . . . only the artificially fed infants, and . . . only a relatively small percentage of these.' According to Lane-Claypon the percentage of infants who were breast-fed was 'fairly high' in England, but she conceded that 'the available data are scanty [and] it appears to vary considerably in the different localities depending upon the occupation of the mothers.' Then, too, although 'in almost all the towns it was found that the death rate among the infants receiving the depot milk was greatly less than in the town as a whole, this could not . . . be altogether attributed to the influence of the depot milk.'[79] Lane-Claypon was not the only observer to identify cost as the reason for the limited popularity of milk depots in England. Hugh Ashby (Visiting Physician to the Manchester Children's Hospital), for example, gave the same explanation in his book on *Infant Mortality*.[80]

The cost problem cut two ways, and the small number of children brought to the depots is open to a number of interpretations. It may have been because few were bottle-fed (which, as we have seen, there was some reason to believe), and it may also have been because their parents could not afford the milk. If £1 per head per child was too great a strain on the rates, 2s per infant per week was certainly too large a chunk out of the average working-class household budget (see *Table 3*.) The problem was, neither was there any money for the nutritious food required by a nursing mother. Maud Pember Reeves's simply written but elegantly eloquent study *Round About a Pound a Week* identified this problem precisely. It was in Reeves's home that the Fabian Women's Group was founded in 1908, and the following year she initiated the 'Mother Allowance Scheme in Lambeth'. From 1909 to 1913 Reeves and other members of the Group recorded the daily budgets and lives of thirty-one working-class families in Lambeth through weekly visits to their homes. Explaining how this had come about, Reeves recounted that a sum of money had been given to the Group which enabled them

> 'to study the effect on mother and child of sufficient nourishment before and after birth. Access was obtained to the list of out-patients of a well-known lying in hospital; names and addresses of expectant mothers were taken from the list, and . . . the weekly task of seeing each woman in her own home, supplying the nourishment, and noting the effects [was undertaken].'[81]

The visits were to continue from three months prior to one year after birth, if possible. As they thought that the wives of men receiving over 26s a week would have 'sufficient nourishment, while the wives of men out of work or receiving less than 18s were likely to be living in a state of such misery that the temptation to let the rest of the family share in the mother's and baby's nourishment would be too great', the Group decided to deal only with families with an income between the two figures. They under-estimated: 'after two years' experience they raised the higher limit to 30s.'[82] The women were taught to keep a record of

118

Table 3 *Sample weekly budget of a working-class family of 8 persons (2 parents 6 children) at 20 shillings per week, London, 1913*

General			Food		
rent	8	0	14 loaves	3	2½
burial insurance	1	8	meat	0	10
boot club	1	0	suet	0	2
coal	1	0	dripping	0	6
gas	0	8	3 ozs tea	0	3
wood	0	3	2 lb sugar	0	4
soap, soda	0	4½	2 tins of milk	0	6
			1 quartern flour	0	5
			potatoes	0	6
			greens	0	4
	12	11½		7	0½

(*Source*: Maud Pember Reeves (1913/1982) *Round About a Pound a Week*, p.134.)

their weekly expenditures, and the book was based upon the visitors' observations and an analysis of these accounts.

One of the more sensitive as well as sensible chronicles of the grim grind of normal everyday working-class poverty among the 'respectable men in full work, at a more or less top wage, young, with families still increasing' and their 'quiet and decent' wives, Reeves challenged many contemporary platitudes and prejudices. With regard to the gospel of cleanliness, for example, she reminded her middle-class readers that 'to manage a husband and six children on round about £1 a week needs, first and foremost, wisdom and loving-kindness, and after that as much cleanliness and order as can be squeezed in.'[83] Similarly, she made short shrift of allegations of lower-class slothfulness, imprudence, or stupidity.

'That the children of the poor suffer from insufficient attention and care is not because the mother is lazy or indifferent to her children's well-being. It is because she has but one pair of hands and but one overburdened brain. She can just get through her day if she does everything she has to do inefficiently. . . . In fact, one woman is not equal to the bearing and efficient, proper care of six children. . . . She would need not only far more money, but far more help. The children of the poor suffer . . . because there is not enough to pay for [necessities]. They also suffer from want of cleanliness, want of attention to health, want of peace and quiet, because the strength of their mother is not enough to provide these necessary conditions.'[84]

Happily lecturing her readers, Reeves pursued the subject, clarifying her position further. 'To put down all the miseries and crying wants of the children of the poor to the ignorance and improvidence of the mothers is merely to salve an uneasy conscience by blaming someone else.'[85]

More specifically, Reeves elucidated particular points of middle-class and medical ignorance with regard to proletariat habits. The original focus of the book was on the children, hence the problem of not having enough money for milk for babies or for food for nursing mothers was of central concern. Poor women realized that milk was the proper food for infants, Reeves emphasized; they did not get milk for the same reason that they did not have adequate heat, housing, or clothing. It was simply too expensive.

> 'A healthy child ought to be able to use a quart of milk a day, which means a weekly milk bill for that child of 2s 4d – quite an impossible amount when the food of the whole family may have to be supplied out of 8s or 9s a week. Even a pint a day means 1s 2d a week, so that is out of the question, though a pint a day would not suffice for a child of a year old.'[86]

The borough of Lambeth had opened a milk depot in 1905, of which Reeves spoke highly. Nevertheless, she pointed out that the cost of the milk (as at others we have discussed) ranged from 9d per week for very young infants to 3s for older babies. 'When it can be afforded, its results are excellent,'[87] Reeves commented. But as she had shown, this was rarely the case. In fact, the weekly budgets had revealed that the food costs for the entire family except the father (the breadwinner) were less than 3d per head per day, or 1s 9d per week, or less than the charge for depot milk for infants over six months. It was a luxury impossible to afford. Thus the milk depot did not provide the aid needed. Too expensive for the family to afford for the sole use of the baby, it was not provided for mothers either. 'Unfortunately, the nursing mother is not helped . . . and it is she who requires milk for the needs of the baby she is nursing.'[88]

It is clear from the letters sent by working women in response to an appeal by Margaret Llewelyn Davies (General Secretary of the Women's Co-operative Guild from 1889 to 1921) for direct experiences of childbirth and rearing (to be used in a campaign to improve maternal and infant health services), that they understood the nutrition dilemma very well. The letters were written in 1914 but, depending upon the age of the woman, they described events which had occurred a certain number of years previously. One woman, who described herself as 'nearly used up' from hard work, worry, and seven children, described how easy birth and nursing should have been, if only the requisite conditions could have been afforded. 'Give a woman a quiet home and an easy conscience and good plain food, and I see no reason why both mother and child should not do well.'[89] 'A mother wants good food before the birth as well as after, but how can it be done out of so little money? If father takes his food it must be as good as can be got; then the children come next and mother last,'[90] another woman explained. 'There is another point; the mother who works and worries generally loses the milk which is so necessary for the baby,'[91] a third pointed out. And a fourth gave a personal experience of precisely this problem. 'I fed them all as long as I could, but I was too harassed, domestic duties too heavy, and the income too limited to furnish me with a rich nourishing milk.'[92]

These women did not discuss feeding practices, but it seems probable from their statements that they, like a fifth, were forced to resort to some form of artificial feeding. 'Being unable to nurse them', this mother wrote, 'I resorted to patent foods. . . . As a result of my experience, my advice is that mothers unable to suckle their children should shun all patent foods, rusks, etc. as they would shun the devil himself, for an infant will have to be born with a digestion like a horse if it is to digest solid food in the early stages.' This woman declared that she was convinced that milk and milk only 'human if possible, and animal if human fails' was the only safe food for infants.[93] But milk was much more expensive than patent foods, and the latter were far better commercially advertised than the former.[94] It was precisely women such as she who needed the high quality milk depots supplied, but could not afford it.

In the final analysis, what was the significance of the milk depot in the infant welfare movement? If, as the Salford study indicated, Lane-Claypon claimed, and Reeves observed, the majority of infants were breast-fed, the depot idea was, from the beginning, built on a shaky basis. At the turn of the century, studies of feeding practices had not been undertaken (indeed, writing in 1913 Lane-Claypon observed that data on this subject were still scant) and it was commonly believed that bottle-feeding was both prevalent and on the increase. This may have been partially true, but it may also have been an echo of the general anxiety that the nation was suffering a decline. Seen within the context of the rhetoric of physical deterioration and fear for the future of the Empire (even if racial degeneration was not actually accepted), it is understandable that both physicians and public commentators jumped on bottle-feeding as an important element in the national devitalization. What did not exist, and what people at that time (with a few exceptions) did not think to obtain was evidence to show, first, what percentage of living infants were breast- versus bottle-fed, and second, precisely when during the first year of life a diarrhoea death occurred in relation to the feeding method for that individual infant. There were, by contrast, plenty of studies to prove that the infant mortality rate from all causes, and from diarrhoea in particular, was several times higher among bottle- as compared with breast-fed babies.

Given this perception of the situation, and the pervasive anxieties and fears, it makes sense that the French consultations de nourrissons and Gouttes de Lait appeared to be reasonable solutions to the English problem. But Drew Harris, Hope, McCleary, and Newman did not critically analyse the different conditions found in France and England. They saw that the French, like the English, suffered a low birth rate and a high infant mortality rate, with a large proportion of deaths due to epidemic diarrhoea. They realized that France, like England, was concerned about the prospect of depopulation and its consequences for the nation. What they did not perceive was that France, with its established wet-nurse system,[95] had different infant rearing practices which had a direct bearing on feeding customs and therefore on epidemic diarrhoea; it was no accident that in France (but not in England) this was the greatest cause of infant mortality.

The milk depot system was thus imported on a weak foundation. But this should not be pushed too far. It may have been that a rather small number of infants were brought to the depots because there were relatively few bottle-fed babies, but this is purely hypothetical. Even if an infant were breast-fed it is not known how long this continued. Medical practice in England commonly dictated a maximum of nine months. If mothers agreed, did those newly weaned infants then contract diarrhoea during the last quarter of their first year of life? In any case, as has been seen, there were two definite reasons for the depots' failure to solve the infant welfare problem. The milk sold was too expensive to be purchased by those women who, due to their own lack of nutrition, most needed to find a substitute or supplement for their own supply in order to feed their infants. Then, too, the depot system with daily milk collection and return of empty bottles was not convenient. A further reason for the failure of the depot to flourish in England may have been because there was no ardent philanthropist, comparable to de Rothschild in France or Nathan Straus in America devoted to the idea and actively supporting it. The milk depot idea may have been popular in France and America because it was *made* to be popular: it was successfully sold both to the public and the profession. A sufficient market existed in England, but the price was not right and the advertising inadequate.

To return to the question, what was the value of the milk depot, built as it was on a dubious basis, too expensive and, except for Liverpool, far too restrictive in the number of children it reached or even attempted to reach? In the first place, simply the fact that the depot existed was important; it was a concrete structure which represented infant welfare work. The establishment of milk depots provided a focus and, consequently, a stimulus for those interested in this aspect of public health or paediatric medicine. Furthermore, it was a beginning from which alternative systems could, and did, develop. Even as a negative model it provided an impetus for the study of alternatives. And, finally, not all aspects of the milk depot system failed. While the provision of milk without supervision came to be seen as having only limited usefulness, health visitors were increasingly incorporated into the scheme to teach the principles of infant care to the depot mothers. It was this hygiene education which became the unique and lasting English contribution to infant welfare work.

V

Maternalism: the conservative solution

The Finsbury Infants' Milk Depot was closed in 1909 and 'instead . . . two health visitors were appointed'[1] to solve the problem the depot had failed to answer adequately. 'The primary fact' which had led to the establishment of milk depots had been the 'high infant mortality' (as George Newman had explained in his *Special Report*).[2] But for various reasons the milk depot system did not reach as many infants as was desirable, and consequently did not affect the infant mortality rate as much as it could have done. As has been seen, they were expensive to run, the milk they supplied was too dear for those who most needed it to afford, and the system was inconvenient for the mothers. This was especially true in Finsbury where, in addition to having to go each day to return the previous day's bottles and collect the new supply, mothers were obliged to bring their infants once a fortnight to be weighed and examined in order to be allowed to continue to purchase the depot milk. For women who worked outside the home this was clearly impracticable. And for women with more than one or two children, the daily household chores as described by investigators such as Maud Pember Reeves as well as by the women themselves, demanded such precise timing and management that the additional tasks of daily collection and fortnightly attendance were also impossible to accomplish.

That such welfare work had the capacity to reduce the number of infant deaths was, if not proven by the depot statistics, at least demonstrated well enough to be accepted as true. Those who were involved in public health, paediatric work, or social work were convinced by the results obtained that attention devoted to infants was rewarded by an improvement in both the morbidity as well as the mortality statistics. And as mothers would not, or could not, bring their children to the depots, nor take advantage of the sale of specially sterilized and humanized milk, many authorities decided to expand their out-reach activities which, until that time, by and large had been limited to depot-enrolled infants. For example, the Liverpool Health Committee appointed lady inspectors 'to teach [depot] mothers the proper method of feeding infants'.[3] In Battersea also 'the homes of the children fed on the [depot] milk [were] visited by the lady sanitary inspectors, who [endeavoured] to secure that the instructions [were] properly carried out.'[4] And in Finsbury, where the depot was opened under the auspices of the Social Workers' Association, 'each child fed on the depot milk [was] visited in its own home once a week, and in some cases more frequently.'[5] Indeed, Newman averred, 'I attribute much of the success of the depot to these personal visits and assistance. They have been of the greatest value to both mothers and infants.'[6]

Home visiting for the purpose of health education originated long before the first milk depot was established (1899) in England, but infant welfare work systematized and rationalized this branch of sanitary instruction. A peculiarly British institution which, as McCleary claimed, 'neither in origin nor development [owed] anything to foreign influence or example',[7] health visiting began in the industrial heartland of England. In 1852 the Manchester and Salford Sanitary Association was founded and ten years later (1862), on the suggestion of Mr Turner, a leading surgeon in the area, an affiliated society was formed which was initially called The Ladies' Sanitary Reform Association of Manchester and Salford, and was later known as The Ladies' Public Health Society. The purpose of this organization was, in the first instance, to popularize knowledge with regard to sanitation in particular and its general goal was 'the elevation of the people physically, socially, morally and religiously'.[8]

The Ladies' Sanitary Association handed out tracts and pamphlets, and in 1875 began a series of penny *Health Lectures for the People*. Finding that the distribution of leaflets by 'ladies of position' was not having the desired effect or result, the Association hired a 'respectable working woman' to 'go from door to door among the poorer classes of the population, to teach and help them as opportunity offered'.[9] In his autobiography Robert Roberts described the form this aid often took in the early years of the twentieth century. 'The Ladies' Health Society worked bravely among us,' he recollected. 'They visited "the lowest classes"' and lent out lime and whitewash to 'sweeten and purify' houses. They also sold carbolic soap and powder at a much reduced price to help people fight against the ubiquitous bugs and vermin. According to Roberts, the Society did not merely preach and sell the Gospel of Cleanliness, they tried to effect it as well.[10]

The Society increased the scope of their work and employed additional (paid) home visitors. Organizing a system for efficiency and comprehensiveness, they divided Manchester and Salford into districts and assigned a lady superintendent to each area to be in charge of a paid working-class health visitor and a body of voluntary helpers. By 1890 there were eleven paid visitors living and working in eleven separate districts. That year the Society and the Manchester Corporation agreed on a mutually beneficial arrangement whereby the health visitors were supervised and directed by the medical officer of health and in return the sanitary authority undertook to pay half the salaries. A few years later a similar arrangement was made with the Salford Corporation.

At the same time, other authorities began to employ women who were to a greater or lesser degree specifically or specially educated for the job of health visiting. In 1890, on the initiative of Florence Nightingale, the North Buckinghamshire Technical Education Committee organized a course of instruction followed by an examination for candidates for such positions, and two years later (1892) the Buckinghamshire County Council appointed three graduates as full-time health visitors.[11] In 1897 the Worcestershire County Council employed five 'lady health missioners' (of indeterminate education) to 'go from house to house [amongst the poor] and school the parents in regard to feeding, clothing, and the rearing of children.'[12]

The Worcestershire lady health missioners were the first visitors to be devoted solely to infant and child welfare work. But as anxiety and disquiet grew regarding the decreasing birth rate, the stationary (if not increasing) infant mortality rate, and the physical condition of those children of the poor who survived the perils of early life, the duties of health visitors focused more and more on infant and child care and maternal education. The evolution of health visiting, like the increased interest in the quality of the milk supply or the establishment of milk depots, was a reflection of contemporary concern about the health of the young, or in other words, the future of the nation. In 1901 Dr Tattersall (the Medical Officer of Health for Salford) assigned the specific task of visiting homes with new babies to the women working in his district. The following year James Niven requested the same concentration of attention from the Manchester visitors. According to the *Annual Report* of the Ladies' Public Health Society for 1902, the reason was all too obvious. 'The abnormally high death rate among babies has led to this special work being undertaken,'[13] the chairwoman, Mrs Redford, explained.

Mrs Worthington, an active member of the Society, corroborated this trend when she was called before the Inter-Departmental Committee on Physical Deterioration on 29 February 1904 to give evidence. Asked if 'the care and nurture of infants [was] the special work of [the] society above all others?' Mrs Worthington replied that 'it was only one of many originally, but the medical officer has been taking such an extreme interest in that of late that the work for him has taken rather that form.'[14] Information was obtained with regard to the birth of an infant from the medical officer of health who, in turn, was sent a list each week from the registrar of births. As the *Annual Report* (1902) stipulated, the goal of the Society was to visit each baby, to note the food received, how the infant was clothed, and the condition of the surroundings. The visitor was to help solve specific problems and to educate the mother generally. Mrs Bostock, who had been working as a health visitor in the South Ancoats district of Manchester for fourteen years when she was called before the Inter-Departmental Committee, specified her duties: she tidied up and taught infant care and the art of economical cooking 'to the best of [her] ability'.[15]

At this time, there was no statutory authority to appoint health visitors. Sanitary inspectors were therefore employed to fulfil these functions. Ironically, traditional ideas about the role of women led to the opening of a field of paid professional work just for females. The concept that the proper sphere of working women was with women and children was matched by the notion that only women could successfully carry out the duties of health visiting, devoted as it was to domestic hygiene and child care. Notices of, or references to jobs for women began to appear with increasing frequency. For instance, on 12 October 1901 the *BMJ* reported that

> 'with a view to encouraging the sanitary authorities to employ female sanitary inspectors who, in addition to their other duties, would take opportunities of inculcating habits of cleanliness and the best methods of utilising food, the [London County] Council informed the Local Government Board that it was willing to pay half the salary of such inspectors.'[16]

Similarly, at a conference on sanitary reform, in celebration of the jubilee of the Manchester and Salford Sanitary Association in April 1902, Mrs H.J. Tennant (previously the Chief Woman Inspector of Factories) delivered a paper on 'Women's Work in Sanitary Reform'. The neglect of infant life, she argued, was one of the worst of the public health evils, and 'the work which was being done in the homes of Manchester by the women workers of the municipality and of the various voluntary societies could not be done properly by men.'[17]

In an article on 'Women as Sanitary Inspectors', J. Spottiswoode Cameron (MOH for Leeds and at the time (1902) President of the Society of Medical Officers of Health) explained that this subject 'has interested me more or less for upwards of a dozen years'. Conversations with John Tatham when he was MOH for Salford and then for Manchester 'in both of which towns women had been employed, led me to talk over the matter with . . . the Chairman of the Leeds Sanitary Committee'. In December 1897 Cameron submitted a report to the committee detailing the particular duties for which he felt the appointment of women inspectors was necessary. If only one were hired 'her most obvious duties would be in connection with workshops and work-places where women are employed,' as practical difficulties had arisen with the male inspectors. Cameron stipulated that 'the duties of a woman inspector would be . . . those of an ordinary workshop inspector,' although her scope was circumscribed to the sphere of female manufacture.[18]

There were, however, additional tasks which required the appointment of a second woman inspector. Her job would be to visit all houses in which children under two years of age had died. Cameron felt that there would be many benefits to such a system.

> 'One principal advantage of her visit would be her oversight of the condition of the house in regard to cleanliness – a matter in which, as it seems to me, a woman is apt to have a higher standard than a man. She would also find out the methods of diet to which the children were subjected, and would deal generally with what might be called the domestic side of hygiene, in addition to the part dealing more directly with so-called sanitary appliances. She should, for instance, be a woman competent to advise mothers what symptoms to be on the look-out for when infective disease was in the neighbourhood, and would have a sufficient knowledge of the early indications of infantile disease to give useful hints to parents. . . . The place for keeping food, and especially milk; the necessity of scalding the latter, particularly in hot weather; the thorough cleansing and disinfection of the feeding-bottle, are all matters on which her advice . . . ought to be valuable.'[19]

Cameron was not immediately successful in stimulating his committee to act. But a further report and personal persuasion finally induced them to appoint two women in May 1899. Equally well qualified (the Inspectors' Certificate of the Sanitary Institute or that of the London or Scottish Board was required) and paid (starting salary of 33s a week) as their male colleagues, these women were trained in the Leeds methods 'as is our usual practice with all new inspectors'. Cameron stressed that he 'was particularly anxious that they should not take simply the position of health visitors, as in some towns, but that they should be thoroughly competent in every respect to discharge the duties of an ordinary . . . inspector'.[20]

Evidently the arrangement worked well; by 1902 five women were on the staff and a sixth was expected as a trainee. The tasks assigned were consonant with the theoretical basis for their employment. They investigated the causes and conditions of infantile mortality generally, and undertook special studies as to the feeding of infants who had died from epidemic diarrhoea. The lady inspectors also enquired into all cases of puerperal fever, inspected all premises where women were employed, and did a great deal of house-to-house visiting. Cameron was enthusiastic. Pleased with the individual abilities of the women who had been hired, he pointedly remarked that while 'the Committee have in no case inserted any conditions in their advertisement other than those for men inspectors,' the women who responded were better educated. Treading carefully, Cameron concluded, 'Although the salary offered is not larger than that given to the men holding similar appointments, our women inspectors are to some extent selected persons, and in every case women who have a strong desire to assist in improving the health of the community.'[21]

Other health authorities followed this plan, and it became increasingly common to hire women sanitary inspectors. At the turn of the century the number of inspectors employed – male and female – in most metropolitan areas increased substantially, and a significant proportion of these new additions to the staff were women. In London, for instance, there were 188 inspectors in 1893 and by 1904 this number had risen to 313. Since the metropolitan boroughs were formed in 1900 a total of sixty inspectors had been taken on, twenty-eight of whom were female. Working in twenty-one of the twenty-eight districts, their duties were similar to the job description of the Leeds female sanitary inspectors. As the *BMJ* reported in July 1904, 'For the most part' they were employed 'in the inspection of work-shops in which women are employed and in the routine work of the prevention of infant disease and death.'[22] In an editorial on Shirley Murphy's (MOH for the Administrative County of London) 1904 *Report*, the *Lancet* elaborated on this development. Commenting upon 'the general increase of organised effort to reduce the mortality of infants which is now observable in London', they specifically noted that 'in many districts specially trained women inspectors systematically visit the homes of the poor and tender to the mothers practical advice concerning the proper feeding, clothing, and management of young children.'[23] As we shall see in greater detail, professional dissatisfaction with the milk depot system helped to create a new field of employment for women, as maternal education through health visiting became the preferred solution to the infant morbidity and mortality problem.

The disillusionment with the form the transplanted Goutte de Lait concept had taken in England, and the gradual but growing tendency towards an emphasis on education, were reflected in both the public and professional press. The fact that the milk depot system (except in Liverpool) did not reach a large percentage of the necessitous infants, and that, at least initially, only milk was provided and not, as in France, medical supervision and maternal education as well, led to the proposal for health visiting in the homes of all needy infants and not just those who were enrolled at a depot. This hygiene education was to be undertaken either by voluntary or paid workers, donating time to or employed by a particular organization, such as The Manchester and Salford Ladies' Public Health Society or, preferably, by female sanitary inspectors hired by the local authority.

In general, as has been seen, the milk depot idea was applauded and supported in the press. However, not all articles were favourable and a number of those which praised the scheme nevertheless called for additional activities, specifically maternal hygiene education. A series of articles on 'Infantile Mortality' published in *The Times* during the autumn of 1904, for instance, considered possible remedies to the problem.[24] Arguing deductively, the author submitted that the example of Preston, where the infant mortality rate had decreased following the employment of two lady health visitors and the organization of a large number of voluntary workers, proved that it was not poverty or the concomitant sanitary condition but 'improper feeding' due to lack of maternal education which was the primary factor in causing infant death.[25] A letter to *The Times* in response to the series picked up this theme of instruction. Signed by Henry Scott Holland (1847–1918), Canon of St Paul's who, as a supporter of both the Oxford House Settlement in Bethnal Green and the Christ Church Mission in Poplar, had much contact with poor mothers, this letter spoke less of the faults of the uneducated and more of the responsibilities of the educated. 'Our first duty is to teach the art of motherhood,' he wrote, and he praised the Douglas Nursery at Hoxton as 'a school in motherhood'.[26]

Couched in varying degrees of moral doctrine, the principle of pedagogy was clearly becoming the most popular remedy – sometimes at the cost of milk depot support. Edmund Cautley, physician to the Belgrave Hospital for Children, had a great deal to say in this regard. The author of two paediatric texts, one devoted exclusively to the problem of feeding, Cautley believed that having clean milk for sale was not enough. To maximize efficiency and effect the greatest change, he suggested that 'a system of home visitation . . . be instituted, and trained women appointed to visit the homes of cases selected by physicians, and there preach cleanliness, show how the foods should be prepared, and how the child should be washed and clothed.'[27] Cautley clarified the role he expected the municipality to play in his system. It was assuredly not that of a milk depot, which provided humanized and sterilized milk. 'The diet for the infant under my scheme', he declared

'only depends upon the municipal authorities to the extent that they shall provide a good milk. It is not even suggested that they are to recommend the milk in any particular form or modification. I am strongly opposed to such bodies acting as dry nurses and relieving the mothers of the responsibility of preparing the infant's food, and the medical practitioner of his proper function of ordering a diet suitable in quality and quantity for the particular child.'[28]

Reginald Dudfield, who as the MOH for Paddington and not a practitioner like Cautley, was not so anxious as the latter about the usurpation of the physician's role, nevertheless was not completely convinced by the idea of depots and advocated education. Dudfield recognized that urgent problems required immediate remedies, and he approved of 'the establishment of municipal depots as a temporary measure', pending the institution of the 'proper procedure' of education 'in the duties of wifehood and motherhood'.[29]

The medical profession, as reflected in various journal editorials, was moving in the direction Dudfield had indicated. A *Lancet* article on 'Infantile Diarrhoea' of September 1904 (a period of unusually high mortality from this cause) explained that 'diarrhoea is essentially a symptom dependent on various morbid causes', and that 'the presence of a pathogenic organism has been frequently sought for and many forms of microbes have been isolated from the stools.' The editors specifically noted also that 'one of the most important aetiologic factors concerned in this affection is undoubtedly the ignorance of the mothers. A very large number of women, more especially among the poorer classes, have not the least idea of the proper management of children and if the natural food – human milk – cannot be supplied the lot of the infant is often hard indeed.' The measures suggested in response to the problem included supervision of cowsheds and dairies and bacteriological research. The editors praised especially the 'excellent example' set by Liverpool 'in establishing depots from which parents can obtain sterilised milk' claiming that 'this plan has proved successful in diminishing the death-rate from diarrhoea.' Nevertheless, in their opinion

'the most important matter . . . is to try to adopt some means by which instructions could be given to women as to the proper management of children. . . . If classes could be formed at which instruction could be given in those matters, not only to the married women amongst the poorer classes but also to district nurses and visitors, who might in their turn convey the necessary instructions to the mothers in their own homes, doubtless beneficial results would follow. . . . A little instruction to the mothers . . . would doubtless do much [they reiterated] in the prevention of one of the most fatal of infantile diseases.'[30]

By 1906 even George McCleary, that staunch advocate of milk depots, had begun to reassess the value of these institutions as they had developed in England. He had always urged the medical management of depot infants but now he said he saw no reason 'why the advantages of this systematic . . . supervision . . . need be restricted to the babies fed on the depot milk'. In the paper he delivered before the first National Conference on Infantile Mortality, he discussed possibilities for expanded and improved out-reach work, especially through education and instruction, with the depot as the co-ordinating centre of infant welfare activities 'for the purpose not of curing but of preventing disease'.[31]

Although a number of commentators discussed education through health visiting in relation to, within the context of, or in comparison with milk depots, most observers perceived this form of infant welfare work as an independent endeavour to be judged, and found worthy of support, on its own merits. This was especially true of reports of activities in Manchester and Salford, where no depot had been established and where health visiting was well developed. In August 1903 the *BMJ* reviewed the annual *Report* of the MOH for Salford. Noting that there had been 'a great improvement in the rate of infant mortality', the editors announced that 'an interesting experiment' in relation to that problem had 'met with success'. Citing the report, they explained that in one district 'visiting and keeping under observation each newly-born child has produced a considerable amount of information, and has . . . proved useful in reducing the infant mortality' in that area.[32]

Positive commentaries such as these on the influence of health visiting on infant mortality continued throughout the period of our study. In 1907, for example, the *BMJ* noted that in Salford 'the death-rate amongst the 956 infants visited by the health visitors was only 119.2 per 1,000 as compared with 162 for the whole borough.'[33] And again in 1908 the editors reported that 'there can be little doubt that the systematic work of the health visitors . . . has had a very considerable effect; the greatest importance is rightly attached to the work of the health visitors in the instruction of mothers in the feeding and tending of infants.'[34] By that time, the impoverished Greengate district which in 1899, prior to the commencement of health visiting specially devoted to baby welfare, had the highest infant mortality rate in the city, could boast of a lower rate than in the borough as a whole.[35]

The value of education and instruction was also praised by other commentators elsewhere. We have noted before the attitude of the Inter-Departmental Committee on Physical Deterioration with regard to this genre of remedy. It is therefore not surprising that in their *Report* they urged action along these lines.

> 'While laying special stress on the need for education of the young in the matters of hygiene and domestic economy, the Committee believe even more may be done in the direction of training the mothers of the present generation in these matters. To this end, Health Societies on the lines of the Manchester and Salford Ladies' Health Society should be formed all over the country. Enough has been said of the value of the system by competent judges to justify the Committee in urging upon every locality the adoption of similar methods.'[36]

This was precisely the sort of solution the Committee most sincerely – and ardently – endorsed.

It was also the type of activity most in consonance with that influential and ubiquitous social work institution, the Charity Organisation Society (COS), which had been established in 1869 to bring order to the chaos of unrestricted and unregulated alms-giving.[37] Helen Bosanquet, a prominent member of the society, forcefully urged the nostrum of maternal education and instruction in a paper on 'Pauperization and Interests' delivered before the Section of State Medicine at the 1904 annual meeting of the BMA. Bosanquet's arguments were framed within the construct of the COS creed: she minimized and disparaged the philosophy that 'dirt, overcrowding, insanitary houses, foul air, and insufficient or inappropriate food and clothing' were due to poverty. She had found that 'these evils frequently exist where there is no poverty to account for them.' The 'real cause' she asserted was 'the absence of those dispositions, faculties, and interests, which we are apt to sum up in the word "character".' Hence she proposed that 'the true method of attack is to strike straight at the root of the evil, and by education and the healthy stimulation of interests to arouse the energies and knowledge which will lead the backward into the ranks of the forward.' Bosanquet specifically decried the provision of sterilized milk for babies as a means of reducing infant mortality as an example of the incorrect approach. 'The true policy', she said, 'lies in the better training of women and girls in the arts of housekeeping and child-rearing; and more especially in some knowledge of proper feeding.'[38]

A special meeting of the council of the Charity Organisation Society was held (February 1907) in London to discuss the question of 'Health Visiting in Relation to Infant Mortality'. Practitioners and medical officers of health as well as non-medical people attended. It is noteworthy that the consensus of this group was that 'the principal factor in the cause of infantile mortality was poverty.' Robert Hutchison, author of *Food and the Principles of Dietetics* and an expert on the problems of the artificial feeding of infants, maintained that, broadly speaking, 'the causes of infantile mortality were poverty in the home, negligence of the parents or ignorance on the part of the mother. Poverty was the chief among these.' He contended that although breast-feeding was theoretically preferable 'it often happened that working-class women were compelled to resort to artificial feeding merely from inability' to nurse. He himself had frequently advised mothers 'to wean their children because owing to the conditions in which the mothers lived the children were not doing well on the natural method of feeding'. He believed that 'poverty was part of the social problem and as the condition of the working class improved infantile mortality would decrease.' These sentiments, this perception of the problem so fundamentally antagonistic to the Bosanquet analysis, was echoed by other participants. Nevertheless, the immediate resolve was to opt for the remedy of health visitors to educate the poor 'in the subject of the rearing of infants'. And as 'maternal hygiene could only be taught to mothers by women, it was very valuable . . . to have as health visitors women with a special understanding of maternal hygiene'.[39]

This tension between a recognition of poverty as the primary underlying cause of infant death, and support for the solution of maternal education rather than radical measures to improve the financial situation of the working class reverberated in the paper delivered by J.S. Cameron (MOH Leeds) at the first National Conference on Infantile Mortality. As we have seen, Cameron was an enthusiastic advocate for the employment of women sanitary inspectors, and the experience of the Leeds health department had, in his opinion, proven his case. In this lecture he concentrated on 'the assistance [they] rendered in the case of young and living children'. He said that in Leeds they had not found 'that the employment of women before their confinement has been associated very specially with the deaths of their infants'. To the contrary, 'the wage earned by these expectant mothers is perhaps sometimes of considerable value to the health of the coming child' as 'it has been made clear to us that . . . infantile deaths are to a large extent connected with . . . poverty on the part of the mother.' Cameron did not elaborate on this and immediately turned to the visiting system he had developed. Information as to the birth was obtained from the registrar: 'the average period from . . . birth to the date of our hearing of it' was forty-two days. The female sanitary inspectors visited each child to help and give advice to the mothers. They found that (confirming the observations of Maud Pember Reeves), in one particular poor district in which the infant mortality was highest, 'whilst, as a rule . . . the mother is quite willing to nurse her child, she not infrequently finds after she begins to get up and about that she has not the requisite milk to do so.' In these cases, the inspectors provided milk from a charitable association for the mothers to drink so that they could continue to nurse. In conclusion, Cameron emphasized once again that he believed 'this actual visiting of the children and influencing their diet' helped to reduce infant mortality.[40]

Clearly the concept of maternal education and instruction through health visiting had amassed broad-spectrum support. From reports of voluntary organizations such as the Manchester and Salford Ladies' Public Health Society to editorials in the public and professional press to commentaries from practitioners, the Inter-Departmental Committee on Physical Deterioration, the Charity Organisation Society, and the municipal employers of the women visitors, the account was the same: a significant number of infant deaths could be, and was, prevented through maternal education by health visitors. Health visiting elicited a uniformity of approval that the milk depot system never even approached. For contemporaries, the direction future infant welfare work should take was unmistakeable.

The question was, how should health visiting be instituted most effectively? As Cameron had pointed out, the infants were already on average forty-two days old before the Sanitary Office was informed of their birth. He had explained, moreover, that 'in a considerable number of cases the birth and the death were registered at the same time; whilst in a few and not altogether inconsiderable number of cases the death of the infant has actually been registered before its birth.'[41] To be maximally influential it was obvious that a more prompt procedure for notification had to be developed.

Samson G. Moore, the Medical Officer of Health for Huddersfield, took the problem of infant mortality and the search for reductive measures seriously. An account of his work is, in short, a history of the determined introduction of systematized health visiting in English infant life protection schemes. Shortly after his appointment in 1901, Moore began to scrutinize 'the returns of [infant] deaths from all causes in the sanitary district with a view to the selection of a disease, or group of diseases, likely to repay special measures for its (or their) prevention'.[42] At the same time he also collected information about infant welfare programmes in operation in Great Britain and abroad. In the Milroy Lectures he delivered in 1916 before the Royal College of Physicians of London he recollected that

'During my early inquiries into the subject I saw a statement in a medical paper to the effect that at Villiers-le-Duc . . . the infant mortality figure had been zero for ten years. I did not believe the statement. It was incredible. Yet I wrote to the French Academy of Medicine and inquired if they had any information on the subject. With the customary courtesy of our neighbours and gallant Allies, the Academy sent me a very full and complete answer confirming the fact, not merely by affirmation, but also by means of a print of a report to the Academy made by a special Commissioner, with the additional facts that during the same period no mother had died in child-bed, and at the date of the report all were vivant et vigoureux.'[43]

The account to which Moore referred was presented by A. Pinard on 15 March 1904. Pinard had already delivered a short communication on the subject on 26 January, but the Academy, like Moore, found the phenomenon so astonishing that they decided to enquire further into the means and methods by which this dramatic accomplishment had been achieved. The mayor of the commune, Morel de Villiers (a physician), confirmed the statistical record with tables showing precisely the number of births and deaths under twelve months of age for each year from 1894 to 1903. He explained that he had devised a ten-point programme for this purpose. The first item clarified the theoretical basis and practical implications of the scheme:

'Toute femme enceinte, mariée ou non, domiciliée dans la commune, ne possédant pas les ressources suffisantes pour lui permettre de prendre à sa charge les dépenses qu'entraîneraient les mesures nécessaires pour assurer, autant que possible, non seulement sa propre existence, mais aussi celle de l'enfant à naître pourra demander l'assistance de la commune.'[44]

This was a comprehensive statement of intention, of the role or responsibility of the commune in relation to pregnant women and their children.

The additional nine measures specified the assistance offered and regulations enacted in order to protect maternal and infant life. Pregnant women wishing to take advantage of the municipal benefits registered at the Town Hall. These included the gratuitous provision of midwifery services in prenatal and delivery care in the case of normal pregnancies, and the attendance of a physician if the midwife ascertained any pathological condition. Both the midwife and the physician were chosen by the pregnant woman herself and paid for 'sur le crédit ouvert au budget de la commune pour l'assistance médicale gratuite et sans participation de l'État ou de département'. Wet-nurses were charged with new obligations. All infants under their care were to be weighed once a fortnight and records of their growth were kept at the municipal offices. All cases of illness which occurred among the babies had to be reported within twenty-four hours. If the nurse used cows' milk to feed, she had to obtain a sterilizing apparatus loaned free of charge and returned after weaning. Finally, numerous financial incentives and deterrents were included. Women remaining in bed for ten days after delivery (then considered optimal practice to preserve maternal health) were awarded a grant of one franc (about 10d) per day for the entire rest period, and mothers or wet-nurses successfully rearing a child by breast or bottle were given two francs (1s 8d) per month from the time they began to care for the child until the first birthday was reached. Punitively, qualifying certificates were withdrawn from wet-nurses who failed to comply with the regulations.[45]

Pinard's report to the Academy elaborated upon the feeding and general care instructions distributed to the mothers and nurses, the recommended procedure for milk sterilization, and the weight increase table adopted by the commune as normal. He analysed the charts and tables Morel de Villiers had sent him, and pointed out various aspects of the programme, such as the provision for ante-natal care, which were particularly praiseworthy. In conclusion Pinard said, 'C'est le plus bel échantillon de puériculture que je connaisse. L'œuvre de M. Morel de Villiers est digne de respect et d'admiration. C'est le plus bel exemple qu'on puisse et qu'on doive donner à toutes les communes de France.'[46]

Samson Moore was equally convinced. In his special *Report on Infantile Mortality* (1904) to the health committee, he gave a detailed analysis of the situation in Huddersfield and of the infant welfare systems which had been developed in Britain, France, and Germany. He explained that according to the classification of the Registrar-General, causes of infant mortality were considered to be preventable, non-preventable, or doubtfully so.* Given this division, examination of the cause of the 324 infant deaths which had occurred in Huddersfield in

* Preventable causes: diarrhoea, inflammation of the bowel, whooping cough, tabes mesenterica, accident and negligence, other infectious diseases.

1902 revealed that 76 were subsumed under the first category, 65 the second, and 183 the third.[47] Turning to preventive programmes, Moore paid particular attention to the practical French contributions and to the role of the French government in stimulating and supporting such work. 'The importance which the French government attaches to the subject of Infantile Mortality, and the concern with which they view the subject indicate clearly that they realise the need for doing all that can be done to prevent the wastage which tends to occur,'[48] Moore declared approvingly. Passing from the national to the local level, he described the work in Villiers-le-Duc in considerable detail and his concluding recommendations mirrored his admiration for this system. He advised the early notification of births, the appointment of at least two lady health visitors, the establishment of a milk depot and a day nursery, and the increase of statutory powers to provide financial inducements to nurse, among other measures.[49]

In the spring of 1904 when this report was submitted, Benjamin Broadbent was the Chairman of the Huddersfield health committee. In November of that year he was elected mayor and, while the committee continued to deliberate over Moore's proposals, Broadbent immediately announced that he himself would pay one guinea to each child upon his first birthday. As the *Lancet* reported, this experiment excited interest,[50] and it may perhaps have been the catalyst needed to move the committee into action. In any case, in April 1905 the sanitary authority approved 'a scheme of work against infantile mortality' which included 'the voluntary notification of births to the medical officer of health and the visitation *in their homes* of *all* newly born infants *immediately* after birth by women doctors, followed by voluntary workers'.[51] Work began on a somewhat limited scale: 'the payment of 1s to the midwife . . . secured the prompt notification of about one-third of the total births.' This was followed up with visits from 'competent ladies'.[52]

A special Act of Parliament enabled the corporation (as of 1 November 1906) to make compulsory the notification of births to the MOH within forty-eight hours of delivery. During the first year of operation 94 per cent of all births were notified. The plan of working was simple, and similar to that operant both in Manchester and Leeds, as the Huddersfield system combined municipal and voluntary efforts. Upon receipt of the information of birth, one of the two female assistant medical officers of health went to the address given and 'if the case is one where help or advice is likely to be of use this visit affords the opportunity. Cards and leaflets of advice on the care of infants, very

---

Non-preventable causes: immature birth, non-inflation of the lungs, congenital defects.

Doubtfully preventable: debility, wasting, inanition, convulsions, bronchitis, inflammation of the lungs, of the brain and membranes (Samson G. Moore, *Report on Infantile Mortality*, Huddersfield, Daily Chronicle Printing Works, 1904, p.14).

carefully thought out, are generally left. Wherever practicable breast feeding is urged, and if there is any difficulty in this respect help and advice are proffered.' This initial contact was followed by repeated visits by 'lady helpers' of the Public Health Union. In keeping with the philosophy of divorcing education from material goods, the *BMJ* emphasized that 'the visit is a visit to the baby, and for its health, and it is a rule that no dole shall be given in any shape.'[53] This was a step further away from the Goutte de Lait system which supplied milk as well as medical supervision, and it was also a significant departure from the Villiers-le-Duc scheme, with its fixed financial awards.

Moore claimed a fair degree of success for the programme. For the first thirty-nine weeks of 1907 the infant mortality rate was 85 per 1,000 in comparison with 138 per 1,000 during the corresponding period in 1906, and a mean of 135 throughout the same months in the ten years 1897 to 1906. Another achievement of the system was the publicity it generated and the positive response it elicited. As the *BMJ* explained:

> 'The scheme . . . appears to have been so carefully thought out and to involve so little expenditure that we . . . hope that other towns in Great Britain may be fired to do similar work on equally good lines. The scheme is interesting if only to demonstrate the possibility of the smooth and successful working together of public and private bodies. . . . Huddersfield is attacking the child problem at the root, for no amount of after-care will undo the mischief done to infants in the first months of their lives.'[54]

The editors concluded by once again urging the establishment of similar systems 'in all our towns'.

The key to the Huddersfield system was the early notification of births. In Villiers-le-Duc women registered themselves at the town hall to obtain the benefits provided, but this was a small town with a correspondingly close knit society, and the medical and financial aid offered by the municipality was significant. Huddersfield, a larger community with greater anonymity and offering nothing but instruction, could not rely upon self-registration and therefore established compulsory notification so that the public health department would know whom to visit. Indeed any town, like Huddersfield, wishing to combat infant mortality through a programme of maternal education had to introduce the early notification of births. This basic, fundamental measure upon which the whole system depended, predicated on sound public health principles and positive statistical results was, unfortunately, opposed by the medical profession. Initially supportive, then cautious, the press reaction finally crystallized into hostility and resistance.

In 1906, shortly after Huddersfield had obtained Parliamentary sanction to require the early notification of births, the *Lancet* remarked, 'With every wish for the success of the proposed experimental legislation . . . it may be presumed that the probability of the enactment of similar provisions operating generally throughout England and Wales must practically depend upon clear proof of their beneficial effect in Huddersfield.'[55] In the event, this took place all too soon to suit either the *BMJ* or the *Lancet*. In early 1907 legislation to provide for the early notification of births was introduced into the House of Commons by Robert Cecil as a private Bill, and was subsequently taken over as a government measure. The proposed regulations (which were mandatory) required that the father if in residence, or in his absence 'any person in attendance upon the mother at the time of birth or within six hours thereafter . . . send or give notice of the birth to the medical officer of the district in which the child is born within 48 hours after such birth.' Furthermore, 'any person who fails to give or send notice of a birth in accordance with this section shall be guilty of an offence and shall be liable on summary conviction to a penalty not exceeding twenty shillings.'[56]

Initially framed as a compulsory statute, 'the Government, after considering the Bill fully, had come to the conclusion . . . that it should be optional . . . for the local authorities to adopt it within their areas.'[57] The government also reduced the notification period to thirty-six hours. John Burns, as President of the Local Government Board, introduced these amendments, which were carried. The medical profession had specific objections, and particularly opposed the provision compelling the birth attendants to furnish the notification in the absence of the father and the imposition of a fine in the case of failure to inform. Parliamentary representatives of the profession, especially John Batty Tuke and G.J. Cooper, MRCS pressed an amendment to relieve medical practitioners from the obligation to notify. The activists for the profession were ultimately out-manoeuvred. They agreed to withdraw their opposition on the understanding that the alterations they desired would be accepted by the government. John Burns, however, sensed correctly that the House was willing and ready to pass the bill as it stood and he announced that 'they could not by an understanding or bargain between themselves withdraw the Bill from the purview of the House.'[58] As the *BMJ* subsequently reported, 'Dr Cooper, who has worked indefatigably in the defence of professional interests in this matter, finally in despair asked the promoters of the Bill to drop the amendment, understanding, as we have no doubt, that the feeling of the House was strongly against it; but it was persevered in' with the result that it was defeated by eighty-seven to nineteen votes. The Act itself was then passed without problem in both Houses and received the Royal assent on 28 August 1907.[59]

Needless to say, reaction in the medical press was not favourable. An editorial in the *BMJ* angrily reiterated the objections of the profession.

'The Act . . . imposes on every medical man a new obligation, and any failure to meet this obligation within thirty-six hours will expose him to the risk of suffering the indignity of being summoned to the police-court and fined anything up to 20s. . . . The provision with its penalty was defended on the ground that the duty imposed is a civic and not a professional duty. The flimsiness of this excuse was exposed. . . . To talk about this new obligation as a civic duty is . . . nonsense, and the promoters of the Bill practically allowed that it was nonsense . . . but the House of Commons, with the amiable air of the man who slaps you on the back and picks your pocket [rejected the amendment and passed the Act].'

The editors concluded plaintively (and self-pityingly), 'It is a very unsatisfactory ending, and we fear exemplifies only too well the unsympathetic attitude which the House of Commons is ready to assume towards the medical profession.'[60]

The *Lancet* response was only marginally less acrimonious. It too objected to the requirement of notification under pain of a penalty and without any positive remuneration for the service. However, unlike the *BMJ*, the *Lancet* addressed the problem the Act had been passed to help solve.

'As to the utility of such a measure there can be no question and members of the medical profession were amongst the first to call attention to the great good which is likely to follow on its adoption. . . . We cordially approve of the principle of this measure and agree that adequate steps cannot be taken to preserve the life of children of whose very existence the local authorities only too often are quite ignorant.'[61]

The prospect and subsequent passage of the Notification of Births Act generated a lively correspondence in both the *BMJ* and the *Lancet*. These letters expressed a greater range of opinion than that held by the editors of the journals. The first to write was Benjamin Broadbent, who naturally supported the bill. Speaking from his own experience, he claimed that 'the early notification of births seems obviously the first step towards combating infantile mortality. Every authority on the subject is absolutely agreed upon this point.' It was only common sense he argued. 'If you are to try to save the lives of infants it is necessary to know that they are in being.' Given that 'it is the first thing that the practical administrator of public health finds that he needs,' Broadbent was at a loss to understand the 'hostility' to the measure on the part of the profession. He pointed out that physicians were in attendance at a maximum of 30 per cent of all births, and that the fathers were in residence in the vast majority of these families. Thus, realistically speaking, very little notification work would devolve upon the profession, 'probably not in more than 1 per cent of the total number of births would any obligation fall upon the medical man.' In Broadbent's opinion the passage of the bill was literally a question of life or death for many infants and he sharply rebuked physicians for blocking its passage. 'That medical men should object to such a measure seems to me a contradiction, an outrage upon the nature of things, . . . it is murder to kill [these infants] and merely to let them die is not free from some blame.'[62]

In the first issue of the *BMJ* subsequent to the passage of the Act (31 August) several irate and indignant letters were published. John Batty Tuke wrote to complain of how he was 'outmanoeuvred' by John Burns.[63] Others protested that the state demanded from physicians 'without remuneration and under penalty, a service for which any other profession than ours would be paid as a matter of course'.[64] As a third practitioner put it, 'Are lawyers treated like this?' Conceding that 'the notification of births within a shorter period than now obtains is desirable' this man nevertheless argued that 'the method proposed is in accordance with the usual slimness of Governmental authorities in dealing with our profession.' In answer to Broadbent's letter he emphasized that 'medical men are not opposed to the Bill . . . but to the method of putting it into practice.'[65]

In light of the long-established home visiting organized by the Manchester and Salford Ladies' Public Health Society, the response of the profession in that area is especially interesting. Actively opposing local adoption of the bill, a deputation from the Manchester and Salford Joint Divisions of the BMA waited on the Sanitary Committee of the Manchester Corporation to explain why the city should not do so; at the same time, a letter of protest was sent to the local newspapers. Their objections were not new and the complaints of 'an unjustifiable interference in their confidential relations with patients', the 'penalty for non-performance', and the lack of 'fee or reward' for compliance were reiterated.[66] The position of the Manchester and Salford physicians was forcefully supported by the *BMJ*. In their report on activities in this area the editors commented:

'If the Act is adopted in Manchester, it is difficult to say what the result will be. If we may judge by the present temper of the general practitioners, something like passive resistance is not at all unlikely to occur. The very idea of penalizing an honourable profession for not performing someone else's duty has aroused a feeling of bitter resentment which augurs very badly for the success of the Act, so far as it depends on medical men. No profession has done more gratuitously for the good of humanity. . . . It is not even as though the notification were a confidential sort of document sent to the registrar; it is nothing of the sort, . . . and practitioners are saying very plainly that they will refuse to be Government spies, either with a fee or without a fee.'[67]

It is not surprising that the Notification of Births Act was not adopted in Manchester until 1912, and was never voluntarily accepted in Salford. The volitional notification by midwives since 1907 in the first instance, and 1899 in the latter, partly compensated for this however.

Not all local professional organizations were hostile to the bill, and not all reports in the medical press were so contentious. Despite continuing criticism in some quarters, the positive results obtained in those areas which adopted this legislation were persuasive. Huddersfield, as the originator of the scheme, thus attracted a great deal of attention. On 14 September, for instance, the *Lancet* published a favourable report on the decrease in the number of infant deaths in that city. 'In view of the new Act . . . the effect of the local measure . . . on infant mortality acquires much importance,' the editors explained. Analysing the relevant data, they concluded that in their opinion the statistics seemed 'to point to the successful administration of the Huddersfield local Act since the beginning of this year as the cause of the recent reduction of infant mortality in that town'.[68] This report was followed by another two months later, stressing the restrictions within which the system operated. Only if the baby '*is not under medical care*', the Leeds correspondent emphasized, was the initial visit followed up. And he hastened to add, 'Great care has been taken both by the public health authorities and by the voluntary association not in any way to make their services obtrusive and always to make it clear that it is fully within the right of anyone to decline the services and advice which are offered to them.'[69] Similarly, a short note in the *BMJ* on the working of the Act in Huddersfield pointed out that 'it has not led to friction'.[70] And a paper given at the Brighton and Sussex Medico-Chirugical Society on the importance of the Act as a factor in the diminution of the infant death rate dismissed the objections raised by the medical profession in light of the benefits to infants 'as proved by the Huddersfield experiment'.[71]

By the end of the year, four months after the Act was passed, the *Lancet* was, in the main, reconciled to the idea. In the 'Annus Medicus' section, summing up the major events of the past twelve months, the editors went so far as to review this particular event rather favourably.

'This onward movement is the first which endeavour[s] to get at . . . the bed-rock of disease, ill-health, and incapacity. Compared to this all our previous efforts have been rather of a patchwork or apologetic character, which have left untouched that great wave of infant mortality.'

The editors emphasized the prevalence of '"ignorance": ignorance of the importance of cleanliness, of light, of fresh air, of the value of different foods – in a word, ignorance of how to live.' Neither the words nor the concept of 'poverty' or 'indigence' were once mentioned. The value of the Act was that it made possible 'the necessary organization whereby the effects of this disastrous ignorance might be mitigated'.[72]

Many communities evidently were convinced of the wisdom or prudence of adopting early notification regulations. In a statement to the House of Commons in early March 1908, after the Act had been in effect for approximately half a year, John Burns reported that 113 local authorities had adopted the measure.[73] Four months later (9 July) he provided more detailed information; in total 107 boroughs and urban districts, 16 metropolitan borough councils and the common council of the City of London had adopted the Act.[74] By January 1909 according to the *Lancet*

> '126 sanitary authorities [have secured] the prompt notification . . . of all births. . . . The act was adopted in 18 of the 29 metropolitan boroughs, and . . . is now under consideration in several of the remaining 11 of those boroughs. Of the 75 large English and Welsh towns . . . 44 have already adopted the Act in addition to Huddersfield.'[75]

One of the reasons why so many communities adopted the Act was because it helped to rationalize programmes they had already developed which required health visiting. At the same time as Huddersfield introduced its version of the Villiers-le-Duc system, other infant welfare workers were organizing a variety of maternal and child health schemes based primarily on the principle of education. The first such endeavour in London was the establishment in 1904 of the Westminster Health Society. In many respects similar to the Manchester and Salford Ladies' Public Health Society, especially with regard to practical arrangements, the Westminster Health Society was devoted to the improvement of infant health through maternal aid and instruction. David Forsyth, physician to the Evelina Hospital for Sick Children and one of the founders of the Society, explained the problem and the remedy as perceived by those involved in this effort. Forsyth recognized that indigence as well as ignorance was the cause of many infant deaths: 'If it were possible tomorrow for each infant to find its home clean and healthy, the problem of the poor would have been solved: conversely, if the problem of the poor were solved, excessive infant mortality would cease to trouble us.' Therefore he maintained that 'infant mortality, and with it infant disease, must be attacked from two directions – the legal and the social.'[76] The purpose of the health society was to fulfil the second of these functions. Forsyth did not view mothers as feckless or slovenly – although he certainly gave them full marks for ignorance. Like other physicians we have discussed who worked with poor women, Forsyth saw these mothers as woefully uneducated but eminently educable and, more importantly, loving towards their children. The Westminster Health Society, in co-ordination with the public health authority and the local charitable and social work agencies, organized a system of home visiting, prepared and distributed leaflets, and arranged frequent lectures to mothers on such topics as food, child care, and children's ailments. Withal, home visiting was 'the main object of the society' and of greatest 'practical value'.[77]

In 1904 the Society's attempt to reach pregnant women prior to the birth of their babies was unique. A list of impending maternity cases was obtained from the various hospitals in the area, and one of the staff of voluntary lady visitors 'trained to the work and chosen for their tact, patience, and perseverance' paid a call on each woman. Practical aid was provided in addition to instruction. If the 'environment' was found to be 'unsatisfactory' additional visits were made 'in order to improve the condition of the home'. Furthermore, 'extra nourishment is provided if necessary at the time of confinement, and facilities are given for mothers who wish to save money for their lying in.' Information with regard to children already born was obtained from registrar lists. All babies were visited and calls were repeated as found necessary, with a minimum of once a month for the first three months and once a quarter thereafter. According to Forsyth 'the practical result of this undertaking has been to establish a very satisfactory difference between the infant mortality in the visited homes and that in the city generally.'[78] Unfortunately he did not describe the system in detail; and we do not know what the 'extra nourishment' consisted of, from where it was obtained, or who paid for it. Nor did he provide any information with regard to medical care.

The Westminster Health Society does not appear to have been very influential, at least initially, outside its own community. (Later on, in 1912, they opened a consultation for children under five years old which attracted a great deal of attention.) Of greater consequence for the child care movement was the St Marylebone Health Society. Started in 1905,[79] this organization radically increased the scope of activities normally undertaken with the establishment of 'a centre under medical supervision to which infants could be brought for periodic examination and advice', attached to the Marylebone General Dispensary.[80] The initiative for this institution was taken by Eric Pritchard, physician to the dispensary, an eminent paediatrician and the author of a number of widely read texts on infant feeding and management. The Borough of St Marylebone Health Society, like that in Westminster, was organized in co-ordination with the local public health department, hospitals, dispensaries, and charitable and social work institutions. Its purpose was 'the prevention of the spread of tuberculosis and the saving of infant life by means of voluntary effort – to inaugurate, in fact "a system of voluntary service in a municipal setting"', he explained citing Beatrice Webb. To accomplish this end the society instituted 'a service of voluntary workers for the whole district'.[81]

The practical working of this system was similar to that established elsewhere. The borough was divided into districts and subdistricts, an independent committee was formed for each area, and workers were assigned to a specific locale. Pritchard emphasized the importance of securing and training appropriate health visitors. The 'first work' he later recalled, 'was to find suitable volunteers for this service'.[82] These were chiefly recruited 'from the ranks of the large contingent of retired nurses who were resident in the Borough and many of whom had married members of the medical staff of the hospital where they had been trained'.[83] 'Having obtained recruits . . . we arranged a very complete series of lectures and demonstrations, covering all the subjects that would be useful or necessary for the work.'[84] Lists of births were obtained from the registrar, and all babies in the borough were visited.

It quickly became clear that this arrangement, while useful, was not accomplishing all that was desired and was certainly not competent to cope with difficult cases. The society decided that 'the work in Marylebone would be greatly furthered [with] some central station where infants could be referred for medical inspection, advice, and treatment', but it was to be, above all, an educational institution. It was not just the mothers who needed to be educated, infant welfare workers also were all too often ignorant of much that was relevant to their profession.[85]

Influential as was the system devised by Eric Pritchard and his colleagues in St Marylebone, the establishment of the School for Mothers in St Pancras was of even greater consequence because it caught the interest of a wide spectrum of observers, and perhaps also because it was the collective work of a number of people. The foundation was laid by John F. Sykes, the Medical Officer of Health for the borough, who was especially interested in infant and maternal health. At the turn of the century he had organized a programme of distribution of advice cards supplemented by home visits from two women sanitary inspectors and their voluntary assistants. He soon found to his 'astonishment and horror' that this leaflet which, while stressing breast-feeding also described 'in detail the best method of bottle feeding', was having the opposite effect to that intended. 'Mothers were sedulously weaning their babes in order to follow the detailed advice *of the medical officer of health* in the method of hand-feeding.' Sykes promptly stopped the distribution of this information sheet, and considered alternatives.[86]

In late 1904 the *BMJ* reported that a meeting organized by the Infants' Health Society, 'to discuss the formation of a milk depot for the supply of modified milk in St Pancras' had been held. Ralph Vincent had urged its establishment, and recommended that it be run in accordance with Rotch's milk laboratory principles.[87] Sykes, however, was not convinced. To the contrary, 'I came gradually to the conclusion that distributing bottled milk for infants of suckling age would be putting into concrete form the abstract teaching of the leaflet which I had already so gladly destroyed', he explained a few years later. He believed that 'faulty maternal hygiene [was] the main factor in maintaining a high infantile mortality, this factor producing its greatest effect in the summer quarter.' He maintained, moreover, that it was a 'physiological law that infant life is dependent upon the mother from nine months before birth until nine months after birth'. Therefore she became 'the centre' of attention in his plans for infant welfare systems.[88] But he did not know how to proceed; any projects he may have had remained ideas. Throughout 1905 and 1906 he continued the programme of home visiting and emphasized breast-feeding, but did not introduce anything new.

Just at this time new methods were being tried elsewhere which fitted well into Sykes's theories. L'Œuvre du Lait Maternel, an association devoted, as its name implies, to the promotion of breast-feeding, was formed in Paris on 31 October 1904 and without wasting any time opened its first restaurant to provide free meals for nursing mothers the following day. Between December 1904 and May 1905 four more restaurants were established, supported by government subsidies and charitable contributions. Henri Coullet who, with his wife, was of central importance in initiating and carrying out the scheme, emphasized that 'any mother is welcome to come in. She will have to give neither name nor address nor reference of any kind.She has but to show that she feeds her baby.' Two meals were served each day, one at noon and the other in the evening. In addition soup or bread and cheese were provided upon application in the morning. Except for the meat portions, the food offered was not limited.[89]

An enthusiastic article in *The Times* of 26 December 1905[90] describing the work of the Coullets inspired Mrs W.E. Gordon to open (28 January 1906) a similar 'kitchen' in Chelsea where nursing mothers were offered a dinner of meat, vegetable, and pudding for the price of one penny. In October Mrs Gordon extended the scope of her work to include women in the last three months of pregnancy, and in January she opened a second restaurant.[91]

At the same time Alys Russell (the wife of Bertrand Russell), one of 'a party of members of the Women's Co-operative Guild who had gone to Belgium to study the work of foreign co-operative and socialist societies', published an article on 'The Ghent School for Mothers' in *The Nineteenth Century* which attracted a great deal of attention. Russell reported that the extremely high infant mortality rate of 333 per 1,000 births in Ghent had stimulated the Vooruit (Forwards) Society of Socialists, and one physician in particular, Dr Miele, 'to devise a complete system which should not only save the infants of the present, but should also prepare the young mothers of the future for their responsibilities'. Miele developed a multi-faceted programme which included operating a dispensary for the medical supervision of well and ill children (with 1,000 babies presented annually), training mothers who were themselves working women to be health visitors, running a medical insurance plan, providing milk either for the babies if weaned or the mothers if nursing, and holding lectures, classes, and practical courses on various aspects of child care. In conclusion Russell contended, 'Children under twelve months of age die in England today in as great numbers as they did seventy years ago. . . . This means that we are suffering not only a loss of 120,000 infant lives every year, while our birth-rate is declining, but it also indicates a prevalence of those causes and conditions which in the long run determine a serious degeneration of race.' And she challenged, 'Which of our philanthropic societies will be the first to follow his example in England, or will the work be undertaken by friendly or co-operative societies, or by trade unionists, or perhaps by wealthy individuals?'[92]

In the event, this question did not go unanswered very long. On 1 May 1907 a meeting was held attended by all those interested in starting some type of infant welfare scheme in St Pancras. Gordon presented an account of the Chelsea dinners for nursing mothers and Russell described what she had seen in Ghent. The *BMJ* reported that 'it was decided to organize and carry out a scheme comprising features of both institutions for the benefit of mothers and infants of the Somers Town district of East St Pancras, and to invite inhabitants of the neighbour-hood and other friends to subscribe.'[93] Calling themselves the St Pancras Mothers' and Infants' Society, this group opened the Mothers' and Babies' Welcome on 4 June 1907. And they recounted contentedly:

'Since then the work has gone on diligently. Babies flocked in and recruits for the dinners were discovered by the doctor amongst the pale-faced, weakly mothers. Ladies from all parts offered their services. From the first a cup of tea and a biscuit was given at each meeting, and that practice has been maintained throughout. It promotes conversation and friendliness, and leads mothers to stay and have a chat instead of hurrying off as soon as their turn at the weighing is over.'[94]

In an attempt to address the problem of infant disease in a comprehensive manner, and focusing primarily on the mother, the Welcome offered many services that were far removed from the earlier milk depot schemes. Women were encouraged to become members of the 'Welcome Club', the infant consultation service, at the price of one penny per fortnightly attendance. Another penny entitled the mother to join all or any of the classes; thus a fully attending member paid a penny a week. The clinic was run by a female physician two afternoons a week. Her job was to weigh the infant and advise the mother; she provided medical supervision and advice but not care. Cases of illness were referred to the family practitioner, or the local dispensary or hospital. The classes were designed to give practical instruction. Women were taught the principles of nutrition, and cookery lessons were given using an open fire (rather than a stove which few of the families had). Similarly, they were taught to cut out and sew simple clothes, to fashion

Plate 4 Leaflet distributed at mothers' meetings and by health visitors to women in St Pancras, announcing the establishment (1907) of the Mothers' and Babies' Welcome

Bring your Baby

to be Weighed!

MOTHERS' & BABIES' WELCOME.

6, Chalton St., Euston Road,

(for Babies under 12 months of age).

Hours for Weighing, etc.

Tuesdays and Fridays, from 2.15 to 3.30 o'clock.

The lady doctor attends to weigh babies and mothers, and to give advice on their feeding, clothing, and general management. If baby is not increasing in weight there is something wrong. Cases of illness are referred to doctors, dispensaries, or hospitals.

Welcome Club. 1d. per week.

Mothers are invited, with their Babies, to join the Club, and come regularly once a fortnight, on Tuesdays *or* Fridays. There are also talks and lessons on health, cooking, sewing, etc., on other days. Girls over school age may attend as visitors.

Dinners for Nursing-Mothers.

Dinners for expectant and nursing-mothers— to be eaten at the Club—are provided on medical recommendation at a charge of 1½d. a day, every day except Sunday, from 1.30 to 3 o'clock.

(*Source*: Evelyn M. Bunting (1907) *A School for Mothers*, p. 17.)

Plate 5 The weighing department of the St Pancras Mothers' and Babies' Welcome, 1907

(*Source*: Evelyn M. Bunting (1907) *A School for Mothers*, facing p. 42.)

Plate 6 London County Council lecturer giving a cooking lesson at the St Pancras Mothers' and Babies' Welcome, 1907

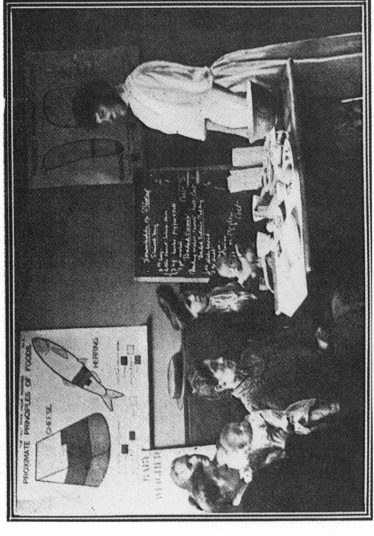

(*Source*: Evelyn M. Bunting (1907) *A School for Mothers*. facing p. 62.)

Plate 7 Leaflet distributed house-to-house in St Pancras advertising the establishment of a Provident Maternity Club at the Mothers' and Babies' Welcome, 1907

A Provident Maternity Club

HAS BEEN STARTED AT

THE MOTHERS' AND BABIES' WELCOME,

Chalton Street, N.W.

And expectant Mothers are earnestly invited to join.

Its object is to help such Mothers to lay by small sums of money week by week in preparation for the coming confinement, so that, in addition to SKILLED ATTENTION at child-birth and proper BABY CLOTHES for the infant, they may also have :—

1.—Help in the Home.
2.—Extra Nourishment.

1.—A Mother needs ENTIRE REST for AT LEAST A FORTNIGHT after child birth, and should do NO WASHING OR SCRUBBING for a MONTH. For WANT OF HELP in the Home, Mothers constantly get up too soon, thus often causing themselves life-long ill-health.

2.—Mothers, after confinement, need plenty of nourishing food and drink, such as Milk, Gruel, etc. (NO BEER or STOUT, and particularly NO SPIRITS.) For want of extra nourishment Mothers often lose their milk, or it gets so poor that the baby is not satisfied. Then foolish people who are very IGNORANT about babies, say "Feed the Child"; if they were wise they would say "FEED THE MOTHER."

The Management of the "Welcome" will add a Penny to every Shilling saved (under certain conditions), and the earlier expectant Mothers join, the greater the benefits they receive.

The Lady Superintendent is at the "Welcome" every day from 1.30 to 2.30, and will gladly give particulars of Rules and Benefits.

(*Source*: Evelyn M. Bunting (1907) *A School for Mothers*, p. 57.)

Plate 8 Bathing the baby lesson at the St Pancras Mothers' and Babies' Welcome, 1907

(*Source:* Evelyn M. Bunting (1907) *A School for Mothers,* facing p. 58.)

Plate 9 The dining room of the St Pancras Mothers' and Babies' Welcome, 1907

(*Source*: Evelyn M. Bunting (1907) *A School for Mothers*, facing p. 34.)

a cradle out of an orange crate, and the daily care of the baby: bathing, dressing, feeding. Fathers were also invited to attend.

In the St Pancras scheme mothers literally became, as Sykes had hoped, 'the centre round which all agencies revolved for the protection and preservation of the health of both mother and child'.[95] Unlike the French Goutte de Lait or the English milk depot which supplied pure milk for infants, one of the most important aspects of the St Pancras scheme was the adoption of the Coullet-Gordon restaurant innovation, and meals for women during the last three months of pregnancy and throughout the nursing period were provided. The founders of the Welcome were emphatic about the importance of nutrition both for the individual mother and child and, in a larger context, for the future of the race. 'There is a strong tendency in English women of all classes to underrate the importance of food,' they claimed. In their opinion this 'extraordinary tendency' of women to starve themselves arose from the fact that they did not 'think enough of themselves'. Women had to eat: 'there can never be a really strong race of Britons' until they did.[96]

Despite this insistence upon the importance of proper nutrition, the meals at the Welcome were not (as in Paris) offered free of charge. The price was 1½d per day and this 'sum is only remitted after close enquiry, generally kindly undertaken by the Charity Organisation Society'. (One can just imagine precisely how 'kindly' the COS enquiry was likely to have been.) In fact the women who ran the society found that far from desiring free meals 'one of our greatest difficulties has been to persuade the most deserving mothers to come at all when they cannot pay for themselves.' Like Pritchard, Forsyth, or Budin the founders of the St Pancras scheme described the women with whom they worked as loving towards their children, and eager to learn. They also recognized that indigence as well as ignorance was the cause of much illness, and they spoke of 'the demon of unemployment and its attendant poverty' and the 'tragedy' of 'no employment to be found'.[97]

The activities of the Mothers' and Babies' Welcome were co-ordinated (as elsewhere) with the public health department, particularly with the health visiting programme Sykes had established. The visitors urged the new mothers with whom they came into contact to go to the Welcome and the administrators of the St Pancras scheme referred follow-up cases to the visitors.[98] Clearly, passage of the Notification of Births Act aided the infant welfare efforts of organizations such as the Mothers' and Babies' Welcome, the St Marylebone Health Society, and the Westminster Health Society. The earlier information was obtained with regard to a birth the sooner the mother could be visited, instructed at home, encouraged to breast-feed, and pressed to attend the classes and consultations. St Pancras had in fact instituted a system of voluntary notification of births late in 1906 and adopted the Act shortly after it was passed in 1907.[99] St Marylebone followed in early 1908 and Westminster in 1909.

The passage of the Notification of Births Act was a decisive step in the history of the child health movement in England; it crystallized and consolidated the relatively amorphous trends and varied activities which had been undertaken until that time. Henceforth, infant welfare work was increasingly seen as a maternal problem or a question of motherhood: the instruction and well being of the mother was the first objective. Speaking in February 1907, prior to the passage of the Act, H.O. Pilkington, the MOH for Preston, described the frustrating situation he constantly encountered in his attempts to reduce infant mortality, and his expectations from the proposed legislation.

> 'The appointment of women health visitors, now so general in all large towns, affords a means of conveying instruction to the poorer households; and a little assistance and a few words of kindly advice, given . . . at the right time, will often prove of great service to the mother and her infant. But since many of the children are weakly and ailing from the time of birth, this help should be given as soon as possible, and the interval of six weeks which often elapses before the birth is registered, and so brought to the notice of the medical officer of health, not seldom renders the information worthless. . . . Shorten[ing] the period which may elapse between the birth and registration . . . or requir[ing] notification to be given to the health authorities at once . . . will [do] something towards reducing [that] infantile mortality.'[100]

Reports in the professional press indicated that adoption of the Act could fulfil these expectations.[101] An article in the *BMJ* on the annual report of John Robertson, the MOH for Birmingham, noted that he claimed that 'undoubtedly the greatest of all the causes of infant mortality is the ignorance of the parents as to how children should be reared.' Explaining that the health committee 'employs the services of paid women health visitors who can give sensible advice to mothers', Robertson affirmed that 'the Notification of Births Act (1907) will enable such visits to be paid at a time when advice may most opportunely be given.'[102] Birmingham adopted the Act in 1908; a woman physician (Jessie Duncan) and two health visitors were appointed to undertake the work this involved. According to Lane-Claypon, 'The results were almost at once apparent. . . . The mortality results were highly satisfactory. . . . The general health of the children . . . and that of their mothers . . . greatly improved as a result.'[103]

An article on the adoption of the Act in Liverpool reported that it had led to the employment of more female staff 'to visit the homes of the newly-born babies at an early date to give advice and help, whereas formerly visits could not be made until seven weeks or more had elapsed'. The scope of activity Niven encouraged in this department was similar to that undertaken by the milk depot system he had developed.

In both branches of infant welfare work his goal was to reach as many babies as possible. By September 1908 Niven maintained that

'15,000 homes had been visited since the beginning of the year, and the result was that good advice had been acted on in time, and the children were kept cleaner and were more intelligently looked after, while the food provided by the corporation was available as soon as it was required. All these were exceedingly important factors in bringing about a reduction in the rate of mortality among infants.'[104]

One year later (August 1909) Alfred Robinson, the Medical Officer of Health for Rotherham, presented the 'startling' results obtained in his area. Rotherham adopted the Notification of Births Act in 1908 and a voluntary health association was formed 'consisting of a lady superintendent for each of the nine wards in the borough, with two or three lady helpers, according to the number of births in each ward'. Robinson emphasized that 'the greatest care is exercised to avoid touching upon the domain of the family doctor – these were never visited – except by request of the usual medical attendant.' He estimated that physicians attended 25 per cent and certificated midwives 50 per cent of all births. (The remaining 25 per cent were attended by 'unqualified women, etc.'.) 'The births reported by medical men and "other agencies" have been ignored,' he explained, only cases attended by midwives were visited. Nearly 1,000 births were notified to the health association, and between 3,000 and 4,000 visits were paid throughout the year. The infant mortality rate among these babies was 92 per 1,000 births, while the rate among the other 50 per cent of the babies born in Rotherham was 195 per 1,000. In sum Robinson concluded, 'The work of the midwife has been co-ordinated with that of the female health visitor, and the Act has become a potent measure for the prevention of infantile mortality.'[105]

One of the (undoubtedly unanticipated) consequences of the passage of the Notification of Births Act was that it opened a large number of jobs for women all over the country. In the beginning of this chapter we noted that the impetus towards maternal education helped to create a new profession for women. The Act consolidated and amplified this development; it meant that these municipal positions were here to stay and that more such posts would be created. Health authorities that applied to the Local Government Board for permission to adopt the Act immediately it was passed also asked for clarification as to whether they might hire health visitors, what qualifications such workers ought to have, and who was to pay for them. Health visitors were a new class of (female) public service employees, and legal regulation with regard to their payment and training was yet to be instituted. A 16 November 1907 department note written by William H. Powers, then Principal

Medical Officer of the LGB, in response to a request by Bermondsey to adopt the Act illustrates the uncertainty both in Whitehall and locally.

'Bermondsey, judged by its infant mortality rate . . . would seem to be a proper district for utilization of the Notification of Births Act, provided suitable machinery is set up for making the Act suitably operative.

'But Bermondsey does not possess a Health Visitor or Visitors, though appointment of a female Sanitary Inspector appears to be contemplated for workshop and "out-worker" purposes under the Factory Acts.

'In the present, and in regard of infant mortality, . . . it is to personal advice rendered to mothers by competent and tactful women that I am looking for useful and adequate results from adoption of the Act.

'Unhappily it appears to be doubtful whether Bermondsey, or any Metropolitan Borough, is competent to pay for the services of a "Health Visitor"; at least I understand that one of the Board's Auditors has officially raised the question. . . . From the Public Health point of view the Board should I think do all they can to remove the dead-lock actual or prospective, arising through audit considerations. I would suggest that . . . the Board express willingness to sanction under Local Authorities Expenses Act any reasonable expenditure incurred in the payment of health visitors during (say) the next two years. This matter is pressing as the Board are already receiving applications for assent to adoption of the Act and it is necessary to decide the policy to be followed in dealing with such applications.'[106]

A year and a half later, on 28 June 1909, the Metropolitan Borough of Stepney wrote to the LGB to ask if they had decided on regulations regarding health visitors. The Board replied that these were 'under consideration'. After waiting nearly two months, Stepney wrote again to enquire when such a decision would be forthcoming. 'The Borough Council are desirous of appointing a female officer to deal . . . with matters relating to infantile mortality', the town clerk explained, and 'the Council are desirous that the proposed appointment shall be made at an early date.'[107]

While these issues were being resolved, the only certainty was that such a position should be filled by a woman. As there was no statutory authority to appoint health visitors per se, many local authorities chose to employ female sanitary inspectors for this purpose. A number of councils undertaking infant welfare work hired women rather than men when an inspectorship became vacant which, upon occasion, created tension, as in the example of Woolwich. On 13 July 1906 Woolwich appointed a female sanitary inspector, to which the Sanitary Inspectors Association objected in no uncertain terms. In a letter to the LGB the Association asked that the Board refuse its sanction. 'In the advertisement of this post', the Association secretary F. Harris Deans wrote, 'it is stated that candidates must have satisfactory experience in sick nursing, etc. The duties, it is stated, will include those known generally as "Health Visiting".' The problem was that 'this appointment is to fill the position vacated by a Male Sanitary Inspector', Deans complained. 'I trust it may appear unsatisfactory to your Board that duties other than those performed by the Male Inspector, in the shape of "Health Visiting", should be included amongst the duties of his successor.' In short, what the Association desired was that, rather than hire a second woman sanitary inspector, 'the duties of Health Visiting should be vested in one Female Inspector; the other performing only those duties of a Sanitary Inspector as laid down under the Public Health Acts' – in other words, duties a male could undertake.

Woolwich Council, for their part, argued forcefully and, in the event persuasively, in favour of their resolve to appoint a second woman inspector and not to replace the position with a male officer. The woman sanitary inspector already on the staff, the council explained to the LGB, would be 'fully occupied with the inspection of houses let in lodgings, workshops where women are employed, factories for female sanitary conveniences, homes of out-workers, restaurant and eating-house kitchens, ladies' lavatories at same, and public and railway lavatories for women'. Such activities were more than enough work for one person. Infant welfare work was an addition to the public health office's duties, the council reminded the LGB: 'The President of the Local Government Board in his recent address to the Congress on Infant Mortality emphasised the importance of Sanitary Authorities taking steps to diminish Infant Mortality, and the [Public Health] Committee felt that it was most important that an Inspector should be appointed who would be able to devote time to this work.'[108]

The need to hire women sanitary inspectors to carry out infant welfare work,[109] or to hire health visitors to do so, continued to grow and, as a result, increasing attention was paid to the health visitor as a new and independent category of worker with specialized training and a unique function. This topic was discussed at the first National Conference on Infantile Mortality in 1906. Following Cameron's paper on the work of the women inspectors at Leeds, John Robertson (MOH for Birmingham) 'urged that health visitors should be paid and not voluntary workers'. Leslie MacKenzie then proposed a resolution 'affirming that the appointment of qualified women specially trained in the hygiene of infancy was necessary as an adjunct to public health work'. Cameron seconded the motion, which was then passed.[110]

The transition from voluntary lady worker to paid professional, accepted as a part of the public health system, was in fact relatively easy and unproblematic. It is remarkable that, given physicians' opposition to the Notification of Births Act there was surprisingly little resistance to health visitors. Of course, the Act required under pain of a penalty a service without a compensating fee, but health visitors could have been perceived as a threat to business, as occurred in Keighley. At a meeting of the Keighley town council in July 1907 the health committee recommended that

> 'a lady health visitor be advertised for at an annual salary of £80, the person appointed to be a trained nurse and certificated midwife, and to hold the certificate of the Royal Sanitary Institute. The infantile death-rate . . . in 1906 was 149, and it was suggested that a lady qualified as suggested might do something to reduce it. It was pointed out by one or more of the speakers that some of the suggested visitor's duties infringed on the domain of the medical man, and on being put to a vote the motion was negatived by 9 to 6.'[111]

(Keighley adopted the Notification of Births Act and hired a health visitor the following year.)

Two weeks later the *BMJ* published a letter from Charles Whitby, a Bath practitioner, complaining that 'in most of our large towns what I consider distinctively medical functions are, in daily increasing measure, being assigned by the health authorities, with hearty support from their medical officers, to unqualified persons. I refer in particular to the growing army of "health visitors", paid by the municipalities.' Whitby apologized that his 'conscience' would not permit him to 'advocate an attitude of uncompromising hostility' as the claims of poor children were paramount, but he insisted that 'the functions discharged by health visitors are *medical* functions', and he recommended that unemployed physicians be hired for this work whenever possible.[112] This correspondence was short-lived. Some weeks later a letter from a Manchester physician[113] in support of Whitby was published, as was a letter from the Bath MOH, W.H. Symons, who protested that the emoluments of general practitioners would certainly not be reduced by the work of health visitors.

> 'The prescribing chemist and the vendor of patent medicines may have some cause to fear her influence, but the legitimate practitioner of medicine should certainly extend a welcome to a trained nurse visiting young mothers and trying to induce them to pay more attention to what they are inclined to regard as trivial ailments.'[114]

(Bath adopted the Notification of Births Act in 1908.) The *BMJ* basically agreed with Symons; their fear was not that the health visitors would undermine the physicians' practices, but that they would not be sufficiently educated to undertake the work properly. 'In view of the work which lady health visitors may have to do in future . . . under the Notification of Births Act,' the editors began 'one would like to be assured that the lady superintendents and health visitors themselves are properly qualified to undertake the teaching of others.' And they continued, 'Unless there is some good guarantee that the health visitors have been properly trained themselves, they may do as much harm as good.'[115]

To obviate this problem, Emilia Kanthack, a midwifery instructor, published *The Preservation of Infant Life: A Guide for Health Visitors* in 1907. This appears to have been the first of many health visitors' manuals. In the preface John Sykes explained that the book was a compendium of the lectures Kanthack delivered to the voluntary health visitors in St Pancras. Beginning with a discussion of the relation between infant mortality and health visiting, Kanthack emphasized the imperial importance of their task of securing the healthy development of infants – 'the nation's asset and England's future working men and future mothers'. To fight against 'race-deterioration and race-degeneration . . . we want not only to keep babies *alive*, but we want them to be healthy young animals.' The mother was the focus of their effort, she explained. 'We . . . see very clearly that if we want to safeguard the baby and give it a good start in life, it is the baby's *mother* we must look after during the first nine months of the baby's life.' Turning to the hygiene of pregnancy, Kanthack emphasized the necessity of proper nutrition, which continued throughout the lactating period, and she advocated 'an enormous multiplication of such small centres for feeding . . . mothers as Mrs W.E. Gordon has established in Chelsea'.[116] Kanthack also covered such topics as bathing and dressing the baby, the practical and theoretical problems of infant nutrition, and she described the common diseases and minor ailments to which infants were subject.

The question of the requisite education needed to be a health visitor, linked to the move from voluntary effort to paid professional, remained unsettled for the next decade. In 1908 the London County Council obtained Parliamentary powers which allowed the metropolitan borough councils to appoint health visitors to look into domestic hygiene and the nurture and care of young children. The Local Government Board was to determine the qualifications and duties of these visitors. The following year (1909), the LGB issued regulations, which represented the first step towards a standardization of proficiency. Health visitors, the Board decided, should have a medical degree, be fully trained nurses, have a certificate from the Central Midwives Board or a health visitor's certificate from a society approved by the Board, or have previous experience in a similar position with a local authority. No comparable legal requirements were set up outside London until the passage of the Maternity and Child Welfare Act in 1918,[117] but many local authorities used the London regulations as guidelines. This training was not considered to be so rigorous as that required of sanitary inspectors, and health visitors were paid lower salaries. This made them more attractive to local authorities for infant welfare work than women sanitary inspectors, and could have created a similar tension to that which had arisen earlier between men and women inspectors. That such disputes were rare, the prime examples being only those of Southwark and Bethnal Green, testifies to the general acceptance of health visiting as a new dimension of public health work. In fact, the Southwark and Bethnal Green cases illustrate the increasing differentiation between, and definition of, specifically sanitary inspector and health visitor functions and duties.

In a letter of 30 May 1912 Southwark Council informed the LGB that a woman sanitary inspector was resigning, and that they wished to appoint a health visitor in her place.[118] To this the Women Sanitary Inspectors' Association objected strenuously. 'There is undoubtedly great need for the work of Health Visiting in Southwark,' the secretary Ethel J. Charlesworth agreed, 'and the Council are presumably acting in response to this need. But,' she continued, 'we consider it very regrettable that the Council, whilst making arrangements to carry out this important work, should not have continued to do so in the same efficient manner as before.' The Association's position was straightforward professional protectionism.

'As a result of our experience we are convinced that [the] method of combining the duties of Sanitary Inspection and Health Visiting in one and the same person is much more satisfactory and economical than that of limiting a woman official to the status and work of Health Visiting. We consider this proposal to substitute a Health Visitor for a Woman Sanitary Inspector a distinctly retrograde step, which will tend to lower the quality of the work.'[119]

The LGB staff notes relating to this correspondence elucidate the vested interests and guild anxieties of the women sanitary inspectors as well as their sincere concern that health visitors would not be able to do the job adequately as they did not have the legal power of inspectors and, on another level entirely, that women as professional public health workers not lose status. It is interesting that the protests against the replacement of women sanitary inspectors by health visitors were not solely from the former; this was an industrial relations matter and other organizations became involved. As a note of 13 June commented, 'There were some representations to the President lately in another London case from the Women's Industrial Council that the substitution of a woman HV [health visitor] for a woman SI [sanitary inspector] involved loss of status, in title and pay.' With regard to the Southwark case, the LGB were not concerned as they were convinced that the MOH, Dr Millson, would 'get an H.V. who has good qualifications for the post . . . to make her function in no way inferior to that of the woman S.I.'[120] The particulars of the other London case, as well as the thinking of the LGB on this matter generally, was explained in a note of 26 June.

'The only case of this kind in 1911 & 1912 is that at Bethnal Green. The B.C. [Borough Council] there said that the sanitary inspection could be adequately carried out by the male inspectors.

161

The Women's Industrial Council protested that a S.I. had more legal power than a H.V., and also received a higher salary and had better status, and therefore could better look after the public health. They desired the offices of S.I. & H.V. to be held in conjunction.

Dr Manly visited the Boro' and reported that the prime influence with the Women's Industrial Council was the salary and status of a S.I. He himself favoured the proposal because a H.V. was looked upon rather as a "friend", while a S.I. was regarded as a "fault-finder".

The Christian Social Union and the Industrial Law Committee also protested against the proposal to the President. The reply in each case was that the woman S.I.'s duties had been practically those of a H.V. before and therefore no objection could be taken.'[121]

As Bethnal Green and Southwark were the only two cases which had arisen in 1911 and 1912 this problem clearly was rather minor, and health visitors were accepted into the public health system with relative ease and alacrity. Indeed, by 1916 the Women Sanitary Inspectors' Association had enlarged to include health visitors and was renamed the Women Sanitary Inspectors' and Health Visitors' Association. Together they encouraged local authorities to decrease their dependence on voluntary organizations[122] and to municipalize infant welfare work – a position supported by the LGB as it allowed for greater control over quality and direction. In the meantime, however, while increasing numbers of health visitors became integral members of the official public health staff, there was a great deal of work to be done and still too few formally trained to do it and too little money to pay for them, so relations remained amicable between the municipal and voluntary organizations.[123]

By 1908 the pattern of future infant welfare work in England had been established. This system, which consisted of a maternity and child welfare centre offering a number of services (primarily a consultation, classes, milk, and meals) and operating in conjunction with domiciliary health visiting, developed rapidly throughout the next decade. As we have seen, all of these elements were present in 1908; by 1918 they simply had coalesced more effectively and had become increasingly municipalized. For instance, in January 1912 the Westminster Health Society opened a Medical Inspection Centre for Children under School Age under the direction of David Forsyth which was co-ordinated with the work of the one municipal and many trained voluntary health visitors of the society. By 1913 Lane-Claypon reported that 'in St Marylebone, where the relations between the municipal and the voluntary workers are . . . most friendly' all notified births were visited by either one group or the other. In St Marylebone, as elsewhere, the usual practice was for the paid, professional, municipal employee to make the initial contact, and for the voluntary visitors to pay subsequent calls. 'The difficult cases are referred to the consultations, of which there are two held in different centres on several days of the week. . . . About 500 cases are referred . . . every year.'[124] The St Marylebone Health Society ran a mothers' club with lectures and classes, and dinners for pregnant and nursing women were provided by the Social Service League. In St Pancras, where the most developed centre had been established, more emphasis was placed on improving out-reach activity. 'This new work is the teaching of domestic subjects, more particularly cookery, in the homes of the people by means of actual work, in which only the utensils and resources of the home are used,' Miss Bibby, one of the founders of the St Pancras scheme, explained. She went on to clarify that cookery lessons had always been given at the Welcome, but the health visitors had found that few if any of the women were putting the lessons into practice. Consequently, it was decided to send Miss F. Petty, 'The Pudding Lady', into the homes of the poor of that area (Somers Town).[125]

In his second report on infant and child mortality (1913), Arthur Newsholme tabulated that 74 of the 98 formally designated large towns had adopted the Notification of Births Act and 'in six further towns there is a system of voluntary notification by midwives.' Of the 111 small towns, 67 had adopted the Act, and a 'few' were about to do so. All the metropolitan boroughs adopted the Act in 1909 by Order of the Local Government Board (although many had previously done so). Newsholme explained that health visiting was carried out to a varying extent in 87 large towns (74 in connection with compulsory, 6 with voluntary, and 7 without any system of notification), 67 small towns (61 compulsory, 2 voluntary, and 1 without any system of notification) and in 27 of the 28 metropolitan boroughs.[126] Infant consultations under either municipal or voluntary auspices were held in 32 large towns, 13 small towns, and 14 metropolitan boroughs. A number of communities without consultations had 'baby weighings' which were run by municipal health visitors. Meals for pregnant and nursing mothers were provided in at least 6 small and 21 large towns, and 15 metropolitan boroughs.[127] Indeed by this time, so many communities had organized or wished to initiate infant welfare programmes that a central co-ordinating society, the Association of Infant Consultations and Schools for Mothers, had been established (1911), with Eric Pritchard as the first chairman. 'At its conferences, discussions and committee meetings', he observed, 'we have not only many opportunities for the exchange of experience and the comparison of statistics, but we have all the machinery for the direct and rapid dissemination of new and useful knowledge.'[128] In 1912 this and other societies merged to form the National Association for the Prevention of Infant Mortality which, in 1917, became the National League for Healthy Maternity and Child Welfare.

The third National Conference on Infant Mortality was held in

Liverpool on 2 and 3 July 1914, and the proceedings reflect the establishment of the trend, which we traced in this chapter, towards a focus on maternal education as the means to reduce infant mortality. 'One of the most effective means of combating infant mortality is the spread of knowledge of mothercraft [and] the care and education of the expectant mother' the conference formally concluded, and they resolved to support all measures to further this end.[129] Speaking specifically on 'The Scope and Functions of Schools for Mothers' Eric Pritchard claimed that the decrease in infant mortality which had occurred between 1904 and 1914 was due to an increase in mothercraft. 'The spread of knowledge of mothercraft through the agency of the Public Health Service, through the research and propaganda work of the Schools for Mothers, and through other educational channels' was the key he said. In short, 'the most effective weapon with which to fight infant mortality is good mothercraft.'[130] The foundation upon which all this educational work rested, according to Lane-Claypon, was the Notification of Births Act. Speaking in 1913 she affirmed that 'the beneficial effects of this act have been, and continue to be, far-reaching. It has led to a vast and always increasing amount of effort on the part of the municipalities in the prevention of infantile mortality.'[131]

The last question to be answered is how the mothers (especially working-class mothers, who were the initial target population) responded to these aid and instruction schemes. The letters from working women collected by the Women's Co-operative Guild to be used in a campaign for improved maternal and infant health services revealed a widespread desire for and appreciation of education, maternity centres, and 'baby welcomes'. Furthermore, the women themselves saw the mother as the key to infant welfare. In her introduction, Margaret Llewelyn Davies (the editor of the book and the General Secretary of the Guild) stressed this point:

'It has become more and more clear that if you wish to guard the health of the infant, you must go back from it to the mother; it is the circumstances of the mother – her health, her knowledge, her education, and her habits – before the child is born no less than at the time of and after birth, that again and again determine whether the child is to have health or disease, to live or to die.'[132]

The women used the rhetoric of the future of the Empire to emphasize their needs. One mother, for instance, declared that 'the best thing that could happen would be a system of State Maternity Homes, where working women could go for a reasonable fee and be confined, and stay for convalescence. . . . It would be a recognition of the importance of our women as race-bearers, and lift her to a higher plane than at present.' And she concluded, 'There is nothing that is done can ever be too much if we are to have going a race in the future worthy of England, but it will not be until the nation wakes up to the needs of the mothers of that future race.'[133] As another woman who described herself as 'a wreck at thirty' put it:

> 'I do feel most strongly that women should be able to get advice and help during pregnancy. Our children are a valuable asset to the nation, and the health of the woman who is doing her duty in rearing the future race should have a claim upon the national purse. Ample provision should be made so that she could give of her best.'[134]

'The child is the asset of the nation, and the mother the backbone', a third asserted. 'Therefore, I think the nation should help to feed and keep that mother, and so help to strengthen the nation by her giving birth to strong boys and girls.'[135]

It is clear that these women wanted education, help, advice, and proper nutrition. Other letters reiterated these requests. A woman, who described her labour as a 'bad experience', wrote: 'after that . . . my feeling is that if it were possible to get Maternity Centres or schools for expectant mothers, it would be a godsend to many a woman; and also to get some little help in nourishing the body, such as a small quantity of fresh milk.'[136] Lack of education was specifically mentioned over and over again. They wanted, they said, instruction with regard to sex, contraception, hygiene, and child-rearing. 'I think ignorance has more to do with suffering than anything,' one woman contended, and she recommended that physicians give lectures to maternity groups.[137] Another claimed that 'from the advice that mothers have been able to get at the "Baby Welcome" here, many babies' lives have been saved.'[138] There is a 'great need for a place where a young mother could go and get advice and, if necessary, nourishment', a third concluded.[139] Women who belonged to the Co-operative Guild may have been more active or politically aware than their neighbours, they may also have been more articulate, but there is no reason to believe that their needs or desires with regard to maternity were any different.

The provision of education (which was here to stay) was undoubtedly a conservative solution, but it was also the best alternative available within the English political and economic structure at the time. It was a solution acceptable, by and large, to practising physicians, medical officers of health, charitable and social work organizations, labour groups (the Women's Labour League opened their own clinic in 1911), and to the women themselves. Coupled with maternity centres or baby welcomes, it also addressed the problem of indigence as well as ignorance, albeit not in a radical or fundamental way. While it was working-class mothers whom the health authorities originally tried to reach, by the time Newsholme published his second report on infant and child mortality in 1913 this appears to have already begun to change. He noted that in the majority of communities which had adopted the Notification of Births Act, over 75 per cent of all births were visited at least once, and in a significant number of towns 90 to 100 per cent were visited. In other words, health visiting (the basis of the maternal education system) which had been started as a class-oriented measure was increasingly brought to bear upon the entire spectrum of society. With its ever more comprehensive approach and state-guaranteed provisions, the infant care movement illustrates the development of a modern welfare system prior to the establishment of the modern welfare state.

VI

School meals and medical inspection

As the news of the rejected Boer War recruits reached the offices of newspaper editors and members of parliament, it raised essential doubts as to the longevity or even viability of Great Britain as an Empire. These statistics, in addition to the alarming reports of a declining birth rate and increased infant mortality rate, made it clear that the country faced fundamental problems which required substantive solutions. The root of the dilemma was the protection of infant life: numbers were needed to populate the Dominions and healthy, efficient people were required to ensure Britain's global pre-eminence. Measures to safeguard the health of babies would both decrease the mortality rate and keep living children well and healthy. While the recruitment statistics focused attention on the care of infants, they also stimulated serious consideration of the possibilities to improve the physical condition of school age children – the soldiers of a single decade rather than twice that period hence. The future of the Empire was not only a long-term theoretical problem, it was an immediate challenge as well. By the end of the Boer War in 1902 England's relations with Germany were rapidly deteriorating, and while the Empire could overcome a humiliation in South Africa, it could not survive a defeat in Europe.

An important factor in the impetus to improve the vigour of school children was the complexity of the infant health puzzle. As we have seen, the problem of morbidity and consequent mortality from epidemic diarrhoea continued to be a conundrum throughout the period of this study. No specific aetiologic agent was identified, and transmission of the disease through the fly vector remained an unproved supposition. The question of child health appeared, by contrast, to be much more straightforward. Among children between the ages of five and fourteen morbidity, not mortality, was the major problem. The diseases from which children suffered were rather well understood, and did not

167

engender any great scientific debates. Then too, children of that age went to school. This provided a specific site where the state's public health arm could reach them without physically invading the privacy of the home. Finally, a precedent for such health work existed, as we shall discuss at greater length below, the city of Bradford had instituted a school medical inspection system in 1893. Furthermore, efforts to reduce the most common – and the most obvious – ailment of school children, malnutrition, had been instituted by philanthropic organizations and individuals both in the capital and the provinces. In short, by the early years of the twentieth century, the institution of a school health system seemed to be almost a bureaucratic matter. A number of issues had yet to be resolved, of course. Was the establishment of such a system justifiable as a necessary antecedent to educational efforts, merely preparing children to go to school so that they might be able to take advantage of the education they compulsorily received? Or was it simply a means to provide health care to a large (20 per cent) and vulnerable portion of the population? What was the appropriate role of the state; at what point would it usurp the responsibility of the parents? And precisely how should a school health service be conducted? What services should be provided, and by whom?

Immediately after the publication of the Boer War recruitment statistics the Royal Commission on Physical Training (Scotland) was appointed to enquire into the purpose of and possibilities for gymnastic education in the state schools 'and to suggest means by which such training may be made to conduce to the welfare of the pupils . . . and thus to contribute towards the sources of national strength'. The Commission presented its report in March 1903, and concluded that so far as elementary schools were concerned, the trouble was not the absence of physical drill, but the condition of the children themselves. Lack of adequate nutrition, the Commissioners said, led to poor physical condition, and the food the children received would have to be improved before exercise would be either useful or beneficial. They recommended that education authorities be empowered to co-operate with voluntary agencies to provide appropriate nourishment for school children. Although they did not suggest that the authorities themselves should provide meals, the Commissioners did advocate that when voluntary contributions were inadequate the authorities should have the power to pay for meals and to secure reimbursements from parents. From an enquiry as to the role of physical training in the improvement of the national physique of the future, the Commission led to the public consideration of the need for the provision of meals for school children and the desirability of instituting a system of school medical inspection.[1]

Just as proper feeding was understood to be the primary factor in maintaining the health of infants and ensuring that they would thrive and grow, adequate nourishment was perceived as the key to preserving and even ameliorating the mental as well as physical condition of school children. During the last quarter of the nineteenth century many reformers had noted the futility of trying to educate hungry children and a few experimental philanthropic programmes had been instituted, but it was not until the country was embarrassed in South Africa and alarmed by the ratio of rejected recruits that the problem received extensive attention. It is not coincidental that it was at this time that data collected some years previously which linked social class, height, weight, and academic achievement began to be reprinted in the public and professional presses. In an article on the 'National Physique', for instance, the editors of the *BMJ* reminded their readers of the 1883 report of the Anthropometric Committee of the British Association and the 1895 report of the Royal Commission on Secondary Education. While the former did include certain statistics on the height and weight of school children, the editors explained, these were not as illuminating as the memorandum of a Mr C. Roberts to the Royal Commission which concluded that, 'the more intelligent classes are taller and heavier at corresponding ages than the less intelligent.'[2]

The solution to this problem was obvious: feed the children and they would become taller, heavier, and more intelligent. Before children could be expected to learn, before they could even be expected to reap advantages from physical training, they had to be well nourished. The report of the Royal Commission on Physical Training supported that view, and the number of articles on this theme grew exponentially after its publication in the spring of 1903. The issue of the *BMJ* that reported on the conclusion of the Royal Commission's work, for example, also included a four-page article, complete with dietaries, on 'The Food Factor in Education'. Perhaps, the anonymous author proposed, part of the nervous disease, muscular weaknesses, anaemia, and digestive disorders found among school children could be 'set down to a diet in which the food is often inadequate both in quantity and quality to supply the requirements of growth as well as of mental and physical effort'. This was a general problem: it was a deficiency from which girls as well as boys, and public school as well as board school pupils suffered. The central question was 'whether we English as a nation are sufficiently alive to the importance of diet in education. . . . When the rising generation shows a deficiency in stamina it is certainly time to consider what part an insufficient dietary may play in its production.'[3]

A series of articles on 'National Physical Training: An Open Debate' which ran in the *Manchester Guardian* between April and June 1903 perceived the problem from a similar perspective. The 22 April piece by Sir George Arthur summarized the issue neatly. 'There are many significant indications that public opinion is being sharply aroused to the subject of the physical decadence of the English masses,' he wrote. Noting the work of the Royal Commission, Sir George agreed with their conclusion that children needed food in order to be either trained or taught.[4] Many of the authors of the series concurred. 'Good food must be the foundation of any system of physical training,' Winston Churchill remarked in his article published three days later.[5] C.E.B. Russell, who had run lads' clubs in the slums of Manchester for twelve years, insisted that the boys' poor physique was due to diet, and that physical training was of no value without proper food.[6] Arthur Newsholme also contributed to the series, and it is not surprising that he too contended that 'food [was] the supremely important factor in health', and that children had to be fed before physical training would be of any use.[7]

The nexus between physical deficiency, intellectual inefficiency, and poor nutrition was reiterated with increasing conviction as figures which appeared to correlate the three were presented to the public. In the course of its work, the Royal Commission had enjoined Professor Matthew Hay of Aberdeen and Dr W. Leslie MacKenzie of Edinburgh to investigate the health of school children in those two major industrial centres. In each city, 100 girls and 100 boys in three groups of school ages were examined, comprising a total of 1,200 children. MacKenzie himself conducted a study to compare the physical condition which obtained among a representative group of 150 children from each of four primary schools in Edinburgh. In both cases it was found that the children from the schools in the poorest districts, whose families lived in houses of one and two rooms, were smaller and less advanced scholastically than those who lived in the better-off districts. According to MacKenzie, 'among the factors that produce[d] these differences, housing and food must be regarded as chief. Race,' he stressed, 'can scarcely count for much.' The Commissioners' report clearly reflected Hay's and MacKenzie's results.

> 'We consider that the question of the proper and sufficient feeding of children is one which has the closest possible connection with any scheme which may be adopted for their physical, and equally for their mental, work. It is evident that among the causes which tell against the physical welfare of the population, the lack of proper nourishment is one of the most serious. The subject demands special notice.'[8]

While these revelations were cause for concern, and provided an additional stimulus for the formation of the Inter-Departmental Committee on Physical Deterioration, the statement by the Secretary to the Board of Education, Sir William Anson, that 'there were 60,000 children in London who were physically inferior and who were unable to get the full benefit of the teaching in the schools'[9] caught and held the public's imagination, until a larger number was disclosed a year later. In his testimony before the Inter-Departmental Committee on 18 December 1903, Dr Alfred Eichholz, an inspector of the state's schools, estimated that 16 per cent of the elementary school population of London, or 122,000 children, were underfed. The Johanna Street School in

Lambeth, less than a ten-minute walk from the Houses of Parliament, provided dramatic proof of the plight of poor pupils. According to Eichholz, 92 per cent of the children in that school suffered from some disability which interfered with their studies; most were malnourished and had anaemia.[10]

By the time the Inter-Departmental Committee published their report, politicians, the public, and the medical profession had accepted that, as the *BMJ* editorialized, 'there can be little doubt that one of the chief causes of this degeneracy in young people is to be found in the insufficient food on which it seems to be expected that the hard work of school life should be performed'. Nor did many doubt the *BMJ*'s assertion that 'the whole matter [was] one of national importance'. 'From the highest to the lowest our children are badly fed as compared with those of other great nations', the editors admonished; 'in the race of life the well-nourished will generally beat the half-starved.' And they concluded, 'The degeneracy in physique of the rising generation . . . is best to be combated, there is every reason to believe, by an intelligent employment of the food factor.'[11] The major debate engendered by these discussions centred on the appropriate role of the state in ameliorating the situation. A complicating factor was that it was not clear whether the problem was properly viewed as an educational issue (intellectual inefficiency) or as a question of the physical health of the future nation (degeneration of the population). In the event, both perceptions were reflections of anxiety about the future of the Empire and the health of the nation's children, and both led to similar conclusions about the correct role of the state. On the other hand, there were those who were alarmed by the prospect of state intervention and usurpation of parental responsibility.

The pages of both the popular and the professional press were replete with this controversy from the end of 1903 until early 1905. One of the most vocal advocates for school meals was Sir John E. Gorst who had recently resigned (1902) from his post as Vice President of the Committee of the Privy Council on Education in the Balfour Ministry. A social reformer ardently devoted to change of the state education system, Gorst was returned to Parliament as an independent member in 1903, where he used his position and influence to promote the plight of impoverished school children. Gorst's position was uncomplicated and clearly formulated. 'If the child is not fed,' he wrote in an article published in the *Manchester Guardian* in December 1903, 'neither must it be taught.'[12] The *BMJ* agreed. In an editorial on 'Education and Deterioration' the editors quoted Gorst and clarified their concurring point of view. While compulsory education was a necessity, they explained, all its indirect effects had not been foreseen. 'It can need no argument to prove that the effect of compelling all children to pass many hours a day for some forty weeks in a year in school rooms may be seriously injurious to their physical development . . . if the children themselves are not so fed and supervised as to ensure that their bodies and minds are alike ready to receive with advantage the instruction given.'[13] In the fourth of the *BMJ* special series on *Physical Degeneration*, the author also discussed the potentially harmful effects of compulsory education on ill-fed children, and concluded with a somewhat oblique reference to the use of state funds to provide meals for necessitous pupils. 'In view of the inevitable waste of public money on the education of the physically unfit,' Watt Smyth noted, 'we observe that were such sums of money expended in the first instance upon the building up of their bodies . . . the benefit they [would] derive would be a thousandfold greater than that which these poor starvelings now enjoy.'[14]

While the *BMJ* and the *Lancet* generally accepted the idea that children had to be fed, and that the state would, of necessity, become involved in some measure, the letter columns of *The Times* reflected a broader spectrum of opinion. There were those who, like Dr Farquharson, believed that it was imprudent to overwork underfed children in schools, and that

> 'if we compel children to go to school, we must see to it that they are not physically or mentally injured in the process. . . . Surely the State can provide some machinery by which the poor little waifs and strays who now crowd the benches of our Board schools may get enough food not only to keep body and soul together, but to add the extra margin necessary to meet the demands of their rapidly growing and expanding minds.'[15]

And there were those who, like Jonathan Hutchinson (FRCS) felt that it would be wise to avoid exaggeration on the issue of parental responsibility, as 'responsibility ends where ability ends.' But there were also those who passionately disagreed. Not surprisingly, a Charity Organization Society visitor, Louisa Twining worried about 'pauperizing the poor by free gifts' and 'removing responsibility from [the] parents'. One 'W.A.B.' wondered where it would all end. 'From free education we are to proceed to free food. It is not difficult to see that there will be no finality in free food.' James Cassidy, 'engaged for some years in London visiting the slums of our great city' maintained that this experience taught him 'that what is required is not a wholesale provision of free meals for children sent hungry to school', but the enforcement of the law pertaining to cruelty to children. 'Let some of our justest and strongest-minded magistrates', Cassidy proposed, 'warn such parents that . . . they will be summarily dealt with, no fines being allowed, but a charge attached to their wages . . . and let such magistrates make a few stern examples in the most notorious parishes, and we should very soon hear nothing at all about famished children.' A number of correspondents perceived the problem from entirely different perspectives.

172

Margaret Frere, Chairman of the Tower-Street School Relief Committee, reported that the system of free dinners she had organized and managed for seven winters had not been wanted, and she was, therefore, 'sceptical as to the existence of those 122,000 underfed school children in London alone of whom we have heard so much lately'. Constance Meyerstein had been a School Board manager for many years, and while she did not deny the existence of malnourished pupils, she was 'convinced that "free meals" was not the solution'; parental education was the only real remedy, she insisted.[16]

The specific recommendation of the Inter-Departmental Committee on Physical Deterioration that a state-sponsored system to feed necessitous school children be instituted to ensure that they would be able to take full advantage of the education offered by the state, and John Gorst's persistent advocacy of the Committee's report in general, and of school meals for children in particular, helped to legitimate the notion of a state subvention for meals for students. As the *BMJ* reported,

'Sir John Gorst's remarks at Cambridge on the question of underfed school children have stirred up the public, and drawn from individuals interested and indignant a shower of letters and articles. The outcome of all these opinions is that if the State insists on compulsorily educating children, it is also the duty of the State to see that the children attending school are physically equal to the mental strain they have to undergo.'[17]

The *Lancet* took an especially pragmatic view of the whole problem and, beginning with a pilot article on 17 September 1904, published a series on 'The Feeding of School Children' by 'our special sanitary commissioner' between October 1906 and April 1907.[18] Reprinted in 1907 as a separate pamphlet revealingly entitled *The Free Feeding of School Children*, these pieces were frequently quoted by contemporaries.[19]

The series began in a rather mundane fashion echoing much of the more liberal sentiment prevailing at the time, but was from the outset remarkably practical rather than polemical in approach. Such physical degeneration as did exist, the Commissioner argued, 'must occur notably among those who in their infancy and childhood have been insufficiently or injudiciously fed'. Fortunately, the public schools provided investigators with both the material for studying the problem and convenient sites at which it could be remedied. As, he reasoned,

'the law renders education obligatory, we have in the primary schools a machinery all ready made and at hand permitting full investigation into the facts of the case. There are here also the means of remedying the evil wherever it shall have been proved to exist. Whatever political economists and others may say, no medical man would maintain that it is possible to educate an underfed child without grave risk to his or her health. From the physical point of view there can be no question but that the child must be fed first and educated afterwards. . . . To attempt to teach children thus suffering is to waste public money as well as to injure the child pupils. It is certainly a means of producing physical degeneration. By law and by taxation schools and teachers are provided and yet food is more necessary than either school or teacher. This, of course, will be admitted by everybody.'

To those who insisted that parents ought to feed their own children, the author flatly rejoined 'the obvious fact [is] that some parents either cannot or will not feed their children'. He was most emphatic that it was 'not charity, with its pauperising and degrading influence that is needed, but a national scheme by which, in some way or other, every child shall receive, without imposing any humiliating condition, all that is necessary for its physical as well as its intellectual development'. In any case, he warned his readers, 'if a foreign nation feeds all its children adequately and if all are not fed in England then, in time, we shall stand at a disadvantage when compared with that foreign nation. Now, the nation in question is our nearest neighbour, France.'[20]

As in the case of programmes to protect the health of infants, here too politicians and medical officers of health looked to foreign (and particularly French) examples for help in designing English public welfare schemes. The system of school feeding which had been developed in France during the second half of the nineteenth century provided an inspiration for English officials interested in similar problems; it furnished a model to be copied and adapted for use across the channel. It was also an impetus for action. The fact that France had already begun to work along these lines indicated that she could become an increasingly formidable competitor. Although such programmes had been developed in other countries as well, and indeed were reported in the *Lancet* series in some detail, it was the example of Paris which was continually quoted and to which reference was most frequently made.[21]

In the idealistic days immediately following the Revolution of 1848 the National Guard of the Second Arrondissement of Paris established a philanthropic caisse des écoles, or school fund, to promote the cause of education by paying school fees and by awarding prizes for attendance and for academic excellence. The creation in all communes of such caisses des écoles was permitted by a law enacted in April 1867 which specified that these funds were 'for the purpose of encouraging school attendance by giving rewards to the most assiduous pupils and help to indigent pupils'.[22] Little was done in the three years prior to the Franco-Prussian War, but in the wake of France's bitterly humiliating defeat, and the subsequent attention to the low birth rate and high infant mortality rate, and the general concern for child life, a number of communes took advantage of the 1867 legislation.[23] Finally, the compulsory education legislation enacted in March 1882 required all communes to establish a caisse des écoles to be funded by charitable donations and subventions given by the commune, department, or state. The passage of this Act also provided for free education and mandatory attendance; thus the school funds could be utilized to promote the physical health of the pupils so that they could take full advantage of their studies.

The Paris municipal council had begun, in May 1877, to study the problem of supplying one wholesome hot meal to all children each day, but at that time the school funds did not have the managerial or financial resources to undertake such a project. Four years later, in May 1881, the Montmartre district began to provide a meal to all children whose parents were in receipt of poor relief. After the passage of the 1882 law the idea was adopted by all the communes. By September 1904, when the *Lancet* Commissioner examined the system *in situ* he found that the institution of cantines scolaires, or school canteens, had 'become universal and experience had taught that the cost need not be more than 15 centimes or 1½*d* per meal of soup, meat, and vegetable'. The author took great pains to explain the payment policy and system. First of all, he emphasized, 'the principle now adopted is to encourage all children, whether poor or not, to eat their meals together'. Second, 'in no case was the child to be humiliated or troubled in any way and on no pretext whatsoever should the food he needed be refused.' Every morning a ticket was given to each child individually for the meal; only those who could afford the fifteen centime price paid it. Those who could not afford the entire sum paid on a graduated scale. The parents of children who received free meals were visited and investigated, but the predominant concern of the programme was that 'the children must be fed'. As private philanthropy did not cover the cost of the dinners, nor were they self-supporting, the Paris municipal council supplied the school funds of the city with the required balance. During the three-year period of 1901 through 1903 these subventions amounted to £40,000. The *Lancet* commissioner was highly enthusiastic about the French system and endorsed it both in principle and in practice. He concluded with a warning:

> 'Is there not in all this the making of a healthy people and a strong race? Can we in England afford to ignore the example here given? Is it not safe to argue, as the managers of the school funds in Paris argue, that whatever the faults of the parents . . . still the children are blameless? Therefore, and without hesitation, if we would preserve the race, without the loss of a moment and without making a single exception, every hungry child must be fed.'[24]

That the *Lancet* articles were immediately well received and reiterated was very possibly due to the fact that they did not burst upon an entirely unprepared audience. As we have seen, the problem of malnutrition in school children and the solution of the provision of meals had been discussed extensively by politicians, physicians, and the public for well over a year. Furthermore, during the second half of the nineteenth century a number of experimental programmes had been instituted (albeit in a more or less desultory fashion) in England itself, and very recently a few communities, but none more than Bradford, had begun to work seriously in this area. Predictably, even the initial schemes were French-inspired. The results of a commission appointed in 1848 by the French government to enquire into the prevention of rickets, scrofula, and anaemia so impressed the novelist Victor Hugo that he decided to provide warm meals in his own home in Guernsey for the children who attended a nearby school. This personal eleemosynous practice was reported in *Punch* on 16 January 1864 and was the catalyst for the formation of the Destitute Children's Dinner Society. Within a month this society began to provide dinners for the pupils at a ragged school in Westminster. Throughout the decade they expanded their activities; between October 1869 and April 1870 the society opened fifty-eight dining rooms.[25]

The number of charitable organizations devoted to the provision of meals increased after the passage of the 1870 Education Act. The *Referee* fund, for example, was started in 1874 by Mrs Burgwin, the head teacher of the Orange Street School in Southwark. Publicized by George R. Sims in his articles on 'How the Poor Live' (which were originally printed in the *Referee* before they were reissued in book form), this charity funded dinners for children throughout the winter and it was found that, contrary to prior experience, the pupils were healthier and attended school more regularly in winter than in summer. The correlation between increased attendance, improved academic perform- ance, and the provision of a meal was corroborated by the equally well-known efforts of Sir Henry Peek who, in the autumn of 1876, organized a system of self-supporting penny dinners for the children attending the schools on his estate at Rousdon in Devonshire. Working actively to promote the COS-approved self-supporting principle, Sir Henry failed in his larger objective of forming a central body to secure co-operation between children's dinner agencies, but he was successful in bringing the matter to public attention.[26]

Peek was not alone in his failure to consolidate efforts and avoid overlapping. In the capital, efforts to feed children were so disjointed that in 1889 the London School Board was prompted to address the matter. The Special Sub-Committee on Meals for School Children appointed by the Board concluded that the supply of food was both insufficient and badly distributed. At best, necessitous students received one meal once or twice per week. In light of their rough estimate that 43,888 or 12.8 per cent of the children attending Board schools were habitually in want of nourishment, with less than half that number receiving any food at all, they recommended the establishment of a central committee to co-ordinate feeding programmes. The London Schools Dinner Association was formed with representatives from the School Board and a number of the organizations which provided meals for children such as the Self-Supporting Penny Dinner Council, the Poor Children's Aid Society, and the South London Schools Dinner Fund. Other agencies like the Destitute Children's Dinner Society maintained their autonomy, and even the most sanguine contemporaries perceived that 'little more unity or increased efficiency has been caused'.[27]

Two more attempts by the London School Board to rationalize and systematize feeding efforts also came to nought. In December 1894 the Board appointed another Special Committee, this time on Underfed Children. Its report was issued in 1895 and reiterated the 1889 assessment that there was a lack of supplies and co-ordination, and a plethora of needy children. Again no changes ensued, and in 1898 the Board referred the problem to the General Purposes Committee, charging it to determine the number of underfed children attending public elementary schools in London and to ascertain if voluntary agencies were able to cope satisfactorily. Finding, as their predecessors had done, that there were more students who required meals than the extant societies could feed, the committee came to the logical conclusion that the provision of meals had to become a public endeavour. They proposed 'that where it is ascertained that children are sent to school "underfed"' (i.e. 'in a state unfit to get normal profit by the school work . . . by reason of underfeeding') it should be part of the duty of the authority to see that 'they are provided . . . with the necessary food. . . . In so far as such voluntary efforts fail to cover the ground the authority should have the power and the duty to supplement them.' The idea that school dinners would pauperize the parents or destroy parental responsibility was they said, 'a mere theoretic fancy'.[28]

Although the Board rejected these proposals and did nothing more than establish a permanent Joint Committee on Underfed Children, the interminable reports of the past decade helped to elucidate and emphasize the exigency of the issue and the need for aid for the pupils. They also amply illustrated that charitable agencies alone simply could not handle the magnitude of the problem and that, consequently, the provision of meals for necessitous students had to become a responsibility of the state. Finally, the committees and their inevitable documents focused attention on the continued failure in England in general and London in particular to solve this problem. Thus, when the *Lancet* articles publicized the success of the French, most especially in Paris, to provide meals through an amalgamation of private philanthropy and state subvention it appeared in sharp contrast to the English impotence to ameliorate the situation at home.

While John Gorst pleaded the cause of the hungry school child and urged that the provision of meals was a responsibility of the community, Thomas J. Macnamara, who had been on the last two of the three London School Board committees, proposed the institution in England of an adaptation of the cantines scolaires system. Macnamara had been an elementary school teacher and, from 1892 to 1907, an editor of the publication of the National Union of Teachers, *The Schoolmaster*. As of the 1900 election he was, like Gorst, a member of parliament (Liberal MP for North Camberwell) and, again like the older man, he used his position and power to press the cause of educational reform. Both men spoke and wrote prodigiously and at every opportunity. Given their convergent interests, it was not unusual for them to appear on the same platform. Thus, on 27 October 1904 Gorst presided at a meeting of the Childhood Society held at the Sanitary Institute of London and Macnamara opened the debate. Claiming that 80 per cent of the working-class children were in fine physical condition, indeed that they 'were never so well off as they were today', he turned his attention to the remaining 20 per cent, the canonical submerged fifth. He went on to explain in detail his 'plan for adapting the "Cantine Scolaire" system, which worked well in Paris'.[29] As the *Lancet* reported, 'Dr Macnamara starts on the principle that no child should remain unfed and he proposes (1) that all parents who can must make suitable provision for the feeding of their children . . . and (2) that children of parents who are unable through misfortune to make such provision shall be assisted at the public expense.' Macnamara suggested that, as in France, all children should be urged to take school meals and that coupons for the dinners be sold to those who could afford to pay and given to those who could not.[30] Much of what Macnamara proposed he had published previously and he would advocate again. If his writings and speeches sound very much like each other, it is important to remember that he was a politician, not a creative artist. His themes, facts, figures, and political principles remained the same. And liberal as he was, lest anyone mistake him for a radical theorist, Macnamara set the record straight: 'All this sounds like rank Socialism – a consideration which doesn't trouble me very much,' he assured his audience. 'But as a matter of fact it is, in reality, first-class Imperialism.'[31]

That educationalists, political theorists, many philanthropists, and large segments of the public were willing not only to accept Macnamara's proposals, but to go even further in their demands for state action and responsibility was demonstrated at the Guildhall Conference on Feeding School Children in January 1905. The meeting was well covered by the *Lancet* as, they noted, 'it would seem that the full description given in these columns of the feeding of all the children attending the primary schools of Paris influenced many of the speakers. Constant reference was made to the *cantines scolaires* and to the Paris schools.' John Gorst presided over the congress, which was attended by approximately 250 delegates representing labour and other

178

organizations with a total membership of about two million. 'On the fundamental point at issue the entire conference was unanimous,' the *Lancet* editors declared, 'all the trade unionists, the Socialists, the Fabians, the philanthropists, and the educationists, one and all, were absolutely and most emphatically of opinion that somehow or other every child must be fed and no child allowed to study without first having sufficient food.' All but thirteen of the delegates adopted a proposal in favour of the free maintenance of school children by the state, with national rather than local funds, 'so that the burden might be more evenly divided throughout the whole community'.[32] The minority was headed by Macnamara, who insisted that it was a parochial, not a state question, and that such work should be supported by the local rates.

With so many convinced that the provision of school meals was an important and eminently justified undertaking,[33] appropriately within the sphere of state activity, the single greatest problem was the government itself. Technically, this was not a very difficult endeavour: those who had concerned themselves with the question knew what to do (supply meals) and how to do it (adapt the French system). All that was needed was political action. As John Gorst, who had set himself the task of moving Whitehall explained – and complained – the government could

'with great ease, and at little cost put an entire stop to destitution and suffering. It has been established beyond the region of controversy that a large proportion of children attending the public elementary schools, and thus under the daily observation of public authority . . . are suffering from habitual underfeeding. Some are compelled to go through their daily lessons whilst in a state of actual starvation. Evidence to this effect was given by the highest medical authorities and school experts before the Committee on Physical Deterioration, and filled everyone who read it – except the Government, who have been officially cognisant of the fact for so many years that they have grown callous – with consternation and alarm.

The effects produced by . . . defrauding helpless children of their legal rights, and forcing them on an empty stomach to learn . . . must be witnessed to be believed. It is the apotheosis of official stupidity and cruelty. Four Education Acts have been passed by Parliament within the last three years. . . . In not one of these has power been given to the local education authority even to feed hungry school children before setting them to learn lessons or perform physical exercises, notwithstanding the testimony of medical and school experts before the Royal Commission on Physical Training in Scotland in 1902, and of the above-mentioned Committee on Physical Deterioration in 1904. If a starving horse or ass were treated in the same way as hundreds of starving children are daily treated by public authority in our public elementary schools, the offender would be taken up and punished by the Criminal Law.'[34]

William Anson, Gorst's successor as Secretary to the Board of Education, was a sincere reformer and personally favoured the proposal to provide meals to school children. Unfortunately, he had been told by Balfour that, so far as socially progressive changes were concerned, he could 'be as sympathetic as he liked, but there would be no increase in the rates'.[35] Furthermore, the Marquis of Londonderry, who as Anson's chief was the President of the Board of Education, opposed reform legislation nearly as steadfastly as Gorst promoted it. In response to public and political pressure (primarily by Gorst and Macnamara), Londonderry sidestepped the problem by appointing yet another committee. On 14 March 1905 the Inter-Departmental Committee on Medical Inspection and Feeding of Children Attending Public Elementary Schools was formed and charged to enquire into 'the methods employed by various voluntary agencies for feeding such children, and whether relief of this character could be better organized without any charge upon the public funds'.[36]

Naturally enough, Gorst took a dim view of this official ruse, and he expostulated against it both in print and in person. 'The Government', he fumed,

'have done little to help in the elucidation of the problem. On the contrary, by appointing a Committee of junior officials to revise the conclusions of the former Committee of senior officials and of the Royal Commission, and ruling the application of public funds for the purpose of school meals as outside their scope of reference, the Board of Education has done its best to block the way to official action in the matter.'[37]

The climax, if not the final act, in this by now purely political drama was a sensational performance, engineered by Gorst, and guaranteed to force the government to address the issue. Shortly after the appointment of this last committee, Gorst organized 'a descent . . . by Lady Warwick, Dr Macnamara, MP, Dr Robert Hutchison, MD, Physician to the Hospital for Sick Children, Great Ormond Street, and myself upon the Johanna Street School of the London Council, situated in a very poor part of Lambeth'. (It may be remembered that the Johanna Street School had already figured prominently in the proceedings of the Inter-Departmental Committee on Physical Deterioration.) After inspecting the students, Dr Hutchison selected twenty boys whom he certified as 'unfit to do any school work' as 'they were actually suffering from hunger'. Nourishment, he said, was urgently and immediately required. According to Gorst's account, 'the party then proceeded to the offices of the Lambeth Board of Guardians . . . and demanded that the relieving officers should be directed to proceed to the school and furnish food immediately to the boys. . . . This application was granted.'[38]

Gorst had calculated correctly. In light of this somewhat spectacular success, he presented a resolution in the House of Commons, which was passed, to the effect that 'local authorities should be empowered . . . for ensuring that all children at any public elementary school . . . shall receive proper nourishment before being subjected to physical or mental instruction.'[39] From that point, the state took responsibility for the provision of meals to malnourished school children, albeit initially through the Poor Law Guardians. Within a year, in February 1906, the Education (Provision of Meals) Bill was introduced which transferred that duty to the local education authority. Receiving the Royal Assent on 21 December 1906, this Act provided that 'a Local Education Authority . . . may take such steps as they think fit for the provision of meals for children in attendance at any public elementary school in their area.' The Act authorized the creation of school canteen committees to undertake this work and the use of public money (within a limit of a rate of one halfpenny in a pound) to defray the cost of the food; equally important, it forbade the disfranchisement or the deprivation of any right or privilege of parents who failed to pay what the authority thought they could afford.[40]

As the 1 January 1907 circular issued by the Board of Education clarified, the Act was 'purely permissive' and 'imposed no duty' where it was considered unnecessary. Robert Laurie Morant, the Permanent Secretary to the Board of Education and the author of the circular, assured the local education authorities that the legislation was 'primarily of an educational character. Its object,' he explained, was

> 'to ensure that children attending public elementary schools shall, so far as possible, be no longer prevented by insufficiency of suitable food from profiting by the education offered in our schools, and it aims at securing that for this purpose suitable meals shall be available just as much for those whose parents are in a position to pay as for those to whom food must be given free of cost.'

Morant was a dedicated reformer who, with Sidney and Beatrice Webb among others, worked ceaselessly and more or less quietly the whole of his civil service life to establish a central public health agency.* It is, therefore, not surprising that the circular stressed the innovative nature of the legislation, albeit in rather conservative language.

> 'It is obvious that the passing of this Act opens up possibilities of a most beneficial nature, if its operation is handled with full circumspection and on carefully thought-out lines by the local authorities and voluntary agencies to whom these great responsibilities are entrusted by Parliament; since it furnishes unrivalled opportunities to the earnest, yet wise, social reformer for mitigating some of the deepest

---

* Morant left the Board of Education in 1911 to become Chairman of the National Health Insurance Commission. He was appointed First Permanent Secretary of the newly created Ministry of Health in 1919.

physical injuries that beset the children of the rising generation, particularly in "slum areas," without necessarily involving . . . undue intervention by the State in the sphere of parental responsibilities or in the duties and influences of any properly-ordered home.'[41]

One of the first towns to apply for authority to levy a rate to support the provision of meals was Bradford.[42] This industrial town in the north of England had already acquired a reputation for remarkable school health work. In 1893 the Bradford School Board had appointed Dr James Kerr as a full-time medical officer; he was the first elementary school doctor with responsibility to care for the health of the students and not simply for the hygiene of the physical premises. Kerr had instituted a number of activities to improve the health of the pupils and the teachers, and he came to be recognized as a leader in the field, whose example could be followed with success. A year after Kerr took up his position, Margaret McMillan, a member of the Independent Labour Party and of the Fabian Society, was elected to the Bradford School Board. During her eight-year tenure (she held this office until she left Bradford in 1902) McMillan promoted the cause of physical health and hygiene. She introduced the use of school baths, instituted programmes to provide meals for students, and it was she who, with Kerr, undertook the first recorded medical inspection of elementary school children in England.[43]

In an article on 'The Provision of Meals for School Children' Ralph Crowley (who had succeeded Kerr as school medical officer in Bradford when the latter moved to London in 1902) described his work in this field in an effort to urge other medical officers to undertake similar endeavours. Crowley explained that for many years large numbers of children had been fed during the winter by one agency or another. 'At the commencement of this year (1907), however, the Education Authority decided to adopt the Education (Provision of Meals) Act, 1906,' he reported.

'As there seemed much room for improvement, both in the character of the food provided and in the manner of its provision, i.e. from both the scientific and educational points of view, it seemed to me that something in the nature of a feeding experiment might prove useful'.

He was, he said, 'anxious to note the effect of feeding on the children, other conditions remaining unaltered'. Forty children in schools in the poorest area of the city, who were 'apparently most in need of meals', were chosen by Crowley and the head teachers to receive breakfast and dinner five days a week from 17 April to 24 July, except during the school holidays. Breakfast consisted of oatmeal porridge with milk and treacle, bread and margarine or dripping, and milk to drink. The superintendent of domestic subjects, Miss Marian E. Cuff, devised seventeen two-course dinners which were practical to prepare and serve, cost between 1*d* and 1½*d*, and contained Atwater's 'universally accepted standard' of 68 grammes of protein and 41 of fat each day. The effect of the meals was judged by changes in general appearance and in weight. With regard to the former, improvement 'was more or less apparent in all, and very obvious in some of the children, who visibly filled out and brightened up. The reverse process was equally apparent when the children were seen after the summer holiday, during which time no special meals had been provided.' Weight gain was compared with a control group of sixty-nine children; it was found that those who received the meals gained approximately 1.2 kilogrammes, while the other children gained less than half (0.4) a kilo during the experimental three-month period. 'It may be pointed out', Crowley reminded his readers, 'that the average gain per year of children of this class and size is not more than 2 kilos . . . for the whole year.' From this experiment Crowley concluded that feeding alone could do much to improve both the mental and physical condition of school children.[44]

On the basis of this study, and of the medical officer's examination of 1,840 children which revealed that probably about 11 per cent of the entire school enrolment was malnourished, the Bradford authorities instituted a general programme for the provision of meals. First, all children were encouraged to take meals. And second, either the parents or the teacher could apply for free meals for a child. A poverty standard was fixed: students were entitled to receive such meals if, after deducting the rent from the weekly earnings of the family, less than 3*s* per person remained.[45] As such eligibility tests went, this was relatively liberal; many of the children of the families whose budgets were recorded by the Women's Co-operative Guild or the Fabian Women's Group would have qualified.[46]

Crowley was not the only medical officer to conduct this type of study. A number of similar investigations were undertaken in various cities and towns throughout the country, but despite strongly analagous results showing considerable malnutrition and need, the provision of meals was not institutionalized and made mandatory before the First World War.[47] When the Provision of Meals Act was passed there were 322 local education authorities in England and Wales. During the first fifteen months of its operation (ending 31 March 1908) only 40 authorities had taken advantage of the option to levy the halfpenny rate to pay for meals. The next year this figure more than doubled to 85, but by 1912 only 131 of the 322 had instituted programmes for the feeding of students.[48] Of these, 95 spent rates for food and administrative costs, 19 for administrative expenses only, and 17 authorities met all costs with voluntary funds. Although there was little uniformity as to the method of selection, use of poverty scales, case review procedures, or even whether to serve breakfast or dinner or both, one principle remained fairly constant: most towns stayed well within the halfpenny limit.[49] In short, the trans-channel journey of the cantines scolaires was only somewhat more successful than the Gouttes de Lait model. Unlike the Gouttes de Lait, school meals eventually did become a regular feature of the English education system, but between 1906 and 1914 the idea of a school restaurant for all the students, so successful and popular in France, never really got off the ground in England. This was partly because of the difference in state support for the venture in the two countries, but undoubtedly also because of different cultural attitudes about the importance of food in daily life. Between the passage of the original Act and the eve of the First World War several stronger bills, which would have required local education authorities to provide food under certain conditions, were regularly introduced and as regularly defeated. It is not coincidental that it was in June 1914 that a bill which empowered the Board of Education to compel local authorities to feed malnourished pupils, allowed a 50 per cent grant-in-aid from the Exchequer for this work and removed the halfpenny rate limitation was passed and made law. Perhaps Macnamara was right, and programmes which sounded 'terribly like rank Socialism' were nothing more than 'first-class Imperialism'.

The Education (Administrative Provisions) Act which authorized the medical inspection of school children was passed just one year (1907) after the Education (Provision of Meals) Act. The movements to provide meals for and to institute medical examination of elementary school pupils were based on the same irrational as well as rational reasons, involved many of the same people, raised a number of corresponding questions and, in short, share a parallel history. In some ways the introduction of medical inspection, which at first sight might appear to be a more radical enterprise, was for contemporaries of the early years of the twentieth century a more acceptable reform measure: while feeding a child clearly was a parental responsibility, the state had already become involved in personal health with such legislation as the Contagious Diseases Acts. Thus controversy as to the appropriate role of the government in the medical examination of students is notably absent from the public and professional press. Then too, medical inspection followed the provision of meals; the battle had been fought, there was little more to say or about which to quarrel. Finally, and perhaps most importantly, the actual legal measures to authorize the medical inspection of school children were couched in terms so wonderfully vague and buried in the bill with such consummate skill that they hardly raised a ripple in the House. Indeed, for reformers medical inspection was never the real issue: treatment for the defects discovered was their goal. Whether viewed as an imperial measure to safeguard the future of the race, a medical measure to alleviate physical distress, or an educational measure to ensure that pupils could profit from the instruction they received, medical examination followed by appropriate treatment of school children was wanted.

In the first instance, however, the principle of school medical inspection had to be presented in a positive fashion to politicians, the public, the medical profession, and educators. And it was, couched in the rhetoric of concern for the future of the empire, financial prudence and common sense, or public responsibility, the argument in favour of the medical examination of students was vigorously adduced. The first major government body to speak to this issue (just as it was the first to have addressed the question of the provision of meals for students in the state schools) was the Royal Commission on Physical Training. The Commissioners reported (1903) that they were convinced that the school children's health problems revealed by the 'medical data now available point to a very serious defect in our organisation to which we desire to call special attention. This consists in the absence of any general or adequate system of medical inspection.' The Commissioners emphasized that 'such a system [was] urgently demanded mainly for remedial objects, but also in order to make available information of the highest value both for ascertaining the facts of national physique and the means that may be adopted for its improvement, or for retarding such degeneration as may be in progress.'[50] And, as the *BMJ* noted with

Plate 10 Nit parade, 1910

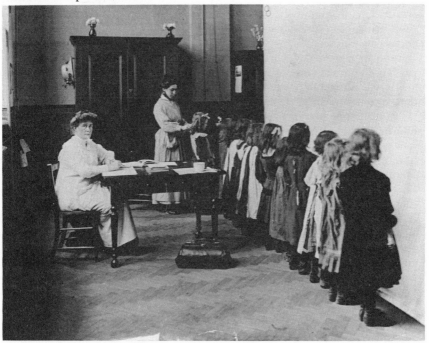

approval, the Commission recommended the appointment of 'a certain number of Sub-Inspectors, to make occasional visits to the schools for the purpose of examining their sanitary conditions, and the health and cleanliness of the scholars.' It is interesting to note that the Commissioners specified that 'the assistance of women might often be useful in this work, so far as it regards the girls and infants, and the effect of physical training in their case.'[51] As we shall see, it was precisely this reasoning, and the assumptions in which it was grounded, that led to the creation of new opportunities for women as health professionals.

A year after the Commission issued its *Report*, W. Leslie MacKenzie, a physician and politician who had undertaken investigations for the Royal Commission (and went on to devote his professional life to school health studies and reform activities), published a book on *The Medical Inspection of School Children* in which he discussed the body's work in great detail. 'The main purpose of the Commission', MacKenzie explained, 'was to establish, as it were, a "first case", clear and convincing, for a medical inspection of children attending State schools in Scotland.' He explained further that 'the general data before the Royal Commission had already persuaded them that a medical inspection of schools was, from many standpoints, eminently desirable; the data accumulated in the special investigation revealed the matter as one of urgency.' MacKenzie hastened to clarify that 'not from the standpoint of military fitness alone, nor yet from the standpoint of industrial endurance, but from the standpoint of educable capacity is the medical inspection of school children seen to be of primary importance to the commonwealth'.[52]

Each of the reasons adduced by MacKenzie claimed adherents. The primary role of the national reaction to the Boer War recruitment statistics at home, and to the army's losses on the field, has been detailed in other areas of child health reform. It is not surprising, therefore, that the rhetoric of national deterioration was used to effect change and, conversely, that school medical inspection was suggested as a remedy for this great malady. In a paper on 'Physical Degeneration in Children of the Working Classes' delivered before the Section of State Medicine at the annual BMA meeting in 1903, Herbert H. Tidswell (MRCS, LRCP) proposed, rather reasonably, the general sentiment that 'no one will deny that the standard of health amongst school children in our large towns is lower than it ought to be.' Unlike others, he did not believe in progressive deterioration; he would 'not be so rash as to assert that [the standard] is lower than it used to be; but it certainly is not so high as it ought to be, considering the advances in all departments of sanitary legislation and the improvements in hospitals and dispensaries for the free treatment of the poor'. As a remedy Tidswell suggested that

'all schools be under systematic medical inspection, let a medical officer be attached to each school, who shall inspect each class as it assembles to detect infectious or other diseases in the early stage, who shall examine the eyesight, the hearing, and general condition of each child and keep a report of the same, who shall visit any pupil at home in case of sudden illness and give certificate to same. A measure of this kind would entail cost, but in the end it would be true economy, it would save a vast amount of suffering and ill-health, and it would help to raise the standard of the national health.'[53]

While many writers and speakers agreed with the general correlation between school medical inspection and improvement of the national health, others had more specific reasons for introducing a system of medical examination of students. For instance, in March 1904 F.G. Haworth of Darwen wrote to the editors of the *BMJ* that his 'short experience as medical officer to the Education Committee' had brought the 'prevalence of adenoids in school children' to his attention, and he believed that these problems not only could but should be ameliorated. 'In my opinion', Haworth declared, 'it is very important to have a medical inspection of all the scholars in the elementary schools with regard to development as revealed by the weight and height of the children, the teeth, eyesight, hearing, skin in regard to diseases, and the mental condition'.[54] J.H. Crocker, MOH for the Borough of Richmond, agreed with Haworth as to the advisability of school medical inspection, but unlike the latter he was not so much interested in the individual ailments of the pupils as he was concerned that schools were centres for the transmission of infectious and contagious diseases. Crocker elaborated on this idea in a report he presented to the Richmond Education Committee. 'As children are compelled to attend elementary schools, reasonable precautions should be taken to ensure that infectious cases are excluded from such schools,' Crocker argued.

'In the past . . . the School Attendance Committee of a local authority, whilst compelling children to attend such schools, have had no powers for the medical inspection of scholars. . . . The result of this was that the teachers had no authority to obtain a medical opinion as to the condition of any child whom they may have suspected was suffering from an infectious or contagious complaint whilst attending school.'

As Crocker pointed out, this state of affairs could – and did – have a deleterious effect on the health of the entire student body. 'It is evident that prompt action in dealing with first cases may often avoid the more serious consequence of closure of the whole school, but heretofore the Medical Office of Health has experienced great difficulty in obtaining the information necessary.' One example of the benefits medical inspection could provide had occurred in the year before when he had exceeded his statutory duties and, with the consent of the school managers, had examined the pupils. He discovered one child whom he recognized as suffering from a mild case of scarlet fever. 'The child was isolated, and as a result no other cases arose in connection with the scholars of that school, and thus the closure of the school was avoided.' Crocker explained that such instances were more numerous than initially would appear.

'In addition to the diseases scheduled under the Infectious Diseases Act, which must legally be notified to the Medical Officer of Health by the parents or medical practitioner, there are other non-notifiable diseases which may assume an epidemic character and thus lead to closure of a school, such as measles, whooping cough, chicken-pox, mumps, ringworm, ophthalmia, scabies, etc.'

According to Crocker, the educators in his district favoured school medical examinations. 'From conversations with various managers and teachers of the elementary schools', he said, 'I am convinced they would appreciate any arrangement by which they could have a medical opinion under such circumstances, and would readily acquiesce in the periodic inspection of the scholars.'[55] The *BMJ* applauded Crocker's arguments, conclusions, and recommendation to the Education Committee to appoint a medical officer for the inspection of children attending the elementary schools and for the performance of other duties under the Education Act. In a notice on his report, the editors expressed their 'hope that the recommendations of the medical officer of health will be accepted'.[56]

The *BMJ* consistently supported the medical inspection of school children although, at least initially, the journal did not address the issues of exactly who was to be hired to conduct the examinations nor what was to be done to ameliorate the uncovered ills. Despite these editorial blind spots, the *BMJ* maintained a favourable position with regard to school health systems, and frequently urged their introduction in the journal columns. In an article on 'Physical Education in Elementary Schools', for example, the editors argued that medical examination was more important than gymnastic exercise. Until 'medical inspection in schools . . . is introduced, the best possible conditions cannot be attained', they asserted. Referring to Aimée Watt Smyth's series of articles, the editors reminded their readers of the work done in other countries. 'As our Commissioner in the course of the inquiry into national deterioration pointed out some months ago, the first thing insisted upon in Sweden, America and other countries, is the medical inspection of school children, and it was shown that the cost was small.' There were many advantages to such a system: 'in this way not only is the spread of infectious disease checked, but underfed children can be singled out.' Indeed, the matter was so urgent, that 'the Council of the British Medical Association has resolved to represent to the Board of Education that not only the Board itself but also every local educational authority should be provided with a medical adviser.' The editors were sure that 'the medical adviser would no doubt find it necessary to organize a system of inspection of schools in each district by medical men practising in the neighbourhood' and, they remarked, 'expense happily need not stand in the way.' The nation, the editors concluded, 'would be vastly the gainer . . . in the matter of physical fitness could it but be brought to recognize the unwisdom of the "penny-wise-and-pound-foolish" policy.'[57]

The threefold argument that, if such work were undertaken, children would be in better condition to profit from the education they compulsorily received; the nation would be saved the expense of trying to educate children who, due to physical ailments, could not learn; and in any case this health system had been undertaken successfully in other countries which might bode ill for the Britain of the future, was adduced both in support of the introduction of school medical inspection and (as we have seen) in support of the introduction of the provision of meals for students. In other words, the claims of education, a profitable national economy, and apprehension about the future of the nation were the concerns which motivated health reform activity, and they were reiterated with increasing frequency. In a *BMJ* commentary on Dr Kerr's report on the work of the medical department of the London School Board, the editors stressed that

'as an institution the school doctor has been slowly taking root on the Continent for many years. Within five years in Germany 676 school doctors have been appointed in 234 towns and districts, the regulations for medical examination of school children having been approved by the Minister of Education. Much is also accomplished in Switzerland, Austria, and in Northern European countries, and in America; but in England very little has yet been done.'

The editors urged the adoption of 'the Boston system under which a local practitioner attends the schools for an hour every morning'. The benefits of such a plan, they contended, were that as infectious or contagious diseases would be checked, 'children would have some chance of avoiding unnecessary disease, and of benefiting by compulsory education, while the nation would be saved the shame and expense of maintaining on the school benches those 60,000 children of whom Sir William Anson speaks as being unfit to benefit by education.' They ended by quoting the *Report* of the Inter-Departmental Committee on the Model Course of Physical Exercises to the effect that, 'no form of educational organization can be considered to be complete which does not make provision for the systematic reference of questions of school hygiene and the special treatment of individual scholars to medical experts.'[58]

The editors of the *BMJ* were not the only ones to propose these arguments in support of school medical inspections. One of the most important advocates was the Inter-Departmental Committee on Physical Deterioration. In their 1904 *Report* the Commissioners affirmed their support for student health examinations in no uncertain terms. Giving similar reasons for the introduction of such a health programme, the Committee concluded by stressing its urgency. 'The Committee', they wrote, 'consider that a systematised Medical Inspection of children at school should be imposed as a public duty on every school authority', and 'a contribution towards the cost should be made out of the Parliamentary Vote.'[59] In his Presidential Address to the Preventive Medicine Section of the BMA, W.J. Tyson sounded the same note.[60] And it is no surprise that both T.J. Macnamara and John Gorst also insisted on the importance of this health measure for school children which, they contended, was a state responsibility. 'The medical examination from time to time of the children . . . is a matter of communal obligation,' Macnamara declared. 'In contrast to our *laissez*

Plate 11 Central Street cleansing station waiting room, 1914

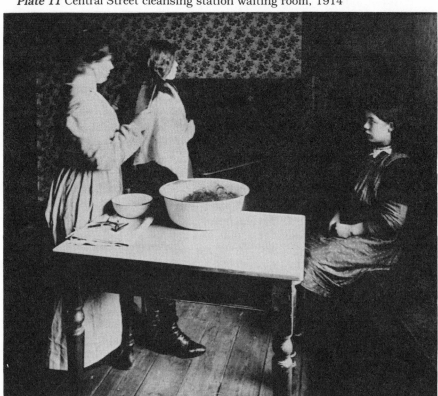

190

faire attitude towards the children, I may direct attention to . . . what the people of Brussels consider to be their duty to the children.' In that city 'every school child is medically examined once every ten days. Its eyes, teeth, ears, and general physical condition are overhauled. If it looks weak and puny they give it doses of cod-liver oil or some suitable tonic.'[61]

While agreeing with Macnamara as to the necessity for school medical inspection, Gorst addressed the issue of treatment more directly and at greater length than did his colleague. Children in schools, Gorst reasoned, were 'placed continuously under the eye of authority'. There was, he said,

'neither reason nor excuse for ignoring their ordinary human claim upon society, which could so easily perform its obligations towards them in these circumstances. In the first place, the health and condition of all children in the national schools should be regularly and systematically inspected. Their growth, weight, hearing, sight, physical defects, etc., should be investigated and recorded by qualified medical inspectors. . . . Children requiring special treatment [should be] placed under medical care either at the expense of the parent or of the public. Medical relief, it should be noted, does not pauperise the parent, and there is no excuse for robbing the child of its right to it. . . . Medical examination does not in any way undermine parental responsibility; and, whereas the cost is small, the economic consequences of neglect are so enormous as to be beyond calculation'.[62]

For Gorst, school medical inspection, treatment, and the provision of meals were all component parts of one single comprehensive system. His plan was that

'every child, on entering school, should be medically examined; the ailing ones classified; and their condition recorded. Treatment, medicine, appliances and diet should be prescribed for those that need medical aid; and the School Authorities should see that they obtain that which is ordered for them either from their parents or, if their parents fail, from the public.'[63]

As public discussion of the reasons for and benefits of medical inspection grew more intense, increasing attention was paid to school health systems developed in other countries which could serve as models for similar work in England. In her book on *Physical Deterioration* Watt Smyth described the procedures that had been developed in Boston where a local practitioner visited the schools in a given neighbourhood early each morning.[64] A 'special sanitary commissioner' writing for the *Lancet* investigated 'The Medical Control of Schools at New York'. In a two-part article published in March 1905 the author explained in some detail the comprehensive scheme which had been instituted in Manhattan in 1902. The most important features of the New York plan were the thoroughness with which the work was undertaken, and the co-ordination and co-operation which evolved between the teachers, medical inspectors, and a new group of health professionals, school nurses. According to the *Lancet* author, the city health department appointed inspectors to visit the schools each day at a ratio of 'approximately one inspector for every 5,000 children'. Every morning each inspector visited the schools assigned to him where he conducted 'two sorts of examination, first, that of the children who are suspected [by their teachers] of being ill and consequently have not been allowed into the class-room; and secondly, that of the children who are believed to be in good health and who are in the class-room'. A nursing system was organized at the same time, and initially eight nurses were appointed 'to attend to children who, though suffering from communicable complaints, are nevertheless admitted to the schools. This permission is granted notably in cases of pediculosis, conjunctivitis, and some forms of the diseases of the skin.' It quickly became apparent that these nurses were essential to the school health service. 'Before six weeks had elapsed the staff of nurses had to be doubled,' and their numbers continued to increase. These new health professionals established clinics in the schools where they treated a number of minor but communicable complaints such as favus, molluscum contagiosum, scabies, ringworm, and impetigo as well as pediculosis and conjunctivitis. Furthermore, as the *Lancet* commissioner explained, 'these school nurses were destined to render great service apart from the mere treatment of the afflicted children.' Not only did they care for the students at school, they also followed up cases in the pupils' own homes, and as visiting nurses they assumed a pedagogical function. In conclusion, the author compared the work done abroad with that undertaken in Britain.

> 'If we compare the medical inspection of the children attending the New York schools and the very successful feeding of all the children attending the schools in Paris with what prevails at home, it will have to be acknowledged that in Great Britain, and especially in London, there remains still much to be done.'[65]

So much interest in the question of school medical inspection had been aroused by the end of 1905 that the Office of Special Inquiries and Reports at the Board of Education sent William Harbutt Dawson to Germany to investigate the role of the school doctor in that country. Dawson's report was issued in February 1906, and in a prefatory note he explained that serious consideration of how to implement a school health system had stimulated curiosity as to the schemes instituted elsewhere. 'The careful record of the physical development of children in schools was recently advocated by the Inter-Departmental Committee on Physical Deterioration,' Dawson reminded his readers, and they advised the introduction of systematized medical inspection of students. 'But the practical fulfilment of this recommendation is not free from difficulties.' Unlike in England, 'the problem in Germany so far as it affects primary schools has been solved in all its main outlines.' Therefore, 'although the institution of the School Doctor is not peculiar to Germany, it has been introduced so widely and with so much success in that country, that German experience and methods may be studied with special advantage.'[66]

By the time the Board of Education pamphlet was published, a number of local authorities had begun to institute school health systems. Between thirty and forty education authorities, or approximately 10 per cent of the whole number, had hired a school doctor who carried out some form of medical inspection.[67] But, as the *BMJ* complained, this was far too few.

> 'If the county councils are taken as important and representative local education authorities, we find that out of 48 of these in England responsible for 12,774 schools with an average attendance of 1,776,022 two [Surrey and the West Riding of Yorkshire] alone have approved of an organized scheme of medical inspection. . . . We find that 31 county authorities, with 7,950 schools and an average attendance of 1,030,524 have not even discussed the question. In the remaining 15 counties, with 3,701 schools and 530, 266 scholars, the question has been discussed generally very briefly, and then either dropped or indefinitely postponed.'

In the editors' view it was 'evident that the authorities have in most cases been unable to apprehend the grave importance of the subject, and that without a definite lead from the Board of Education no improvement is likely to be made'. Therefore, they urged most strenuously that, first and foremost, a Medical Department at the Board of Education needed to be created: 'the health and well-being of the elementary school population has long suffered for want of this reform'. Second, the editors advocated that 'no grant should be made on account of any school not included in a scheme of medical inspection approved by the Board.' In conclusion they noted that the government had 'pledged itself to deal at an early date with the educational system of the country'. And, they warned their readers, 'whatever changes or improvements may be introduced, the provision of such a scheme . . . is a matter upon which depends much of our future welfare as a nation.'[68]

In the event, these reforms were not long in coming. As we have noted earlier in the chapter, the first major amendment to ameliorate the physical condition of school age children was the Provision of Meals Act of December 1906. The next significant step which was taken to protect their health was the unproblematic passage of the Education

(Administrative Provisions) Bill on 28 August 1907. The key clause of this legislation, Section 13, provided that

> 'the powers and duties of a local education authority . . . shall include . . . the duty to provide for the medical inspection of children immediately before or at the time of or as soon as possible after their admission to a public elementary school, and on such other occasions as the Board of Education direct, and the power to make such arrangements as may be sanctioned by the Board of Education for attending to the health and physical condition of the children educated in public elementary schools.'

Concomitant with the passage of this legislation, the post of Chief Medical Officer of Health to the Board of Education was created, primarily due to the efforts of Robert Morant. This innovation meant that while the health care of infants and pre-school age children was under the aegis of the Chief Medical Officer of the Local Government Board, medical services for school age children would be under the direction of his counterpart at the Board of Education.

By the end of 1907 Morant knew, through his friendship with those most influential Fabians Beatrice and Sidney Webb, that it was very likely that the Royal Commission on the Poor Laws (of which Beatrice was a member) would eventually present both a Majority and Minority Report. Written by Beatrice Webb, the Minority Report would advocate the abolition of the old Poor Law and, consequently, of that department responsible for administering it, the LGB. In its place, Webb would recommend the organization of a number of individual agencies which would address specific aspects of poverty. Of greatest interest to Morant was the plan for a separate, general public health agency. Morant supported this idea and conceived of such an agency as having responsibility for the health of children of all ages. In the meantime, however, as the break-up of the LGB appeared possible, and in any case it was a weak department with cumbersome official machinery, he felt it should not be trusted with the responsibilities of a national school health service. Or, as Beatrice Webb quoted Morant as having asserted at a private dinner with her, 'He says he will be forced to start a medical department because of the incapacity of the LGB to do the necessary work.'[69]

George Newman was appointed to the post of Chief Medical Officer of Health to the Board of Education in September 1907.[70] Two months later the Board issued circular 576, 'A Memorandum on Medical Inspection of Children in Public Elementary Schools' to explain the purpose and operation of the new legislation. Morant had taken great pains to prepare the circular so that it would stimulate appropriate activity. In his attempt to perfect the draft he turned (among others) to Margaret McMillan who, in 1902, had moved from Bradford to London where she had continued her fight for medical inspection of, and more especially treatment clinics for school children. 'I wanted to ask', he wrote to her on 28 October,

> 'if you would come and see me for a good talk in Whitehall on the inauguration of Medical Inspection under the new Act, and help me by going through my draft circular with me, for I am very anxious to keep the zealous interest of those who care for this new development, so that we may get it started right, and that it shall neither hang fire nor get started on wrong or futile lines. Would it be asking too much to beg you to give me the benefit of your criticisms, and to have first, a good straight talk on the matter?'[71]

The net result of Morant's drafts, conferences, and rewrites was a remarkable document which addressed the long-term goals as well as the immediate objectives of the Act. The three themes of national salvation, the claims of compulsory education, and true economy were skilfully woven together and used to maximum effect.

Morant began the circular with a statement which clearly delineated the Board's hopes and expectations.

> 'The Board of Education desire at the outset to emphasize that this new legislation aims not merely at a physical or anthropometric survey or at a record of defects disclosed by medical inspection, but at the physical improvement, and, as a natural corollary, the mental and moral improvement, of coming generations. The broad requirements of a healthy life are comparatively few and elementary, but they are essential, and should not be regarded as applicable only to the case of the rich. In point of fact, if rightly administered, the new enactment is economical in the best sense of the word. Its justification is not to be measured in terms of money, but in the decrease of sickness and incapacity among children and in the ultimate decrease of inefficiency and poverty in after life arising from physical disabilities.'

Morant explained that, practically speaking, the organization of the school health service was in the hands of the local education authorities, and it would be their task to appoint medical officers to carry out the annual inspection. Although new personnel would have to be hired to undertake school hygiene work (and it is interesting that Morant specified that 'it should be noted that there are many cases in which women are likely to be specially suitable'), co-ordination and co-operation with other branches of local government work was necessary. 'In view of the varied influences which affect, directly or indirectly, the health of the children of the nation, it is manifestly of the highest importance that the administration of this Act should rest upon a broad basis of public health,' Morant insisted. The local education authorities should 'use to the utmost extent the existing machinery of Medical and Sanitary Administration, developing and supplementing it as required, rather than supplanting it by bringing into existence new agencies, partially redundant and possibly competing'. Morant was very clear about the central role of the MOH in school health work, and indeed that school hygiene was simply one of the community's public health services.

'The Board view the entire subject of school hygiene not as a specialty or as a group of specialties existing by and of themselves, but as an integral factor in the health of the nation. The application of this principle requires that the work of medical inspection should be carried out in intimate conjunction with the Public Health Authorities and under the direct supervision of the Medical Officer of Health.'

Morant not only addressed the theoretical issues raised by the introduction of a national school health service, he also delineated precisely what was to be done to implement this work. In the first year, he admitted, the inspection of newly admitted students and those leaving school would be a sufficiently ambitious undertaking. This was especially true as examination was only one part of school hygiene.

'The aim of this Act is practical and it is important that Local Education Authorities should keep in view the desirability of . . . formulating . . . schemes for the amelioration of the evils revealed by medical inspection, including . . . the establishment of school surgeries or clinics, such as exist in some cities of Europe. . . . It is clear that to point out the presence of uncleanliness, defect, or disease does not absolve an Authority from the consequent duty of so applying its statutory powers as to secure their amelioration and to prevent . . . their future recurrence or development.'[72]

Despite these instructions, and indeed upon occasion precisely because of them, questions arose as to who should be entrusted with the task of school medical inspection and, practically speaking, precisely how it should be done. The *BMJ*, for example, which consistently had approved of the principle of a school health service, was appalled by the circular which, the editors said, called for 'medical inspection falling into the hands of sanitary authorities'. The central problem was that the Board of Education had advised 'that the work should be everywhere organized under the medical officer of health, and that when the actual work of inspecting is more than he can undertake unaided it should be carried out by special assistants working under his supervision.' The editors objected most vehemently to, as they sarcastically put it, the 'confusion in the mind of the writer of the memorandum between public-health administration and school hygiene and the special study of diseases in children'.[73]

For the Board of Education, the problem of explicating what medical inspection should entail was more urgent than specifying who was to do it. Within two months of the publication of memorandum 576, Morant issued circular 582, a 'Schedule of Medical Inspection'. Explaining that the schedule had been 'drawn up in response to requests which the Board of Education had received for further and more definite guidance as regards the details of the work of medical inspection', Morant nevertheless stressed that this form was merely a model. Although the Board had been 'pressed by many Local Education Authorities to issue a complete set of forms for use in carrying out the work' they thought it 'expedient to leave considerable latitude . . . in regard to the particular forms or schedules to be used in different cases or circumstances'. Morant identified the issues, formulated the problem, gave general guidelines, and concluded by telling the local education authorities to resolve the situation according to their own needs. The chief difficulties, he said, were 'administrative rather than educational or scientific'. A number of considerations had to be taken into account.

'The existing resources of Local Education Authorities [were] not unlimited, the feelings and prejudices of parents [had] to be considered, and a new element [had] to be introduced into school life and organization with the least possible disturbance and inconvenience. Moreover, in this case, two departments of local public administration [were] brought for the first time into organic connection – those of public health and of public education.'

Basically, what the local authorities had to keep in mind was that the primary purpose of school medical inspection was to determine 'the fitness of the individual child for school life' and 'to prepare the way for measures for the amelioration of defects in the child or its environment'.[74]

This circular was followed by a number of articles in the medical press detailing local experiences with school medical inspection and providing suggestions as to how to record the findings (the form to be used) as well as precisely what the examination should entail. Given James Kerr's early school hygiene work in London, it is not surprising that one of these papers dealing with practical matters was written by an assistant medical officer to the Education Department of the London County Council, C.J. Thomas. Focusing first on the history and then on the practice of school inspection, Thomas offered several sensible suggestions. In terms of records he recommended that registers be eschewed as they were unwieldy and imposed a certain rigidity. Only cards and cabinets, which offered more flexibility as to the information noted and in terms of addition and removal of individual student's records, should be used. Turning to the inspection itself, he urged a two-step approach of a preliminary run followed by a return visit to examine each child who warranted closer attention; in these cases the presence of the parent was, he thought, highly desirable. Thomas went on to enumerate the particulars he found most important to examine, including assessing the standard of clothing, nutrition, and cleanliness, the condition of the child's teeth, vision, and hearing, and the presence of nose or throat obstructions, or external eye disease.[75] An article by W. Lloyd Edwards, a school medical officer in Barry, on 'Medical Inspection of Schools: Some Notes on Organization' was even more technical in character. 'As so many medical men are now about commencing the medical inspection of schools, it may be interesting to give a few notes as to the methods to adopt on starting,' Edwards began. 'There will be a large amount of clerical work,' he continued, 'and it is therefore highly important that medical men should make use of all modern business methods which will simplify the work and save time and labour.' Edwards agreed entirely with the practice of using a card filing system, and his article mainly addressed the issues of how these cards should be designed and what information should be included on them. One full page of the article was devoted to a reproduction of the two sides of Edwards's model design.[76]

While the practical details of school medical inspection was the first problem the Board of Education addressed, the issue of who was to undertake this work was debated much more heatedly. In the first place, it opened a new field for public health workers to which, as we have seen, the official organ of the BMA (the *BMJ*) objected. In the second, the traditional ideas about the special relation between women and children which we saw operant elsewhere were influential here too in helping to create new opportunities for women as school medical officers and school nurses. This trend had begun even prior to the passage of the 1907 Act. In the annual report for 1903 of the London School Board's Medical Department, for example, the importance of nursing care in ameliorating the problem of ringworm was discussed at some length.

'In the course of last year three additional nurses were appointed to visit schools and to draw attention to ringworm infection and other similar conditions among children. . . . The nurses are doing useful work without in any degree weakening the responsibility of parents in regard to the care of their children. The nurses' visits are in a measure educational for scholars and teachers alike, for they direct attention to matters of cleanliness.'[77]

After the 1907 Act was passed, the practical consequences of the philosophy that, as the *BMJ* remarked, 'the school is really an annexe of the home, where woman reigns supreme',[78] became increasingly visible. The issue of the role of women as participants (in one capacity or another) in the school health service specifically because of their gender was raised at a number of local meetings to organize the medical inspection of school children. For instance, at a conference to discuss various practical proposals held in Warwick on 16 March 1908, between the Education and Sanitary Committees of the County Council, as well as representatives of town and district councils, the question of the employment of women was considered. One of the participants, a Dr Twomey, 'suggested that one woman doctor should be employed for the work [as] he believed the parents would prefer the inspection of the children should be made by a woman'. At about the same time, the Birmingham Education Committee adopted a proposal to appoint three medical practitioners (gender unspecified) at a salary of £250 and three 'women attendants' at a salary of £50 per annum.[79]

Before local authorities could decide on the finer issues of gender, however, precisely who was to undertake the medical inspection of school children, the functions of such a 'school medical officer' as recognized for the first time in the Education Code of 1908, and the scope of the arrangements for attending to the health and physical condition of school children had to be clarified. The Board of Education's earlier directives established that school medical inspection was to be conducted under the aegis of the local medical officer of health, and that this work was to be seen as part of the larger sphere of public health work rather than a speciality unto itself. The Society of Medical Officers of Health and their journal, *Public Health*, welcomed this conception; it was a major development in the growth of their field of expertise. Contact and communication between public health professionals was quickly recognized to be advantageous and both the journal editors and the society itself responded appropriately. 'In view of the important duties which the recent development of school hygiene now imposes on medical officers of health, the Society have thought it desirable to enlarge *Public Health*, in order to provide for the insertion of additional matters relating to that subject,' the editors announced in March 1908. 'It is to be hoped', they added, 'that those who are engaged in this most important branch of public health work will take advantage of the opportunities thus afforded, and will make the columns of this Journal the medium for communicating to their colleagues the results of their experience in the work of school hygiene.'[80] Less than four months later the Society addressed the issue of membership. At an extraordinary general meeting on 19 June it was 'unanimously decided that the full privileges of the Fellowship of the Society should be open to "Medical officers appointed by Education Authorities"'. Whether technically medical officers of health or not, school doctors were thus invited to participate in the activities and government of the Society. In their announcement of this decision the editors of *Public Health* explained its significance in some detail.

'The Society, in taking the first opportunity thus to extend the basis of its membership, is but acting in accordance with the view that it has consistently upheld, namely, that school hygiene is not a distinct speciality, but is an integral part of our system of public health administration. This is the view expressed by the Board of Education in their memorandum on the medical inspection of school children,

199

and it is a view which the events of the last few months justify us in saying has been generally adopted in the country.'[81]

The role and function of these new public health professionals, school medical officers, was described in circular 596, written by Robert Morant and issued by the Board of Education on 17 August 1908. According to the Board, the task of these officers was 'to concentrate and organize . . . all matters of school hygiene, including medical inspection'. Practically speaking, this meant that one person, appointed by the local education authority, was to be 'charged with the organization and control of the whole machinery of the School Medical Service' and was to be 'in a position to take responsibility for the acts of all persons taking part in the work, including those of Assistant Medical Officers, School Nurses, Attendance Officers, and Teachers so far as they perform any functions in connexion with the School Medical Service'. Part of their task was to write an annual report reviewing the hygienic condition of the schools in their area and the arrangements which were made 'for the co-relation of the School Medical Service with the Public Health Service and for the organization and supervision of medical inspection'. Furthermore, such officers were also to devise schemes 'for the amelioration of the evils' revealed by examination of the children.[82]

The role of women in the school health service as medical officers and as nurses was recognized by Morant, both tacitly and in a straightforward manner. By speaking of duties 'specifically assigned to him (or her)' with regard to the school medical officer, Morant acknowledged that such a position was open to women as well as to men. The subject of school nurses was addressed much more directly. It was assumed that they would be women, and the Board of Education wholeheartedly supported their appointment. 'A School Nurse is capable of performing very useful and important functions', Morant reminded his readers. Following the example of school nurses in New York City, many common conditions found among the pupils could be cared for by these health workers. 'Such matters as the antiseptic treatment of discharging ears, the treatment of sores and minor skin diseases, or minor diseases of the eye, such as blepharitis and conjunctivitis, the treatment of slight injuries resulting from accident, will fall within the scope of the work of the School Nurse,' he explained. Her role was so integral a part of the school health service as envisioned by Morant that, he said, 'the sanction of the Board to her employment was not [even] required'. Furthermore, although approval was required for nurses hired not just to help with school medical inspection but specifically to treat the students or to visit them in their homes to give advice, Morant assured his readers that the Board would have 'no difficulty in sanctioning any well-considered scheme for these purposes'.[83]

Clearly women were slated to participate in the new school medical service – to some extent and in one capacity or another. As we have seen, this issue already had been raised by a number of local authorities in their deliberations over the establishment of school hygiene programmes. Just as the passage of the Notification of Births Act increased opportunities for the employment of women as sanitary inspectors and gave rise to a whole new field of (female) professional work, health visiting, the Education (Administrative Provisions) Act also, quite inadvertently, opened new positions for women both on a par with men as school medical officers and as a new cadre of subordinates, school nurses. The desire, and the need, for women workers continued to be expressed throughout the period of this study.

The example of Manchester elucidates contemporary notions of the special suitability of women to work with children, and the younger the child the more appropriate to the domain of women. At a meeting in late September 1908 of the Manchester Education Authority 'considerable discussion arose on the question of the appointment of a medical woman' as one of the three assistant medical officers to be hired at a starting salary of £250 per year. The headmistress of the Manchester High School for Girls, Miss Burstall, favoured this idea. Explaining that

Plate 12 School doctor and nurse, 1910

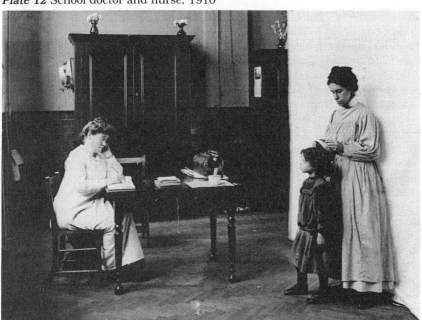

she thought 'these were appointments where the services of medical women might be extremely useful', she moved an amendment that at least one of the medical officers should be a woman. She was told that 'the number of assistants would certainly have to be doubled in course of time, and when the arrangements were made the work would be specialized, and certainly a department for infants would be made which might well be placed under the charge of a lady doctor.' Miss Burstall withdrew her amendment, but the *Manchester Guardian* picked up where she left off. Arguing that medical women were extremely well suited to school health work as at least half the children and the teachers were female, the editors contended further that 'the active sympathy of mothers will be accorded more readily if their daughters are to be examined by qualified women, while the women teachers can hardly display fullness of confidence and freedom from restraint when discussing the girls under their charge with a man.' The cause was taken up also by the Committee of the Federation of University Women which adduced the same arguments in favour of a woman inspector, adding that women had been appointed in other towns and had organized their own departments successfully, and furthermore that there was 'no reason for artificially restricting the appointments to one sex'. The agitation ultimately was successful, and a woman inspector was appointed at a salary equal to her male colleagues.[84]

This employment of female physicians was not so problematic in some districts such as the West Riding, where four of the ten newly appointed school medical inspectors were women. In most areas, however, women were not hired to be colleagues of men, but in subordinate positions. By the end of 1909, when 307 of the 328 local education authorities had instituted a school medical inspection scheme approved by the Board of Education, only 68 of the 750 assistant school physicians were women. While this was hailed as a positive advance by Robert Morant and was, perhaps, one of the reasons for the decision by the Society of Medical Officers of Health to open their membership to women,[85] it represents a much smaller proportion than either Manchester's one-third or the West Riding's four-tenths. By and large, the great openings for women as a result of the 1907 Act were as school nurses and, in a roundabout way, as health visitors.

The appointment of women to the position of school nurse or health visitor with the responsibility to follow the care of pupils in their homes, and the need to hire more such personnel, was regularly reported in the medical press and in the annual reports of individual medical officers of health. An October 1908 *BMJ* article on 'The Health of Salford', for instance, noted that a school nurse had been 'appointed to assist in the inspection, and so far her main duty has been the detection of pediculosis and assisting at the special examination of children and teachers'.[86] Three months later, in a talk given as one of a course of lectures on the medical inspection of school children organized by James Kerr, H. Meredith Richards (MOH for Croydon) discussed 'the co-ordination of medical inspection with public health work'. Richards argued that health visitors were ideal liaisons between the public health and education departments. 'In many towns qualified women with hospital training have long been engaged in giving advice as to infant feeding,' Richards pointed out. It was, he claimed, 'a simple matter to combine the office of health visitor and school nurse'. Such health workers would have five major duties with regard to school children.

'(1) In the school they would act as school nurses and assist at the inspections.
(2) They would investigate illness among absentees.
(3) They would act as a medium between the medical inspectors and the parents, and keep children under observation until the advice given had been followed.
(4) They would give detailed advice in the home on dietetics, domestic hygiene, and so forth.
(5) They would assist at the school clinic.'

'Personally,' Richards affirmed, 'I have found this combination of health visitor and school nurse extremely valuable. After a time, the health visitor gets to know the families in her district, and can often give invaluable information to the inspector, especially when the parents are not present at the medical examination in the schools.'[87]

Richards's conception of health visitors as the connection between the school and the home, the educational system and the public health department, was endorsed by other medical officers of health. In an article on the 'Co-Relation of the School Medical Service and the Public Health Service', E.W. Hope discussed the system he had instituted in Liverpool, recommending it for adoption by other local authorities. 'A still further linking up of the two departments', he contended, 'takes place where the sanitary authority is able to allow a trained female sanitary inspector to be present at the time of the examination; an inspector familiar with the district, and who in all likelihood knows some at least of the children, and who can pay a visit to any home which the school medical officer may desire a visit to be paid to.'[88]

The practice of utilizing the services of sanitary inspectors or health visitors for school health work became increasingly common, especially after the passage of the Children's Act in 1908 which empowered local authorities to cleanse verminous children (section 122). Indeed, this mode of procedure had become so institutionalized that in the 1912 annual report of the MOH for Woolwich, Sidney Davies argued that for this reason alone more women sanitary inspectors needed to be hired. There were two women sanitary inspectors for Woolwich, Davies explained, and one of them was 'specially a health visitor'. The other 'originally inspected houses registered under the by-laws, workshops where women are employed, restaurants, and eating-houses, re kitchens, etc.' However, he pointed out, 'during recent years special efforts have been made by the school authority to deal with verminous children, and for these efforts to be successful it has been necessary to inspect the homes of such children, and arrange for the cleansing of those found to be verminous.' This job 'naturally' fell on the second woman sanitary inspector 'and has grown to such an extent as to take up the greater part of her time'. As the work she used to do was given over to a male inspector, the MOH concluded that there was 'very great need for an additional woman inspector for registered houses, infectious disease, and other work done by female inspectors'.[89]

As greater numbers of health visitors were hired, this dual function devolved on them. For example, when the Durham County Council finally adopted the Notification of Births Act in 1912 the MOH, T. Eustace Hill divided the county into twenty-five areas with one health visitor for each district. The visitors were responsible for three major tasks: seven-twelfths of their time was devoted to infant welfare work, two-twelfths to school health duties, and the remainder was spent on tuberculosis visiting and dispensary attendance.[90] While a number of local authorities chose to fragment the health visitors' time between tasks, others, such as Birmingham, hired two sets of visitors. As Blanche Gardiner, the superintendent of health visitors in that city explained in the MOH's annual report for 1914, 'Since the appointment of the first four Health Visitors in 1899 there has been a gradual evolution of the term; and so now it is necessary to discriminate between those Health Visitors who do *general* Health Visiting and those Health Visitors who specialize in Infant or Tuberculosis work.' The nineteen general health visitors attended to the health of school children. The system operant in Birmingham was for either the school health officer, the school nurse, or the headteacher to report students in need of attention to the health department. Such pupils had been found to be verminous or suffering from an ailment which required follow-up care in the home. Unlike the schemes developed by other local authorities, the general health visitors in Birmingham also went into the schools to investigate and deal with reported or discovered cases of lack of cleanliness, but this comprised only about 10 per cent of their work. In 1914, 20,580 cases were reported from the schools 'to be dealt with by the Health Visitors . . . during the year 4,575 cases of vermin were reported by the Head Teachers, etc., and were visited both in the homes and schools' (an estimated 2,100 school visits were paid).[91]

By the time the Great War had begun three new, more or less distinct types of female public health workers had evolved and were employed in ever greater numbers: school nurses, infant health visitors, and general health visitors or specialized visiting nurses. Not only did the Education (Administrative Provisions) Act open the field of school nursing to help with the medical inspection of students, but the obligation to institute systems sanctioned by the Board for the amelioration of the discovered ills led to the establishment of school clinics, many of which were run by a nurse under the direction of the medical officer. These clinics arose, as George Newman noted in his annual reports as Chief Medical Officer of the Board of Education, necessarily and inevitably out of the arrangements for medical inspections. They provided treatment for cases which otherwise would never have received attention, as well as more continuous care with greater individual solicitude than was ordinarily available to afflicted students. Expediting treatment without delay, lengthy journeys, or long waits, such clinics ensured a minimum leakage between inspection and treatment and facilitated both control of care and regularity of attendance. That school nurses were central to this system of supplying 'frequent, sometimes daily, treatment' at a cost 'much lower than if each child were taken separately to a specialist,' was emphasized by Newman in his report for 1913. 'The School Nurse is an essential officer of the Treatment Clinic,' he insisted. 'She is actually responsible for the carrying out of minor and incidental treatment; further her presence is necessary at all hours when the clinic is working, for assisting in medical treatment, and in general arrangements.'[92] According to L.D. Cruikshank's 1913 study of *School Clinics at Home and Abroad*, there were approximately 118 centres in England 'where treatment schemes or school clinics are in operation.'[93] This meant that the work of school nurses, to an increasing degree, was primarily in the clinic itself. Infant health visitors, on the other hand, followed the health of babies both in the home and through contact with maternity and child welfare centres. And general health visitors, or specialized visiting nurses, followed the care of school children in their homes. These jobs were not particularly exciting or powerful; in the main they dealt with routine, run of the mill problems. Furthermore, they were subordinate positions, usually under the supervision of a more highly trained and better paid male superior. Nevertheless, they were definite and real opportunities for employment in the public sphere as professional health workers, and they provided women who held these positions with economic independence.

The history of the school health movement is not an especially complicated story. Unlike the case of the infant welfare movement, even to contemporaries the school hygiene issues were straightforward. The problems were basically bureaucratic and, well within the expertise of a Robert Morant, could be resolved. This was rather different from the scientific impediments to infant health care; the aetiology and mode of transmission of epidemic diarrhoea were conundrums beyond the expertise of physicians and bacteriologists during the period of our study. Furthermore, the diseases from which school children suffered (malnutrition, dental caries, minor skin problems, verminous conditions, external eye infections) were well understood and easily remedied.

All that was required was the establishment of a scheme or system to identify and treat the children who suffered from these ailments.

Many reasons were adduced to support a school medical service (which included the provision of meals and medical inspection), and a number of these arguments were found to be irrelevant or non-essential. As in the case of the infant welfare movement, the impetus for the adoption of such a programme was the frightening Boer War recruitment statistics and the spectre of general progressive physical deterioration. More specifically, the institution of a school health service was urged on the basis of the need for anthropometric surveys, which were found to be less valuable than initially appeared. The suppositions that medical inspection would make the school buildings more sanitary and prevent or materially alter the course of outbreaks of epidemic disease were also found to be incorrect. The two most important arguments for a school health programme were those of education and the maintenance of health itself. First, children who suffered from debilitating ailments, however minor, could not profit from the education the state provided as they would do if they were in good physical condition. The second but really primary reason was quite simply the protection of the health of school children as an end in itself. As E.W. Hope put it, the real object of the 1907 Act was not merely to tabulate statistics with regard to height, weight, or physical defects, nor was it fundamentally a disciplinary or educational measure. The purpose of this legislation was, he insisted, to protect and ameliorate the health of that one-fifth of the entire population who were school children.[94]

The school health movement was nearly contemporaneous with the infant welfare movement, but in some sense it was dependent upon the latter. That the health of children was recognized as a problem at all was, to some degree, a sequela of infant hygiene work. Having begun to care for the health of babies, it was logical to continue this work by providing medical inspection and treatment through the school system for older children. More than simply sensible, it was necessary to undertake such school hygiene activities; had it not been done, the infant welfare movement would have lost or been robbed of its legitimacy. It would have operated in a vacuum and led nowhere.

The question is, was the establishment of health care services for infants and children incipient Socialism, the beginnings of the modern welfare state with programmes to provide care for the whole of society? Or was it, as Macnamara had claimed, first-class Imperialism? This is not just a question of semantics, it reflects contemporaries' concepts of the future of the state and of their society. Early twentieth-century efforts to prevent illness in the youngest members of society, to keep the well baby healthy, and to address the problems of disease and malnutrition in school children, was a particular response to a perceived crisis. Having faced that specific emergency, there was no intrinsic commitment or compulsion to take any other action. A society may choose, as did Britain in the early years of this century, to confront the problem of ill-health in infants and children without accepting responsibility for mature adults. Thus the infant and child welfare movement did not in any way necessitate or make inevitable the development of a modern welfare state, but it did inaugurate the establishment of a modern welfare system.

Conclusion

Or war is good for babies – and other young children

The singularly disheartening and depressing reverses suffered by the British army during the first years of the Great War engendered a renewed sense of urgency for the establishment of a comprehensive infant and child welfare system. The power of a global Empire seemed as nought in the mud of northern France. A generation of men, bred to exercise the rule of the thistle and the rose in the farthest corners of the earth, found a grave under the poppies of Flanders field. Participation in the bloodiest and most lethal war in European history not only raised once again the spectre of Imperial decline, it also aroused a sense of foreboding that a new, vital generation capable and competent to take on the work of their parents would not be born at all: too many fathers killed, too many children unborn.

The statistics of the Registrar-General appeared to justify this fear, and by the end of the first year of the war it was evident that the birth rate had suffered a precipitous decline. That this decrease was due to the war was well understood, and it was commonly accepted that the diminished number of children born made it imperative to protect the life of each infant. In an article specifically addressing 'The War and the Falling Birth-Rate', the editors of the *BMJ* stressed the exigency of the situation:

> 'We are all apt to be depressed by the quickly-following lists of casualties and by the hope deferred that soon these melancholy indications of the war will cease with the establishment of a hardly earned but honourable and lasting peace, and that instead of the fathers there will be the children. But will there be the children to fill the places of the fathers? The question cannot be answered with the confidence that one would like to feel. . . . *The falling birth-rate has been a casualty list.*'[1]

Explaining that 'these matters have become suddenly urgent on account of the war, and of the times which must follow it,' the editors maintained that 'the birth-rate of a nation . . . is a vital question in every sense of the word.' Agreeing with the obstetrician John Ballantyne (whom they quoted), the editors argued that 'in the ultimate issue of things babies are of greater import than battalions, and they are the true dreadnoughts of a nation.' The state must, they said looking to the future, prepare for peace in the midst of war; protection of the health of the next generation was essential so that they could 'play their part worthily for their country, and for her high destiny in the years which are to follow'.[2]

The experience of the war was reflected in more general works on the causes of and remedies for infant mortality as well as those concentrating on the immediately obvious decreased birth rate. Indeed, the public and professional protective reaction towards the youngest members of society when putting at greatest risk the lives of those on the verge of realizing their potential and reaching productivity meant, in short, that war was good for babies. 'It may seem like a cold-blooded thing to say,' S. Josephine Baker (1873–1945) wrote on the eve of the Second World War,

> 'but someone ought to point out that the World War was a backhanded break for children – a break originating in the world's dismay at the appalling waste of human life, both at the front and behind the lines. As more and more thousands of men were slaughtered every day, the belligerent nations, on whatever side, began to see that new human lives, which could grow up to replace brutally extinguished adult lives, were extremely valuable national assets. When father had been torn apart by shrapnel or smothered by poison gas, his small sons and daughters, the parents of the future, took the spotlight as the hope of the nation. That is the handsomest way to put it. The ugliest way – and, I suspect, the truer, is to say flatly that it was the military usefulness of human life that wrought the change. When a nation is fighting a war or preparing for another . . . it must look to its future supplies of cannon fodder.'[3]

Baker was a competent commentator; in September 1908 she had been appointed Chief of the Division of Child Hygiene of the New York City Health Department, the first government agency anywhere in the world devoted exclusively to child health. An innovative and imaginative as well as energetic to the point of indefatigable activist in child care work, she held this position until her retirement from the Health Department in 1923. It was Baker's task both to create and to engender support for infant health schemes, and she found that in Europe and America enthusiasm for such public health programmes was much more easily roused and maintained far longer during belligerent as compared with peaceful times.

209

Plate 13 Poster used by the American Red Cross in France in 1918 to encourage the use of infant welfare centres.

(*Source: Maternity and Child Welfare* (1918). vol.2, p.228.)

CONCLUSION, OR WAR IS GOOD FOR BABIES

The increased concern for infant welfare was expressed in a number of publicity campaigns which, in their turn, aroused public interest in the nation's babies; thus a cyclical process was created. The most extraordinary of these publicity campaigns was the National Baby Week held in early July 1917. In his article on 'The Impact of the First World War on Civilian Health in Britain', J.M. Winter has briefly described the major events of the week, and the accompanying rhetoric:

> 'The week opened with an exhibition at Central Hall, Westminster, attended by the Queen. She was received by a guard of honour of 120 mothers and children, who were drawn from 80 maternal and infant welfare centres in London. On the same day, the Bishop of London spoke at a meeting of the Fulham Babies Hospital and Training Centre for Mothers. His address brought out well the mixture of philanthropy and patriotism which lay behind what *The Times* called the growing "cult of the child". The Bishop told his audience that "While nine soldiers died every hour in 1915, twelve babies died every hour, so that it was more dangerous to be a baby than a soldier.* The loss of life in this war had made every baby's life doubly precious".'[4]

In a more pragmatic way, the quickened interest in infant health aroused by the Great War was reflected in the increase in the number and variety of services which were made available. In 1914 local authorities employed 600 health visitors, and by 1918 this figure had more than quadrupled to 2,577. Whereas 300 municipal and 350 voluntary maternity and child welfare centres had been established by the beginning of the war, 700 of the former and 578 of the latter were in operation in 1918.[5] Not only had the total number risen, but the proportion of work undertaken by the public and private sectors respectively had reversed within a few years. The scope of activities carried on by the centres also expanded: more attention was paid to ante-natal work, medical consultations were extended from infants to include all pre-schoolers, milk and meals for toddlers as well as for pregnant and nursing women were more commonly offered, and dental care for mothers and children began to be provided at a number of clinics. Naturally the amount of money spent rose with the multiplication of services. In a statement to the House of Commons on 2 May 1918, William Hayes Fisher, President of the Local Government Board, announced that while in 1916 voluntary agencies had spent £40,000 on maternal and infant welfare programmes, the projected budget for the current year was £70,000; the corresponding figures for local authority expenditure were £96,000 in 1916 and £279,000 in 1918.[6]

One of the results of this considerably augmented government

---

* Josephine Baker also coined a rhetorical contrast phrase at about the same time: 'It's six times safer to be a soldier in the trenches of France than to be born a baby in the United States' (*Fighting for Life*, p.170).

211

expenditure on maternal and child health projects was a concomitant increase in official control over such programmes. This trend from voluntary independence to greater municipalization is clearly visible in the record of Liverpool work between 1914 and 1918. Three Liverpool site reports by LGB investigators elucidate this general tendency, even though the national growth pattern of charitable and public health department efforts was reversed in that city. (In the country generally, the number of municipal centres grew at a greater rate than did voluntary services; in Liverpool the latter increased more rapidly.) Janet Lane-Claypon (by this point a member of the LGB staff) visited Liverpool in 1914 and, in her analysis of infant welfare work in the city, she noted that there was 'no co-ordination between the various agencies, but the work requiring to be done is so vast and the amount done so comparatively small that it is hardly possible there can be any appreciable degree of overlapping'.[7] A year and half later, in January 1916, Lane-Claypon paid a return visit. She noted that while 'municipal work was started many years ago . . . voluntary effort does not appear to have begun until about five years ago, or so, and at first developed slowly. During the last three years however, it has grown greatly'; i.e. more or less coinciding with the war. According to Lane-Claypon the MOH, Dr Hope, was 'beginning to get a little anxious as to the number of voluntary agencies which want to start work and I said that I would ask the Board not to promise grants to agencies other than those now existing . . . without consulting him as to the necessity for the centre'. She recommended that 'no further centres should be established in Liverpool beyond those now contemplated by the municipality.'[8] By the time the last of these three site visits was undertaken by Dr Cameron in October 1917, Hope had been fairly successful in getting the situation under his control. 'The steady growth of more or less independent centres with separate committees of management led the MOH to consider a scheme for the co-ordination of all the agencies for child welfare work,' Cameron reported. 'It is not to be denied that the work of co-ordinating the various agencies at work was an extremely difficult one,' she continued. Cameron tested Hope's success according to three criteria: the establishment of amicable relations, the accomplishment of work, and the absence of overlapping effort. 'Considered generally,' she concluded, Hope's 'attempt to co-ordinate the numerous activities carried on voluntarily' with municipal efforts and public health department policy had been successful.[9] They were now all operating under his general aegis and supervision.

Given the renewed sense of the importance of child life, it is to be expected that legislation central to their welfare was passed in an improved and more extensive form during this time. As we have seen, the early notification of births was the basis upon which the English infant care system depended, and therefore it is not surprising that the permissive 1907 Act was made compulsory in 1915 with the passage of the Notification of Births Extension Act. The association between this legislation and the current state of war was explicitly elucidated. 'Although not a war measure, at no time in our history has it been ever more desirable that we should do everything to assist mothers or promote the health of infants so that they may become healthy men and women,' the President of the LGB announced.[10] The bill was passed without problems in the Commons and the Lords, and received the Royal Assent at the end of July. The Education (Provision of Meals) Act of 1914, which empowered the Board of Education to compel local authorities to feed necessitous school children, removed the halfpenny rate limitation and authorized a regular 50 per cent grant-in-aid from the Exchequer, had enjoyed the same fate a year earlier and for similar reasons. 'The summer of 1914', George Newman noted in his annual report as Chief Medical Officer to the Board of Education, 'has seen the beginning of a new stage in the evolution of the movement for providing meals for children in the Public Elementary Schools.' The outbreak of war raised fears of a general economic crisis, and the government moved quickly to ensure that school children would be fed. A memorandum of 15 August 1914 issued by the Board of Education addressed these potential problems directly. 'It is unnecessary to emphasise the importance of securing that, in case of necessity, effective and economic provision shall be made for supplying school meals for children.' This was, the circular stressed, simply part of the machinery of education, and 'the Board . . . emphasised the national importance of carrying on the public education system of the country with as great regularity as possible'.[11] Nor was it either accidental or coincidental that the Milk and Dairies Act of 1914 and the Milk and Dairies Consolidation Act of 1915, which were designed specifically to protect the milk supply from the cow to the consumer, were passed as well. Finally, while the school medical inspection and treatment system was not strengthened legislatively at this time, Britain's entry in the war certainly focused attention upon it, and stimulated its growth. Analysing the situation in 1919 Newman wrote:

'The School Medical Service has emerged from the War . . . bearing not only evidences of the struggle, but also of the complete vindication for its existence and of its recognition as the educational portion of a national system of Preventive Medicine. The returns of the medical examinations of recruits to H.M. Forces, and their import in connection with recruitment and the national physique, directed public attention to the findings and results of the School Medical Service, and drove home the lesson that the nation was suffering from its neglect to detect the earliest beginnings of disease, and to take steps to prevent as far as possible their development into physical disability. As a result of the War there has arisen a new conception of the value of the child to the nation.'[12]

Rhetoric had become reality.

In George Newman's *Annual Report* for 1917 he reviewed the work of the school medical service during the ten-year period from 1908 through 1917. 'At present . . . there is in being a national system of medical care and supervision of the school-children', he noted with satisfaction. 'The system is not complete or adequate, it is not yet being worked perfectly and therefore not yielding its fullest value; but it is available and it is universal.' Repeating himself for emphasis Newman continued, 'The School Medical Service is now a national system (it may be said as complete of its kind and more universal than elsewhere in the world) at work in all the 318 educational areas of England and Wales, [and] in all the 21,000 Public Elementary Schools.' Medical inspection and treatment for discovered ailments were provided to all students in the state schools, regardless of ability to pay or degree of physical distress. As Newman put it, 'the School Medical Service has recognised that the ordinary child is the key to the nation's health, and therefore it has exercised its duty to *all* children of school age.'[13] Clearly, pupils were as entitled to health care as they were to education; the state had assumed the responsibility to provide both.

By the time Newman's report was published, a similarly complete programme to protect the health of younger children was also universally available. In August 1918, close to the end of the war, comprehensive legislation was passed which systematized and regulated the provision of welfare services for pregnant and nursing mothers and children up to school age. The Maternity and Child Welfare Act formalized the establishment of the modern welfare system which had been instituted in an embryonic form in Huddersfield twelve years previously. Like the school medical service, it signified the explicit recognition of the responsibility of the State to protect the health of its citizens regardless of socio-economic status, albeit for one age group only. The assistance offered was made available as a right or privilege, and not a charitable donation or eleemosynary relief, to all who wished to make use of it. Outreach activities were extended to each mother and every child, and the types of services to be instituted, provisions for payment, and qualification guidelines were regulated by statute and guaranteed by the State. Exchequer monies were made available for a spectrum of services including the establishment of lying-in homes, creches, day nurseries and infant welfare centres, salaries for midwives and health visitors, and the provision of milk and food for mothers and children.[14]

The infant welfare system explicitly and definitely structured by the 1918 Act remained essentially intact until it was superseded by the establishment of the National Health Service in 1948. The theoretical (or philosophical) basis of this approach, the ideology of mothercraft, survived concomitantly. At the annual meeting of the BMA in 1923 the

214

Section of Public Health discussed 'factors contributing to the recent decrease in infantile mortality' (in 1922 the infant mortality rate had dropped to 77 per 1,000 births). The opening paper was delivered by James Wheatley, MOH for Shropshire. Wheatley calculated that during the seven years from 1916 to 1922 the infant mortality rate had decreased by approximately 30 per cent, while in the previous fifteen years (1901–15) it had fallen by 40 per cent. He argued that 'this seems to point to some special cause operating during the later period', and immediately added that this 'was the period of greatest child welfare activity'. Wheatley examined the effect of other factors, such as the fall in the birth rate, improved standards of living and general sanitation, climactic conditions and the milk supply, but considered these 'minor'. 'My conclusions', he said in summary, 'are that the fall in the infant mortality rate has been due chiefly to education. . . . It is in education and creation of a sense of responsibility, and not in the material conditions, that so much improvement has taken place.' Not all of the members of his audience agreed with this analysis; nevertheless, all the speakers acknowledged that the education of mothers through the health visiting–infant welfare centre system was a major, if not the sole, factor in the decrease in infant mortality.[15]

Newsholme (1857–1943), Newman (1870–1948), and Pritchard (1865–1943), three prominent activists in the early infant welfare movement, towards the end of their lives assessed the causes of, or reasons for, the decline in the infant mortality rate which they had worked so hard to achieve. More than the other two, Newsholme perceived the problem of infant mortality as complicated and requiring a multifactorial solution, including improved social and sanitary conditions, better quality medical care, and expanded health services. Indigence and ignorance were not, for him, two discrete categories but one continuum: 'no practical line of demarcation could be drawn between the dangers to child health due to ignorance or carelessness of the mother, and those due to conditions over which she was entirely without control.' Newsholme urged 'improved public health measures, improved domestic sanitation, [and] more adequate aid in the relief and prevention of poverty', as well as hygiene education through health visiting and child welfare centres. Writing in 1936 he concluded, 'It is evident that, following on the rapid strides made in child welfare work during post-War years, an even lower figure will be attained in infant mortality rates. . . . But the preceding forecast and my suggested forecast for future years . . . *can only be secured by improving the welfare of every mother*'.[16]

Newman and Pritchard placed greater emphasis on maternal education as compared with Newsholme's concept of maternal welfare, although for all three the mother was (as Sykes described) 'the centre round which all the agencies revolve for the protection and preservation of the health of both the mother and the child'. In his book *The Building*

215

of a Nation's Health (1939), Newman stated his position clearly. He noted that 'from 1901 to 1910 [the infant mortality rate] was reduced to 128 per thousand. But from 1910 it fell, in twenty years, to 60 per thousand births – it was halved.' 'The agency of reform', Newman stressed, 'has not been improved sanitation so much as more enlightened motherhood.' Through the 'simple, practical and, as it proved, far-reaching' instruction of health visitors and schools for mothers, 'several million mothers became "child conscious"; it was this almost universal *maternal awakening* which really began to change the outlook of child health.'[17]

Observing the precipitous decline in the infant mortality rate from 163 per thousand births in 1899 to 50 in 1942 Pritchard, like Newman, asked how 'this miracle' had been accomplished. In answer he professed that he had no doubt but that it was due to improved mothercraft.

'It is quite clear that it has not been due to sanitary reform or to the other hygienic causes which have for some years so favourably influenced the Adult Mortality Rate. It has not been due to improvement in the standard of living or to any lessening in the industrial employment of mothers, or because more infants are breast-fed; it has been due to the discovery that an infant's life depends on the care and skill with which its mother attends to its needs and requirements, in fact, to "the discovery of the Mother".'[18]

The infant welfare movement, Pritchard submitted, had one 'single objective, namely, the instruction of the mother and the easing of her task'.[19]

When we in the 1980s first read these passages, they appear to signify nothing more than the plaintive cry of garrulous old men calling women back to the home. Our initial impression is that 'mothercraft', or maternal aid and education, was the easy solution – for everyone but the mothers. With our prejudices we would accuse these men of having come to this remedy via the smooth route of traditional ethics and morality which required women to cherish their children in only one acceptable fashion: by abandoning the workplace and staying at home. This would be a serious misapprehension. Far from facile, the route to this remedy was tortuous; and far from easy, the solution of maternalism was labour-intensive and expensive. Then too, there is considerable evidence that contemporary women supported and approved of the health visitor–child welfare centre systems. As we saw in Chapter V, the members of the Women's Co-operative Guild expressed their desire for such aid and information programmes in the letters they wrote to their secretary, Margaret Llewelyn Davies. With this mandate Davies went to Whitehall to lobby Arthur Newsholme. A note recording her appointment with the Chief Medical Office reported that she 'and the four women's Associations with which she is associated propose to obtain an influentially signed petition on the subject to be sent to the Board and to Local Authorities'.[20]

Davies explained the women's position in a circular letter sent to anyone and everyone interested in maternal and child welfare. 'May we call the attention of your organisation to the desirability of linking up all work which has relation to Maternity, in such a way as to meet the special needs of this time [i.e. war-time], so that all working class districts throughout the country may be covered by an effective scheme of help?' Her style was sharp and precise. 'There is need for *immediate* action in this case. . . . Short time is being worked. Wives of those sent to the front are applying for Poor Relief. There is no money for the wants of Maternity, which calls for additional expenditure over and above the cost of daily life.'[21] Adamant about the need for maternal and child health services, the Women's Co-operative Guild campaigned vigorously to have them instituted and expanded. In an open letter to the editors of the *Westminster Gazette*, Davies and the President of the Guild, Eleanor Barton, presented their argument even more forcefully.

'The mothers of young children, or those who are shortly going to give birth to babies, have a special claim upon us. We have heard too little of their needs as yet. But we turn just now from the thought of the wreck and waste of young vigorous lives upon the field, with a fresh sense of the value and sanctity of these new lives, and of the imperative need of caring for the mothers and the young children of the race. . . .

'In many towns and boroughs there is the machinery for this work already in the making. Infant consultations, schools for mothers, baby clinics, have been started by municipal or voluntary agencies. Now is the time to extend their work, and where nothing has as yet been done, to make a beginning. . . .

'Working women have seen the need for this development of public service, and through their organisations they are asking for it.'[22]

As Barton and Davies noted, working women's organizations other than the Guild also supported this public health work, and together they did more than write letters, as the example of their activities in Camberwell illustrates. The Borough of Camberwell had been extremely recalcitrant about instituting any sort of maternal and child health system, and the borough council became the object of the women's associations' attentions. Articles in both the *Camberwell and Peckham Times* and the *South London Press* reported that the Camberwell Public Health Committee received a deputation from four different groups on 7 December 1915. Representatives from the Women's Labour League (Dulwich branch), the Women's Co-operative Guild (Dulwich and Peckham branch), Women of the Independent Labour Party (Dulwich and Camberwell branch), and women members of the Borough of Camberwell Trades and Labour Council 'asked that maternity centres should be established . . . and that efficient health visitors might be employed'. No action was taken, and six months later another deputation waited on the council 'to urge the necessity for maternity centres. The wastage of child life', the women argued, 'was far greater than the wastage of war.' They believed that 'maternity centres would tend to dispel the appalling ignorance of many mothers.' While it was true that there were some voluntary maternity centres in Camberwell, they were 'quite inadequate'. Furthermore, the deputation insisted, 'working women did not like to feel that they were receiving anything in the way of charity. They wanted municipal maternity centres into which women could walk just as they now walked into the public library.'[23]

The council remained obdurate and obstinate. Nearly a year later a public meeting of the residents of the Borough of Camberwell was called 'by a joint committee of the Peckham Women's Co-operative Guild and Dulwich Women's Labour League to consider the steps to be taken in view of the inaction of the Borough Council'. The honorary secretary of the committee, Beatrice Warwick, reported the event to the President of the LGB in the hope that it would encourage the Board to pressure the council. 'Representatives of the local places of worship, Schools for mothers, Trade Unions, Co-operative Guilds, Women's Labour League and the Camberwell Trades Council were present in addition to many members of the public. Women largely predominated,' she related.[24] A resolution urging action was passed unanimously:

'That this public meeting of men and women of the Borough of Camberwell calls upon the Borough Council to at once take steps to establish a scheme of Maternity and Child Welfare in the Borough in accordance with the requests of the Local Government Board and thus prevent the unnecessary suffering of mothers and their children, and loss of infant life.

The scheme is imperative if the virility of the nation is to be preserved, in view of the tremendous loss of life caused by the War, the rapidly decreasing birthrate and the new industrial conditions of women.'[25]

Although the council did appoint a special committee to consider the question of maternal and child welfare work, no other action was taken. The committee pondered the problem from June 1917 until February 1918 when they reported that they were not prepared to recommend the appointment of health visitors. Clearly it took more than deputations and public meetings to activate Camberwell Council in the area of maternal and child health care, and no system was instituted until it was statutorily required by the 1918 legislation.[26] Thus the women of Camberwell were not successful in their endeavour to force the borough council to institute a maternal and child health services scheme, but their efforts towards this end signify and demonstrate their wishes and desires. It is manifestly obvious that they wanted health visitors to come to their homes, and maternity centres to which they could bring their children and where they could obtain aid and advice. Although forced to be more active and articulate than their cohorts elsewhere, there is no reason to believe or presume that their needs and wants were any different.

If we marvel at their enthusiasm for such a conservative solution we must remember that there were no simple answers available to them nor, in the immediate future, any more radical remedies. Infants died of many causes, not one of which was readily controlled. As we have seen, epidemic diarrhoea was perceived by contemporaries as the primary preventable cause of infant death, and much research was done to identify the responsible organism before the word 'mothercraft' was even invented (by John Sykes c.1910). However, bacteriologists failed to isolate the aetiologic agent, epidemiologists failed to elucidate precisely the mode of transmission, and no vaccine or specific antidote was developed. Nevertheless, these investigations indicated that improvement of the milk supply was necessary, and at this point the infant welfare movement and the anti-tuberculosis campaign intersected. Unfortunately for both, attempts to reduce morbidity and mortality from contaminated milk were also by and large frustrated. Although a number of local authorities passed Model Milk Clauses, those concerned with the purity of the milk supply were not powerful enough to push national legislation through Parliament. The milk depot system, imported from France, tried to obviate these problems by providing pure milk appropriately modified for infants. Too expensive to afford and too restrictive in the regulations for elegibility, depot milk was unobtainable in practice for those who most needed it, and this solution was found to be ineffectual.

The attempt to combat one disease or one cause of several diseases with a single solution whether bacteriological, legislative, or in the provision of a material good, had failed or proved in some way inadequate. All of these endeavours preceded the development of maternal aid and instruction systems; in the history we have traced, education was the last resort. As Pritchard explained in his memoirs:

'It was my belief that the aim of good mothercraft was to protect the helpless infant from the many sources of infection which assailed him on all sides, one of which, and possibly the more [sic?] important, was contaminated milk, a danger which was inevitably associated with the consumption of milk which had not been artificially sterilized.'[27]

Seen from this perspective we can recognize that education was perceived as the only way to prepare each mother to face the plethora of dangers to which infants were exposed. To use Pritchard's example, until a pure milk supply was achieved, or commercial pasteurization was statutorily regulated, the mother could be taught to sterilize milk. Then too, turning to the mother opened opportunities to confront causes of infant death which were previously considered beyond the scope of either practitioners or medical officers of health: the problems of immaturity and developmental disease. Early research had indicated strongly that feeding and caring for pregnant and nursing mothers would improve the health and viability of the newborn as well as help to maintain maternal milk.

Education was time consuming and laborious. The aids provided (milk, meals, and medical inspection as well as classes, courses, and lectures) were increasingly comprehensive and expensive. It was not a quick and easy solution. It was not a radical solution. But it was successful.

A Note

On the secondary literature pertaining to the history of the infant and child welfare movement in England between 1898 and 1918

The crucial period in the history of the English infant welfare movement, 1899–1914, is wedged firmly between the Boer and First World Wars. The role of national involvement in military action as a stimulus for the enactment of protective provisions for infants and children, the next generation of combatants, has been identified and discussed by three generations of historians. Writing in 1930 Gilbert Slater (*Poverty and the State*) claimed that 'in no respect . . . is the difference between the nineteenth and twentieth centuries in England so marked as in the attitude of the nation towards childhood and towards health.' Listing 'the causes of the change' Slater singled out 'the shock to national complacency supplied by the South African War, which marked the close of the Victorian Age. When the war was over the Transvaal gold mines were almost completely forgotten in the anxiety over the national physique.'[1] Similarly, in his essay on 'War and Social Policy' (1958) Richard Titmuss submitted that 'it was the South African War, not one of the notable wars in human history to change the affairs of man, that touched off the personal health movement' in general and 'the school medical service, the school feeding of children in elementary schools [and] a campaign to reduce infant mortality' in particular.[2] That scholars of the 1980s agree with Slater's and Titmuss's perception of the importance of the Boer War revelations in establishing health programmes for infants and children is made clear by Pat Thane's assessment in *The Foundations of the Welfare State* (1982). 'The Boer War brought problems concerning children into greater prominence,' she asserted.[3]

While there appears to be a consensus among historians with regard to the general thesis that, to paraphrase S. Josephine Baker, war is good for babies and, more particularly, that the experience of the South African War was an example of this principle, no such agreement exists as to the role played by the resultant legislation to protect infant and child health in the formation of the welfare state. Many scholars, it is true, hold as Titmuss deduced that 'the personal health movement . . . led eventually to the National Health Service in 1948' – a basic element of the welfare state.[4] Bentley B. Gilbert, for example, developed this theme. In his book on *The Evolution of National Insurance in Great*

Britain (revealingly sub-titled *The Origins of the Welfare State*) he too discussed the effect of the Boer War as a stimulus for social reform. According to Gilbert, the 'Boer War seemed to have proved [that] an unhealthy schoolchild was a danger to all society, that it was in society's selfish, non-humanitarian interest to see that the child was [medically] treated.'[5] Therefore, legislation was passed to provide meals for necessitous and medical inspection for all state school children. 'The passage of the Education (Provision of Meals) Act of 1906 and the Education (Administrative Provisions) Act of 1907', he argued, 'marked the beginning of the construction of the welfare state.'[6] This was 'a breach in the wall of absolute personal responsibility for one's own fate'. In short, he reiterated in conclusion, 'the feeding and medical inspection of schoolchildren were the first elements of the welfare state.'[7]

While in no way wishing to diminish the significance of the passage of infant and child health legislation in early twentieth century England, it is difficult to accept Gilbert's hypothesis that this action meant that 'the dyke had been breached and the trickle of 1906 became in the next few years a roaring flood which swept away the few figures who stood against all unconditional State aid'.[8] The thesis of his later book, *British Social Policy 1914–1939*, that the basis for the welfare state had been established prior to the First World War and that the inter-war years were simply a period of consolidation,[9] is a problematic proposition. The results of this study suggest that the infant and child welfare movement inaugurated the establishment of a modern welfare system but did not in any way necessitate or make inevitable the development of a modern welfare state. As Eric J. Evans has explained in his book on the origins of the welfare state (1978), the Edwardian era was

> 'a period of strife, crisis and tension. Many changes in the role of the State are responses to that crisis, not deeply matured plans receiving natural majority assent in course of time. The "national efficiency" crisis, precipitated by the standards of recruits for the Boer War, persuaded the . . . government to enact measures designed to improve the stock by providing greater care for children. . . . Liberal reforms are, thus, pragmatic rather than reflective.'

Pointing out that the early twentieth century welfare legislation was both permissive and piecemeal, Evans cautioned that 'we should beware of grandiloquent claims that the Liberal Party created the Welfare State between 1906 and 1914.' He emphasized that while 'many of the policies . . . were integral to the establishment of the Welfare State, by themselves . . . they did not herald its event'; indeed, 'the emergence of the Welfare State was by no means inevitable by 1914.'[10]

The introduction of legislation to protect infant and child health may, however, have presaged the establishment in 1919 of the Ministry of Health. It is reasonable to claim, as does Frank Honigsbaum in both *The*

Struggle for the Ministry of Health (1970) and *The Division in British Medicine* (1979), that maternal and child services were the field on which the battle was fought for the Ministry of Health, and between the principle of an insurance system versus a municipal service. In these meticulous studies Honigsbaum has elucidated the controversy between two reform strategies. One plan, personified by George Newman (Chief Medical Officer for the Board of Education), urged the unification of all the public health services provided by the local authorities, boards of guardians, and insurance committees. The second option, favoured by Arthur Newsholme (Chief Medical Officer of the Local Goverment Board), called for the extension of municipal services. Within this framework, Honigsbaum has interpreted the LGB-sponsored Maternity and Child Welfare Act of 1918 which formalized the establishment of the modern welfare system that had been developed to address the problem of infant mortality, as a reactionary measure 'to kill all hope of a Ministry of Health'.[11]

A fundamental weakness of the assessment of the significance of the introduction of maternal and child health services in studies of the origin of the welfare state or the Ministry of Health is that they fail to address the questions contemporaries had to answer as to the causes of, and consequently the possible remedies for, infant and child morbidity and mortality. Such studies assume that there were no alternatives to the health services which were instituted. This was not the case at all. To give a concrete example, in the first years of the twentieth century epidemic diarrhoea was perceived to be the single greatest preventable cause of infant mortality and the most amenable to ameliorative action. The question was, what was the most fruitful way to proceed? If, for instance, a vaccine had been developed, the promotion of this specific clearly would have been the route taken.

At the turn of the century, the decreasing birth rate and, among infants only, the slightly increasing mortality rate throughout the past two decades alarmed physicians, politicians, and the public, who saw the annually diminishing net population gains with alarm. These fears grew in the fertile ground primed by the publication of the new exploratory sociological studies of George R. Sims, Andrew Mearns, Charles Booth, William Booth, and B. Seebohm Rowntree which had revealed the vast extent to which abject poverty and concomitant ill-health and disease prevailed.[12] Exacerbated further by the Boer War reverses in the field, the poor physical condition of would-be soldiers found by recruitment officers at home, the propaganda of eugenics, and the philosophy of national efficiency, this anxiety roused the public to clamour for something to be done, politicians to reassess social policy, and physicians to examine the immediate causes of infant mortality and potential preventive measures.[13] Thus while politicians came to recognize the 'poverty which undermines physical ill-health and self-respect . . . as a social peril',[14] and began to reject, as Peter Keating has explained 'the mid-Victorian faith in the ability of voluntary organizations to solve problems', to become aware 'of the failure of some of the most cherished mid-Victorian ideals, the Church, Philanthropy, and Self-Help',[15] physicians began to study seriously the factors influencing the diminishing net population gains. Realizing that there was little they could do to increase the birth rate, the medical profession turned their attention to the specific prevention of infant deaths, particularly those due to epidemic diarrhoea.

This aspect of the problem has been discussed by F.B. Smith. In his book on *The People's Health, 1830-1910* Smith examined contemporary understanding of the relation between modes of feeding and diarrhoea, but unfortunately did not provide a general picture of the common consensus with regard to either feeding practices or epidemic diarrhoea. Smith neglected to investigate closely the bacteriological research conducted at the turn of the century to identify the aetiology of this disease, and he implied that physicians were either ignorant of or hostile to the new science of bacteriology.[16] He assumed, and suggested, that the work of Escherich in Germany, Lesage in France, and Booker in the United States on the bacteriology of diarrhoea in infants was neither known nor discussed in England. And, turning to England itself, the name of Edward Ballard was not once mentioned or cited; his seminal work at the end of the 1880s on the pathology of diarrhoea was completely overlooked in Smith's account.

In some sense Smith's analysis, which implied that turn of the century medical understanding of epidemic diarrhoea ignored or was ignorant of contemporary laboratory research on this problem, is consonant with Thomas McKeown's theory that science really has not made much difference in the provision of effective medical care. McKeown, like Smith, ignored the history of bacteriology at the turn of the century and its relation to and incorporation in the infant and child health care systems which were developed at that time; in other words, how science informed the (successful) action to reduce infant morbidity and mortality. 'The rapid decline of mortality from diseases spread by water and food since the late nineteenth century owed little to medical intervention,' McKeown asserted in *The Role of Medicine* (1979).[17]

'For many years the decline of gastro-enteritis presented a problem (a central one in the interpretation of infant mortality) which arose from uncertainty about the infective nature of the disease. It is now clear that the provision of a safe milk supply was the main reason for the reduction of deaths from gastro-enteritis and contributed substantially to the fall of infant mortality from 1900.

'The other water- and food-borne disease which contributed to the reduction of mortality was non-respiratory tuberculosis. . . . The abdominal cases were caused largely by infected milk, and their decline can be attributed to elimination of tuberculous cattle and to the more general measures taken to protect milk supplies after 1900.'[18]

These claims are packed with a number of assumptions which are not addressed but are adduced as fact. McKeown has alleged, but has cited no evidence to prove, that physicians and medical scientists were 'uncertain' that gastro-enteritis (or epidemic diarrhoea) was an infectious illness long after the mortality it caused began to decline. Like Smith, McKeown does not explain contemporary understanding of the aetiology and transmission of epidemic diarrhoea. He has contended that 'a safe milk supply' was available after 1900, but this too has not been substantiated in any way. The only reference given for the entire discussion of 'water- and food-borne diseases' and 'other diseases due to micro-organisms' was one meagrely researched paper on 'Population, Infant Mortality and Milk' by M.W. Beaver. Beaver's 'main thesis' was that 'the cornerstone of the infant welfare movement was a safe supply of milk and the emphasis was on safe artificial feeding.'[19] There are several objections to this assertion (what does Beaver mean by 'infant welfare movement'; what system was developed and how did milk provision fit in as a component?), the most important being the assumption that there was an improvement in milk purity during the early years of the twentieth century, which has been based on exactly four secondary sources, and not a single primary one.[20] One of these actually adduced evidence to the contrary of Beaver's assertion. In *This Milk Business* (1943) Arthur Enock contended that 'milk should be *clean and safe.*'[21] 'Unfortunately, numerous milk-borne epidemics have occurred from time to time. . . . The British Medical Association, after having overcome strong opposition in the daily Press to their determination to make the facts known, issued an announcement in February, 1938.'[22] This notice was reprinted in full in the text, and the headline, in enormous letters, read, 'IS ALL MILK SAFE TO DRINK?' Citing various facts with regard to milk contamination, such as that 'during the past 24 years there have been over 100 outbreaks of epidemic diseases . . . all borne by unsafe milk', the broadcast ended with the warning 'MILK MUST BE MADE SAFE'.[23] Given such a rebuttal, one is left questioning – even doubting – McKeown and Beaver's basic explicatory principle.

An examination of one more assertion from McKeown will suffice to illustrate an image of his theories as scaffolding with more empty space than structure. In the introduction to *The Role of Medicine* McKeown argued:

'Medical science and services are misdirected, and society's investment in health is not well used, because they rest on an erroneous assumption about the basis of human health. It is assumed that the body can be regarded as a machine whose protection from disease and its effects depends primarily on internal intervention. The approach has led to indifference to the external influences and personal behaviour which are the predominant determinants of health.'[24]

According to many historians who have studied the infant welfare movement in England, however, the systems which were established in the early years of this century were predicated precisely upon the principle of influencing personal behaviour. Jeanne Brand, for example, maintained that 'it was clear to those at the beginning years of the century that civic cleanliness campaigns aided in reducing diarrhoea death tolls, and studies of the disease made in the first decade of the twentieth century emphasized the significance of domestic cleanliness in the feeding of infants.'[25]

Indeed, the early twentieth century insistence upon the 'personal behaviour' of mothers as the 'predominant determinant' of the health of infants and children has led scholars such as Anna Davin, Carol Dyhouse, and Jane Lewis to complain that 'medical science and services' were working to control the conduct of women. Their historical interpretations[26] are diametrically opposed to McKeown's analysis of the failure of medicine, as an institution, to be concerned with nutrition, environment, and personal behaviour which, he has claimed, are the main influences on health. To the contrary, Davin and Dyhouse have perceived the contemporary medical understanding of the problem of infant health to have focused specifically on the determinant of personal (the mother's) behaviour.

In their work, Davin, Dyhouse, and Lewis have analysed the solution of maternalism within the construct of social control. This thesis, or interpretation of history, has been so forcefully emphasized by all three scholars that rather long passages will be quoted to illustrate the encompassing sweep of this exegesis.

'Because of the declining birth rate motherhood had to be made to seem desirable; because high infant mortality was explained by maternal inadequacy the standards of mothers must be improved. A powerful ideology of motherhood emerged in relation to these problems of the early 20th century, though it was firmly rooted of course in nineteenth-century assumptions about women, domesticity and individualism. Motherhood was to be given new dignity: it was the duty and destiny of women to be the 'mothers of the race', but also their great reward. But just as it was the individual mother's duty and reward to rear healthy members of an imperial race, so it was her individual ignorance and neglect which must account for infant deaths or sick children. Thus moral blackmail, exploiting the real difficulties and insecurities of many mothers, underpinned their new lofty status. Nor did the elevation mean an end to subordination. To be good mothers they now needed instruction . . . in the skills of what came to be known as mothercraft, as they were being defined by the medical profession. Doctors, district nurses, health visitors, were all asserting their superior knowledge and authority, establishing moral sanctions on grounds of health and the national interest, and denigrating traditional methods of child care – in particular care by anyone except the mother: neighbours, grandmothers, and older children looking after babies were automatically assumed to be dirty, incompetent and irresponsible. The authority of state over individual, of professional over amateur, of science over tradition, of male over female, of ruling class over working class, were all involved in the redefining of motherhood in this period.'[27]

Dyhouse has similarly argued that 'explanations of high infant mortality rate in terms of married women's work or the ignorance of mothers [were] knitted into the fabric of contemporary assumptions about social class and the nature of family life.' She adduced two reasons for the 'popular opposition to married women's work'. One was 'the middle-class ideal of family organization – wife securely ensconced in the home by a husband working for a family wage'. The second was 'the anxieties of male Trade Unionists' who feared women as 'cheap competition'. Dyhouse claimed further that the middle-class 'vision of social order' was so firmly entrenched that 'even when faced with the near-impossibility of marshalling any convincing evidence in support of the theory that the employment of mothers meant a significant loss of infant life, many authorities refused to abandon their conviction that this *must* be the case.'[28]

Jane Lewis neatly formulated the goal of maternalism in her study of *The Politics of Motherhood* (1980): 'The ideology of motherhood persuaded married women that their role in the home was of national importance and that motherhood was their primary duty.'[29] She contended that 'neither changes in medical practice nor in social policy' based on this ideology, which were 'important in determining the shape of maternal and child welfare services, can be assumed to have been benevolent'.[30] Lewis, like Davin and Dyhouse, perceived the remedy of maternalism as a restrictive social control solution, and she too noted its nineteenth century origins.

> 'The emphasis put on the question of maternal efficiency by those involved in child and maternal welfare work cannot be adequately explained by . . . their belief that domestic dirt caused excessive infant mortality. . . . The emphasis on maternal responsibility gained its legitimacy from an ideology of motherhood rooted in the nineteenth-century doctrine of spheres, which made women's proper place the home. Now that the welfare of the next generation was recognized to depend on the mother, the rhetoric of motherhood at once insisted on and elevated her maternal duties and status.'[31]

Given the unanimity of scholarly opinion on this issue one hardly

227

dares to question its veracity. Yet, doubt arises: is the social control model particularly illuminating? How does it fit in with contemporary medical understanding of the causes of infant mortality? Lewis, Davin, and Dyhouse (like Smith and McKeown) have not addressed the relevant bacteriological research which impinged upon these issues. Furthermore, according to these historians, maternalism was the only solution which was adopted; at any rate it is the only one they have discussed. There were, however, other attempts, based on alternative ideologies, to reduce infant mortality. It is impossible to understand the choice to institute one or another system if we ignore precisely that which was of greatest importance to turn of the century medical care providers: effectiveness in reducing the number of infant deaths. Reading the analyses of Davin, Dyhouse, and Lewis one begins to doubt the sincerity of official concern with the problem of infant mortality: everyone appears to have been more concerned with controlling women than saving babies.

One of Lewis's main contentions was that the medical profession blithely – and resolutely – disregarded the fact that indigence was a primary cause of infant mortality. She claimed physicians paid attention to infant mortality *rates* but neglected the conditions which these figures represented.

'Having defined the problem of infant . . . welfare in terms of . . . rates, policies were increasingly aimed at improving the rates as such, rather than solving the problems which they attempted to quantify. Because of this, the attempt to prevent the clinical causes of . . . infant . . . deaths was made without due attention to the underlying social, environmental and biological causes.'[32]

More specifically, Lewis asserted, 'medical officers of health and LGB officials adopted an untenable position when . . . they argued that . . . neither poverty nor environmental factors played an important part in causing infant mortality.' Elaborating on this allegation she said that

'medical officers of health, physicians and Local Government Board officials skirted, and even denied, the influence of factors such as low incomes, poor housing conditions and sanitation, and contaminated milk. Those involved in the child and maternal welfare movement held women responsible for all infant deaths that were due to preventable causes. In their view, women's chief duty was to their infants and anything that detracted from this, such as work outside the home, was to be discouraged.'[33]

This sweeping condemnation is astonishing. Contemporaries understood the risk of 'contaminated milk' to infants very well. And while it is true that physicians never radically addressed the problem of poverty, we can only accuse them of being as conservative as most, and a bit less than some of their peers. There is abundant evidence that they recognized in a way Charity Organisation Society officials, for instance, did not that indigence was a critical and fundamental factor in the health of infants and children. Lewis cited Arthur Newsholme as a specific example of this obdurate single-mindedness.[34] Yet even a cursory examination of his numerous articles on public health problems and special reports on infant mortality reveals his extremely sensitive appreciation of the numerous factors militating against infant life among the poor. In chapter 13 of his 1913 *Report*, appropriately entitled 'Poverty and Infant Mortality', Newsholme stated this recognition clearly and unequivocally.

> 'Whatever other influences are at work, and they are many and important, one thing is certain: infant mortality is high among the poor, and low among the well-to-do. It is highest among the most densely populated and poorest wards in any given town, and in the poorest and most crowded parts of a given ward.'[35]

Section 11 ('Circumstances of Environment Favouring Excessive Infant Mortality') of his 1916 *Report* directly contradicted Lewis's indictment.

> 'Maternal ignorance is sometimes regarded as a chief factor in the causation of excessive child mortality. It is a comfortable doctrine for the well-to-do person to adopt; and it goes far to relieve his conscience in the contemplation of excessive suffering and mortality among the poor.'[36]

Towards the end of his life he repeated what he had written in 1914; 'Poverty, and what it implies, is commonly a more potent influence than ignorance.'[37]

Nor did Newsholme confine his observations to general remarks about the correspondence between poverty and infant mortality; his reports also addressed the issues of 'poor housing conditions and sanitation, and contaminated milk'. One example will suffice to illustrate his concern with these factors as well. Speaking of 'sanitary conditions' he explained:

> 'Although the facts as to the retention of the conservancy system, as to the existence of unsatisfactory water-closets and as to the inadequate removal of domestic and stable refuse cannot be considered alone, they stand first in importance in their association with excessive infant mortality. The association is too regular to allow of doubt.'[38]

Clearly Newsholme, whom Lewis specifically cited, does not fit her description of contemporary medical officers of health and LGB officials – and he was both. The rest of the profession conformed more closely to his example than to her views. When we judge them, it is important to remember that physicians were trained to be medical care providers; if they concentrated on the clinical aspects of health problems they were but addressing simply and precisely that which they knew how to do best.

The last hypothesis proposed by Davin, Dyhouse, and Lewis which is questionable is their contention that, as Davin put it, 'The focus on mothers provided an easy way out. It was cheaper to blame them and to organize a few classes than to expand social and medical services.'[39] Lewis also adduced finance as a reason for the introduction of maternal instruction, claiming that 'such programmes were attractive because they were cheap and could be implemented quickly'.[40] This is not true; the solution of maternalism was not just a cheap and easy remedy. It is clear that maternal education was not a solution which required or even called for fundamental social change, but it was something more than 'a few classes'. The systems which were established provided a number of 'social and medical services' in addition to instruction.

Health visiting was a primary component of the infant welfare system developed during the early years of this century, and it is odd that while there is a substantial literature on the history of other medical care and social service providers, relatively little has been written about the evolution of this profession in the twentieth century. The antecedents of modern health visiting in eleemosynary activity have been well documented by F.K. Prochaska in his extremely interesting study of *Women and Philanthropy in Nineteenth-Century England*. Prochaska has elucidated how the visiting societies, whose 'aim was nothing less than to prevent distress and to promote social harmony . . . had very old traditions in England'. He explained that what these societies (which gained 'enormous public support in the nineteenth century') 'added to customary practice was system'.

> 'Geared to cities and towns, where suffering was most concentrated, they divided communities into districts, more often than not based on parish boundaries. Dividing the districts into streets, and the streets into households, they assigned visitors to each district. . . . Armed with the paraphernalia of their calling – Bibles, tracts, blankets, food and coal tickets, and love – these foot-soldiers of the charitable army went from door to door to combat the evils of poverty, disease, and religion. . . . In its thoroughness it was a system that must have warmed the heart of Jeremy Bentham.'[41]

According to Prochaska 'most of the early female visiting societies specialized in lying-in and sick visiting. But several of them branched out into more general visiting in the early nineteenth century.'[42] During the period of our study, a century later, the reverse trend is visible. Maternal and infant welfare work increasingly became the focus of concentration for visitors. As Prochaska's study ended with the close of the nineteenth century, this development was not of interest to him and the question remains as to how and why this occurred. Whereas during the nineteenth century 'there were as many types of visiting society as there were denominations and distresses',[43] beginning in the early years of this century only one variety continued to flourish – health visiting. It was this form which was professionalized and incorporated into the provision of municipal services.

There was a veritable boom in the health visiting business during the First World War when, as Richard Titmuss put it, 'public concern about the standard of fitness of men of military age move[d] out . . . to embrace concern about the health and well-being of the whole population and, in particular, of children – the next generation of recruits.'[44] Like the Boer War, the First World War also turned out to be beneficial for babies. In his article on 'The Impact of the First World War on Civilian Health in Britain', J.M. Winter has precisely analysed to what degree it was advantageous for infants in terms of decreased mortality rates. Explaining why and by what means this 'wartime decline' occurred, Winter noted that 'one reason was an improvement in standards of care of pregnant women and infants' both just before and during the war. In an attempt to effect this change, the LGB offered to pay half the cost of a number of services including the establishment of ante-natal, infant, and child-care clinics, and the salaries for home visitors for expectant mothers and families with young children.[45] Thus, unlike the Boer War experience, when infants were of public interest only after the conflict had ended, during the war years 1914–18 infant welfare was a significant issue. Documenting the action taken by health officials and the propaganda campaigns launched by various groups and individuals, Winter concluded that although 'we ought not exaggerate . . . the immediate effectiveness of these measures', we should recognize that 'what had changed during the war were attitudes to infant welfare.'[46] As his paper did not examine the history of interest in infant welfare, one must ask if this assertion is correct. Attitudes did not change during the First World War, but the emphasis on infant health, so visible during those years, was the result of a recrudescence of an already extant concern.

There are a number of illuminating works which, although not directly addressing the issues discussed here, should not be ignored by anyone interested in this area of concern. One general category can be classified as literature focusing on attitudes towards children. Ivy Pinchbeck and Margaret Hewitt's classic *Children in English Society* (especially the second volume) is of primary importance to any work in this field.[47] Pinchbeck and Hewitt have admirably described and charted changing attitudes towards children and how this has been reflected in the impetus for protective legislation and the development of social services. Unfortunately they did not deal very extensively with the narrower but corresponding evolution of medical care systems to preserve infant and child health. In contrast to the broad sweep of

231

Pinchbeck and Hewitt's study, George K. Behlmer[48] concentrated on the interpretation of the significance of the establishment and work of one particular organization devoted to safeguarding children, the National Society for the Prevention of Cruelty to Children. In his highly informative dissertation Behlmer has related contemporary perceptions of children and their role and function in English society to the development of the child protection movement in the late Victorian period.

The question of the availability of contraception (which may be related to attitudes towards children and the practical realities of infant care) is the focus of another general category of literature. In *Silent Sisterhood*, Patricia Branca[49] has correlated changing attitudes towards reproduction and child care, and has postulated a direct relationship between the proliferation of child-rearing advice literature at precisely the same time as the size of middle-class families in late Victorian England decreased. Equally interesting, but less clearly related to this study are the two books by J.A. Banks and J.A. and Olive Banks respectively. In *Prosperity and Parenthood*[50] and *Feminism and Family Planning* the Bankses studied the interaction between the concomitant developments of a rising standard of living (with simultaneous increased cost of domestic help), a growing feminist movement, and the conscious limitation of families. In their studies of both the economic and socio-political (they defined 'feminism' as 'the deliberate attempt to achieve equality between the sexes in the political, economic and domestic spheres')[51] factors or motivations to control family size, they, like Branca, focused on the English Victorian middle class.

Gareth Stedman Jones's *Outcast London*, a sensitive analysis of contemporary perceptions of and anxieties about the poor in London during the second half of the nineteenth century, also anticipates the period I discuss (excepting his last two chapters). Nevertheless, it is an illuminating history of attitudes towards the concept and reality of poverty which were still highly influential during the early years of this century. Similarly, Jones's discussion of middle-class knowledge and understanding of poverty and the poor, and the solutions they devised to these complex problems (such as the establishment of university settlement houses and the formation of the Charity Organisation Society) is very helpful in understanding the background to various controversies (indigence versus ignorance, for example) which plagued the infant welfare movement.[52]

Finally, every social historian of the Edwardian period is indebted to Robert Roberts, Katharine Chorley, Thea Thompson, and Paul Thompson for their evocative descriptions of the normal everyday lives of ordinary people. In his book Paul Thompson used oral histories as documentary evidence, skilfully weaving quotations from his interviewed sources into his general historical discussion. In addition to aiding his analysis these passages helped to depict the noise, smells, colours, and rhythms of the past – the feel or sense of the Edwardian era.[53] Thea Thompson's *Edwardian Childhoods* complements P. Thompson's study. This collection of nine accounts of childhood were selected from 560 interviews with people born before 1906. 'Chosen rather to illuminate the past of Edwardian families than to speak for classes or categories', these recollections provide a wealth of information about the experiences, remembered perceptions, thoughts, and feelings of children born during the rise of the infant welfare movement.[54] They, like Katharine Chorley's autobiographical *Manchester Made Them*[55] and Robert Roberts's equally personal *The Classic Slum*[56] are a reminder that the problems addressed in this study were the troubles of real people, and the solutions and remedies attempted and implemented affected the lives of human beings who are almost with us today.

Notes

Chapter I

1 Arthur Newsholme, *The Elements of Vital Statistics*, 3rd edn, London, Swan Sonnenschein, 1899, p.73.
2 Arthur Newsholme, *The Elements of Vital Statistics*, 4th edn, London, George Allen & Unwin, 1923, p.115.
3 See, for example, the discussion of the importance of the falling birth rate in the *BMJ*, 2 March 1901, p.55.
4 G.B., P.P., *39th Annual Report of the Registrar-General* (for 1876), C. 2075, London, HMSO, 1878; G.B., P.P., *60th Annual Report of the Registrar-General* (for 1897), C. 9016, London, HMSO, 1899.
5 Arthur Newsholme, *Vital Statistics*, 4th edn., 1923, p.115.
6 Arthur Newsholme, 'Infantile Mortality. A Statistical Study from the Public Health Standpoint', *The Practitioner*, October 1905, pp.489–91.
7 George Newman, *Infant Mortality*, London, Methuen, 1906, p.13.
8 George Frederick McCleary, *Infantile Mortality and Infant Milk Depots*, London, P.S. King, 1905, p.6.
9 *BMJ*, 11 May 1901, p.1159.
10 See, for example: Herbert Spencer, *The Principles of Sociology*, 3rd edn, London, Williams & Norgate, 1885; idem, *A Rejoinder to Professor Weismann* [i.e. to the 'All Sufficiency of Natural Selection'], London, Williams & Norgate, 1893; idem, *Weismannism Once More* [A Reply to Dr Weismann's Romanes Lecture of 2 May 1894], London, Williams & Norgate, 1894.
11 August Weismann, *Studies in the Theory of Descent* (with a preface by Charles Darwin), London, Sampson Low & Co., 1880–82.
12 For a more detailed discussion see, *inter alia*, C.P. Blacker, *Eugenics: Galton and After*, London, Duckworth, 1952; Donald MacKenzie, 'Eugenics in Britain', *Social Studies of Science*, vol.6, 1976, pp.499–532; G.R. Searle, *Eugenics and Politics in Britain: 1900–1914* (especially Chapter I), Leiden, Nordhoof International Publishing, 1976; Bernard Semmel, *Imperialism and Social Reform* (especially Chapter 2), London, George Allen & Unwin, 1960.
13 Francis Galton, 'Eugenics: Its Definition, Scope, and Aims', *Nature*, vol.70, 1904, p.82.
14 Letter from Galton to Darwin, reproduced in full in C.P. Blacker, *Eugenics, Galton and After*, p.83.
15 Francis Galton, *Essays in Eugenics*, London, Eugenics Society, 1909; idem, *Hereditary Genius* (2nd edn), London, Macmillan, 1892.
16 Karl Pearson, 'Socialism and Natural Selection' in *The Chances of Death and Other Studies in Evolution*, vol.I, London, Edward Arnold, 1897; idem, *Darwinism, Medical Progress and Eugenics*, The Cavendish Lecture, 1912,

London, Eugenics Laboratory Lecture Series no.9, 1912; idem, 'Socialism and Sex' in *The Ethic of Freethought* (2nd edn), London, Adam & Charles Black, 1901; idem, *Eugenics and Public Health*, London, Questions of the Day Series no.6, University of London, 1910; idem, *The Groundwork of Eugenics*, London, Eugenics Laboratory Lecture Series no.2, 1909; idem, *Nature and Nurture: The Problem of the Future*, London, Eugenics Laboratory Lecture Series, no.6, 1910; idem, *The Problem of Practical Eugenics*, London, Eugenics Laboratory Lecture Series no.5, 1909.

17 Karl Pearson, 'Socialism and Sex' in *The Ethic of Freethought*, p.424.

18 Ibid., p.417.

19 G.R. Searle, *Eugenics and Politics in Britain*, p.20.

20 Sir Charles Wentworth Dilke, *The Present Position of European Politics*, London, Chapman & Hall, 1887, p.306. See also: idem, *Army Reform*, London, Service & Paton, 1898; idem, *The British Army*, London, Chapman & Hall, 1888; idem, *The British Empire*, London, Chatto & Windus, 1899.

21 R.C.K. Ensor, *England, 1870–1914*, Oxford, The Clarendon Press, 1936; 1963 edn, pp.197–98.

22 G.R. Searle, *The Quest for National Efficiency*, Oxford, Blackwell, 1971, p.8.

23 T.H. Huxley, 'The Struggle for Existence: A Programme', *The Nineteenth Century*, vol.23, no.132, February, 1888, pp.169–80.

24 See, for example: D.H. Aldcroft (edn.), *The Development of British Industry and Foreign Competition, 1875–1914*, London, George Allen & Unwin, 1968; Eric John Hobsbawm, *Industry and Empire, An Economic History of Britain Since 1750*, London, Weidenfeld & Nicolson, 1968; John Ecclesfield Tyler, *The Struggle for Imperial Unity, 1868–1895*, London, Longman, 1938; Ernest Edwin Williams, '*Made in Germany*', London, W. Heinemann, 1896.

25 G.R. Searle, *The Quest for Efficiency*, p.12.

26 Bernard Semmel, *Imperialism and Social Reform*, p.53.

27 For a more detailed discussion see, *inter alia*, Norman and Jeanne MacKenzie, *The First Fabians*, London, Quartet Books, 1979, especially pp.276–78, 285–92, and Chapter 20, 'Wire pullers', pp.296–313; H.C.G. Matthew, *The Liberal Imperialists*; G.R. Searle, *The Quest for National Efficiency*; Bernard Semmel, *Imperialism and Social Reform*, especially Chapter 3, 'A Party of National Efficiency: The Liberal-Imperialists and the Fabians'; George Bernard Shaw (edn.), *Fabianism and the Empire*, London, G. Richards, 1900.

28 Sidney Webb, *The Difficulties of Individualism*, Fabian Tract no.69, London, The Fabian Society, 1896, p.16.

29 Ibid., p.19.

30 Ibid., p.17.

31 'National Health and Military Service', *BMJ*, 25 July 1903, p.208.

32 Aimée Watt Smyth, *Physical Deterioration, Its Causes and the Cure*, London, John Murray, 1904, preface, p.vii.

33 Ibid., p.3.

34 Arthur Newsholme, 'Alleged Physical Degeneration in Towns', *Public Health*, vol.17, 1905, p.292.

35 Arnold White, 'Efficiency and Empire', *The Weekly Sun*, 28 July 1900, p.5.

36 Arnold White, *Efficiency and Empire*, London, Methuen, 1901, pp.xiii, 100, 109.
37 Ibid., pp.102–3.
38 Ibid., pp.103, 106–7.
39 Karl Pearson, *National Life from the Standpoint of Science*, London, Adam & Charles Black, 1901, pp.26–8.
40 See Francis Galton's Huxley Lecture, 'The Possible Improvements of the Human Breed under the Existing Conditions of Law and Sentiment', given by invitation at the Anthropological Institute in October 1901.
41 Sidney Webb, 'Lord Rosebery's Escape from Houndsditch', *The Nineteenth Century*, September 1901, pp.375–77.
42 B. Seebohm Rowntree, *Poverty: A Study of Town Life*, London, Macmillan, 1901, p.viii.
43 Ibid., p.133.
44 Ibid., p.26.
45 Ibid., p.117.
46 Ibid., pp.133–34.
47 Ibid., pp.216–18.
48 Ibid., p.221.
49 See, for example, Arthur Newsholme's review, 'Poverty in Town Life' in *The Practitioner*, vol.16, N.S., July–December 1902. More of a précis of the book than an analytical review, it runs a full thirteen pages (pp.682–94). See also the review by W.T. Stead in *The Review of Reviews*, vol.24, December 1901, pp.642–45.
50 'Miles', 'Where to Get Men', *The Contemporary Review*, vol.81, January 1902, pp.78–81.
51 Ibid., pp.81–6.
52 Frederick Maurice, 'National Health: A Soldier's Study', *The Contemporary Review*, vol.83, January 1903, p.41.
53 Ibid., p.44.
54 Ibid., p.55.
55 G.B., P.P., *Report of the Royal Commission on Physical Training Scotland*, vol.I: Report and Appendix, Cd 1507, London, HMSO, 1903, p.25.
56 G.B., P.P., *Report of the Inter-Departmental Committee on Physical Deterioration*, vol.I, Appendix I, 1904, Cd 2175, XXXII, p.95. The medical press reported this issue extensively. The memorandum was issued as a Parliamentary Paper by the War Office in July, and press coverage consequently increased during that month. Note, for example, 'Medical Notes in Parliament: The Physique of the People', *BMJ*, 11 July 1903, pp.99–100; the abstract of the memo: *BMJ*, 25 July 1903, pp.202–03; and the editorial 'National Health and Military Service', *BMJ*, 25 July 1903, pp.207–08.
57 Ibid., p.95.
58 Ibid., pp.98–9. Note also coverage in *BMJ*, 8 August 1903, p.345, 24 October 1903, p.1101 and 21 November 1903, pp.1339–340.
59 Ibid., pp.92–3.
60 Sidney Webb, *The Decline in the Birth-Rate*, Fabian Tract no.131, London, The Fabian Society, 1907.
61 'Physical Deterioration', *BMJ*, 6 February 1904, pp.319–20.
62 *BMJ*, July 1904, p.140.

Chapter II

1 *BMJ*, July 1904, p.140.
2 Reginald Dudfield, 'The Milk Supply of the Metropolis', *Public Health*, March 1904, p.353.
3 Arthur Newsholme, 'Infantile Mortality', *The Practitioner*, October 1905, p.489.
4 Ibid., p.494.
5 *BMJ*, 12 January 1901, p.127.
6 George Newman, *Infant Mortality: A Social Problem*, London, Methuen, 1906, pp.50–1.
7 G.B., P.P., *Report of the Inter-Departmental Committee on Physical Deterioration*, vol.I, 1904, Cd 2175, Appendix Va, Table A, p.131.
8 Ibid., p.130.
9 Newman, *Infant Mortality*, p.47.
10 John William Ballantyne, *Ante-Natal Pathology and Hygiene*, Edinburgh, W. Green & Sons, 1902. See also: idem, 'The Problem of the Premature Infant', *BMJ*, 17 May 1902, pp.1196–200; idem, *Expectant Motherhood*, London, Cassell, 1914.
11 D. Noel Paton, 'The Influence of Diet in Pregnancy on the Weight of the Offspring', *Lancet*, 4 July 1903, pp.21–2.
12 George Frederick McCleary, 'The Influence of Antenatal Conditions on Infantile Mortality', *BMJ*, 13 August 1904, p.321.
13 Letter from Thomas Dutton to the *Lancet*, 6 July 1901, p.49. See also, *inter alia*, the following letters to the *Lancet* editors: 6 July 1901, p.50; 13 July 1901, pp.102–03; and 20 July 1901, pp.169–70.
14 W. Cecil Bosanquet, 'Summer Diarrhoea of Infants', *Practitioner*, vol.69, N.S.16, p.155. See also, for example, H.T. Hicks, 'On the Treatment of the Summer Diarrhoea and Vomiting in Infants', *Lancet*, 15 August 1903, pp.455–56; and G.A. Sutherland, 'Infantile Diarrhoea', *Practitioner*, October 1915, pp.501–9.
15 W.B. Ransom, 'Should Milk Be Boiled?' *BMJ*, 22 February 1902, p.440.
16 William J. Howarth, 'The Influence of Feeding on the Mortality of Infants', *Lancet*, 22 July 1905, p.212.
17 Précis of annual *Report* of Dr J.J. Buchan, MOH St Helens, *Lancet*, 8 July 1905, p.106.
18 'Special Correspondence: Liverpool', *BMJ*, 27 August 1904, p.468.
19 'Classification of "Diarrhoea" Deaths', *Public Health*, May, 1899. p.545.
20 'The Classification of Deaths from Diarrhoea', *BMJ*, 3 February 1900, p.269.
21 'The Classification of Diarrhoea Deaths', *BMJ*, 21 April 1900, p.977. See also, *inter alia*, Bosanquet, 'Summer Diarrhoea of Infants', pp.139–40; and, in the same volume, Newsholme, 'The Public Health Aspects of Summer Diarrhoea', pp.162–65.
22 Newsholme, 'Public Health Aspects of Summer Diarrhoea', *The Practitioner*, August 1902, p.167.
23 Newman, *Infant Mortality*, p.174.
24 Ransom, 'Should Milk Be Boiled?', p.440.
25 E.W. Hope, 'Observations on Autumnal Diarrhoea in Cities', *Public Health*, July 1899, pp.661–62.

26 H. Meredith Richards, 'The Factors Which Determine the Local Incidence of Fatal Infantile Diarrhoea', *Journal of Hygiene*, vol.3, 1903, pp.330–31.

27 Arthur Newsholme, 'Remarks on the Causation of Epidemic Diarrhoea', *Transactions of the Epidemiological Society, London*, N.S.22, 1902–3, p.37.

28 'Report of the Medical Officer of Health of Birmingham', *Lancet*, 11 February 1905, pp.380–81.

29 William J. Howarth, 'The Influence of Feeding on the Mortality of Infants', *Lancet*, 22 July 1905, p.212.

30 Richards, 'The Factors Which Determine the Local Incidence of Fatal Infantile Diarrhoea', p.329.

31 Newsholme, 'Remarks on the Causation of Epidemic Diarrhoea', pp.37–8.

32 Howarth, 'The Influence of Feeding', pp.212–13.

33 'The Prevention of Infantile Mortality', *BMJ*, 14 December 1907, p.1727.

34 G.B., Ministry of Health, *42nd Annual Report of the Local Government Board, 1912–1913*. Supplement . . . Containing a Second Report on Infant and Child Mortality, by the Medical Officer of the Board (Arthur Newsholme), London, HMSO, 1913, pp.82–8.

35 G.B., Ministry of Health, *Reports to the Local Government Board on Public Health and Medical Subjects*, N.S. no.56, 'Dr F.J.H. Coutts's Report to the Local Government Board on an Inquiry as to Condensed Milks; with Special Reference to their Use as Infants' Foods', Food Reports, no.15, London, HMSO, 1911, pp.31–2.

36 G.B., Ministry of Health, *Reports to the Local Government Board on Public Health and Medical Subjects*, N.S. no.80, I. 'On the Use of Proprietary Foods for Infant Feeding', by Dr F.J.H. Coutts; II. 'On the Analysis and Composition of some Proprietary Foods for Infants', by Mr Julian L. Baker, Food Reports, no.20, London, HMSO, 1914, p.35.

37 Herbert Jones, 'Back-to-Back Houses', *Public Health*, vol.5, 1892–93, p.347.

38 Ibid., p.348.

39 Arnold Evans, 'Back-to-Back Houses', *Transactions of the Epidemiological Society, London*, vol.15, 1896, p.98.

40 Ibid., pp.98–9.

41 John F.J. Sykes, 'The Influence of the Dwelling Upon Health', *BMJ*, 2 March 1901, p.508.

42 Ibid., p.508.

43 *Report on the Health of Birmingham*, 1904, pp.38–9.

44 Howarth, 'The Influence of Feeding', p.212.

45 G.B., Ministry of Health, *Report on Back-to-Back Houses*, by Dr L.W. Darra Mair, Cd 5314, London, HMSO, 1910, pp.20–1.

46 George Reid, 'Infant Mortality and the Employment of Married Women in Factories', *BMJ*, 17 August 1901, pp.411–12.

47 George Reid, 'Infantile Mortality and the Employment of Married Women in Factory Labour Before and After Confinement', *Lancet*, 18 August 1906, pp.423–24.

48 'Infantile Mortality and the Employment of Married Women in Factories', *Lancet*, 22 September 1906, p.818.

49 G.B., Ministry of Health, *17th Annual Report of the Local Government Board*, 1887–88, Supplement in Continuation of the Report of the Medical

Officer for 1887, 'Diarrhoea and Diphtheria', Cd 5638, London, HMSO, 1889, pp.3, 7, 5.
50 Ibid., pp.6, 8–9.
51 Newsholme, 'Public Health Aspects', pp.166–67.
52 Ibid., p.174; idem, *A Contribution to the Study of Epidemic Diarrhoea*, London, Rebman, 1900, p.28.
53 Newsholme, 'Public Health Aspects', p.173.
54 Newsholme, 'Remarks on the Causation', p.42.
55 Ibid., pp.39–40.
56 Arthur Newsholme, 'Domestic Infection in Relation to Epidemic Diarrhoea', *Journal of Hygiene*, vol.6, 1906, pp.143, 145, 146.
57 This article was published simultaneously in two journals: Sheridan Delépine, 'The Bearing of Outbreaks of Food Poisoning upon the Etiology of Epidemic Diarrhoea', *Journal of Hygiene*, 1903, pp.68–94. Sheridan Delépine, 'The Bearing of Outbreaks of Food Poisoning upon the Etiology of Epidemic Diarrhoea', *Transactions of the Epidemiological Society, London*, N.S. 22, 1902–3, pp.11–33. As the *Journal of Hygiene* is easier to obtain than the *Transactions*, pagination will be given for this edition. See pp.73–4. See also the report of this paper in the *BMJ*, 21 February 1903, pp.456–59, and in the *Lancet*, 14 February 1903, pp.461–62.
58 J. Spottiswoode Cameron, 'Diarrhoea in Some Lancashire and Yorkshire Towns in 1892', *Public Health*, vol.6, October 1893–September 1894, p.153.
59 E.W. Hope, 'Summer Diarrhoea', *Public Health*, March 1899, p.436.
60 E.W. Hope, 'Observations of Autumnal Diarrhoea in Cities', *Public Health*, July 1899, p.664.
61 F.J. Waldo, 'The Milroy Lectures on Summer Diarrhoea', Lecture III, *Lancet*, 26 May 1900, p.1494.
62 Delépine, 'The Bearing of Outbreaks of Food Poisoning', p.71.
63 M.H. Gordon, 'The Bacteriology of Epidemic Diarrhoea and Its Differential Diagnosis from Other Similar Diseases', *The Practitioner*, August 1902, pp.181–82.
64 Theodor Escherich, 'Die Darmbakterien des Neugeborenen und Säuglings', *Fortschritte der Medicin*, vol.3, no.16, August 1885, p.516.
65 Ibid., vol.3, no.17, September 1885, p.549.
66 Idem, *Die Darmbakterien des Säuglings*, Stuttgart, Ferdinand Enke, 1886, p.176.
67 William D. Booker, 'A Study of Some of the Bacteria Found in the Faeces of Infants Affected with Summer Diarrhoea', *Transactions of the American Pediatric Society*, vol.1, 1889, p.199.
68 Idem, 'A Study of Some of the Bacteria found in the Dejecta of Infants Afflicted with Summer Diarrhoea', *Transactions* of the International Medical Congress, 9th Session, vol.III, Washington DC, 1887, p.616.
69 Idem, 'A Bacteriological and Anatomical Study of the Summer Diarrhoeas of Infants', *Johns Hopkins Hospital Reports*, vol.6, 1897, p.251.
70 Shiga, 'Über den Erreger der Dysenterie in Japan', *Centralblatt für Bakteriologie, Parasitenkunde, und Infektionskrankheiten*, vol.24, 1898–99, pp.599–600, 817–28, 870–74, 913–18; idem, 'Studien über die epidemische Dysenterie in Japan, unter besonderer Berücksichtigung des Bacillus dysenteriae', *Deutsche Medicinische Wochenschrift*, vol.27, 1901,

pp.741–43, 765–68, 783–86. See also Simon Flexner and Lewellys F. Barker, 'Report upon an Expedition Sent by the Johns Hopkins University to Investigate the Prevalent Diseases in the Philippines', *Bulletin of the Johns Hopkins Hospital*, vol.11, no.107, February 1900, pp.37–41; and Kruse, 'Weitere Untersuchungen über die Ruhr und die Ruhrbazillen', *Deutsche Medicinische Wochenschrift*, vol.27, 1901, pp.370–72.

71 Charles W. Duval and Victor H. Bassett, 'The Etiology of Summer Diarrhoea in Infants', *Studies from the Rockefeller Institute for Medical Research*, vol.2, 1904, p.24.

72 Simon Flexner and L. Emmett Holt, eds, 'Bacteriological and Clinical Studies of the Diarrhoeal Diseases of Infancy with Reference to the Bacillus Dysenteriae (Shiga)', *Studies from the Rockefeller Institute for Medical Research*, vol.2, 1904, pp.1–202. See also the article on the Rockefeller Studies in the *BMJ*: 'Infantile Diarrhoea', *BMJ*, 17 December 1904, pp.1653–654.

73 H. de R. Morgan, 'Upon the Bacteriology of the Summer Diarrhoea of Infants', *BMJ*, 21 April 1906, pp.908–9, 911.

74 Idem, 'Upon the Bacteriology of the Summer Diarrhoea of Infants', (second communication), *BMJ*, 6 July 1907, p.19.

75 Idem and J.C.G. Ledingham, 'The Bacteriology of Summer Diarrhoea', *Proceedings of the Royal Society of Medicine*, vol.2, no.2, 1909, p.145.

76 This quote is taken from a précis by Nuttall of his monograph and printed in the *BMJ*. George H.F. Nuttall, 'The Part Played by Insects, Arachnids, and Myriapods in the Propagation of Infective Diseases of Man and Animals', *BMJ*, 9 September 1899, p.642. In his monograph published at Johns Hopkins, where he had been an Associate in Hygiene, this sentiment is expressed in different words. See idem, 'On the Role of Insects, Arachnids, and Myriapods, as Carriers in the Spread of Bacterial and Parasitic Diseases of Man and Animals. A Critical and Historical Study', *Johns Hopkins Hospital Reports*, vol.8, 1899, pp.1–125.

77 J.T.C. Nash, 'The Etiology of Summer Diarrhoea', *Lancet*, 31 January 1903, p.330.

78 *Transactions of the Epidemiological Society, London*, N.S. 22, 1902–3, pp.44–5.

79 Newsholme, 'Remarks on the Causation of Epidemic Diarrhoea', p.40.

80 Newsholme, 'Domestic Infection in Relation to Epidemic Diarrhoea', p.142–43, 145.

81 J.E. Sandilands, 'Epidemic Diarrhoea and the Bacterial Content of Food', *Journal of Hygiene*, vol.6, 1906, pp.78–9. See also the lead article 'Infant Feeding and Epidemic Diarrhoea' in the *Lancet*, 24 February 1904, p.533, and Dr Sandilands's reply, 'Infant Feeding and Epidemic Diarrhoea', *Lancet*, 10 March 1904, p.707.

82 Sandilands, 'Epidemic Diarrhoea', pp.83, 89.

83 William H. Hamer, 'Nuisance from Flies', *Report* of the Public Health Committee of the London County Council, nos 1138 and 1202, London, 1908.

84 G.B., Ministry of Health, *Reports to the Local Government Board on Public Health and Medical Subjects*, N.S. no.5, 'Report on the Breeding of the Common House Fly during the Winter Months' by Mr Jepson, London, HMSO, 1909; G.B., Ministry of Health, *Reports to the Local Government*

Board on Public Health and Medical Subjects, N.S. no.16, 'Preliminary Note on Examinations of Flies for the Presence of Bacillus coli' by Dr Graham Smith, London, HMSO, 1909; G.B., Ministry of Health, Reports to the Local Government Board on Public Health and Medical Subjects, N.S. no.16, 'Abstracts of Literature and Bibliography' by Professor Nuttall and Mr Jepson, London, HMSO, 1909.

85 J.T.C. Nash, 'House Flies as Carriers of Disease', Journal of Hygiene, vol.IX, no.2, September 1909, p.150.

86 J.E. Sandilands, 'The Communication of Diarrhoea from the Sick to the Healthy', Proceedings of the Royal Society of Medicine, vol.3, part 2, 1910, pp.120–21.

87 James Niven, 'Summer Diarrhoea and Enteric Fever', Proceedings of the Royal Society of Medicine, vol.3, part 2, April 1910, pp.141, 153–54.

88 O.H. Peters, 'Observations upon the Natural History of Epidemic Diarrhoea', Journal of Hygiene, vol.10, 1910, pp.607–18.

89 Ibid., pp.633–57.

90 Ibid., pp.657–64, 765.

91 Ibid., pp.667–82, 765–66.

92 Ibid., pp.702–7, 715–18, 766.

93 Ibid., pp.687, 707–09, 717–18, 727–33, 766–67.

94 Henry Ashby and George A. Wright, The Diseases of Children (1st edn), London, Longmans Green & Co., 1889, pp. 66–7.

95 Ibid. (2nd edn), 1892, p.79.

96 Ibid. (4th edn), 1899, pp.92–3.

97 Hugh T. Ashby and Charles Roberts, Ashby and Wright's Diseases of Children (6th edn), London, Henry Frowde and Hodder & Stoughton, 1922, p.75. See also the similar development in the editions of The Diseases of Infancy and Childhood by the American paediatrician L. Emmett Holt. (These texts were published in London as well as New York.)

98 Topley and Wilson, Principles of Bacteriology and Immunity (2nd edn), London, Edward Arnold, 1936, p.1254.

99 John S.B. Bray, 'Isolation of Antigenically Homogeneous Strains of Bact. Coli Neapolitanum from Summer Diarrhoea of Infants', Journal of Pathology and Bacteriology, vol.57, 1945, pp.239–47. See also: idem and T.E.D. Beaven, 'Slide Agglutination of Bacterium Coli Var. Neapolitanum in Summer Diarrhoea', Journal of Pathology and Bacteriology, vol.60, 1948, pp.395–401; and Bray, 'Bray's Discovery of Pathogenic Esch. coli as a Cause of Infantile Gastroenteritis', Archives of Disease in Childhood, vol.48, 1973, pp.923–26.

Chapter III

1 Remark by Dr Driver during discussion following the paper by G. Leslie Eastes, 'The Pathology of Milk', BMJ, 11 November 1899, p.1342.

2 Report of the meeting of the Bradford Medico-Chirugical Society. Précis of a paper on the supply of pure milk by Dr Crowley, BMJ, 22 June 1901, p.1550.

3 W.J. Tyson, 'Presidential Address to the Preventive Medicine Section', Journal of State Medicine, vol.12, no.9, 1904, p.530.

4 William Hallock Park, 'The Great Bacterial Contamination of the Milk of

Cities. Can it be Lessened by the Action of Health Authorities?', *Journal of Hygiene*, vol.1, 1901, p.392.

5 Eastes, 'The Pathology of Milk', p.1341.

6 Ibid., p.1342.

7 Walter C. Pakes, 'The Application of Bacteriology to Public Health', *Public Health*, March 1900, p.428.

8 Ibid., p.431. See also the précis of Pakes's paper in the *Lancet*, 3 February 1900, p.312. The editors used the phrase 'not fit for human, much less infants' food'.

9 F.T. Harvey, 'Some Points on the Hygiene of the Udder, and the Conditions of Milk Production in Rural Districts', *Journal of State Medicine*, December 1902, pp.753–55.

10 Edward F. Willoughby, *Milk, Its Production and Uses*, London, Charles Griffen & Co., 1903.

11 Harold Swithinbank and George Newman, *The Bacteriology of Milk*, London, John Murray, 1903.

12 'A Report on the Milk Supply of Large Towns', *BMJ*, (1) 21 March 1903, pp.678–80; (2) 28 March 1903, pp.739–42; (3) 4 April 1903, pp.801–02; (4) 11 April 1903, pp.876–78; (5) 18 April 1903, pp.933–34; (6) 25 April 1903, pp.973–77; (7) 2 May 1903, pp.1033–037.

13 *BMJ*, 5 December 1903, p.1477.

14 *BMJ*, 21 March 1903, p.678.

15 Ibid., p.678.

16 Ibid., p.680.

17 Frederick Maurice, 'Where to Get Men', *The Contemporary Review*, vol.81, January 1902, p.80.

18 Smyth, 'A Report on the Milk Supply', *BMJ*, 21 March 1903, p.680.

19 The correlation between feeding practices and national health is implicit in the preface. 'This work [deals with] a subject which has made such extensive progress within recent years and is of such vital importance to the health and well-being of the nation. The child's future health and strength commonly depend upon the way it has been fed during the first few years of life.' Edmund Cautley, *The Natural and Artificial Methods of Feeding Infants and Young Children*, London, J. & A. Churchill, 1897, p.iii.

20 *BMJ*, 21 November 1903, p.1352.

21 Aimée Watt Smyth, 'Physical Degeneration: The Food Factor in Deterioration', *BMJ*, 5 December 1903, p.1471.

22 'Milk and Men', *The Pall Mall Gazette*, 12 April 1904, p.2.

23 'Our Milk Supply', *The Daily Chronicle*, 14 July 1904, p.5.

24 See in particular 'Milk and Disease: Sources of Contamination', *The Daily Chronicle*, 15 July 1904, p.3.

25 See in particular 'Milk and Disease: The Law as Dead Letter', *The Daily Chronicle*, 18 July 1904, p.3.

26 See in particular 'Milk and Disease: Lessons from Abroad', *The Daily Chronicle*, 19 July 1904, p.3.

27 'Milk and Disease: "Culpable Homicide" ', *The Daily Chronicle*, 16 July 1904, p.3.

28 'Milk and Disease: A Summary', *The Daily Chronicle*, 22 July 1904, p.3.

29 'Pus as a Beverage', *BMJ*, 5 December 1903, pp.1477–478.

30 'Interdepartmental Committee on Physical Deterioration', *BMJ*, 6 August 1904, p.297.
31 G.B., P.P., *Report* of the Inter-Departmental Committee on Physical Deterioration, vol.I, Cd 2175, London, HMSO, 1904, pp.53–4.
32 Ibid., p.89.
33 Ernest Hart, 'The Influence of Milk in Spreading Zymotic Disease', *Transactions* of the International Medical Congress, 7th session, vol.4, London, J.W. Kolckmann, 1881, pp.491–544.
34 See, *inter alia*, Arthur Guy Enock, *This Milk Business: A Study From 1895 to 1943*, London, H.K. Lewis & Co., 1943, especially Chapter IV, 'Bacterial Infection and Contamination of Milk', pp.67–97; W. Leslie MacKenzie, 'The Hygienics of Milk', *The Edinburgh Medical Journal*, N.S. vol.5, 1899, pp.372–78 and 563–76; George Newman, 'The Control of the Milk Supply', *BMJ*, 27 August 1904, pp.421–29; George Newman, *The Health of the People*, London, Headley Brothers, 1907, pp.50–2; Charles E. North, 'Milk and its Relation to the Public Health', in *A Half Century of Public Health* edited by Mazÿck Ravenel, New York, American Public Health Association, 1921, pp.236–89; George Rosen, *A History of Public Health*, New York, MD Publications, 1958, pp.358–60; William G. Savage, *Milk and the Public Health*, London, Macmillan, 1912, especially Chapter V, 'Milk and the Acute Infectious Diseases', pp.71–102; Swithinbank and Newman, *Bacteriology of Milk*, especially pp.210–391.
   There are, in addition, a great number of specific studies of bacterial contamination of milk in the *Reports* of the Medical Officer of the Local Government Board, the *Reports* of the Medical Officer of the London County Council, and in the various medical journals, especially the *Journal of Hygiene*. News of epidemics can be found in the *BMJ* and *Lancet*, and epidemiological studies of individual epidemics or outbreaks are to be found primarily in *Public Health*.
35 Savage, *Milk and the Public Health*, p.301.
36 See, *inter alia*, A.K. Chalmers, 'The Increase of the Power of Local Authorities with Regard to Milk Supply', *Lancet*, 18 August 1906, pp.425–26; Charles Harrington, 'Infantile Mortality and its Principal Cause – Dirty Milk', *The American Journal of the Medical Sciences*, vol.132, no.6, December 1906, pp.811–35; H. Meredith Richards, 'Some Observations in Regard to the Control of the Milk Trade', *Public Health*, May 1903, pp.457–63; Savage, *Milk and the Public Health*, Chapter 17, 'Legal Powers in England Applicable to Milk', pp.298–320; Willoughby, *Milk*, especially pp.90–111; J. Mitchell Wilson, 'Regulations under the Dairies Cow-sheds and Milk-shops (sic) Orders', *Public Health*, May 1903, pp.441–56.
   See also the coverage of the failure of current legislation to deal adequately with particular epidemics in the medical press. For example, 'Scarlet Fever and Milk Supply', *BMJ*, 25 May 1901, pp.1289–290; 'The Spread of Scarlet Fever by Milk', *BMJ*, 8 June 1901, pp.1427–428; 'A Milk Outbreak of Scarlet Fever in London', *BMJ*, 23 November 1901, pp.1555–556.
   The coverage of legal cases concerning infected milk supplies is of particular interest. See, for example, 'Typhoid Fever and Milk', *BMJ*, 5 November 1904, p.1265; 'The Control of the Milk Supply: Frost v. The

Aylesbury Dairy Company', *BMJ*, 12 November 1904, pp.1329–340.

37 George Newman, *Infant Mortality*, London, Methuen, 1906, p.46.

38 Arthur Newsholme, *The Elements of Vital Statistics*, 3rd edn, London, George Allen & Unwin, 1923, p.370.

39 J.C. Harley Williams, *A Century of Public Health in Britain, 1832–1929*, London, Adam & Charles Black, 1932, p.116.

40 German Sims Woodhead, 'Tuberculosis and Tabes Mesenterica', *Lancet*, 14 July 1888, pp.51–2.

41 Ibid., p.52. See also G.B., Registrar-General's Office, *Supplement to the 45th Annual Report of the Registrar-General, 1871–1880*, C.4564, London, HMSO, 1885, Table 5, pp.cxiv–cxv.

42 Ibid., p.52.

43 Ibid., pp.52–4.

44 J. Walter Carr, 'The Starting Points of Tuberculous Disease in Children', *Transactions of the Medical Society of London*, vol.17, 1894, pp.299, 290, 297, 301.

45 German Sims Woodhead, 'The Channels of Infection in Tuberculosis', *Lancet*, 27 October 1894, p.960.

46 Sheridan Delépine, 'Tuberculosis Infection Through the Alimentary Canal', *Medical Chronicle*, vol.3, 1895, pp.144–48.

47 Ibid., pp.147–48.

48 G.B., P.P., *Report of the Royal Commission Appointed to Inquire Into the Effect of Food Derived from Tuberculosis Animals on Human Health*, Part I: Report, Cd 7703, London, HMSO, 1895, p.9.

49 Ibid., pp.10, 17, 20, 10.

50 Ibid., p.21.

51 J. Walter Carr, 'A Protest Against the Use of the Term "Consumptive Bowels" in the Wasting Diseases of Infants', *BMJ*, 21 September 1895, p.717.

52 G.B., P.P., *Report of the Royal Commission Appointed to Inquire Into the Administrative Procedures for Controlling Danger to Man Through the Use as Food of the Meat and Milk of Tuberculous Animals*, Part II: Minutes of Evidence and Appendices, Cd 8831, London, HMSO, 1898, p.357.

53 Richard Thorne-Thorne, 'The Administrative Control of Tuberculosis', The Harben Lectures for 1898, *Public Health*, December 1898, p.201. See also the reports in the *BMJ* and *Lancet*: 'The Prevention of Tuberculosis', *BMJ*, 5 November 1898, pp.1458–459; 12 November 1898, p.1502; 19 November 1898, p.1580; 'The Administrative Control of Tuberculosis', *Lancet*, 12 November 1898, pp.1288–290; 26 November 1898, p.1411. See also the *Lancet* editorial which emphasized Tatham's statistics adduced by Thorne: 3 December 1898, pp.1489–490.

54 Idem, 'The Administrative Control of Tuberculosis', *Public Health*, December 1898, pp.201–02.

55 Sheridan Delépine, 'Tuberculosis and the Milk Supply', *Lancet*, 17 September 1898, pp.733, 735.

56 J. Walter Carr, 'What is Tabes Mesenterica in Infants?', *Lancet*, 17 December 1898, p.1662.

57 Leonard G. Guthrie, 'The Distribution and Origin of Tuberculosis in Children', *Lancet*, 4 February 1899, p.290.

58 Richard Douglas Powell, 'Recent Advances in Practical Medicine', *BMJ*, 5

August 1899, p.336.

59 George F. Still, 'Observations on the Morbid Anatomy of Tuberculosis in Childhood', *BMJ*, 19 August 1899, p.457.

60 J. Walter Carr, 'Tuberculosis in Childhood', *BMJ*, 2 September 1899, pp.626–27.

61 H.B. Donkin, 'Tuberculosis in Childhood', *BMJ*, 9 September 1899, p.685.

62 George F. Still, 'Tuberculosis in Childhood', *The Practitioner*, July 1901, pp. 94, 102.

63 G.B., P.P., *Report of the Royal Commission Appointed to Inquire into the Administrative Procedures for Controlling Danger to Man through . . . Tuberculous Animals*, Part I: Report, Cd 8824, London, HMSO, 1898, pp. 1, 2, 12.

64 Ibid., pp. 13, 15–23.

65 Ibid., pp. 15–23.

66 Delépine, 'Tuberculosis and the Milk Supply', p.736.

67 James Niven, 'Tuberculous Milk and Meat', *Public Health*, March 1899, pp.430–32.

68 James Niven, 'The Administration of the Manchester Milk Clauses', *BMJ*, 3 August 1901, p.314.

69 G. Sims Woodhead, 'Prevention of Tuberculosis', *Public Health*, May 1899, p.582.

70 Robert Koch, 'An Address on the Fight Against Tuberculosis', *BMJ*, 27 July 1901, pp.190–91.

71 'Second General Meeting: Tuesday, July 23rd', *BMJ*, 27 July 1901, p.206. See also 'Important Views on the Relation Between Bovine and Human Tuberculosis', *Lancet*, 3 August 1901, p.301.

72 Ibid., p.206.

73 Ibid., p.206.

74 'Professor Koch and Tuberculous Milk and Meat', *Lancet*, 27 July 1901, p.217.

75 Woodhead, 'Prevention of Tuberculosis', 1899, p.50.

76 G.B., *38th Annual Report of the L.G.B.*, 1908–9, Supplement . . . Report of the Medical Officer, Appendix B, no.5, 'Report by Professor Delépine on Investigations in the Public Health Laboratory of the University of Manchester upon the Prevalence and Sources of Tubercle Bacilli in Cow's Milk', Cd 4935, London, HMSO, 1909, p.393.

77 John McFadyean, 'Tubercle Bacilli in Cows' Milk as a Possible Source of Tuberculous Disease in Man', *Lancet*, 3 August 1901, pp.268–69.

78 Ibid., p.270.

79 Mazÿck P. Ravenel, 'The Comparative Virulence of the Tubercle Bacillus from Human and Bovine Sources', *Lancet*, 17 August 1901, p.447.

80 'Human and Bovine Tuberculosis', *BMJ*, 26 October 1901, p.1282.

81 Sheridan Delépine, 'The Communicability of Human Tuberculosis to Cattle', *BMJ*, 26 October 1901, p.1224.

82 D.J. Hamilton, 'A Discussion on the Relationship of Human and Bovine Tuberculosis', *BMJ*, 27 September 1902, pp.946–47.

83 Ibid., p.947.

84 'The Royal Commission on Tuberculosis', *BMJ*, 9 February 1907, pp.330–32.

85 G.B., P.P., *Royal Commission on Tuberculosis (Relation Between Human*

and Animal), Second Interim Report, Cd 3322, London, HMSO, 1907, pp.14–15, 36.

86 Alfred Hillier, *Tuberculosis*, London, Cassell, 1900.

87 Letter to the editor from J. Alfred Coutts, *BMJ*, 10 August 1901, p.381.

88 Letter to the editor from Alfred Hillier, *BMJ*, 10 August 1901, pp.380–81.

89 See, for example, C.H. Cattle, 'Remarks on the Relations of Human and Bovine Tuberculosis', *BMJ*, 22 February 1902, pp.443–45; and Hubert Armstrong, 'A Note on the Infantile Mortality from Tuberculous Meningitis and Tabes Mesenterica', *BMJ*, 26 April 1902, p.1024.

90 'Tuberculosis in Infancy and Childhood', *BMJ*, 26 April 1902, p.1041.

91 Alfred Hillier, *The Prevention of Consumption*, London, Longmans Green & Co., 1903, p.64.

92 Ibid., p.64.

93 See, for example, the articles by Dr Nathan Raw (a member of the International Committee for the Prevention of Consumption, and a physician at the Mill Road Infirmary and the Sanatorium for Consumption in Liverpool) and the response they engendered. Raw repeatedly quoted Thorne-Thorne in detail, as well as the percentages of tuberculous cases presumed to have been derived from contaminated milk which had been adduced by Ashby, Still, and Woodhead to support his own position regarding the pathogenicity of infected milk. The latter three were cited to demonstrate that primary tuberculosis of the mesenteric glands, abdomen, and intestine had been found in a significant proportion of those children who had tuberculosis. Thorne-Thorne was cited to prove that the frequency of this occurrence had increased. Thus the danger of such milk was greater than ever, and had to be taken seriously at once. No one quarrelled with the post mortem figures, but Thorne-Thorne's argument invariably raised objections. Nathan Raw, 'Human and Bovine Tuberculosis', *BMJ*, 31 January 1903, pp.247–48; idem, 'Human and Bovine Tuberculosis', *BMJ*, 14 March 1903, pp.596–98; idem, 'Discussions on Tuberculosis in Children and its Relationship to Bovine Tuberculosis' (Section of the Diseases of Children of the BMA), *Lancet*, 15 August 1903, pp.473–74; and *BMJ*, 29 August 1903, pp.470–74 (including discussion); letters in response from Sidney Davies (MOH, Woolwich) published in the *Lancet*, 12 September 1903, p.788 and *BMJ*, 19 September 1903, p.692 and from Frank C. Madden (Professor of Surgery, Egyptian School of Medicine, Cairo), *BMJ*, 17 October 1903, p.1016; Raw, 'Human and Bovine Tuberculosis', *BMJ*, 8 October 1904, pp.907–09.

94 L. Kingsford, 'The Channels of Infection in Tuberculosis in Childhood', *Lancet*, 24 September 1904, pp.889–91.

95 G.B., P.P., *Second Interim Report of the Royal Commission on Tuberculosis*, Cd 3322, 1907, pp.36–7.

96 G.B., Ministry of Health, *Reports to the Local Government Board on Public Health and Medical Subjects*, N.S. no.88, (I) 'The Incidence and Bacteriological Characteristics of Tuberculous Infection in Children', by Arthur Eastwood and Fred Griffith; (II) 'An Enquiry . . . into the Occurrence and Distribution of Tuberculous Infection in Children', by A. Stanley Griffith, London, HMSO, 1914, p.2.

97 Ibid., p.i.

98 Ibid., p.iv.

99 Ibid., p.iv.
100 George Newman, 'The Milk Supply of a London Borough', *Public Health*, February 1904, pp.282–84.
101 George Newman, *Report on the Milk Supply of Finsbury, 1903*, London, Thomas Bean & Son, 1903, p.44.
102 'Our Milk Supply', *The Daily Chronicle*, 14 July 1904, p.5.
103 'The Tubercle Bacillus in Milk', *BMJ*, 30 March 1907, p.763; 'Dirty and Tuberculous Milk', *Lancet*, 2 May 1908, p.1284; 'The Contamination of Milk', *BMJ*, 18 July 1908, p.155.
104 G.B., Ministry of Health, *38th Annual Report of the L.G.B.*, 1908–9, Supplement . . . Report of the Medical Officer . . . Report by Professor Delépine, London, HMSO, 1909, Cd 4935, pp.343, 411.
105 'Pus as a Beverage', *BMJ*, 5 December 1903, p.1477. See also the text of the replies, 'The Milk Supply of Large Towns', *BMJ*, 5 December 1903, pp.1488–492.
106 L.M. Bowen-Jones, 'The Control of the Milk Supply', *Public Health*, February 1909, p.172.
107 H. Meredith Richards, 'Some Observations in Regard to the Control of the Milk Trade', *Public Health*, May 1903, pp.459–60.
108 James Crichton-Browne, 'Milk for the Multitude', *The Sanitary Journal*, no.227, 1904, p.226.
109 *The Daily Chronicle*, 18 July 1904, p.3.
110 G.B., Ministry of Health, *38th Annual Report of the L.G.B.*, 1908–9, Supplement, Cd 4935, pp.413–14.
111 William G. Savage, *Milk and the Public Health*, London, Macmillan, 1912, p.337.
112 Ibid., p.337.
113 For a discussion of the legislation of 1914–15, see Arthur Guy Enock, *This Milk Business*, London, H.K. Lewis & Co., 1943, pp.33–4, 71 and Appendix no.5; J.C. Harley Williams, *A Century of Public Health in Britain*, London, Adam & Charles Black, 1932, pp.175–81; and G.B., P.P., Committee on the Production and Distribution of Milk, *Final Report*, Cd 483, London, HMSO, 1919.
114 Nathan Raw, 'Bovine Tuberculosis in Children', in Kelynack (ed.), *Tuberculosis*, p.41.
115 Hugh T. Ashby, *Infant Mortality*, Cambridge, Cambridge University Press, 1915, pp.163–64.

Chapter IV

1 Arthur Newsholme, *The Elements of Vital Statistics*, 4th edn, London, George Allen & Unwin, 1923, pp.92–3.
2 Arthur Newsholme, *The Elements of Vital Statistics*, 3rd edn, London, Swan Sonnenschein, 1899, pp. 78, 97, 95.
3 Henri de Rothschild, *Dépopulation et protection de la première enfance*, Paris, Octave Doin, 1900, p.4. This was in fact true. See Jacques Bertillon, *Élements de demographie*, Paris, 1896, p.28. See also idem, *La Dépopulation de la France: ses consequences, ses causes, et mesures à prendre pour la combattre*, Paris, Librarie Félix Alcan, 1911.

4 Albert Balestre and A. Gilletta de Saint-Joseph, *Étude sur la Mortalité de la Première Enfance dans la Population Urbaine de la France de 1892 à 1897*, Paris, Doin, 1901.

5 Lesage, 'De la diarrhée verte des enfants du premier âge', *Bulletin de Médecine*, vol.26, 1887, p.10.

6 François-Joseph Herrgott, *Annales de la Societé Obstétricale de France*, 1901, Variot, 'La Goutte de Lait', *La Clinique Infantile*, 1 November 1903, and English reports of the work: George Carpenter's editorial, 'La Goutte de Lait', *British Journal of Children's Diseases*, vol.1, no.5, May 1904, p.167; George Frederick McCleary, 'The Infants' Milk Depôt: Its History and Function', *Journal of Hygiene*, vol.4, no.3, July 1904, p.330; idem, *The Early History of the Infant Welfare Movement*, London, H.K. Lewis & Co., 1933, pp.43–4; George Rosen, *A History of Public Health*, New York, MD Publications Inc., p.354; G. Variot, 'Gouttes de Lait et Consultations de Nourrissons', *BMJ*, 14 May 1904, p.1125.

7 Pierre Budin, 'Note sur l'alimentation des enfants', *Bulletin de l'Académie de Médecine*, vol.51, 5 January 1904, p.23; see also idem, 'La Mortalité Infantile', p.27.

8 Pierre Budin, *The Nursling*, London, The Caxton Publishing Co., 1907 (originally *Le Nourrisson*, 1900), p.148.

9 Idem, 'Sur le lait stérilisé', *Bulletin de l'Académie de Médecine*, vol.37, 1 June 1897, p.685. See also idem, 'Note sur l'alimentation des enfants', pp.23–4; idem, *The Nursling*, p.147.

10 *The Nursling*, pp.153, 142; see also Planchon, 'Résultats obtenus à la Consultation de Nourrissons de la Clinique Tarnier', *L'Obstétrique*, vol.5, January 1900, p.37.

11 Ibid., p.148–49.

12 Budin, 'Sur un mémoire de MM. les Drs M. Balestre et A. Gilletta de Saint-Joseph, intitulé: 'Étude sur la mortalité de la première enfance', *Bulletin de L'Académie de Médecine*, Vol 45, 11 June 1901, p.663; idem, 'La mortalité infantile', pp.28–9; idem 'Note sur l'alimentation des enfants', pp.38–9; A.-L. Peyroux, 'Consultations de nourrissons et Gouttes de Lait', *La Semaine Medicale*, 24 December 1902, p.421; Planchon, 'Résultats obtenus', pp.37–49.

13 Gaston Variot, 'Gouttes de Lait', *BMJ*, 14 May 1904, pp.1125–126; see also 'Dr Variot's Goutte de Lait', *Lancet*, 19 November 1904, pp.1458–459 and especially Gaston Variot, 'L'Élevage des enfants atrophiques par l'emploi méthodique du lait stérilisé', *Revue Scientifique*, vol.17, no.8, 22 February 1902, pp.225–35. This article explains the problems presented by his particular patient population and the system he devised in response.

14 Porak, 'Rapport au nom de la Commission permanente de l'Hygiene de l'enfance, sur les mémoires et travaux envoyés à cette Commission en 1902', *Bulletin de l'Académie de Médecine*, vol.48, 30 December 1902, pp.786–88.

15 Budin, 'Précis de *Consultations de nourrissons* par Charles Maygrier', *Bulletin de l'Académie de Médecine*, vol.50, 10 November 1903, p.266.

16 Quoted in Porak, 'Rapport au nom de la Commission permanente de l'Hygiene de l'enfance, sur les mémoires et travaux envoyés à cette Commission en 1901', *Bulletin de l'Académie de Médicine*, vol.46, 10 December 1901, pp.753–54.

17 Reprinted in McCleary, 'The Infants' Milk Depôt', p.332.
18 McCleary, 'The Infants' Milk Depôt', p.332.
19 Léon Dufour, 'L'Oeuvre de la Goutte de Lait', *Bulletin de l'Académie de Médecine*, vol.38, 30 November 1897, pp.530–31; see also Budin, *The Nursling*, p.154.
20 Porak, 'Rapport', 1902, pp.789–90. See also Variot's discussion of 'Les deux operations faites dans le même but' in 'L'Avenir des Gouttes de Lait', *Archives de Médecine des Enfants*, vol.6, 1903, pp.209–20.
21 Budin, *The Nursling*, p.155. See also Dufour, 'L'Oeuvre de la Goutte de Lait', pp.531–32.
22 Leonard Robinson, 'Consultations for Infants in France', *Practitioner*, October 1905, p.485.
23 Budin, *The Nursling*, p.155 and Dufour, 'L'Oeuvre de la Goutte de Lait', pp.529–32.
24 'La Goutte de Lait', *Journal of State Medicine*, vol.4, 1898, pp.612–14.
25 F. Drew Harris, 'The Supply of Sterilised Humanised Milk for the Use of Infants in St Helens', *BMJ*, 18 August 1900, p.427.
26 Ibid., pp.428, 430.
27 Ibid., pp.429–30.
28 A.A. Mussen, 'Supply of Sterilized Humanized Milk for Infants', *Journal of State Medicine*, vol.11, no.10, 1903, p.607 and 'Public Health and Poor Law' section in the *Lancet*, 22 October 1904, p.1173.
29 'Liverpool Medical Institution', *Lancet*, 26 March 1904, p.873.
30 'Liverpool' (From our own Correspondent), *Lancet*, 30 April 1904, p.1237. See also the report of the paper given by Councillor Shelmerdine (Liverpool) at the Congress of the Royal Institute of Public Health, *Lancet*, 30 July 1904, p.315.
31 'Liverpool Medical Institution', *BMJ*, 2 April 1904, p.785.
32 McCleary, *The Early History*, p.75.
33 Idem, *Infantile Mortality and Infants' Milk Depots*, London, P.S. King & Son, 1905, pp.77–80.
34 Idem, 'The Municipal Feeding of Infants', *Practitioner*, October 1905, p.473.
35 Aimée Watt Smyth, 'A Report on the Milk Supply of Large Towns: VI. Sterilized and "Humanized" Milk for Infants in England', *BMJ*, 25 April 1903, p.973.
36 McCleary, 'The Municipal Feeding of Infants', p.474.
37 Idem, *The Early History*, p.80.
38 Idem, 'The Infants' Milk Depot', *Journal of Hygiene*, vol. 4, July 1904, p.339.
39 Ibid., pp.364–65.
40 Idem, 'The Public Supply of Pure or Specially Prepared Milk for the Feeding of Infants', *Lancet*, pp.422–23.
41 Idem, 'The Infants' Milk Depot', p.349. See also the 'Public Health and Poor Law' Section in the *Lancet*, 22 October 1904, p.1172.
42 'Public Health and Poor Law Medical Services', *BMJ*, 15 June 1907, p.1463.
43 'Special Correspondence: Paris', *BMJ*, 29 June 1901, p.1643. See also 'The Vital Statistics of France', *BMJ*, 9 March 1901, p.597; 'Special Correspondence: Paris', *BMJ*, 14 December 1901, p.1778; 25 January 1902, p.236; 15

February 1902, p.423; 'Education or Charity', *BMJ*, 10 January 1903, pp.95–6; 'Depopulation and the Marriage-Age', *BMJ*, 31 January 1903, pp.267–68.

44 Smyth, 'A Report on the Milk Supply', pp.973–77.

45 'Municipal Infant Milk Depots', *Lancet*, 25 April 1903, p.1184.

46 T.D. Lister, 'On the Utilization of Infants' Milk Depots', *BMJ*, 29 August 1903, p.469.

47 'Organized Efforts for the Diminution of Infantile Mortality in France and Belgium', *BMJ*, 26 September 1903, pp.764–65.

48 'The Systematization of Efforts to Reduce Infantile Mortality', *BMJ*, 26 September 1903, p.747.

49 G.B., P.P., Inter-Departmental Committee on Physical Deterioration, Cd 2210, vol.II: *Minutes of Evidence*, p.442. See also Ralph Vincent, *The Nutrition of the Infant*, 2nd edn, London, Ballière Tindall & Cox, 1904; idem, *Lectures on Babies*, London, Ballière Tindall & Cox, 1908, and the following sample of his letters: *BMJ*, 7 February 1903, p.339, 15 August, p.396, 28 November, p.1436; *Lancet*, 16 July 1904, p.173, 8 October, p.1046. In addition, see his article 'The Milk Laboratory and its Relation to Medicine', *BMJ*, 13 October 1906, pp. 937–39.

The work of Thomas Morgan Rotch (the 'percentage feeding' paediatrician) was well publicized in England as well as America. In 1902 he was invited to present a paper to the Section of Diseases of Children of the BMA, which was subsequently published as 'A Discussion on the Modification of Milk in the Feeding of Infants', *BMJ*, 6 September 1902, pp.653–72. See also: *Pediatrics: The Hygienic and Medical Treatment of Children*, Philadelphia, J.B. Lippincott, 1896 (3rd edn, 1901; 5th edn, 1907).

50 Letter from Duchess Margaret of Teck, President, W.H. Goschen, Treasurer, Sara Fletcher, Honorary Secretary, and Flora Weld-Blundell, 'National Physique and the Feeding of Infants', *Manchester Guardian*, 30 June 1903, p.10.

51 Letter from Portland, Mansfield, W.H. Goschen, Frederick Maurice, Harold Boulton, Henry Ashby and J.S. Fletcher, 'The Infants' Health Society', *The Times*, 25 April 1904, p.6.

52 The Infants' Health Society, *The Present Conditions of Infant Life*, Ballière, Tindall & Cox, 1905, p.12.

53 George Carpenter, 'The Milk Supplied to Infants', *British Journal of Children's Diseases*, vol.1, 1904, pp.76–9; idem, 'Milk Dispensaries for Children's Hospitals', *British Journal of Children's Diseases*, vol.1, 1904, pp.123–28; idem, 'La Goutte de Lait', *British Journal of Children's Diseases*, vol.1, 1904, pp.167–75; and idem, 'Municipal Milk Supplies', *The British Journal of Children's Diseases*, vol.1, 1904, p.216–19.

54 Ibid., p.174.

55 'Milk and Men' (By an Expert), *The Pall Mall Gazette*, 12 April 1904, p.2.

56 'Our Milk Supply', *The Daily Chronicle*, 14 July 1904, p.5; 'Milk and Disease', 16 July 1904, p.3; 19 July 1903, p.3; 22 July 1903, p.3.

57 'Milk and Disease: A Summary and a Suggestion', *The Daily Chronicle*, 22 July 1904, p.3.

58 Inter-Departmental Committee on Physical Deterioration, vol.II: *Minutes of Evidence*, see the testimony, in chronological order, of Aimée Watt Smyth, 18 January 1904, especially pp.58–61; Thomas Frederick Young, 20

January, p.92; J.B. Atkins, 27 January, pp.127–29; R.J. Collie, 10 February, p.175; Archibald K. Chalmers, 22 February, p.244; James Niven, 22 February, p.253; Eustace Smith, 7 March, p.319; Henry Ashby, 9 March, p.330; Robert Hutchison, 14 March, p.363; Ralph Vincent, 25 April, pp.446–50.

59 G.B., P.P., *Report of the Inter-Departmental Committee on Physical Deterioration*, vol.I, Cd 2175, London, HMSO, 1904, pp.54, 57.

60 George Newman, *A Special Report on an Infants' Milk Depot*, London, Thomas Bean & Son, 1905, p.9.

61 Idem, *Infant Mortality*, London, Methuen, 1906, p.290.

62 Idem, *A Special Report*, pp.11–14.

63 Ibid., p.17.

64 Idem, *Infant Mortality*, p.298.

65 Idem, *A Special Report*, p.20.

66 Idem, *Infant Mortality*, pp.302–15. See also the précis of Newman's report in the 'Public Health and Poor Law' section of the *Lancet*, 3 March 1906, p.619.

67 McCleary, *The Early History*, p.103. See also, idem, *The Development of British Maternity and Child Welfare Services*, London, published by the National Association of Maternity and Child Welfare Services and for the Prevention of Infant Mortality, 1945, pp.7–8; idem, *The Maternity and Child Welfare Movement*, London, P.S. King & Son, 1935, pp.9–10.

68 Presidential address of John Burns reprinted in full in the Appendix (pp.151–68) of McCleary's *The Early History*, pp.154–65.

69 Archibald K. Chalmers, 'The Increase of the Power of Local Authorities with Regard to Milk-Supply', *Lancet*, 18 August 1906, pp.425–26, and George Frederick McCleary, 'The Public Supply of Pure or Specially Prepared Milk for the Feeding of Infants', *Lancet*, 18 August 1906, pp.422–23.

70 Caleb W. Saleeby, 'The Human Mother', *Report of the Proceedings of the Second National Conference on Infantile Mortality*, P.S. King & Son, 1908, pp.30–2.

71 Ibid., p.32.

72 See the *BMJ*, 26 December 1903, pp.1657–658.

73 G.B., Ministry of Health, *42nd Annual Report* of the Local Government Board, Supplement . . . containing a 'Second Report on Infant and Child Mortality' by the Medical Officer of the Board, Cd 6909, London, HMSO, 1913, pp.390–91.

74 Janet Lane-Claypon, 'Phases in the Development of the Infant Welfare Movement in England', *Transactions* of the Fourth Annual Meeting of the American Association for the Study and Prevention of Infant Mortality, Washington DC, GPO, 1914, p.389.

75 This was by no means true of all the milk depot news items. To the contrary, both the *BMJ* and *Lancet* reported favourably upon the initiative to establish new stations and the results of existing ones. See, for example, with regard to: Bradford, *BMJ*, 24 September 1904, pp.768–69 and 21 July 1907, pp.168–69; Lambeth, *Lancet*, 6 January 1906, pp.44–5 and 3 November 1906, p.1227; Leicester, *Lancet*, 17 March 1906, p.802; Leeds, *BMJ*, 14 September 1907, p.697.

76 'The Borough of St Helens', *Lancet*, 22 October 1904, p.1172.

77 'Manchester', *BMJ*, 23 September 1905, p.752.

78 Sidney Davies, 'Notes on Infants' Milk Depot Statistics', *Public Health*, vol.22, December 1908, pp.93–4.

79 Lane-Claypon, 'Phases in the Development', p.389–90. Although very little information was available at the turn of the century with regard to breast-feeding habits, more came to be known as a consequence of local adoption of the Notification of Births Act (1907), and especially following the mandatory Notification of Births Extension Act (1915). The 'Schedules for Inquiry into Maternity and Child Welfare Work' designed by the LGB and used by their medical staff when on site visits to investigate the local working of the Act provide a plethora of information about many aspects of infant care. With regard to breast feeding, see *inter* alia:

M.H. 48 no.182 Birmingham County Borough. Maternity and Child Welfare File, 1915–18. Schedule for Inquiry completed by Dr S. Seekings, following a site visit of 16 October 1917. In 1916, 87 per cent of the infants seen by health visitors were breast-fed at the time of the first visit; 38 per cent were breast-fed at the end of six months.

M.H. 48 no.262 Middlesborough County Borough. Maternity and Child Welfare Scheme. Site visit of 25 May 1916. In both 1914 and 1915, 97 per cent of the infants seen by health visitors were breast-fed at the time of the first visit.

N.B. This information would tend to confirm the hypothesis that a small percentage of infants were initially bottle-fed. It does not tell us at what age the majority of infants were weaned and whether it was those who were newly weaned who contracted epidemic diarrhoea. Furthermore, it is important to note that there is every reason to believe that feeding practices may have been very different during the early years of twentieth century from those during the war years.

80 Hugh T. Ashby, *Infant Mortality*, Cambridge, Cambridge University Press, 1915, p.142.

81 Maud Pember Reeves, *Round About a Pound a Week*, London, Virago Press, 1979 (first published 1913 by G. Bell & Sons, London), p.8.

82 Ibid., pp.8–9.

83 Ibid., pp. 3, 19.

84 Ibid., pp.174–75.

85 Ibid., p.220.

86 Ibid., p.99.

87 Ibid., p.101. See also 'A Municipal Milk Depot for Lambeth', *Lancet*, 6 January 1906, pp.44–5; 'The Lambeth Municipal Milk Depot', *Lancet*, 3 November 1906, p.1227, and 'Municipal Milk Shops', *The British Journal of Children's Diseases*, vol.1, 1904, pp.450–52.

88 Ibid., pp.102–3.

89 Margaret Llewelyn Davies (ed.) *Maternity: Letters from Working Women*, London, Virago Press, 1978 (first published 1915 by G. Bell & Sons, London), Letter no.29, p.57.

90 Ibid., Letter no.30, pp.58–9.

91 Ibid., Letter no.75, p.102.

92 Ibid., Letter no.20, p.45.

93 Ibid., Letter no. 51, pp.78–9.

94 G.B., Ministry of Health, *Reports* to the Local Government Board on Public

Health and Medical Subjects, N.S. no.80, 'On the Use of Proprietary Foods for Infant Feeding' by F.J.H. Coutts, especially pp.36–9; and 'On the Analysis and Composition of some Proprietary Foods for Infants', by Julian L. Baker, pp.49–79, London, HMSO, 1914.

95 George Sussman, 'The Wet-nursing Business in Nineteenth-Century France', *French Historical Studies*, vol.9, no.2, Autumn, 1975, pp.304–28.

Chapter V

1 Hugh T. Ashby, *Infant Mortality*, Cambridge Public Health Series, Cambridge, Cambridge University Press, 1915, p.142.

2 George Newman, *A Special Report on an Infant's Milk Depot*, London, Thomas Bean & Son, 1905, p.5.

3 A.A. Mussen, 'Supply of Sterilized Humanized Milk for Infants', *The Journal of State Medicine*, vol.11, no.10, 1903, p.607. Also reported in the *Lancet*, 22 October 1904, p.1173.

4 George Frederick McCleary, 'The Infants' Milk Depot: Its History and Function', *Journal of Hygiene*, vol.4, no.3, July 1904, p.338.

5 Newman, *A Special Report*, p.20.

6 Idem, *Infant Mortality*, London, Methuen, 1906, p.301.

7 George Frederick McCleary, *The Maternity and Child Welfare Movement*, London, P.S. King & Son, 1935, p.25.

8 William S. Craig, *Child and Adolescent Life*, Edinburgh, E. & S. Livingstone, 1946, p.42.

9 Quoted from Mrs Hardie, President of the Working Committee from 1891 to 1902, in George F. McCleary's, *The Early History of the Infant Welfare Movement*, London, H.K. Lewis, 1933, p.85.

10 Robert Roberts, *The Classic Slum*, Manchester, Manchester University Press, 1971, pp.57–8.

11 See, *inter alia*, Craig, *Child and Adolescent Life*, pp.42, 156; McCleary, *The Development of British Maternity and Child Welfare Services*, London, published by the National Association of Maternity and Child Welfare Centres, 1945, pp.10–11; idem, *Maternity and Child Welfare*, pp.26–7; G.H. Owen, 'Health Visiting' in Peta Allan and Moya Jolly (eds), *Nursing, Midwifery and Health Visiting Since 1900*, London, Faber & Faber, 1982, pp.92–105.

12 G.B., P.P., Inter-Departmental Committee on Physical Deterioration, vol.II: *Minutes of Evidence*, Cd 2210, London, HMSO, 1904, evidence of G.H. Fosbroke, MOH for Worcestershire County Council, p.262, para.6614.

13 Manchester and Salford Sanitary Association, *Annual Report*, 'Report of the Ladies' Public Health Society', Manchester, Sherratt & Hughes, 1902, pp.4–5.

14 Committee on Physical Deterioration, vol.II, Cd 2210, Evidence of Mrs Worthington, p.284, para.7312.

15 Ibid., Evidence of Mrs Bostock, pp.286–89.

16 'The London County Council', *BMJ*, 12 October 1901, p.1102.

17 'Manchester and Salford Sanitary Conference', *BMJ*, 3 May 1902, p.1113.

18 J. Spottiswoode Cameron, 'Women as Sanitary Inspectors', *The Journal of State Medicine*, vol. 10, no. 12, 1902, p.743.

19 Ibid., pp.745–46.

20 Ibid., pp.746–47.
21 Ibid., p.750.
22 'Sanitary Inspectors', *BMJ*, 16 July 1904, p.141.
23 'Report of the Medical Officer of Health of the Administrative County of London', *Lancet*, 20 January 1906, p.171.
24 'Infantile Mortality', *The Times*, 17 September 1904, p.8; 26 September 1904, p.6; 1 November 1904, p.15; 9 November 1904, p.4.
25 Ibid., 22 September 1904, p.6.
26 Letter to *The Times* signed by Henry Scott Holland, 15 November 1904, p.15.
27 'Out-Patient Departments and the Rearing of Children', *BMJ*, 21 November 1903, p.1352.
28 Letter from Edmund Cautley to the *BMJ*, 5 December 1903, p.1496.
29 Reginald Dudfield, 'The Milk Supply of the Metropolis', *Public Health*, March 1904, pp.353–54.
30 'Infantile Diarrhoea', *Lancet*, 17 September 1904, pp.839–40.
31 George F. McCleary, 'The Public Supply of Pure or Specially Prepared Milk for the Feeding of Infants', *Lancet*, 18 August 1906, p.423.
32 'Special Correspondence: Manchester', *BMJ*, 8 August 1903, p.337.
33 'Manchester and Salford', *BMJ*, 10 August 1907, p.336.
34 'Manchester', *BMJ*, 29 August 1908, p.624.
35 'Manchester and Salford', *BMJ*, 3 October 1908, p.1038.
36 Inter-Departmental Committee on Physical Deterioration, vol.I: *Report*, pp.89–90. See also pp.58–9 and vol.II: *Minutes of Evidence*, Cd 2210, in chronological order, the testimony of Dr Eichholz, p.28; Mrs Watt Smyth, pp.57–8; Dr Edward Mallins, p.140; Dr R.J. Collie, p.171; Mr T.C. Horsfall, pp.221–22, 229–30; Mr G.H. Fosbroke, pp.262–64; Mrs Worthington, pp.282–86; Mrs Bostock, pp.286–89; Mrs Greenwood, pp.315–17.
37 See Helen Bosanquet, *Social Work in London 1869–1912*, Brighton, Harvester, 1973.
38 Helen Bosanquet, 'Pauperization and Interests', *BMJ*, 27 August 1904, pp.435–36. This argument was reiterated repeatedly by the COS in general, and Helen Bosanquet in particular. See Helen Bosanquet, 'Physical Degeneration and the Poverty Line', *The Contemporary Review*, vol.85, January 1904, pp.65–75.
39 'Infantile Mortality and its Prevention', *Lancet*, 16 February 1907, p.475.
40 J. Spottiswoode Cameron, 'The Appointment of Qualified Women with Special Reference to the Hygiene and Feeding of Infants', *Lancet*, 4 August 1906, pp.290–91.
41 Ibid., p.290.
42 Samson G. Moore, 'Infantile Mortality and the Relative Practical Value of Measures Directed to its Prevention', *Lancet*, 22 April 1916, p.850.
43 Ibid., 6 May 1916, p.943.
44 A. Pinard, 'Sur un ârrete municipal pris par M. Morel de Villiers, médecin et maire de la commune de Villiers-le-Duc (Côte-d'Or)', *Bulletin de l'Académie de Médecine*, vol.51, 15 March 1904, p.223.
45 Ibid., pp.223–24.
46 Ibid., pp.235–36.
47 Samson G. Moore, *Report of the Medical Officer of Health on Infantile Mortality*, Huddersfield, Daily Chronicle Printing Works, 1904, p.19.

48 Ibid., pp.29–30.
49 Ibid., pp.102–4.
50 'Manchester: Reduction of Infant Mortality at Huddersfield', *Lancet*, 9 December 1905, p.1732. See also the *Lancet*, 24 February 1906, p.520; 5 May 1906, p.1261; and 17 November 1906, p.1381.
51 Moore, 'Infantile Mortality', p.850.
52 'Society of Medical Officers of Health', *Lancet*, 24 February 1906, p.520.
53 'Infantile Mortality: The Huddersfield Scheme', *BMJ*, December 1907, p.1658–659.
54 'The Huddersfield System', *BMJ*, 7 December 1907, p.1677.
55 'Infant Mortality and Birth Notification', *Lancet*, 5 May 1906, p.1263.
56 'Parliamentary Intelligence', *Lancet*, 4 May 1907, p.1265.
57 'Parliamentary Intelligence', *Lancet*, 8 June 1907, p.1618.
58 'Medical Notes in Parliament: The Early Notification of Births Bill', *BMJ*, 31 August 1907, p.545. See also 'Parliamentary Intelligence', *Lancet*, 27 July 1907, p.266, and 7 September pp.742–43; and 'Chelsea and the Notification of Births Act', *Lancet*, 1 February 1908, p.390.
59 'Early Notification of Births Act', *BMJ*, 31 August 1907, p.541.
60 Ibid., p.541.
61 'The Early Notification of Births Act', *Lancet*, 7 September 1907, p.717.
62 Letter from Benjamin Broadbent, *BMJ*, 10 August 1907, p.364.
63 Letter from John Batty Tuke, *BMJ*, 31 August 1907, p.553.
64 Letter from Victor Horsley, *BMJ*, 31 August 1907, p.553. See other letters in the same issue.
65 Letter from J.D. Willis, *BMJ*, 31 August 1907, p.553.
66 'Manchester and Salford', *BMJ*, 2 November 1907, pp.1271–272. See also 'The Notification of Births Act', pp.1266–267.
67 'Manchester and Salford', *BMJ*, 14 September 1907, p.696.
68 'Infant Mortality in Huddersfield', *Lancet*, 14 September 1907, p.784.
69 'Leeds. The Lessening of Infantile Mortality in Huddersfield', *Lancet*, 23 November 1907, p.1499.
70 'Leeds. Infantile Mortality at Huddersfield', *BMJ*, 30 November 1907, p.1614.
71 Précis of paper given (5 February) by L.A. Parry, 'The Notification of Births Act, 1907', *Lancet*, 29 February 1908, p.644.
72 'The Notification of Births Act', *Lancet*, 28 December 1907, p.1846.
73 'Medical Notes in Parliament', *BMJ*, 7 March 1908, p.592.
74 'Parliamentary Intelligence', *Lancet*, 18 July 1908, pp.204–05.
75 'Notification of Births Act', *Lancet*, 23 January 1909, p.256.
76 David Forsyth, *Children in Health and Disease*, London, John Murray, 1909, pp.259, 258.
77 Ibid., pp.259–60.
78 Ibid., pp.260–61.
79 According to Eric Pritchard's memoirs, held in the archives of the Wellcome Institute, the Society was established in 1905. McCleary, however, dates it from February 1906. See Eric Pritchard's manuscript 'The Welfare Movement', p.4, and McCleary, *The Early History*, p.117.
80 Eric Pritchard, *The Infant: Nutrition and Management*, London, Edward Arnold, 1914, p.242.
81 Ibid., pp.255–56.

82 Ibid., p.256.

83 London, Wellcome Institute, Contemporary Medical Archives Centre, Eric Pritchard's papers, 'The Welfare Movement', p.7.

84 Pritchard, *The Infant*, p.256. See also his book *Infant Education*, London, Henry Kimpton, 1911.

85 Pritchard's papers, 'The Welfare Movement', pp.16–17.

86 John F. Sykes, 'The Evolution of the St Pancras Scheme', in Evelyn M. Bunting, *A School For Mothers*, London, Horace Marshall & Son, 1907, p.7.

87 'Medical News', *BMJ*, 26 November 1904, p.1477 and 'Letters, Notes, Etc.', *BMJ*, 3 December 1904, p.1551.

88 Sykes, 'The Evolution', pp.7–8.

89 Henri Coullet, 'The Best Means of Helping the Mother Below the "Poverty" Line', *Proceedings of the Second National Conference on Infantile Mortality*, London, P.S. King & Son, 1908.

90 'How they Fight Infant Mortality in Paris', *The Times*, 26 December 1905, p.2.

91 'St Pancras Mothers' and Infants' Society', *Lancet*, 15 June 1907, pp.1665–666; McCleary, *The Early History*, pp.118–19.

92 Alys Russell, 'The Ghent School for Mothers', *The Nineteenth Century*, December 1906, pp.970, 975. See also *BMJ*, 6 July 1907, p.50.

93 'St Pancras School for Mothers', *BMJ*, 13 June 1908, p.1461.

94 Evelyn Bunting, Dora E.L. Bunting, Annie E. Barnes, and Blanche Gardiner, *A School for Mothers*, p.18.

95 Sykes, 'The Evolution', in Bunting, *A School for Mothers*, pp.8–9. See also reports in the medical press: 'The Prevention of Infantile Mortality', *BMJ*, 12 September 1908, p.775 and 'The Attack on Infantile Mortality', *Public Health*, vol.21, no.1, March 1908, p.43.

96 Bunting, Bunting, Barnes, and Gardiner, *A School for Mothers*, pp.25, 29–30.

97 Ibid., pp.35–6, 41–2, 37–8.

98 Ibid., pp.72–6.

99 'Public Health of London', *BMJ*, 1 February 1908, p.272.

100 H.O. Pilkington, 'The Reduction of Infantile Mortality Without Municipal Milk Depôts', *Public Health*, April 1907, pp.415–16. See also the report of Pilkington's paper in the *BMJ*, 16 March 1907, pp.628–29.

101 The records in the Ministry of Health files provide evidence both of constructive and obstructive local activity. Not all authorities adopting the Notification of Births Act did so to advantage: in a number the legislation remained a dead-letter and nothing the LGB did or wrote ameliorated the situation until the outbreak of the war and the passage of the Extension Act.

For evidence of constructive local activity subsequent to adoption of the Notification of Births Act, see also:

M.H. 48 no.164 Kensington Metropolitan Borough. Maternity and Child Welfare Scheme File, 1907–19.

M.H. 48 no.196 Bradford County Borough. Maternity and Child Welfare Scheme File, 1907–17.

For evidence of local recalcitrance, see *inter alia*:

M.H. 48 no. 23 Cornwall County Council. Maternity and Child Welfare Scheme File, 1913–19.

M.H. 48 no. 161 Camberwell Metropolitan Borough. Maternity and Child Welfare Scheme File, 1907–19. N.B. Local physicians opposed adoption of the Notification of Births Act and the MOH, Francis Stevens, believed that material help was needed, not education. By November 1915 Camberwell was the only borough in London which refused to hire health visitors; this situation did not change through 1918. See especially the controversy surrounding the impassioned plea of Alfred Lucas, Member of Camberwell Borough Council and the Registrar of Births and Deaths, to the Public Health Committee to hire health visitors. Letter of Lucas to LGB, 22 August 1911. Excerpts reprinted in the Public Health Committee agenda of the same date.

M.H. 48 no. 163 Islington Metropolitan Borough. Maternal and Child Welfare File, 1908–19. Despite the active efforts of the MOH A.E. Harris, the Borough Council refused to sanction expenditure for infant welfare work. Note particularly the 1910 *Report* of the MOH, in which Harris '*again advises the Council, as strongly as he can, to appoint a sufficient number of Health Visitors to carry out the intentions of the Notification of Births Act, 1907, which was the instruction of mothers through the means of Health Visitors*': pp. 17–18, also pp. 37–42. Also of special interest: J. Lane-Claypon's site report dated 29 October 1914 and the notes relating to Harris's appointment at the LGB office to discuss his borough's failure to move in the area of infant welfare work, 29 January 1915. And Harris's report to the Public Health Committee on Maternity and Child Welfare Scheme, 29 May 1916.

102 'Birmingham', *BMJ*, 15 August 1908, pp.435–36.
103 Janet Lane-Claypon, 'Phases in the Development of the Infant Welfare Movement in England', *Transactions of the 4th Annual Meeting of the American Association for the Study and Prevention of Infant Mortality*, Washington DC, GPO, 1914, pp.391–92. See also M.H. 48 no.183 Birmingham County Borough. Maternity and Child Welfare Scheme File, 1908–15. M.H. 48 no.182 Ibid., 1915–18.
104 'Liverpool', *BMJ*, 19 September 1908, p.856. See also M.H. 48 no.252 Liverpool County Borough. Maternity and Child Welfare Scheme File 1914–16. M.H. 48 no.251 Ibid., 1917.
105 Alfred Robinson, 'The Trained Midwife; her Effect upon Infantile Mortality', *Public Health*, August 1909, pp.423–24. See also Harold Kerr, 'Modern Educative Methods for the Prevention of Infantile Mortality', *Public Health*, January 1910, pp.129–34, and A.E. Naish, 'Summer Diarrhoea', *Public Health*, vol.23, February 1910, pp.168–73.
106 M.H. 48 no.160 Bermondsey Metropolitan Borough, Maternity and Child Welfare 1907–19. Note by W.H. Power, 16 November 1907.
107 M.H. 48 no.167 Stepney Metropolitan Borough, Sanitary Inspectors 1901–19. Correspondence: 28 June 1909 – Stepney to LGB; 9 July 1909 – LGB to Stepney; 27 August 1909 – Stepney to LGB.
108 M.H. 48 no.169 Woolwich Metropolitan Borough. Sanitary Inspectors 1901–9. Correspondence: 20 July 1906 – The Sanitary Inspectors Association to the LGB; 26 July 1906 – Woolwich to LGB; 6 November 1906 –

Woolwich to LGB. See also relevant correspondence and notes on 4 June and 13 July 1906.

109 See, *inter alia*, George Millson's (MOH, Southwark) impassioned pleas to hire two additional woman sanitary inspectors to do infant welfare work. M.H. 48 no.165 Southwark Metropolitan Borough Council. Sanitary Inspectors 1909–1919; George Millson, *Borough of Southwark Public Health Department Report* for week ending 4 November 1911, p.11; *Report* of the Public Health Department to the Special Sub-Committee of the Public Health Committee of the Borough Council, 11 December 1911, signed by Millson.

110 'National Conference of Infantile Mortality', *Lancet*, 16 June 1906, p.1424.

111 'Proposed Lady Health Visitor for Keighley', *BMJ*, 13 July 1907, p.110.

112 Letter from Charles Whitby to the *BMJ*, 27 July 1907, p.236.

113 Letter from J. Skardon Prowse to the *BMJ*, 10 August 1907, p.365.

114 Letter from W.H. Symons to the *BMJ*, 10 August 1907, p.365.

115 'Ladies and Public Health', *BMJ*, 16 November 1907, pp.1458–459.

116 Emilia Kanthack, *The Preservation of Infant Life*, London, H.K. Lewis 1907, pp. 8–10, 20–22, 52–3.

117 Craig, *Child and Adolescent Life*, p.157.

118 M.H. 48 no.165 Southwark Metropolitan Borough Council. Sanitary Inspectors 1909–19. Correspondence and notes: 30 May 1912 Southwark to LGB.

119 Ibid., 10 June 1912 Women Sanitary Inspectors' Association to LGB.

120 Ibid., 13 June 1912 office note.

121 Ibid., 25 June 1912 office note.

122 See, for example, M.H. 48 no.168 Westminster City Council. Sanitary Inspectors 1911–12. 13 January 1916 letter from the Women Sanitary Inspectors and Health Visitors' Association to the LGB. Westminster City Council had decided 'to delegate its powers to appoint and directly to supervise the work of two Health Visitors to the Westminster Health Society' to which the Association objected.

123 There are a plethora of examples of amicable relations between the municipal and voluntary infant welfare organizations in the Ministry of Health File 48. One particularly noteworthy case was that of Kensington. M.H. 48 no.164. Kensington Metropolitan Borough. Maternal and Child Welfare Scheme File, 1907–19. See, *inter alia*, the site report of J. Lane-Claypon dated 3 July 1914.

124 Lane-Claypon, 'Phases in the Development', p.393.

125 Bibby, Colles, and Petty, *The Pudding Lady*, London, Steads Publishing House, 1910, pp.1–2.

126 Arthur Newsholme, 'Second Report on Infant and Child Mortality', Supplement to the *42nd Annual Report of the Local Government Board*, Cd 6909, London, HMSO, 1913, p. 100.

127 Ibid., pp.387–90.

128 Pritchard, *The Infant*, pp.260–61.

129 Third National Conference on Infant Mortality, *Report of the Proceedings*, London, National Association for the Prevention of Infant Mortality and for the Welfare of Infancy, 1914, p.5.

130 Eric Pritchard, 'The Scope and Functions of Schools for Mothers', in Third National Conference, *Report of the Proceedings*, pp. 55, 62.

131 Lane-Claypon, 'Phases in the Development', p.391.
132 Margaret Llewelyn Davies (ed.), *Maternity: Letters from Working Women*, London, Virago, 1978 (first published 1915 by G. Bell & Sons, London), pp.10–11.
133 Ibid., Letter no. 62, pp.89–90.
134 Ibid., Letter no. 100, p.129.
135 Ibid., Letter no. 122, p.154.
136 Ibid., Letter no. 43, p.70.
137 Ibid., Letter no. 53, p.81.
138 Ibid., Letter no. 115, p.147.
139 Ibid., Letter no. 120, p.152.

Chapter VI

1 G.B., P.P., Royal Commission on Physical Training, vol. I *Report*, Cd 1507, London, HMSO, 1903, p.37.
2 'National Physique', *BMJ*, 28 December 1901, p.1875.
3 'The Food Factor in Education', *BMJ*, 4 April 1903, pp. 797–98, 800.
4 Sir George Arthur, 'National Physical Training: An Open Debate', *Manchester Guardian*, 22 April 1903, p.10.
5 Winston Churchill, 'National Physical Training: An Open Debate', *Manchester Guardian*, 25 April 1903, p.7.
6 C.E.B. Russell, 'National Physical Training: An Open Debate', *Manchester Guardian*, 12 May 1903, p.12.
7 Arthur Newsholme, 'National Physical Training: An Open Debate', *Manchester Guardian*, 27 May 1903, p.12. See also *BMJ* review of this series, 'Manchester', *BMJ*, 13 June 1903, p.1407.
8 Royal Commission on Physical Training, *Report*, Cd 1507, pp.29, 87.
9 'National Physique', *BMJ*, 18 July 1903, p.155. See also, 'Medical Notes in Parliament', *BMJ*, 18 July 1903, p.159.
10 G.B., P.P., Inter-Departmental Committee on Physical Deterioration, vol. II: *Minutes of Evidence*, Cd 2210, Evidence of Dr Alfred Eichholz, pp. 19–39. (See especially pp.22, 26. See also vol. I, Cd 2175, p. 66.)
11 'The Food Factor in Education', *BMJ*, 22 August 1903, pp.424–25.
12 Sir John E. Gorst, 'Is the British Race Degenerating?' *Manchester Guardian*, 10 December 1903, p.12. For a historical assessment of Gorst, see Bentley B. Gilbert, 'Sir John Eldon Gorst and the Children of the Nation', *Bulletin of Historical Medicine*, vol. 28, 1954, pp. 243–51.
13 'Education and Deterioration', *BMJ*, 12 December 1903, p.1541.
14 'Physical Degeneration: Compulsory Education', *BMJ*, 12 December 1903, p.1557.
15 'Physical Deterioration', a letter to *The Times* by Robert Farquharson, MP, MD, 26 December 1903, p. 8.
16 Letters on 'Free Meals for Children' in *The Times* – Jonathan Hutchinson: 20 September 1904, p.8; Louisa Twining: 7 September 1904, p.7; W.A.B.: 12 September 1904, p.9; James Cassidy: 15 September 1904, p.8; Margaret Frere: 20 September 1904, p.7; Constance Meyerstein: 20 September 1904, p.8.
17 'The Problem of Feeding School Children', *BMJ*, 1 October 1904, p.850.
18 'The Feeding of School Children', *Lancet*, 17 September 1904, pp. 860–62;

20 October 1906, pp. 1096–098; 10 November 1906, pp. 1308–310; 1 December 1906, pp. 1547–549; 15 December 1906, pp. 1689–690; 5 January 1907, pp. 53–5; 19 January 1907, pp. 191–93; 13 April 1907, pp. 1042–044. See also two articles by another correspondent on 5 August 1905, pp. 406–08 and 28 October 1905, pp. 1278–280.

19 See, *inter alia*, Ralph H. Crowley, *The Hygiene of School Life*, London, Methuen, 1910, p. 187.

20 'The Feeding of School Children', *Lancet*, 17 September 1904, p. 860.

21 See, *inter alia*, N.A., *Prize Essays on Feeding Children*, London, Sir Joseph Causton & Sons, 1890: Essay I: Frederick Allen, 'Food-Aided Education; or Methods Adopted in Continental or Foreign Countries for Supplying Meals to Underfed School Children'; Essay II: P. César, 'Les Soupes Scolaires or Soup-Kitchens in Schools'; Essay III: Mary E. Huddy, 'This is the Way we Eat our Food'. All three essays discussed the Paris system.

22 'The Feeding of School Children', *Lancet*, 17 September 1904, pp. 860–62.

23 Ibid. Also, note the reference to the 1870–71 war in 'Feeding Children in the Paris Schools', *Lancet*, 31 December 1904, p. 1876.

24 Ibid.

25 For an excellent discussion of the early history of the movement for the provision of meals in England, see M.E. Bulkley, *The Feeding of School Children*, London, G. Bell & Sons, 1914, Chapter I, 'The History of the Movement', pp. 1–49. See also Louise Stevens Bryant, *School Feeding*, Philadelphia & London, J.B. Lippincott, 1913, Chapter I, pp. 14–22.

26 Ibid. See also N.A., *Prize Essays on Feeding School Children*, Introduction by William Bousfield, pp. 5–15.

27 Ibid. See also 'London Schools Dinner Association', *The Times*, 11 December 1901, p. 7, and 'Destitute Children's Dinner Society', *The Times*, 14 December 1901, p. 13.

28 Quoted in T.J. Macnamara, 'Physical Condition of Working-Class Children', *The Nineteenth Century*, August 1904, pp. 308–09.

29 'The Physical Condition of Working-Class Children', *BMJ*, 5 November 1904, p. 1252.

30 'The Physical Condition of Board School Children', *Lancet*, 5 November 1904, p. 1302.

31 T.J. Macnamara, 'Physical Condition of Working-Class Children', p. 311. See also, 'In Corpore Sano', *The Contemporary Review*, February 1905, p. 248.

32 'The Guildhall Conference on Feeding School Children', *Lancet*, 28 January 1905, pp. 235–37.

33 Gertrude M. Tuckwell, 'Trades Union Congress, 1904', *Commonwealth*, vol. 9, October 1904, pp. 307–08. Gorst obtained a resolution in favour of school feeding from the Trades Union Congress in 1904. Of course, there were also those who opposed the idea, most notably the COS and its devotees. See, for example, C.A. Elliott, 'State Feeding of School Children in London', *Nineteenth Century*, May 1909, pp. 862–74; 'The Feeding of School Children', *Charity Organization Review*, vol. 20, July 1906, pp. 30–45; Henry Iselin, 'The Story of a Children's Care Committee', *Economic Review*, vol. 22, January 1912, pp. 42–64; 'A New Poor Law for Children', *Charity Organization Review*, vol. 25, March 1909, pp. 168–72.

34 John Gorst, 'Governments and Social Reform', *Fortnightly Review*, May

1905, pp. 846–47. See also Gorst, 'Physical Deterioration in Great Britain', *North American Review*, July 1905, pp. 1–10.

35 Quoted in Bentley B. Gilbert, 'Health and Politics', *Bulletin of the History of Medicine*, vol. 39, 1965, p. 150. See this article for an excellent historical analysis, pp. 143–53.

36 G.B., P.P., Inter-Derpartmental Committee on Medical Inspection and Feeding of Children Attending the Public Elementary Schools, *Report*, Cd 2779, London, HMSO, 1906, p. 4.

37 John Gorst, 'Children's Rights', *The National Review*, June 1905, pp. 712–13.

38 John Gorst, *The Children of the Nation*, London, Methuen, 1906, p. 86.

39 *Hansard*, vol. 145, 18 April 1905, col. 531.

40 Bryant, *School Feeding*, Appendix A, pp. 299–302.

41 Ibid., Appendix B, pp. 302–11.

42 Bradford already had been supplying meals to some students. See: 'Yorkshire', *BMJ*, 17 February 1906, p. 409 and William Leach, 'School Feeding', *The Crusade*, vol. 2, pp. 192–93.

43 G.A.N. Lowndes, *Margaret McMillan*, London, Museum Press, 1960, pp. 50–9; Albert Mansbridge, *Margaret McMillan*, London, Dent, 1932, pp. 21–52.

44 Ralph H. Crowley, 'The Provision of Meals for School Children', *Public Health*, vol. 20, no. 5, February 1908, pp. 325–35.

45 Crowley, *The Hygiene of School Life*, Chapter XI, 'The Provision of School Meals', especially pp. 193–201. See also Bryant, *School Feeding*, pp. 46–57 and Bulkley, *The Feeding of School Children*, pp. 184–86.

46 See, for example, Margaret Llewelyn Davies, *Maternity: Letters from Working Women*, London, Virago, 1978; and Maud Pember Reeves, *Round About a Pound a Week*, London, Virago, 1979, especially Chapter VI, 'Budgets', pp. 75–93.

47 See for example, Bryant, *School Feeding*, pp. 31–7; Bulkley, *Feeding of School Children*, pp. 171–83 and most especially pp. 184–201; Arthur Greenwood, *The Health and Physique of School Children*, London, P.S. King & Son, 1913, especially Chapter V, 'The Health of School Children', pp. 45–68; 'School Hygiene: A Comparison of Children in Secondary and Elementary Schools', *BMJ*, 16 March 1907, pp. 635–36.

48 For a discussion of local difficulties see, for example, Harry Beswick, 'Feeding the Children', *The Clarion*, 11 October 1912, p.7.

49 Bulkley, *Feeding School Children*, Chapter II, 'The Administration of the Act', pp.50–130; Crowley, *Hygiene of School Life*, pp.191 *et seq.*

50 Royal Commission on Physical Training, *Report*, Cd 1507, p.28.

51 Ibid., p.29. See also 'The Report of the Royal Commission on Physical Training (Scotland)', *BMJ*, 25 April 1903, p.984.

52 W. Leslie MacKenzie, *The Medical Inspection of School Children*, Edinburgh, William Hodge, 1904, pp.73–5.

53 Herbert H. Tidswell, 'Physical Degeneration in Children of the Working Classes', *BMJ*, 15 August 1903, pp.356–57.

54 Letter from F.G. Haworth, *BMJ*, 26 March 1903, pp.756–57.

55 J.H. Crocker, 'Medical Officers of Health and Elementary Schools', *Public Health*, April 1904, pp.414–15.

56 'Medical Inspection of Schools', *BMJ*, April 1904, p.850.

57 'Physical Education in Elementary Schools', *BMJ*, 7 May 1904, pp.1091–092.
58 'Medical Inspection of School Children', *BMJ*, 16 July 1904, pp.137–38.
59 Inter-Departmental Committee on Physical Deterioration, *Report*, Cd 2175, p.91.
60 W.J. Tyson, 'Presidential Address to the Preventive Medicine Section', *Journal of State Medicine*, vol.12, no.9, 1904, p.533.
61 Macnamara 'Physical Condition of Working-Class Children', p.311. See also idem, 'In Corpore Sano', pp.245–46.
62 John Gorst, 'Children's Rights', *The National Review*, June 1905, p.711.
63 Idem, 'Physical Deterioration in Great Britain', p.6. In his book, *The Children of the Nation*, Gorst elaborated on these themes; see especially Chapters 1 and 4.
64 Aimée Watt Smyth, *Physical Deterioration*, London, John Murray, 1904, pp.120–22.
65 'The Medical Control of Schools at New York', *Lancet*, 25 March 1905, pp.823–24 and 1 April 1905, pp.888–90.
66 William Harbutt Dawson, Board of Education, Educational Pamphlets, no.4, *School Doctors in Germany*, London, HMSO, 1906, pp.iii, iv, 1.
67 Ibid., p.iii.
68 'Medical Inspection of Schools', *BMJ*, 17 February 1906, pp.400–02. This general argument was voiced by several different speakers in a variety of forums. See, *inter alia*, 'The Physical State of School Children: The Question of Medical Inspection', *Lancet*, 21 April 1906, p.1123; the report of Kerr's address to the Birmingham branch of the Society of Medical Officers of Health in 'Birmingham', *BMJ*, 5 May 1906, p.1066; Helen MacMurchy's address on 'Medical Inspection of Children Attending Elementary Schools', to the Section of State Medicine at the 1906 BMA meeting, *BMJ*, 22 September 1906, pp.675–80; and a paper read before the Medical Officers of Schools Association on 13 December 1906, by Ralph Crowley (and commentary), *The Need, Objects, and Method of the Medical Inspection of Primary Schools*, London, J. & A. Churchill, 1907. See also the *Proceedings* of the second International Congress on School Hygiene which was held 5–8 August 1907 in London.
69 Beatrice Webb, *Our Partnership*, London, Longmans, Green & Co., 1948, p.379. For a discussion of the relation between Robert Morant and the Webbs, and of their shared vision of future social services, see Gilbert, *The Evolution of National Insurance*, London, Michael Joseph, 1966, Chapter 3, 'The Children of the Nation'; Norman and Jeanne MacKenzie, *The First Fabians*, London, Quartet Books, 1979, pp.197–98, 351–60.
70 This appointment was controversial, and led to a great deal of bitterness. Many people thought it should have gone to James Kerr who had done important work in this field both in Bradford, and after 1901, in London. Kerr's views on and plans for future health services did not coincide with those of Morant, and the job went to Newman. For evidence of contemporary bad feeling, see two letters written by Archibald Hogarth, an Assistant Medical Officer (Education) for the London County Concil under Kerr: *BMJ*, 21 September 1907, pp.772–73 and 12 October 1907, p.1019. See also *BMJ* editorial position: 'The Attitude of the Board of Education to School Hygiene', *BMJ*, 21 September 1907, pp.760–61. For a discussion of the disastrous results of this conflict between the Board of Education and

the London County Council see J.D. Hirst, '"A Failure Without Parallel": The School Medical Service and the London County Council', *Medical History*, 1981, pp.281–300.

71 Quoted in Albert Mansbridge, *Margaret McMillan*, London, Dent, 1932, p.66.

72 'The Medical Inspection of School Children', reprint in full of the 'Memorandum on Medical Inspection of Children in Public Elementary Schools' (Circular 576), by Robert Morant, dated 22 November 1907, *Lancet*, 30 November 1907, pp.1555–557.

73 'Medical Inspection of School Children, *BMJ*, 30 November 1907, pp.1604–605.

74 'The Medical Inspection of School Children', a reprint in full of the 23 January 1908 Circular 582 issued by the Board of Education, *Public Health*, vol.21, March 1908, pp.37–9.

75 C.J. Thomas, 'The History and Practice of School Inspection', *Public Health*, vol.21, July 1908, pp.189–93.

76 W. Lloyd Edwards, 'Medical Inspection of Schools', *BMJ*, 18 July 1908, pp.142–44.

77 'The Last School Board Report', *BMJ*, 25 June 1904, pp.1814–815.

78 'The International Congress of School Hygiene', *BMJ*, 17 August 1907, p.403.

79 'Medical Inspection of School Children', see the 'Warwickshire' and 'Birmingham' sections, *BMJ*, 11 April 1908, p.884.

80 'The Official Schedule of Medical Inspection', *Public Health*, vol.21, March 1908, p.1.

81 'The Position of the School Doctor in the Society of Medical Officers of Health', *Public Health*, vol.21, July 1908, p.173.

82 'Medical Inspection of School Children', *BMJ*, Supplement for 12 September 1908, pp.190–92.

83 Ibid., pp.190, 193.

84 'Manchester and Salford', *BMJ*, 3 October 1908, p.1038 and 7 November 1908, p.1464; 'West Yorkshire: Medical Inspection in West Riding Schools', *BMJ*, 3 October 1908, p.1039.

85 'Annual Dinner', *Public Health*, vol.23, November 1909, p.67.

86 'The Health of Salford', *BMJ*, 3 October 1908, p.1039.

87 H. Meredith Richards, 'The Co-ordination of Medical Inspection with Public Health Work', *Public Health*, February 1909, p.166.

88 Edward W. Hope, 'Co-relation of the School Medical Service and the Public Health Service', in T.N. Kelynack (ed.), *Medical Examination of Schools and Scholars*, London, P.S. King & Son, 1910, p.7.

89 M.H. 48 no.169, Woolwich Metropolitan Borough, Sanitary Inspectors 1901–19, 'Extract from the Annual Report of the Medical Officer of Health for the Year 1912', pp.111–12.

90 M.H. 48 no.42, Durham County, Maternity and Child Welfare Scheme 1907–15, 'Summary of Expenditure for the Six Month Period ending 30 September 1914'.

91 M.H. 48 no.182, Birmingham, Maternity and Child Welfare File. *Annual Report* of the MOH for 1914. 'Health Visitors' Work' by Blanche Gardiner, pp.117–18. See also note of I. Cameron to Arthur Newsholme of 5 June 1916.

92 G.B., Board of Education, *Annual Report of the Chief Medical Officer for*

1909, Cd 5426, London, HMSO, 1910, p.118; idem, *Annual Report for 1910*, Cd 5925, p.152; idem, *Annual Report for 1912*, Cd 7184, pp.175–77; idem, *Annual Report for 1913*, Cd 7730, p.136.

93 Lewis D. Cruickshank, *School Clinics at Home and Abroad*, London, National League for Physical Education and Improvement, 1913, p.111.

94 E.W. Hope, 'Co-relation of the School Medical Service and the Public Health Service', p.4.

Conclusion

1 'The War and the Falling Birth-Rate', *BMJ*, 30 October 1915, p.649. See also 'Infant Mortality and the Birth-Rate', *Lancet*, 4 September 1915, p.556.

2 Ibid., pp.649–50. For a more prosaic but similar point of view, see Arthur Newsholme, 'Report of the Medical Officer', *Supplement to the 47th Annual Report of the Local Government Board 1917–18*, Cd 9169, London, HMSO, 1918, pp.xx–xxi.

3 Sara Josephine Baker, *Fighting for Life*, Huntingdon, NY, Robert E. Krieger Publishing Company, 1980 (originally published 1939 by Macmillan), p.165.

4 J.M. Winter, 'The Impact of the First World War on Civilian Health in Britain', *Economic History Review*, vol.30, 1977, p.498. See also London, Wellcome Institute Archives, Eric Pritchard papers, 'The Welfare Movement', in which he has described in considerable detail the first National Baby Week and its yearly successors. For a discussion of other publicity campaigns, see George F. McCleary, *The Maternity and Child Welfare Movement*, London, P.S. King & Son, 1935, pp.18–24.

5 William S. Craig, *Child and Adolescent Life*, Edinburgh, E. & S. Livingstone, p.164.

6 *Maternity and Child Welfare*, vol.2, no.5, May 1918, p.183.

7 M.H. 48 no.252, Liverpool County Borough, Maternal and Child Welfare Scheme File, 1907–16, 'Inquiry into the Local Conditions Affecting Child Welfare' by Janet Lane-Claypon dated 19 August 1914.

8 Ibid., Lane-Claypon's report of a site visit on 20 and 21 January 1916.

9 M.H. 48 no.251 Liverpool County Borough, Maternal and Child Welfare Scheme File, 1917, Report by I. Cameron dated 6 October 1917.

10 'Parliamentary Intelligence: Notification of Births (Extension) Bill', *Lancet*, 17 July 1915, p.155.

11 G.B., Board of Education, *Annual Report for 1913 of the Chief Medical Officer of the Board of Education*, Cd 7730, London, HMSO, 1914, pp.257, 250.

12 G.B., Board of Education, *Annual Report for 1918 of the Chief Medical Officer of the Board of Education*, Cmd 420, London, HMSO, 1919, p.1.

13 G.B., Board of Education, *Annual Report for 1917 of the Chief Medical Officer of the Board of Education*, Cd 9206, London, HMSO, 1918, pp.161, 162, 173.

14 Janet Lane-Claypon, *The Child Welfare Movement*, London, G. Bell & Sons, 1920, Appendix, 'Circular (Maternity and Child Welfare 4)' from the Local Government Board, pp.244–61.

15 James Wheatley, 'Discussion on Factors Contributing to the Recent

Decrease in Infantile Mortality', *BMJ*, 27 October 1923, p.756.

16 Arthur Newsholme, *The Last Thirty Years in Public Health*, London, George Allen & Unwin, 1936, pp.198, 188–94.

17 George Newman, *The Building of a Nation's Health*, London, Macmillan, 1939, pp.245, 247–48, 318. See in particular Chapter IX, 'The Mother and Her Infant', pp.281–321 and pp.234–48.

18 London, Wellcome Institute Archives, Eric Pritchard papers, 'The Welfare Movement', p.3.

19 Ibid., p.4.

20 M.H. 55 no.543, Maternity and Child Welfare: Scope of Grant-aided Service, Notification of Births (Extension) Act, 1915. Office note of 18 August 1914 re: visit of Margaret Llewelyn Davies to Arthur Newsholme.

21 Ibid., M.H. 55 no.543, Draft of letter.

22 Ibid., M.H. 55 no.543, letter to the editor from Barton and Davies, 'The Care of Maternity in War-Time', *Westminster Gazette*, 26 August 1914.

23 Ibid., M.H. 55 no.543, 'Save the Babies', *South London Press*, 30 June 1916; 'Infant Welfare: Camberwell's Mistake', *South London Press*, 30 June 1916; 'Child Welfare', *Camberwell and Peckham Times*, 1 July 1916.

24 M.H. 48 no.161, Camberwell Metropolitan Borough, Maternity and Child Welfare Scheme File, 1907–19. Letter from Beatrice W. Warwick to the President of the LGB, dated 27 March 1917.

25 Ibid., M.H. 48 no.161, Resolution passed unanimously at a public meeting of residents of Camberwell, 15 March 1917.

26 Ibid., M.H. 48 no.161. Notes of 28 August 1916, June 1917, 6 December 1917, February 1918.

27 London, Wellcome Institute, Contemporary Medical Archives Centre, Eric Pritchard papers, 'The Infants' Hospital', p.1.

A note on sources

1 Gilbert Slater, *Poverty and the State*, London, Constable, 1930, p.162.

2 Richard M. Titmuss, *Essays on 'the Welfare State'*, 3rd edn, London, George Allen and Unwin, 1976 (first published 1958), pp. 80–1.

3 Pat Thane, *The Foundations of the Welfare State*, London, Longman, 1982, pp.69, 78.

4 Titmuss, *Essays*, p.80.

5 Bentley B. Gilbert, *The Evolution of National Insurance in Great Britain: The Origins of the Welfare State*, London, Michael Joseph, 1966, p.152.

6 Ibid., p.102.

7 Ibid., p.156.

8 Ibid., p.157.

9 Bentley B. Gilbert, *British Social Policy 1914–1939*, London, Batsford, 1970, p.vii.

10 Eric J. Evans, *Social Policy 1830–1914: Individualism, Collectivism and the Origins of the Welfare State*, London, Routledge & Kegan Paul, 1978, pp.15–17, 2.

11 Frank Honigsbaum, *The Struggle for the Ministry of Health, 1914–1919*, Occasional Papers on Social Adminstration no.37, London, G. Bell & Sons, 1970, p.42. See pp.36–48 for the analysis of the LGB measure v. the Ministry of Health scheme. See also idem, *The Division in British*

Medicine, London, Kogan Page, 1979, especially parts 1 and 2, pp.7–91.

12 See, for example, Charles Booth, *The Life and Labour of the People in London*, 10 vols, London, Macmillan, 1892–7 and idem *Family Budgets*, London, Economic Club, 1896; William Booth, *In Darkest England and the Way Out*, London, International Headquarters of the Salvation Army, 1890; Andrew Mearns, *The Bitter Cry of Outcast London*, edited by Anthony S. Wohl, Leicester, Leicester University Press, 1970 (first published 1883); idem, *London and its Teeming Toilers*, London, Warren Hall & Lovitt, 1885; B. Seebohm Rowntree, *Poverty*, London, Macmillan, 1901; and George Sims, *How the Poor Live and Horrible London*, London, Chatto & Windus, 1889.

13 There is a rich literature on the relationship between imperialism, national efficiency, eugenics, and social reform. See, *inter alia*, Michael Freeden *The New Liberalism*, Oxford, Clarendon Press, 1978, especially Chapter 3, 'Biology Evolution and Liberal Collectivism' and Chapter 5, 'Social Reform and Human Improvement', pp.76–116, 170–94; Gilbert, *The Evolution of National Insurance*, especially part 3 of Chapter 2, 'The Condition of the People' and parts 1 and 2 of Chapter 3, 'The Children of the Nation', pp.72–101, 102–13; Donald MacKenzie, 'Eugenics in Britain', *Social Studies in Science*, vol.6, 1976, pp.499–532; Jeanne and Norman McKenzie, *The First Fabians*, London, Quartet Books, 1979; H.C.G. Matthew, *The Liberal Imperialists*, London, Oxford University Press, 1973; Geoffrey R. Searle, *The Quest for National Efficiency*, Oxford, Blackwell, 1971; idem, *Eugenics and Politics in Britain: 1900–1914*, Leyden, Nordhoof International Publishing, 1976; Bernard Semmel, *Imperialism and Social Reform*, London, George Allen & Unwin, 1960. Less extensive but also of interest are the brief discussions in Jeanne Brand, *Doctors and the State*, Baltimore, Md, The Johns Hopkins University Press, 1965, pp.165–71; Derek Fraser, *The Evolution of the British Welfare State*, London, Macmillan, 1981, pp.135–38; Thane, *Foundations of the Welfare State*, pp.57–62; Titmuss, 'War and Social Policy', *Essays*, pp.75–87.

14 Slater, *Poverty and the State*, p.3.

15 Peter Keating (ed.), *Into Unknown England, 1866–1913*, Manchester, Manchester University Press, 1976, p.19.

16 F.B. Smith, *The People's Health, 1830–1910*, London, Croom Helm, 1979, pp.92–103.

17 Thomas McKeown, *The Role of Medicine*, Oxford, Blackwell, 1979, p.53.

18 Ibid., p.57.

19 M.W. Beaver, 'Population, Infant Mortality and Milk', *Population Studies*, vol.27, 1973, p.253.

20 Ibid. See pp.250–52, fns 40, 41, 44, 45.

21 Arthur Guy Enock, *This Milk Business*, London, H.K. Lewis, p.3.

22 Ibid., p.67.

23 Ibid., p.68.

24 McKeown, *The Role of Medicine*, p.xv-xvi.

25 Jeanne L. Brand, *Doctors and the State: The British Medical Profession and Government Action in Public Health, 1870–1912*, Baltimore, Md, Johns Hopkins University Press, 1965, p.182.

26 Anna Davin, 'Imperialism and Motherhood', *History Workshop*, vol.5, 1978, p.12; Carol Dyhouse, 'Working-Class Mothers and Infant Mortality in England, 1895–1914', *Journal of Social History*, vol.12, 1979, p.251.

27 Davin, 'Imperialism and Motherhood', p.13.
2   Dyhouse, 'Mothers and Infant Mortality', pp.259–60.
29 Jane Lewis, *The Politics of Motherhood*, London, Croom Helm, 1980, p.224.
30 Ibid., p.21.
31 Ibid., p.68.
32 Ibid., pp.27, 68.
33 Ibid., p.81.
34 See Anna Davin's very different view of Newsholme in 'Imperialism and Motherhood', pp.30–2.
35 Arthur Newsholme, 'A Second Report on Infant and Child Mortality', *Supplement to the Report of the Medical Officer of the Local Government Board*, Cd 6909, London, HMSO, 1913, p.73.
36 Idem, 'A Report on Child Mortality at ages 0–5 in England and Wales', *Supplement to the Report of the Medical Officer of the Local Government Board*, Cd 8496, London, HMSO, 1916, p.64.
37 Idem, *The Last Thirty Years in Public Health*, London, George Allen & Unwin, 1936, p.198.
38 Idem, 'A Third Report on Infant Mortality', *Supplement to the Report of the Medical Officer of the Local Government Board*, Cd 7511, London, HMSO, 1914, p.12. See also, for example, Chapter 12, 'Defective Sanitation in Relation to Infant Mortality' in the 1913 report (Cd 6909).
39 Davin, 'Imperialism and Motherhood', p.26.
40 Lewis, *Politics of Motherhood*, p.220.
41 F.K. Prochaska, *Women and Philanthropy in Nineteenth-Century England*, Oxford, Clarendon Press, 1980, pp.97–8. Prochaska himself has noted that 'very little has been written on the visiting movement' (fn. p.97).
42 Ibid., p.101.
43 Ibid., p.103.
44 Titmuss, *Essays*, p.80.
45 J.M. Winter, 'The Impact of the First World War on Civilian Health in Britain', *Economic History Review*, vol.30, 1977, p.496.
46 Ibid., p.498.
47 Ivy Pinchbeck and Margaret Hewitt, *Children in English Society* (2 volumes), London, Routledge & Kegan Paul, 1973.
48 George K. Behlmer, *The Child Protection Movement in England 1860–1890*. Ph.D. dissertation, Stanford University, 1977.
49 Patricia Branca, *Silent Sisterhood: Middle-Class Women in the Victorian Home*, London, Croom Helm, 1975.
50 J.A. Banks, *Prosperity and Parenthood*, London, RKP, 1954.
51 J.A. Banks and Olive Banks, *Feminism and Family Planning*, Liverpool, Liverpool University Press, 1964, p.11.
52 Gareth Stedman Jones, *Outcast London*, Oxford, Clarendon Press, 1971.
53 Paul Thompson, *The Edwardians*, Frogmore, St Albans, Paladin, 1977 (first published by Weidenfeld & Nicolson, 1975).
54 Thea Thompson, *Edwardian Childhoods*, London, RKP, 1981.
55 Katharine Chorley, *Manchester Made Them*, London, Faber & Faber, 1950.
56 Robert Roberts, *The Classic Slum*, Manchester, Manchester University Press, 1971.

Bibliography

Allen, Greta (1908) *Practical Hints to Health Visitors.* London: Scientific Press (also 2nd edn, 1915).

Anderson, Bailie W.F. (1905) A Discussion on Infant Milk Depots (précis). *BMJ* 16 September: 643–44.

Armstrong, Hubert (1902) A Note on the Infantile Mortality from Tuberculous Meningitis and Tabes Mesenterica. *BMJ* 26 April: 1024.

Arthur, Sir George (1903) National Physical Training: An Open Debate. *Manchester Guardian* 22 April: 10.

Ashby, Henry (with Wright, G.A.) (1896) *The Diseases of Children* (3rd edn). London: Longmans Green & Co.

—— (1904) A Case of Scurvy in an Infant Fed on Municipal 'Humanized' Sterilized Milk. *BMJ* 27 February: 479–80.

—— (1905) *Health in the Nursery* (4th edn) London: Longmans Green & Co.

Ashby, Hugh T. (1922) *Infant Mortality* (2nd edn) Cambridge: Cambridge University Press.

Ashby, Lucy E. and Earp, Kate Atherton (1926) *Health Visitor's Guide.* London: Faber & Gwyer.

Association of Infant Welfare and Maternity Centres (1916) *To Wives and Mothers.* London: National League for Physical Education and Improvement (4th edn, 1921).

Astor, Viscount (1931) The Problem of the Milk Supply. *Lancet* 4 April: 771–73.

Atherton, Kate C. (1918) Some Hints on Teaching in Schools for Mothers. *Maternity and Child Welfare* 2 (1), January: 29–31.

Atkins, J.B. (1903) National Physical Training: An Open Debate. *Manchester Guardian* 18 April: 7.

Austen, E.E. (1909) Notes on Flies Examined during 1908. *Reports to the Local Government Board on Public Health and Medical Subjects*, Preliminary Reports on Flies as Carriers of Infection, N.S. no. 5. London: HMSO.

Axe, John Wortley (1904) The Cow in Relation to Public Health. *The Journal of State Medicine* 12 (12): 701–9.

Baginsky, Adolf (1913) Hygiene of City Infants and Babies. *Transactions* of the 15th International Congress on Hygiene and Demography, September 1912, vol. 3. Washington DC: GPO, 69–80.

Baker, Julian L. (1914) On the Analysis and Composition of some Proprietary Foods for Infants. *Reports to the Local Government Board on Public Health and Medical Subjects*, N.S. no. 80, Food Reports, no. 20. London: HMSO.

Baker, S. Josephine (1913) The Reduction of Infant Mortality in New York City. *Transactions* of the 15th International Congress in Hygiene and Demography, September 1912, vol. 3. Washington DC: GPO, 139–52.

—— (1914) The Relation of Baby-Saving Activities to the Department of Health and to Each Other. *Transactions* of the 4th Annual Meeting of the American Association for the Study and Prevention of Infant Mortality,

BIBLIOGRAPHY

Washington DC, 14–17 November 1913. Baltimore, MD: Franklin Printing Co., 351–53.

—— (1915) *The Bureau of Child Hygiene of the Department of Health of the City of New York.* New York: Monograph Series no. 4 of the Department of Health, January.

—— (1923a) *Healthy Babies.* Boston, MA: Little Brown & Co.

—— (1923b) *Healthy Children.* Boston, MA: Little Brown & Co.

—— (1980) *Fighting for Life.* New York: Robert E. Krieger (first published 1939).

Balestre, Paul-Louis (1905) Étude Statistique sur la Mortalité Infantile de 0 à 1 an de 1 à 2 ans à Nice de 1887 à 1904. Indications sur la Prophylaxie de la Mortalité Infantile. Lyon. No publisher noted.

Ballantyne, John William (1891) *An Introduction to the Diseases of Infancy.* London: Simpkin Marshall Hamilton Kent & Co.

—— (1902a) *Ante-Natal Pathology and Hygiene.* Edinburgh: W. Green & Sons.

—— (1902b) The Problem of the Premature Infant. *BMJ* 17 May: 1196–200.

—— (1908) Hospital Treatment of Morbid Pregnancies. *BMJ* 11 January: 65–6.

—— (1914) *Expectant Motherhood.* London: Cassell.

—— (1918) Antenatal and Neonatal Factors in Infantile Mortality. *Maternity and Child Welfare* 2 (10), October: 333–39.

Ballard, Edward (1889) Supplement in Continuation of the Report of the Medical Officer for 1887: The Causation of the Annual Mortality from 'Diarrhoea' which is observed principally in the Summer Season of the Year. *17th Annual Report of the Local Government Board 1887–8*, C. 5638. London: HMSO.

Barclay, James W. (1906) The Race Suicide Scare. *Nineteenth Century* December: 895–99.

Beadles, Hugh S. (1903) Case of Infantile Scurvy. *BMJ* 11 April: 843.

Bennett, Edith M. (1918) Babies in Peril. *Maternity and Child Welfare* 2 (11), November: 370–76; also 2 (12), December: 410–15, 418.

Beresford, Lord Charles (1903) National Physical Training: An Open Debate. *Manchester Guardian* 20 April: 10.

Berry, F. May Dickinson (1904) On the Physical Examination of 1,580 Girls from Elementary Schools in London. *BMJ* 28 May: 1248–249.

Berry, William (1904) Death Certification. *Lancet* 24 September: 893–94.

—— (1906) *Lectures to Teachers on the Prevention of Infectious Diseases.* Bristol: John Wright & Co.

Bertillon, Jacques (1896) *Élements de démographie.* Paris: Société d'Editions Scientifiques.

—— (1911) *La dépopulation de la France.* Paris: Librairie Félix Alcan.

Bertrand, D.-M. (1914) Recherches sur la flore intestinale dans la diarrhée des nourissons. *Annales de l'Institut Pasteur* 28: 121–48.

Beswick, Harry (1912) Feeding the Children. *The Clarion* 11 October: 7.

Bibby, Colles, and Petty (1910) *The Pudding Lady.* Published for the St Pancras School for Mothers, London: Stead's Publishing House.

Birchenough, Henry (1904) Compulsory Education and Compulsory Military Training. *Nineteenth Century* 56 (July): 20–7.

Blagg, Helen (1910) *A Statistical Analysis of Infant Mortality.* London: P.S. King.

Bond, W.A. (1909) The Milk Clauses of the London County Council (General

Powers) Act, 1908. *Public Health* 22 (5), February: 175–77.

Booker, William D. (1887) A Study of Some of the Bacteria Found in the Dejecta of Infants Afflicted with Summer Diarrhoea. *Transactions* of the International Medical Congress, 9th Session, vol. 3, Washington DC, 598–617.

—— (1889) A Study of Some of the Bacteria Found in the Faeces of Infants Affected with Summer Diarrhoea. *Transactions of the American Pediatric Society* 1: 198–227.

—— (1897) A Bacteriological and Anatomical Study of the Summer Diarrhoeas of Infants. *Johns Hopkins Hospital Reports* 6: 159–259.

Booth, Charles (1892–97) *The Life and Labour of the People in London* (10 vols). London: Macmillan.

—— (1896) *Family Budgets.* London: Economic Club.

Bosanquet, Bernard (ed.) (1895) *Aspects of the Social Problem by Various Writers.* London: Macmillan.

Bosanquet, Helen Dendy (1904a) Pauperization and Interests. *BMJ* 27 August: 434–36.

—— (1904b) Physical Degeneration and the Poverty Line. *The Contemporary Review* 85 (January): 65–75.

—— (1906) *The Family.* London: Macmillan.

—— (1914/1973) *Social Work in London, 1869–1912.* Brighton: Harvester (first published in 1914 by John Murray, London).

Bosanquet, W. Cecil (1902) Summer Diarrhoea of Infants. *Practitioner* 69 (16 N.S.), July–December: 139–61.

Bowen-Jones, L.M. (1909) The Control of the Milk Supply. *Public Health* 22 (5), February: 170–75.

Bray, John (1945) Isolation of Antigenically Homogenous Strains of *Bact. Coli Neapolitanum* from Summer Diarrhoea of Infants. *Journal of Pathology and Bacteriology* 57: 239–47.

—— and Beavan, T.E.D. (1948) Slide Agglutination of *Bacterium Coli Var. Neapolitanum* in Summer Diarrhoea. *Journal of Pathology and Bacteriology* 60: 395–401.

—— (1973) Bray's Discovery of Pathogenic *Esch. coli* as a Cause of Infantile Gastroenteritis. *Archives of Disease in Childhood* 48: 923–26.

Brend, William A. (1917a) The Relative Importance of Pre-Natal and Post-Natal Conditions as Causes of Infant Mortality. *The Mortalities of Birth, Infancy and Childhood*, Medical Research Council, Special Report Series no. 10. London: HMSO.

—— (1917b) *Health and the State.* London: Constable.

—— (1918) Atmospheric Pollution and Infant Mortality. *Maternity and Child Welfare* 2 (1), January: 25–9.

Broadfield, E.J. (1903) National Physical Training: An Open Debate. *Manchester Guardian* 21 May: 12

Brownlee, John and Young, Matthew (1922) The Epidemiology of Summer Diarrhoea. *Proceedings of the Royal Society of Medicine* 15 (2): 55–74.

Brunton, Sir Thomas Lauder (1903) National Physical Training: An Open Debate. *Manchester Guardian* 2 June: 10.

—— (1905) The Report of the Inter-Departmental Committee on Physical Degeneration. *Public Health* 17 (February): 274–84; Discussion: 284–92.

Bryant, Louise Stevens (1913) *School Feeding.* Philadelphia & London: J.B. Lippincott.

Budin, Pierre (1897) Sur le lait stérilisé. *Bulletin de l'Académie de Médecine* 37 (1 June): 685–87.

—— (1901) Sur un memoire de MM. les Drs. M. Balestre et Gilletta de Saint-Joseph (de Nice), intitulé: *Étude sur la mortalité de la première enfance. Bulletin de l'Académie de Médecine* 45 (11 June): 661–69.

—— (1903a) La mortalité infantile. *L'Obstétrique* 8 (January): 1–44.

—— (1903b) Précis de *Les Consultations de Nourrissons* par Charles Maygrier (1903) et *Goutte de Lait de Saint-Pol* par M. le Dr. Ausset. *Bulletin de l'Académie de Médecine* 50 (10 November): 266–67.

—— and Planchon, Pierre (1904) Note sur l'alimentation des enfants. *Bulletin de l'Académie de Médecine* 51 (5 January) 23–40.

—— (1907) *The Nursling* (originally *Le nourrisson*, 1900; authorized translation by William J. Maloney). London: The Caxton Publishing Co.

Bulkley, M.E. (1914) *The Feeding of School Children.* London: G. Bell.

Bunting, Evelyn M. (1907) *A School for Mothers.* London: Horace Marshall & Son.

Burgerstein, Leo (1913) Results to Individuals from Medical Inspection. *Transactions* of the 15th International Congress on Hygiene and Demography, September, 1912, vol. 3. Washington, DC: GPO, 245–55.

Burns, John (1903) National Physical Training: An Open Debate. *Manchester Guardian* 27 April: 10.

Byers, J.W. (1901) Introductory Remarks by the President (of the Section of Obstetric Medicine and Gynaecology) on Puerperal Fever, Uterine Cancer, and the Falling Birth-Rate. *BMJ* 5 October: 941–43.

Cameron, J. Spottiswoode (1892/3) Diarrhoea in Lancashire and Yorkshire Towns in 1892. *Public Health* 6: 152–53.

—— (1902) Women as Sanitary Inspectors. *Journal of State Medicine* December: 743–50.

—— (1906) The Appointment of Qualified Women with Special Reference to the Hygiene and Feeding of Infants. *Lancet* 4 August: 289–91.

Campbell, Janet (1910) Board of Education *Memorandum on the Teaching of Infant Care and Management in Public Elementary Schools*, Circular 758. London: HMSO.

—— (1915) Board of Education *Memorandum on Class Instruction at Schools for Mothers*, Circular 912. London: HMSO.

—— (1924) Maternal Mortality. *Reports on Public Health and Medical Subjects*, no. 25. London: HMSO.

—— (1927) The Protection of Motherhood. *Reports on Public Health and Medical Subjects*, no. 48. London: HMSO.

Cantlie, James (1902) The Health of the People. *Practitioner* 68: 259–83.

Carnegie United Kingdom Trust (1917) *Report on the Physical Welfare of Mothers and Children*, Volume I by E.W. Hope, Volume II by Janet M. Campbell. Liverpool: C. Tinling.

Carpenter, George (1903) *Golden Rules for Diseases of Infants and Children.* London: Simpkin Marshall Hamilton Kent.

—— (1904a) The Milk Supplied to Infants (editorial). *British Journal of Children's Diseases* 1 (1) January: 76–9.

—— (1904b) Milk Dispensaries for Children's Hospitals (editorial). *British Journal of Children's Diseases* 1 (4) May: 123–28.

—— (1904c) La Goutte de Lait (editorial). *British Journal of Children's*

Diseases 1 (5) May: 167–75.

—— (1904d) Municipal Milk Supplies (editorial). *British Journal of Children's Diseases* 1: 216–19.

Carr, J. Walter (1894) The Starting Points of Tuberculous Disease in Children. *Transactions of the Medical Society* (London) 17: 280–304.

—— (1895) A Protest Against the Use of the Term 'Consumptive Bowels' in the Wasting Diseases of Infants. *BMJ* 21 September: 717.

Cates, Joseph (1919) *The Welfare of the School Child.* London: Cassell.

Cattle, C.H. (1902) Remarks on the Relations of Human and Bovine Tuberculosis. *BMJ* 22 February: 443–45.

Cautley, Edmund (1897) *The Natural and Artificial Methods of Feeding Infants and Young Children.* London: J. & A. Churchill (also 2nd edn, 1903).

—— (1901) Infantile Scurvy. *Lancet* 20 July: 143–44.

—— (1905) The Artificial Feeding of Infants. *Practitioner* October: 460–61.

—— (1910) *The Diseases of Infants and Children.* London: Shaw & Sons.

Central Council for Promoting Self-Supporting Penny Dinners (1886) *Penny Dinners.* London: Sir Joseph Causton & Sons.

Chalmers, Archibald K. (1898) The Causation of Tuberculosis and its Prevention by Legislation. *Practitioner* June: 690–712.

—— (1906) The Increase of the Power of Local Authorities as With Regard to Milk-Supply. *Lancet* 18 August: 425–26.

—— (1913) The House as a Contributory Factor in the Death-Rate. *Proceedings of the Royal Society of Medicine* 6 (2): 155–90.

Chapin, C.V. (1910) *The Sources and Modes of Infection.* London: Chapman & Hall.

Chapin, Henry Dwight (1902) *The Theory and Practice of Infant Feeding.* New York: William Wood.

—— (1904) The Influence of Breast-feeding on the Infant's Development. *Archives of Pediatrics* 21 (8), August: 576–81.

—— and Pisek, Godfrey Roger (1911–28) *Diseases of Infants and Children.* London: Ballière (2nd edn, 1911, 3rd edn, 1916, 5th edn, 1925 (with Lawrence T. Royster), 6th edn, 1928.)

—— (1917) *Health First.* New York: The Century Co.

Child Conference for Research and Welfare (1910) *Proceedings* of the Conference held at Clark University, 6–10 July 1909. New York: G.E. Stechant.

Chisholm, Catherine (1914) *The Medical Inspection of Girls in Secondary School.* London: Longmans, Green & Co.

Churchill, Winston (1903) National Physical Training: An Open Debate. *Manchester Guardian* 25 April: 7.

Coit, Henry Leber (1909) The Medical Milk Commission on the American Continent. *Public Health* 23 (3) December: 93–7.

—— (1913) The Public School as a Possible Factor in Preventing Infant and Child Mortality. *Transactions* of the 15th International Congress on Hygiene and Demography, September 1912, vol. 3. Washington, DC: GPO, 286–89.

Collins, H. Beale (1904) Health and Empire. *Public Health* 16 (7), April: 401–13.

Colman, Walter S. (1893) The Distribution of Tubercle in Abdominal Tuberculosis. *BMJ* 30 September: 740–42.

—— (1903) Infantile Scurvy. *Lancet* 15 August: 443–46.

Coutts, F.J.H. (1911) Report on an Inquiry as to Condensed Milks; with Special Reference to their Use as Infants' Foods. *Reports to the Local Government*

Board on Public Health and Medical Subjects, N.S. no. 56, Food Reports no. 15. London: HMSO.

—— (1914) On the Use of Proprietary Foods for Infant Feeding. *Reports to the Local Government Board on Public Health and Medical Subjects*, N.S. no. 80, Food Reports no. 20. London: HMSO.

—— (1918) Upon an Inquiry as to Dried Milks, with Special Reference to their Use in Infant Feeding. *Reports to the Local Government Board on Public Health and Medical Subjects*, N.S. no. 116, Food Reports no. 24. London: HMSO.

Crichton-Browne, James (1904) Milk for the Multitude. *The Sanitary Journal* 227: 217–29.

Crocker, J.H. (1904) Medical Officers of Health and Elementary Schools. *Public Health* 16 (7), April: 414–17.

Crowley, Ralph H. (1907) *The Need, Objects, and Method of the Medical Inspection of Primary Schools*, issued by The Medical Officers of Schools Association. London: J.A. Churchill.

—— (1908) The Provision of Meals for School Children. *Public Health* 20: 325–35.

—— (1910) *The Hygiene of School Life*. London: Methuen.

Cruickshank, Lewis D. and MacKenzie, W. Leslie (1913) *School Clinics at Home and Abroad*. London: The National League for Physical Education and Improvement.

Darra Mair, L.W. (1910) *Report on Back-to-Back Houses*, Cd 5314. London: HMSO.

Davies, Margaret Llewelyn (ed.) (1915/1978) *Maternity: Letters from Working Women*. London: Virago (first published 1915).

—— (1931/1982) *Life as We Have Known It*. London: Virago (first published 1931).

Davies, Sidney (1908a) Infant Mortality Statistics. *Public Health* 21 (1), March: 40–1.

—— (1908b) Notes on Infants' Milk Depot Statistics. *Public Health* 22 (December): 93–4.

—— (1918) The Causes of Infantile Mortality: A Criticism of the Report of the Medical Research Committee. *Maternity and Child Welfare* 2 (1), January: 9–11.

Davy, J.S., Newsholme, Arthur and Adair Hore, C.F. (1909) *Public Health and Social Conditions*, Cd 4671. London: HMSO.

Dawson, William Harbutt (1906) School Doctors in Germany. Office of Special Inquiries and Reports, Board of Education, *Educational Pamphlets*, no. 4. London: HMSO.

Delépine, Sheridan (1895) Tuberculous Infection Through the Alimentary Canal. *Medical Chronicle* 3: 144–54.

—— (1898) Tuberculosis and the Milk-Supply, With Some General Remarks on the Dangers of Bad Milk. *Lancet* 17 September: 733–38.

—— (1901) The Communicability of Human Tuberculosis to Cattle. *BMJ* 26 October: 1224–226.

—— (1902–03a) The Bearing of Outbreaks of Food Poisoning upon the Aetiology of Epidemic Diarrhoea. *Journal of Hygiene* 68–94, and also *Transactions of Epidemiological Society* 22 (N.S.): 11–33.

—— (1902–03b) Some of the Dangers of Boracic Acid and Formaldehyde as

Food Preservatives. *Transactions of the Epidemiological Society* 22 (N.S.): 56–9.

—— (1910) Contribution to the Study of the Influences determining the Prevalence of Bovine Tuberculous Mastitis. *Proceedings of the Royal Society of Medicine.* 3 (2), April: 217–43.

—— (1914) Report upon the Effect of Certain Condensing and Drying Processes used in the Preservation of Milk upon its Bacterial Contents. *Reports to the Local Government Board on Public Health and Medical Subjects*, N.S. no. 97, Food Reports no. 21. London: HMSO.

Dilke, Charles Wentworth (1887) *The Present Position of European Politics, or, Europe in 1887.* London: Chapman & Hall.

—— (1888) *The British Army.* London: Chapman & Hall.

—— (1898) *Army Reform.* London: Service & Paton.

—— (1899) *The British Empire.* London: Chatto & Windus.

Divine, Thomas (1906) Some Social Factors in the Causation of Infantile Mortality. *Lancet* 21 July: 142–45.

—— (1907) Sanitary Condition in Relation to Infantile Mortality. *Lancet* 9 February: 358–59.

Doane, C.F. (1904) Economical Methods for Improving the Keeping Qualities of Milk. *Public Health* February: 303–5.

Dobbie, James J. (1918) On the Examination of Milk Powders at the Government Laboratory. *Reports to the Local Government Board on Public Health and Medical Subjects*, N.S. no. 116, Food Reports no. 24. London: HMSO.

Dudfield, Reginald (1904) The Milk Supply of the Metropolis. *Public Health* 16 (March): 345–54.

—— (1912) Diarrhoea in 1911. *Proceedings of the Royal Society of Medicine* 5 (2): 99–148.

Dukes, Clement (1894) *Health at School* (3rd edn). London: Rivington, Percival & Co.

—— (1899) *The Essentials of School Diet.* London: Rivingtons.

Eastes, G. Leslie (1899) The Pathology of Milk. *BMJ* 11 November: 1341–342.

Eastwood, Arthur and Griffith, Fred (1914) The Incidence and Bacteriological Characteristics of Tuberculous Infection in Children. *Report to the Local Government Board on Public Health and Medical Subjects*, N.S. no. 88. London: HMSO.

Elliott, Sir Charles (1909) State Feeding of School Children in London. *Nineteenth Century* May: 862–74.

Escherich, Theodor (1885) Die Darmbakterien des Neugeborenen und Säuglings. *Fortschritte der Medizin* 3 (16 and 17), August, September: 515–22, 547–54.

—— (1886) *Die Darmbakterien des Säuglings.* Stuttgart: Verlag von Ferdinand Enke.

—— (1897) Ueber specifische Krankheitserreger der Säuglings-diarrhöen (streptococcenenteritis). *Wiener Klinische Wochenschrift* 42: 917–20.

Evans, Arnold (1895) Back-to-Back Houses. *Transactions of the Epidemiological Society, London.* 15: 87–99.

Eyre, J.W. (1904) The Bacterial Content of Milk at the Point of Origin and Distribution. *Journal of State Medicine* 12 (12): 728–34.

Ferguson, Margaret (1918) *A Study of Social and Economic Factors in the*

Causation of Rickets, Medical Research Committee, Special Series no. 20. London: HMSO.

Findlay, Leonard (1908) The Aetiology of Rickets: A Clinical and Experimental Study. *BMJ* 4 July: 13–17.

Flewe, H. (1983) Rotavirus in the Home and Hospital Nursery. *BMJ* 27 August: 568–69.

Flexner, Simon and Barker, Lewellys F. (1900) Report upon an Expedition Sent by the Johns Hopkins University to Investigate the Prevalent Diseases in the Philippines. *Bulletin of the Johns Hopkins Hospital* 11 (107), February: 37–41.

Flexner, Simon and Holt, L. Emmett (eds) (1904) Bacteriological and Clinical Studies of the Diarrhoeal Diseases of Infancy. *Studies from the Rockefeller Institute for Medical Research* 2: 1–202.

Forsyth, David (1909) *Children in Health and Disease.* London: John Murray.

Fox, Selina (1912) *Mother and Baby.* London: J. & A. Churchill.

Freeman, Rowland G. (1903) The Reduction in the Infantile Mortality in the City of New York. *Medical News* 83 (10), 5 September: 433–38.

Frere, Margaret (1909) *Children's Care Committees.* London: P.S. King.

Fulton, George C.H. (1904) Infantile Mortality: Its Causes and Prevention. *BMJ* 3 December: 1513–515.

Gordon, M.H. (1902) The Bacteriology of Epidemic Diarrhoea. *Practitioner* 69 (16 N.S.), August: 180–94.

Gorst, John E. (1903) Social Reform. *Nineteenth Century* 53 (March): 519–32.

—— (1905a) Governments and Social Reform. *Fortnightly Review* 87 N.S. (May): 843–55.

—— (1905b) Children's Rights. *National Review* 45 (June): 705–15.

—— (1905c) Physical Deterioration in Great Britain. *North American Review* 81 (July): 1–10.

—— (1906) *The Children of the Nation.* London: Methuen.

Graham-Smith, G.S. (1909) Preliminary Note on Examinations of Flies for the Presence of *Bacillus Coli. Reports to the Local Government Board on Public Health and Medical Subjects,* Further Preliminary Reports on Flies as Carriers of Infection, N.S. no. 16. London: HMSO.

G.B., Board of Agriculture and Fisheries (1905) *Cleanliness in the Dairy,* Leaflet no. 151. London: HMSO (revised 1912).

—— (1907) *The Selection and Milking of Dairy Cattle,* Leaflet no. 187. London: HMSO (revised 1914).

G.B., Board of Education (1905) *Outline Scheme for Teaching Hygiene and Temperance to the Scholars Attending Public Elementary Schools.* London: HMSO (reprinted 1909 and 1912).

—— (1910–21) *Annual Reports* of the Chief Medical Officer of the Board of Education, from the *Report for 1908,* Cd 4986 through the *Report for 1920,* Cmd 1522. London: HMSO.

—— (1911) *Report on the Working of the Education (Provision of Meals) Act, 1906,* for the year ending 31 March 1910, Cd 5724. London: HMSO.

—— (1916) *Education and Infant Welfare,* reprint from the Report of the Chief Medical Officer of the Board of Education, 1914, with additional Appendix. London: HMSO.

G.B., Ministry of Health, *Supplements to the Annual Reports of the Local Government Board, Containing the Report of the Medical Officer,* and the numerous appendices.

—— (1917) *Maternity and Child Welfare: Report on the Provision made by Public Health Authorities and Voluntary Agencies in England and Wales.* London: HMSO.

—— (1930) Departmental Committee on Maternal Mortality and Morbidity, *Interim Report.* London: HMSO.

—— (1931) Memorandum on Bovine Tuberculosis in Man. *Reports on Public Health and Medical Subjects* 63.

—— (1932) Departmental Committee on Maternal Mortality and Morbidity, *Final Report.* London: HMSO.

G.B., Office of the Registrar-General, *Annual Reports of the Registrar-General.*

G.B., P.P. (1895–96) *Report of the Royal Commission Appointed to Inquire into the Effect of Food Derived from Tuberculous Animals on Human Health.* Part I: *Report*; Part II: *Minutes of Evidence*, Cd 7703, 1895; Part III: *Appendix*, Cd 7992, 1896. London: HMSO.

—— (1898) *Report of the Royal Commission Appointed to Inquire into the Administrative Procedures for Controlling Danger to Man Through the Use as Food of the Meat and Milk of Tuberculous Animals.* Part I: *Report*, Cd 8824; Part II: *Minutes of Evidence and Appendices*, Cd 8831. London: HMSO.

—— (1903) Royal Commission on Physical Training, vol. I: *Report and Appendix*, Cd 1507; vol. II: *Minutes of Evidence*, Cd 1508. London: HMSO.

—— (1904) *Report of the Inter-Departmental Committee on Physical Deterioration.* Vol. I: *Report and Appendix*, Cd 2175; vol. II: *List of Witnesses and Minutes of Evidence*, Cd 2210; vol. III: *Appendix and General Index*, Cd 2186. London: HMSO.

—— (1904–11) *Reports of the Royal Commission on Tuberculosis (Relation Between Human and Animal).* London: HMSO.

(1) *Interim Report*, 1904, Cd 2092.

(2) *Second Interim Report and Appendices:* Part I: *Report*, 1907, Cd 3322; Part II: vol. 1, *Pathogenic Effects of Bovine Viruses*, 1907, Cd 3584; vol. 2, *Pathogenic Effects of Human Viruses*, 1907, Cd 3660–3661; vol. 3, *Additional Investigation of Bovine and Human Viruses*, 1907, Cd 3758.

(3) *Third Interim Report and Appendix*, 1909, Cd 4483.

(4) *Final Report*, Part I, *Report*, 1911, Cd 5761.

—— (1906) *Report* of the Inter-Departmental Committee on Medical Inspection and Feeding of Children Attending the Public Elementary Schools, Cd 2779. London: HMSO.

—— (1919) Committee on the Production and Distribution of Milk, *Final Report* of the Committee, Cmd 483. London: HMSO.

Greenwood, Arthur (1913) *Health and Physique of School Children.* London: P.S. King & Son.

Greenwood, M. Jr and Brown, J.W. (1912) An Examination of Some Factors Influencing the Rate of Infant Mortality. *Journal of Hygiene* 12: 5–43.

Greville, Frances Evelyn (Countess of Warwick) (1906) *A Nation's Youth.* London: Cassell.

Griffith, A. Stanley (1914) An Enquiry, based on a series of Autopsies, into the Occurrence and Distribution of Tuberculous Infection in Children, and its Relation to the Bovine and the Human Types of Tubercle Bacilli respectively. *Report to the Local Government Board on Public Health and Medical Subjects*, N.S. no. 88. London: HMSO.

Grimwood, K., Abbott, G.D., Jennings, L.C., and Allan, J.M. (1983) Spread of Rotavirus within Families: A Community-Based Study. *BMJ* 27 August: 575–77.

Guthrie, Leonard G. (1899) The Distribution and Origin of Tuberculosis in Children. *Lancet* 4 February: 286–90.

Haldane, Richard Burdon (1902) *Education and Empire.* London: John Murray.

―――― (1903) National Physical Training: An Open Debate. *Manchester Guardian* 9 May: 6.

Hamer, William H. (1902) *Manual of Hygiene.* London: J. & A. Churchill.

―――― (1908a) Nuisance from Flies. *Report of the Public Health Committee of the London County Council,* no. 1138.

―――― (1908b) Nuisance from Flies. *Report of the Public Health Committee of the London County Council,* no. 1202.

Hamill, J.M. (1923) Notes on the Pasteurization of Milk. *Reports on Public Health and Medical Subjects,* no. 17. London: HMSO.

Hamilton, D.J. (1902) A Discussion on the Relationship of Human and Bovine Tuberculosis. *BMJ* 27 September: 944–48.

Harrington, Charles (1906) Infantile Mortality and its Principal Cause – Dirty Milk. *American Journal of Medical Sciences* 132 (6), December: 811–35.

Harris, F. Drew (1900) The Supply of Sterilized Humanized Milk for the Use of Infants in St Helens. *BMJ* 18 August: 427–31.

Harvey, F.T. (1902) Some Points on the Hygiene of the Udder, and the Conditions of Milk Production in Rural Districts. *Journal of State Medicine* December: 751–61.

Hayward, T.E. (1901) The Mortality from Phthisis and from Other Tuberculous Diseases Considered in Some Aspects which may be Demonstrated by Means of Life-Tables. *Lancet* 10 August: 356–60.

Hecht, Charles E. (ed.) (1912) *Our Children's Health at Home and at School* (The report of a conference on diet and hygiene in public secondary and private schools, held at the Guildhall, London, 13 May 1912). London: National Food Reform Association.

―――― (1921) *The Gateway to Health.* London: The Food Education Society.

Helme, T. Arthur (1907) The Unborn Child: Its Care and Its Rights. *BMJ* 24 August: 421–26.

Hess, Alfred F. (1917) Infantile Scurvy. *American Journal of Diseases of Children* 14 (5), November: 337–53.

Hewitt, C. Gordon (1912a) An Account of the Bionomics and the Larvae of the Flies 'Fannia (Homalomyia) canicularis' L., and 'F. scalaris' Fab. *Reports to the Local Government Board on Public Health and Medical Subjects,* Further Reports (no. 5) on Flies as Carriers of Infection, N.S. no. 66. London: HMSO.

―――― (1912b) Observations on the Range of Flight of Flies. *Reports to the Local Government Board on Public Health and Medical Subjects,* Further Reports (no. 5) on Flies as Carriers of Infection, N.S. no. 66. London: HMSO.

Hewlett, Richard Tanner (1898) *A Manual of Bacteriology.* London: Churchill (2nd edn, 1902; 3rd edn, 1908; 4th edn, 1911; 5th edn, 1914; 6th edn, 1918; 7th edn, 1921; 8th edn, 1926; 9th edn, 1932 by Hewlett and J. McIntosh).

―――― and Murray, H. Montague (1901) On a Common Source of Diphtherial Infection and a Means of Dealing With It. *BMJ* 15 June: 1474–475.

―――― and Barton, George S. (1907) The Results of Chemical, Microscopical and Bacteriological Examination of Samples of London Milks. *Journal of Hygiene* 7: 22–31.

Hicks, H.T. (1903) On the Treatment of the Summer Diarrhoea and Vomiting in Infants. *Lancet* 15 August: 455–56.

Hicks, Reverend Canon (1903) National Physical Training: An Open Debate. *Manchester Guardian* 8 June: 10.

Hildesheim, Oscar (1915) *The Health of the Child.* London: Methuen.

Hillier, Alfred (1900) *Tuberculosis.* London: Cassell.

—— (1903) *The Prevention of Consumption.* London: Longman Green & Co.

Hogarth, Archibald Henry (1909) *Medical Inspection of Schools.* London: Oxford University Press.

Holt, L. Emmett (Senior) (1900) (2nd edn) *The Care and Feeding of Children.* New York: D. Appleton (3rd edn, 1904; 4th edn, 1907, 1910; 7th edn, 1914; 9th edn, 1918; 12th edn, 1923; 14th edn, 1929).

—— (1900) *Diseases of Infancy and Childhood.* London: H. Kimpton (later editions published in New York and London by D. Appleton: 2nd edn, 1902; 3rd edn, 1906; 4th edn, 1908; 5th edn, 1909; 6th edn, 1911; 7th edn, 1916 and 1919; 8th edn, 1922, with John Howland).

—— (1913) Infant Mortality Ancient and Modern. *Archives of Pediatrics* 30 (12), December: 885–915.

Hope, E.W. (1899a) Summer Diarrhoea. *Public Health* March: 435–36.

—— (1899b) Observations on Autumnal Diarrhoea in Cities. *Public Health* July: 660–65.

Howarth, William J. (1905) The Influence of Feeding on the Mortality of Infants. *Lancet* 22 July: 210–13.

Hunter, William (1904) The Occurrence of Primary Tuberculous Infection of the Intestinal Tract in Children. *BMJ* 14 May: 1126–127.

Hutchison, Robert (1900 and 1902) *Food and Dietetics* (4th and 5th edns). London: Edward Arnold.

—— (1903) The Artificial Feeding of Infants. *Lancet* 19 September: 803–05.

Hutt, Cecil Williams (1912) *Hygiene for Health Visitors.* London: P.S. King & Son (2nd edn, 1921).

—— (1914) A Study of Summer Diarrhoea in Warrington in 1911. *Journal of Hygiene* 14: 422–32.

Huxley, T.H. (1888) The Struggle for Existence. *Nineteenth Century* 23 (132), February: 161–80.

The Infants' Health Society (1905) *The Present Conditions of Infant Life and their Effect on the Nation.* London: Ballière Tindall & Cox.

International Congress on Hygiene and Demography, *Transactions* of the Congresses: 10th Congrès International, Paris, 1900; 15th International Congress, Washington, 1913.

International Congress for School Hygiene, *Transactions* of the following congresses:

Internationalen Kongress für Schulhygiene, Nürnberg, 4–9 April 1904.

International Congress on School Hygiene, London, 1907.

Congrès International d'Hygiène Scolaire, Paris, 2–7 August 1910.

International Congress on School Hygiene, Buffalo, 25–30 August 1913.

Iselin, Henry (1909) A New Poor Law for Children. *Charity Organization Review* March: 168–72.

—— (1912) The Story of a Children's Care Committee. *Economic Review* 22 (January): 42–64.

Jepson, J.P. (1909a) Report on the Breeding of the Common House Fly during the Winter Months. *Reports to the Local Government Board on Public Health and Medical Subjects*, Preliminary Reports on Flies as Carriers of Infection. London: HMSO.

—— (1909b) Notes on Colouring Flies for Purposes of Identification. *Reports to the Local Government Board on Public Health and Medical Subjects*, Further Preliminary Reports on Flies as Carriers of Infection, N.S. no. 16. London: HMSO.

—— and Nuttall, G.H.F. (1909c) Abstract of Literature and Bibliography. *Reports to the Local Government Board on Public Health and Medical Subjects*, Further Preliminary Reports on Flies as Carriers of Infection, N.S. no. 16. London: HMSO.

Joint Committee on Milk (1910) *Milk Supply*. National Health Society and the National League for Physical Education and Improvement.

Jones, Herbert (1892–93) Back-to-Back Houses. *Public Health* 5: 347–49.

Jones, J. Howard (1899) The Influence of Preventive Medicine Upon the Evolution of the Race. *Public Health* February: 345–55.

Josias, Albert (1904) Précis de deux brochures: *La lutte contre la mortalité infantile et les consultations de nourrissons dans le Nord et le Pas-de-Calais et la deuxième année de fonctionnement de la Goutte de lait de Saint-Pol-sur-Mer* par M. Ausset. *Bulletin de l'Académie de Médecine* 52 (2 November): 277.

Kanthack, Emilia (1907) *The Preservation of Infant Life*. London: H.K. Lewis.

Kelynack, Theophilus Nicholas (ed.) (1908) *Tuberculosis in Infancy and Childhood*. London: Ballière Tindall & Cox.

—— (1910) *Medical Examination of Schools and Scholars*. London: P.S. King & Son.

Kerley, Charles Gilmour (1906) Prevention of the Acute Intestinal Diseases of Summer. *BMJ* 13 October: 927–29.

Kerr, Harold (1910) Modern Educative Methods for the Prevention of Infantile Mortality. *Public Health* January: 129–34.

Kerr, James (1909) The Medical Officer of Schools, His Work and His Reports. *Public Health* 22 (5), February: 162–65.

—— (1916) *Newsholme's School Hygiene* (14th edn). London: George Allen & Unwin.

Kingsford, L. (1904) The Channels of Infection in Tuberculosis in Childhood. *Lancet* 24 September: 889–92.

Klein, E. (1901) Pathogenic Microbes in Milk. *Journal of Hygiene* 1:78–95.

—— (1909) The Bacterial Character of Sweetened Condensed Milk. *Public Health* 22 (6), March: 222–23.

Koch, Robert (1901) An Address on the Fight Against Tuberculosis. *BMJ* 27 July: 189–93.

—— (1902) An Address on the Transference of Bovine Tuberculosis to Man. *BMJ* 20 December: 1885–889.

Kruse (1901) Weitere Untersuchungen über die Ruhr und die Ruhrbazillen. *Deutsche Medicinische Wochenschrift* 27: 370–72.

Lane-Claypon, Janet (1912) Report upon the Available Data in Regard to the Value of Boiled Milk as a Food for Infants and Young Animals. *Reports to the Local Government Board on Public Health and Medical Subjects*, N.S. no. 63. London: HMSO.

—— (1913a) Report upon the 'Biological Properties' of Milk, both of the

Human Species, and of Cows, considered in Special Relation to the Feeding of Infants. *Reports to the Local Government Board on Public Health and Medical Subjects*, N.S. no. 76. London: HMSO.

—— (1913b) Phases in the Development of the Infant Welfare Movement in England. *Transactions* of the 15th International Congress on Hygiene and Demography, September 1912, vol. 3. Washington DC: GPO, 388–96.

—— (1916) *Milk and its Hygienic Relations*. London: Longmans Green & Co.

—— (1920) *The Child Welfare Movement*. London: G. Bell.

Larson, J.H. (1918) A Maternity and Infant Welfare Program for the United States. *American Journal of Public Health* 18: 482–87.

Leach, William (n.d.) School Feeding. *The Crusade* 2: 192–93.

Lister, T.D. (1903) On the Utilization of Infants' Milk Depots. *BMJ* 29 August: 469–70.

Loane, Margaret (1902) *The Next Street But One*. London: Edward Arnold.

London Schools Dinners Associations (1886) *Prize Essays*. London: Sir Joseph Causton & Sons.

Low, Bruce (1889) An Account of some Instances of Communicable Diarrhoea which occurred in the Rural Sanitary Districts of Helmsley, Yorkshire. *Supplement* in Continuation of the Report of the Medical Officer to the Local Government Board for 1887, C 5638. London: HMSO.

Lust, Maurice (1918) Child Welfare Work in Belgium During the War. *Maternity and Child Welfare* 2: 308–9.

McCaw, John (1901) Remarks on a Case of Infantile Scurvy. *BMJ* 2 November: 1324.

—— (1907) Tuberculosis in Childhood and its Relation to Milk. *BMJ* 21 December: 1758–759.

McCleary, George Frederick (1903) Infant Feeding. *Lancet* 3 October: 945–48.

—— (1904a) The Infants' Milk Depot: Its History and Function. *Journal of Hygiene* 4: 329–68.

—— (1904b) The Influence of Ante-Natal Conditions on Infant Mortality. *BMJ* 13 August: 321–23.

—— (1905a) The Municipal Feeding of Infants. *Practitioner* October: 470–78.

—— (1905b) *Infantile Mortality and Infant Milk Depots*. London: P.S. King & Son.

—— (1906) The Public Supply of Pure or Specially Prepared Milk for the Feeding of Infants. *Lancet* 18 August: 422–23.

—— (1933) *The Early History of the Infant Welfare Movement*. London: H.K. Lewis.

—— (1935) *The Maternity and Child Welfare Movement*. London: P.S. King & Son.

—— (1945) *The Development of British Maternity and Child Welfare Services*. London: published by The National Association of Maternity and Child Welfare Centres and for the Prevention of Infant Mortality.

MacConkey, Alfred (1905) Lactose-Fermenting Bacteria in Faeces. *Journal of Hygiene* 5: 333–79.

McDougall, Alderman (1902) The Relation of Poverty and Disease. *BMJ* 16 August: 447–49.

McFadyean, John (1901) Tubercle Bacilli in Cows' Milk as a Possible Source of Tuberculous Disease in Man. *Lancet* 3 August: 268–71.

—— (1910) The Common Method of Infection in Human and Bovine

Tuberculosis. *Journal of the Royal Institute of Public Health* 18 (12): 705–24.

MacFadyen, Allen (1898) The Relation of Tuberculosis of Animals to Man. *Practitioner* June: 602–8.

MacKenzie, W. Leslie (1899) The Hygienics of Milk. *Edinburgh Medical Journal* N.S. vol. 5: 372–78, 563–76.

—— (1904) *The Medical Inspection of School Children.* Edinburgh & Glasgow: William Hodge.

—— (1906) *The Health of the School Child.* London: Methuen.

—— and Foster, A. (1907) *Report on a Collection of Statistics as to the Physical Condition of Children Attending the Public Schools of the School Board for Glasgow,* Cd 3637. London: HMSO.

—— and Cruickshank, Lewis D. (eds) (1914) *Problems of School Hygiene.* London: W. Hodge.

—— (1926) *The Child at School.* London: Faber & Gwyer.

McKnight, Miss (1906) The Feeding of School Children. *Charity Organization Review* 20 (July): 30–45.

McLean, Russell (1904) The Administration of the Dairies, Cowsheds, and Milkshops Orders. *Public Health* February: 294–301.

Macmillan, J. Shawnet Cameron (1915) *Infant Health: A Manual for District Visitors, Nurses, and Mothers.* London: Oxford University Press.

McMillan, Margaret (1907a) *Infant Mortality.* London: The Independent Labour Party.

—— (1907b) *Labour and Childhood.* London: Swan Sonnenschein & Co.

—— (1911) *The Child and the State.* London: The Socialist Library (vol. 9).

—— (1912) *The Needs of Little Children.* London: Women's Labour League.

—— (1919) *The Nursery School.* London: J.M. Dent.

—— (1920) *Early Childhood* (3rd edn). London: J.M. Dent.

—— (1927) *Life of Rachel McMillan.* London: J.M. Dent.

MacMurchy, Helen (1906) Medical Inspection of Children Attending Elementary Schools. *BMJ* 22 September: 675–80.

Macnamara, Thomas J. (1903) National Physical Training: An Open Debate. *Manchester Guardian* 5 May: 12.

—— (1904) The Physical Condition of Working-Class Children. *Nineteenth Century* 66 (August): 307–11.

—— (1905) In Corpore Sano. *Contemporary Review* February: 238–48.

Manchester and Salford Sanitary Association (1887) *Health Lectures* (2 vols). London: John Heywood.

—— (1892) *Pamphlet Series.* London: John Heywood.

—— (1902a) *Tract Series.* Manchester: Sherratt & Hughes.

—— (1902b) *Annual Report for 1902.* Manchester: Sherratt & Hughes.

Marquis, F.J. (1913) Care Committee Work in Liverpool. *The School Child* September: 11.

Martin, C.J. (1913) Insect Porters of Bacterial Infections. *BMJ* 4 January: 1–8.

Mason, Falkner C. (1899) The Milk of Tuberculous Animals in its Relation to Public Health. *The Journal of State Medicine* 7 (1): 33–8.

Mattick, Elfrieda C.V. and Golding, J. (1931) Relative Value of Raw and Heated Milk in Nutrition. *Lancet* 21 March: 662–67.

Maurice, Frederick (pseudonym 'Miles') (1902) Where to Get Men. *Contemporary Review* 81 (January): 78–86.

—— (1903) The National Health: A Soldier's Study. *The Contemporary Review*

83 (January): 41–56.

Mearns, Andrew (1885) *London and its Teeming Toilers*. London: Warren Hall & Lovitt.

Meath, Earl of (1904) The Deterioration of British Health and Physique. *Public Health* 16 (7), April: 387–92.

Meigs, Grace L. (1917) Infant Welfare Work in War Time. *American Journal of Diseases of Children* 14 (2), August: 80–97.

Metchnikoff, Étienne (1914) Études sur la flore intestinale: les diarrhées des nourrissons. *Annals de l'Institut Pasteur* 28: 89–120.

Michelazzi, A. (1903) On the Toxic Effects of Prolonged Alimentation with Sterilized Milk of Tuberculous Animals. *Public Health* May: 475–76.

Monckton, Copeman S. (1909) Memorandum on Lines of Investigation. *Reports to the Local Government Board on Public Health and Medical Subjects, Further Preliminary Reports on Flies as Carriers of Infection*, N.S. no. 16. London: HMSO.

Monier-Williams, G.W. (1912) Report on Analyses and Methods of Detection of Certain Proprietary Substances Sold as Preservatives for Milk, Cream, etc. *Reports to the Local Government Board on Public Health and Medical Subjects*, N.S. no. 60, Food Reports no. 17. London: HMSO.

Moore, Samson George (1904) *County Borough of Huddersfield, Report of the M.O.H. on Infantile Mortality*. London: Daily Chronicle Printing Works.

—— (1908) Notification of Births. *BMJ* 29 August: 568–70.

—— (1916) Infantile Mortality and the Relative Practical Value of Measures Dedicated to its Prevention (The Milroy Lectures for 1916). *Lancet* 22 April: 849–53; 29 April: 895–900; 6 May: 943–48. Also reported in the *BMJ* 6 and 13 May: 659–60, 693–94.

—— (1921) *This Concerns You*. London: The St Catherine Press.

Morant, Robert (1909) 'Address' at the Annual Dinner of the Society of Medical Officers of Health. *Public Health* 23 (November): 66–8.

Morgan, H. de R. (1906) Upon the Bacteriology of the Summer Diarrhoea of Infants. *BMJ* 21 April: 908–12.

—— (1907) Upon the Bacteriology of the Summer Diarrhoea of Infants. *BMJ* 6 July: 16–19.

—— and Ledingham, J. (1909) The Bacteriology of Summer Diarrhoea. *Proceedings of the Royal Society of Medicine* 2 (2): 133–49.

Mussen, A.A. (1903) Supply of Sterilized Humanized Milk for Infants. *Journal of State Medicine* 11 (October): 599–608.

Nabarro, David (1923) Discussion on Summer Diarrhoea. *BMJ* 10 November: 857–63.

—— (1927) Observations on the Sonne Dysentery Bacillus and *Bacillus Coli Anaerogenes*. *Journal of Pathology and Bacteriology* 30:176–78.

Naish, Albert E. (1908) The Sheffield Dry Milk Scheme. *BMJ* 29 August: 570–73.

—— (1910) Summer Diarrhoea. *Public Health* 23 (February): 168–73.

Nash, J.T.C. (1903) The Seasonal Incidence of Typhoid Fever and of Diarrhoea. *Transactions of the Epidemiological Society of London*, N.S. vol. 22: 110–38.

—— (1904) Some Points in the Prevention of Epidemic Diarrhoea. *Lancet* 24 September: 892. Also: Letter to him: 1 October 1904: 981 and Reply from him: 8 October 1904: 1043–045.

—— (1906) The Prevention of Epidemic Diarrhoea. *Practitioner* 699–710.

—— (1909) House-flies as Carriers of Disease. *Journal of Hygiene* 9 (2),

September: 141–69.

National Association for the Prevention of Infant Mortality and for the Welfare of Infancy (1915) *Mothercraft*. London.

National Conference on Infantile Mortality (Second) (1908) *Report of the Proceedings* of the conference held in the Caxton Halls, Westminster, 23–25 March. London: P.S. King & Son.

—— (Third) (1914) *Report of the Proceedings* of the conference held at St George's Hall, Liverpool, 2–3 July. London: published by The National Association for the Prevention of Infant Mortality and for the Welfare of Infancy.

National League for Physical Education and Improvement (1905) *The Health of the People*. London: published by the League.

—— (1910) *Milk Supply* (3 leaflets prepared by the Joint Committee of the National Health Society and the National League). London: published by the League.

—— (1916) *The Care of the School Child*. London: published by the League.

Newman, George (1903) *Report on the Milk Supply of Finsbury*. London: Thomas Bean & Son.

—— (1904a) The Milk Supply of a London Borough. *Public Health* 16 (5), February: 258–94.

—— (1904b) The Control of the Milk Supply. *BMJ* 27 August: 421–29.

—— (1905) *A Special Report on an Infants' Milk Depot*. London: Thomas Bean & Son.

—— (1906) *Infant Mortality: A Social Problem*. London: Methuen.

—— (1907) *The Health of the State*. London: Headley Bros.

—— (1909) Medical Inspection of School Children. *Public Health* 22 (5), February: 160–61.

—— (1931) *Health and Social Evolution*. London: George Allen & Unwin.

—— (1932) *The Rise of Preventive Medicine*. London: Oxford University Press.

—— (1939) *The Building of a Nation's Health*. London: Macmillan.

Newsholme, Arthur (1887) *School Hygiene: The Laws of Health in Relation to School Life*. London: Swan Sonnenschein (1st edn).

—— (1892) *Hygiene*. London: George Gill & Sons.

—— (1893) *Elementary Hygiene*. London: Swan Sonnenschein.

—— (1899a) *The Elements of Vital Statistics* (revised 3rd edn). London: Swan Sonnenschein.

—— (1899b) A Contribution to the Study of Epidemic Diarrhoea. *Public Health* December; also published in pamphlet form as *A Contribution to the Study of Epidemic Diarrhoea*. London: Rebman Ltd, 1900.

—— (1902–03) Remarks on the Causation of Epidemic Diarrhoea. *Transactions of the Epidemiological Society* N.S. 22; 34–43.

—— (1902a) The Public Health Aspects of Summer Diarrhoea. *Practitioner* 69 (N.S. 16), August: 161–80.

—— (1902b) Poverty in Town Life. *Practitioner* 69 (N.S. 16): 682–95.

—— and Scott, Margaret Eleanor (1902c) *Domestic Economy*. London: Swan Sonnenschein.

—— (1903a) National Physical Training: Is the Nation Physically Degenerating? *Manchester Guardian* 27 May: 12.

—— and Pakes, Walter C.C. (1903b) *School Hygiene: The Laws of Health in Relation to School Life* (9th edn). London: Swan Sonnenschein.

—— (1905a) Alleged Physical Degeneration in Towns. *Public Health* 17 (February): 293–300.

—— (1905b) Infantile Mortality. *Practitioner* October: 489–500.

—— and Stevenson T.H.C. (1905c) An Improved Method of Calculating Birth-Rates. *Journal of Hygiene* 5: 175–84.

—— (1906) Domestic Infection in Relation to Epidemic Diarrhoea. *Journal of Hygiene* 6 (April): 139–48.

—— (1909) Some Conditions of Social Efficiency in Relation to Local Public Administration. *Public Health* 22 (August): 403–14.

—— (1910) Supplement in Continuation of the Report of the Medical Officer of the Board for 1909–10 Containing a Report on Infant and Child Mortality. *39th Annual Report of the Local Government Board, 1909–10*, Cd 5263. London: HMSO.

—— (1911) *The Declining Birth-Rate*. London: Cassell.

—— (1913) Supplement in Continuation of the Report of the Medical Officer of the Board for 1912–13 Containing a Second Report on Infant and Child Mortality. *42nd Annual Report of the Local Government Board, 1912–13*, Cd 6909. London: HMSO.

——, Copeman, Farrar, Lane-Claypon and Manby (1914) Supplement in Continuation of the Report of the Medical Officer of the Board for 1913–14 Containing a Third Report on Infant Mortality dealing with the Infant Mortality in Lancashire. *43rd Annual Report of the Local Government Board, 1913–14*, Cd 7511. London: HMSO.

——, Lane-Claypon, Janet, and Cameron, Isabella (1915) Supplement in Continuation of the Report of the Medical Officer of the Board for 1914–15 Containing a Report on Maternal Mortality in connection with Childbearing and its Relation to Infant Mortality. *44th Annual Report of the Local Government Board, 1914–15*, Cd 8085. London: HMSO.

—— (1916) Supplement in Continuation of the Report of the Medical Officer of the Board for 1915–16, Containing a Report on Child Mortality at Ages 0–5, in England and Wales. *45th Annual Report of the Local Government Board, 1915-16*, Cd 8496. London: HMSO.

—— (1923) *The Elements of Vital Statistics* (new edn). London: George Allen & Unwin.

—— (1927) *Evolution of Preventive Medicine*. London: Ballière Tindall & Cox.

—— (1932) *Medicine and the State*. London: George Allen & Unwin.

—— (1935) *Fifty Years in Public Health*. London: George Allen & Unwin.

—— (1936) *The Last Thirty Years in Public Health*. London: George Allen & Unwin.

Niven, James (1899) Tuberculous Meat and Milk. *Public Health* March: 430–32.

—— (1910) Summer Diarrhoea and Enteric Fever. *Proceedings of the Royal Society of Medicine*. 3 (2), April: 131–216.

Nuttall, G.H.F. (1899a) The Part Played by Insects, Arachnids and Myriapods in the Propagation of Infective Diseases of Man and Animals. *BMJ* 9 September: 642–44.

—— (1899b) On the Role of Insects, Arachnids and Myriapods as Carriers in the Spread of Bacterial and Parasitic Diseases of Man and Animals: A Critical and Historical Study. *Johns Hopkins Hospital Reports* 8: 1–125.

Orr, J.B., Williams, R. Stenhouse, Muray, H. Leith, Rundle, C., and Williams, A.E. (1909) 'Bacillus F': An Organism Obtained in a Case of Epidemic

Diarrhoea. *Lancet* 30 January: 301–4.

—— (1928) Milk Consumption and the Growth of School Children. *Lancet* 28 January: 202–3.

—— and Clark, M.L. (1930) A Dietary Survey of Six Hundred and Seven Families in Seven Cities and Towns in Scotland. *Lancet* 13 September: 594–98.

Pakes, Walter C.C. (1900) The Application of Bacteriology to Public Health. *Public Health* 12 (March): 385–437.

Park, William Hallock (1901) The Great Contamination of the Milk of Cities. *Journal of Hygiene* 1: 391–406.

—— and Holt, L. Emmett (1903) Report upon the Results with Different Kinds of Pure and Impure Milk in Infant Feeding. *Medical News* 83 (23), 5 December: 1066–078.

Parker, W.G. (1913) Infantile Mortality and the Health of Survivors in the Elementary Schools. *Public Health* April: 186–88.

Paton, Noel (1903) The Influence of Diet in Pregnancy on the Weight of the Offspring. *Lancet* 4 July: 21–2.

Pearson, Karl (1897) Socialism and Natural Selection. *The Chances of Death and Other Studies in Evolution*, vol. I. London: Arnold.

—— (1901a) *National Life from the Standpoint of Science*. London: Adam & Charles Black.

—— (1901b) *The Ethic of Freethought* (2nd edn). London: Adam & Charles Black.

—— (1909a) *The Groundwork of Eugenics*. London: Eugenics Laboratory Lecture Series no. 2.

—— (1909b) *Problems of Practical Eugenics*. London: Eugenics Laboratory Lecture Series no. 5.

—— (1910a) *Nature and Nurture: The Problem of the Future*. London: Eugenics Laboratory Lecture Series no. 6.

—— (1910b) *Eugenics and Public Health*. London: Questions of the Day Series no. 6, University of London.

Peters, O.H. (1910) Observations on the Natural History of Epidemic Diarrhoea. *Journal of Hygiene* 10: 602–777.

Peyroux, A.-L. (1902) Consultations de nourrissons et Gouttes de Lait. *La Semaine Médicale* December: 421–22.

Pilkington, H.O. (1907) The Reduction of Infantile Mortality Without Municipal Milk Depots. *Public Health* April: 410–28.

Pinard (1895) Untitled article.*Gazette des Hopitaux* 68 (28 November): 1348–349.

—— (1904) Sur un arrête municipal pris par M. Morel de Villiers, médecin et maire de la commune de Villiers-le-Duc (Côte-d'Or). *Bulletin de l'Académie de Médecine* 51 (15 March): 222–36.

Planchon, Pierre, (1900) Resultats obtenus à la Consultation des Nourrissons de la Clinique Tarnier. *L'Obstetrique* 5 (January): 35–50.

Poore, G.V. (1901) Flies and the Science of Scavenging. *Lancet* 18 May: 1389–391.

Porak, Charles (1901) Rapport au nom de la Commission permanente de l'Hygiene de l'enfance, sur les memoires et travaux envoyés à cette Commission en 1901, and discussion following. *Bulletin de l'Académie de Médecine* 46 (10 December): 668–769.

——— (1902) Rapport au nom de la Commission permanente de l'Hygiene de l'enfance sur les memoires et travaux envoyés à cette Commission en 1902. *Bulletin de l'Académie de Médecine* 48: especially 756–97.

Powell, Richard Douglas (1899) Recent Advances in Practical Medicine. *BMJ* 5 August: 332–37.

Pritchard, Eric (1904) *The Physiological Feeding of Infants*. London: Henry Kimpton.

——— (1911) *Infant Education*. London: Henry Kimpton.

——— (1914) *The Infant: Nutrition and Management*. London: Edward Arnold.

Ransom, W.B. (1902) Should Milk Be Boiled? *BMJ* 22 February: 440–41.

Ransome, Arthur (1899) The Prospect of Abolishing Tuberculosis. *Public Health* January: 293–98.

Ravenel, Mazÿck (1901) The Comparative Virulence of the Tubercle Bacillus from Human and Bovine Sources. *Lancet* 10 and 17 August: 349–56, 443–48.

Ravenhill, Alice (1897) *The Health of the Community and How to Promote It*. London: Women's Co-operative Guild, Public Health Papers no. 1.

——— (1898) *How the Law Helps Healthy Homes*. London: Women's Co-operative Guild, The Housing of the People, no. 1.

——— (1908) *Some Characteristics and Requirements of Childhood*. Leeds: E.J. Arnold & Son.

——— and Schiff, Catherine (1910) *Household Administration*. London: Grant Richards.

Raw, Nathan (1903a) Human and Bovine Tuberculosis. *BMJ* 31 January: 247–48.

——— (1903b) Human and Bovine Tuberculosis. *BMJ* 14 March: 596–98.

——— (1903c) Discussion on Tuberculosis in Children: Its Relation to Bovine Tuberculosis. *BMJ* 29 August: 470–72.

——— (1904) Human and Bovine Tuberculosis. *BMJ* 8 October: 907–9.

Reeves, Maud Pember (1913/1982) *Round About a Pound a Week*. London: Virago Press (first published 1913 by G. Bell, London).

Reid, George (1908) Infantile Mortality and the Employment of Married Women in Factory Labour Before and After Confinement. *Lancet* 18 August: 423–24.

Richards, H. Meredith (1903a) The Factors which Determine the Local Incidence of Fatal Infantile Diarrhoea. *Journal of Hygiene* 3: 325–46.

——— (1903b) Some Observations in Regard to the Control of the Milk Trade. *Public Health* May: 457–63.

——— (1909) Co-ordination of Medical Inspection with Public Health Work. *Public Health* 22 (5), February: 166–69.

Riviere, Clive (1918) The Tuberculosis Threat in Infancy. *Maternity and Child Welfare* 2 (3), March: 101–3.

Robertson, John (1909) Prevention of Tuberculosis Among Cattle. *Public Health* 22 (9), June: 324–28.

Robertson, W. and Mair, W. (1904) On the Bacteriology of So-Called 'Sterilized Milk'.*BMJ* 14 May: 1122–125.

Robinson, Alfred (1908) The Trained Midwife and Her Effect on Infantile Mortality. *Public Health* 21 (1), March: 22–7.

——— (1909) The Trained Midwife; Her Effect upon Infantile Mortality. *Public Health* 22 (11), August: 422–25.

Robinson, Leonard (1905) Consultations for Infants in France. *Practitioner*

October: 479–88.

Ross, F.W. Forbes (1897) *Intestinal Intoxication of Infants*. London: Rebman.

Rotch, Thomas Morgan (1896) *Pediatrics: The Hygienic and Medical Treatment of Children*. Philadelphia: J.B. Lippincott (3rd edn, 1901; 5th edn, 1907).

—— (1902) A Discussion on the Modification of Milk in the Feeding of Infants. *BMJ* 6 September: 653–72.

—— (1903) Hygienic Requirements in the Milk Trade. *Public Health* May: 464–67.

de Rothschild, Henri (1900) *Dépopulation et protection de la première enfance*. Paris: Octave Doin, Editeur.

—— (1902) Hygiene de l'enfance: À propos du lait stérilisé. *Le Progrès Médical* 22 February: 113–16.

Rowntree, B. Seebohm (1901) *Poverty*. London: Macmillan.

—— and Kendall, May (1913) *How the Labourer Lives*. London: Nelson.

Russell, Alys (1906) The Ghent School for Mothers. *Nineteenth Century* December: 970–75.

Russell, C.E.B. (1903) National Physical Training: An Open Debate. *Manchester Guardian* 12 May: 12.

Saleeby, Caleb Williams (1904) *The Cycle of Life According to Modern Science*. London: Harper & Bros.

—— (1906) *Evolution the Master-key*. London: Harper & Bros.

—— (1909) *Parenthood and Race Culture*. London: Cassell.

—— (1914) *The Progress of Eugenics*. London: Cassell.

—— (1921) *The Eugenic Prospect: National and Racial*. London: T. Fischer Unwin.

Sandilands, J.E. (1906) Epidemic Diarrhoea and the Bacterial Content of Food. *Journal of Hygiene* January: 77–92.

—— (1910) The Communication of Diarrhoea. *Proceedings of the Royal Society of Medicine*. 3 (2), February: 95–130.

Savage, William G. (1912) *Milk and the Public Health*. London: Macmillan.

Schereschewsky, J.W. (1914) Heat and Infant Mortality. *Transactions* of the 4th Annual Meeting of the American Association for the Study and Prevention of Infant Mortality, Washington DC, 14–17 November 1913. Baltimore, MD: Franklin Printing Co., 99–132.

Scott, William (1906) The Medical Inspection of Schools. *BMJ* 22 September: 680–85.

Scurfield, Harold (1919) *Infant and Young Child Welfare*. London: Cassell.

Shaw, George Bernard (ed.) (1888) *Fabian Essays in Socialism*. London: Walter Scott.

—— (1900) *Fabianism and the Empire*. London: G. Richards.

Shee, George F. (1903) The Deterioration in the National Physique. *Nineteenth Century* 53 (May): 797–805.

Sherwell, Arthur (1891) *Life in West London: A Study and a Contrast*, Social Question of Today.

Shiga, K. (1898–99) Über den Erreger der Dysenterie in Japan. *Centralblatt für Backteriologie Parasitenkunde und Infektionskrankheiten* 24: 599–600, 817–28, 870–74, 913–18.

—— (1901) Studien über die epidemische Dysenterie in Japan, unter besonderer Berucksichtigung des Bacillus dysenteriae. *Deutsche Medizinische Wochenschrift* 27 (43): 741–43, 765–68, 783–86.

Sims, George R. (1889) *How the Poor Live and Horrible London*. London: Chatto & Windus.

—— (1907) *The Black Stain*. London: Jarrold & Sons.

Sladen, E. Sydney St B. (1901) Pasteurization of Infected Milk. *Lancet* 10 August: 368–70.

Smith, J. Lorrain and Tennant, J. (1902) On the Growth of Bacteria in the Intestine. *BMJ* 27 December: 1941–943.

Smyth, Aimée Watt (1904) *Physical Deterioration, its Causes and the Cure*. London: John Murray.

Spargo, John (1908) *The Common Sense of the Milk Question*. New York: Macmillan.

Spencer, Herbert (1885) *The Principles of Sociology* (3rd edn). London: Williams & Norgate.

—— (1893) *A Rejoinder to Professor Weismann*. London: Williams & Norgate.

—— (1894) *Weismannism Once More*. London: Williams & Norgate.

Stevenson, T.H. Craig (1909) The Administration of School Medical Inspection especially in County Areas. *Public Health* 22 (8), May: 282–95.

Still, George F. (1899) Observations on the Morbid Anatomy of Tuberculosis in Childhood. *BMJ* 19 August: 455–58.

—— (1901a) Tuberculosis in Childhood. *Practitioner* July: 91–103.

—— (1901b) Abdominal Tuberculosis in Children. *Clinical Journal* 19 (8), 11 December: 113–20.

—— (1905) On the Use and Abuse of Condensed Milk and Patent Foods on Infant-Feeding. *Practitioner*, October: 462–69.

Straus, Lina Gutherz (1917) *Disease in Milk, The Remedy Pasteurization (The Life Work of Nathan Straus)* (2nd edn). New York: E.P. Dutton.

Straus, Nathan (1905) Discussion on Infant Milk Depots (précis). *BMJ* 16 September: 644–47.

Strauss, Paul (1918) Puericulture in France. *American Journal of Diseases of Children* 16 (4), October: 207–11.

Stuart, Hackworth (1908) *The Doctor in the Schools*. London: H.K. Lewis.

Sutherland, G.A. (1905) Infantile Diarrhoea. *Practitioner* October: 501–9.

Swithinbank, Harold and Newman, George (1903) *The Bacteriology of Milk*. London: John Murray.

Sykes, John F.J. (1901) The Influence of the Dwelling upon Health. *BMJ* 2 March: 505–8; 9 March: 569–70; 16 March: 638–40.

Taylor, Jonathan (1884) Feeding the Children. *Justice* 13 September: 2; 6 December: 3

Taylor, J.W. (1904) The Diminishing Birth-Rate and What is Involved By It. *BMJ* 20 February: 427–28.

Thomas, C.J. (1908) The History and Practice of School Inspection. *Public Health* 21 (5), July: 189–93.

Thorne-Thorne, Richard (1898a) The Prevention of Tuberculosis. *BMJ* 5, 12 and 19 November: 1458–459, 1502, 1580.

—— (1898b) The Administrative Control of Tuberculosis. *Lancet* 12 and 26 November: 1288–290, 1411.

—— (1898c) The Administrative Control of Tuberculosis. *Public Health* December: 201–05.

Tidswell, Herbert H. (1903) Physical Degeneration in Children of the Working Classes. *BMJ* 15 August: 356–57.

Tomkins, Henry (1889) Report on an Inquiry into the Aetiology of Summer Diarrhoea. *BMJ* 27 July: 180–82.

Topley, William Whiteman Carlton and Wilson, Graham Selby (1929) *The Principles of Bacteriology and Immunity.* London: Edward Arnold (2nd edn, 1936; 3rd edn, 1946; 4th edn, 1955).

Trippel, H.F. (1903) National Physical Training: An Open Debate. *Manchester Guardian* 28 April: 12.

Tuckwell, Gertrude (1904) Trades Union Congress, 1904. *Commonwealth* 9 (October).

Tyson, W.J. (1904) Presidential Address to the Preventive Medicine Section of the BMA. *Journal of State Medicine* 12 (9), September: 525–35.

Variot, Gaston (1902) L'Élevage des enfants atrophiques par l'emploi methodique du lait stérilisé. *Revue Scientifique* (4th series) 17 (8), 22 February: 225–35.

———— (1903a) L'Avenir des Gouttes de Lait. *Archives de Médecine des Enfants* 6: 209–20.

———— and Chatard, Henri (1903b) Rapport sur la mortalité des enfants de un à quatorze ans en France. *Bulletin de l'Académie de Médecine* 50 (7 July): 13.

———— (1903c) La Goutte de Lait. *La Clinique Infantile* 1 (1), 1 November: 1–11.

———— (1904a) Gouttes de Lait et Consultations de Nourrissons. *BMJ* 14 May: 1125–126.

———— (1904b) Valeur nutritive du lait de vache sterilisé à 108° pour l'allaitement artificiel. *Comptes Rendus de l'Académie des Sciences* 139: 1002–003.

Vincent, Ralph (1904) *The Nutrition of the Infant* (2nd edn). London: Ballière Tindall & Cox.

———— (1906) The Milk Laboratory and its Relation to Medicine. *BMJ* 13 October: 937–38 and discussion, 938–39.

———— (1908) *Lectures on Babies.* London: Ballière Tindall & Cox.

Voelcker, A.F. (1907) Some Common Errors in the Diet and General Hygiene of Children. *BMJ* 26 January: 181–86.

Waldo, F.J. (1900) Summer Diarrhoea. *Lancet* 12 May: 1344–350; 19 May: 1426–430; 26 May: 1494–498.

Wallis, I. White (1899) Healthy Education for Brain and Body. *The Humanitarian* 14 (2), February: 101–04.

Warner, Francis (1898) *The Study of Children.* London: Macmillan.

Webb, Beatrice (1979) *My Apprenticeship.* Cambridge: Cambridge University Press (first published 1926).

———— (1948) *Our Partnership.* London: Longmans, Green & Co.

Webb, Sidney (1896) *The Difficulties of Individualism,* Fabian Tract no. 69. London: The Fabian Society.

———— (1899a) *Socialism: True and False,* Fabian Tract no. 51. London: The Fabian Society.

———— (1899b) *Labour in the Longest Reign* (2nd edn), Fabian Tract no. 75. London: The Fabian Society.

———— (1901) Lord Rosebery's Escape from Houndsditch. *Nineteenth Century and After* September: 366–86.

———— (1907) *The Decline in the Birth-Rate,* Fabian Tract no. 131. London: The Fabian Society.

———— (1908) The Necessary Basis of Society. *Contemporary Review* 93 (June): 658–68.

—— and Webb, Beatrice (1910) *The State and the Doctor*. London: Longmans Green & Co.

—— and Webb, Beatrice (1923) *The Decay of Capitalist Civilization* (3rd edn). London: George Allen & Unwin.

Weismann, August (1880–82) *Studies in the Theory of Descent*. London: Sampson Low.

Wells, H.G. (1906) Modern Socialism and the Family. *Independent Review* 11 (November): 165–73.

Wheatley, James (1923) Discussions on Factors Contributing to the Recent Decrease in Infantile Mortality. *BMJ* 27 October: 754–59.

Whetham, W.C.D. and Whetham, C.D. (1909) *The Family and the Nation*. London: Longmans.

—— (1912) *Heredity and Society*. London: Longmans.

White, Arnold (1900) Efficiency and Empire. *The Weekly Sun* 28 July: 5.

—— (1901) *Efficiency and Empire*. London: Methuen.

White, R.G. (1926) A Study of the Effect of Pasteurization on the Infectivity of the Milk of Tuberculous Cows. *Lancet* 30 January: 222–25.

Williams, C. Theodore (1901) A Discussion on the Treatment of Consumption by Climate. *BMJ* 27 July: 198–202.

Williams, Ernst Edwin (1896) *'Made in Germany'*. London: W. Heinemann.

Williams, R. Stenhouse, Muray, H. Leith, and Rundle, C. (1910) Further Researches into the Bacteriology of Epidemic Summer Diarrhoea. *Lancet* 3 September: 730–32.

Willoughby, Edward F. (1903) *Milk, Its Production and Uses*. London: Charles Griffin.

Wilson, J. Mitchell (1903) Regulations under the Dairies, Cowsheds, and Milk-Shops Orders. *Public Health* May: 441–56.

Winder, Phyllis (1913) *The Public Feeding of Elementary School Children*. Birmingham: University of Birmingham Studies in Social Economics.

Winfield, George (1918) Some Investigations Bearing on the Nutritive Value of Dried Milk. *Report to the Local Government Board on Public Health and Medical Subjects*, N.S. no. 116, Food Report no. 24. London: HMSO.

Woodhead, George Sims, (1888) Lectures on Tuberculosis and Tabes Mesenterica. *Lancet* 14 and 21 July: 51–4, 99–102.

—— (1894) The Channels of Infection in Tuberculosis. *Lancet* 27 October: 957–60.

—— (1899) Prevention of Tuberculosis. *Public Health* May: 579–82.

Wright, Almroth (1908) Discussion on the Causation and Treatment of Scurvy, Especially Infantile Scurvy. *BMJ* 31 October: 1365–366.

Yeo, Burney (1896) *Food in Health and Disease*. London: Cassell.

—— (1901) Introductory Address Mainly on the Classification of Cases. *BMJ* 27 July: 202–5.

Yoxall, J.H. (1903) National Physical Training: An Open Debate. *Manchester Guardian* 29 April: 10.

Secondary sources

Aldcroft, D.H. (ed.) (1968) *The Development of British Industry and Foreign Competition, 1875–1914*. London: George Allen & Unwin.

Allan, Peta and Jolley, Moya (eds) (1982) *Nursing, Midwifery and Health Visiting*

Since 1900. London: Faber & Faber.

Andrewes, F.W. (1930) *A System of Bacteriology in Relation to Medicine,* vol. 1. London: HMSO.

Ariès, Philippe (1962) *Centuries of Childhood* (translated by R. Baldwick). London: Cape.

Baldry, Peter (1976) *The Battle Against Bacteria: A Fresh Look.* Cambridge: Cambridge University Press (first published 1965).

Banks, J.A. (1954) *Prosperity and Parenthood.* London: Routledge & Kegan Paul.

—— and Banks, Olive (1964) *Feminism and Family Planning in Victorian England.* Liverpool: Liverpool University Press.

Beaver, M.W. (1973) Population, Infant Mortality and Milk. *Population Studies* 27: 243–54.

Behlmer, George Kinkel (1977) *The Child Protection Movement in England, 1860–1890.* PhD. thesis, Stanford University.

Bigger, Joseph W. (1941) *Man Against Microbe.* London: The Book Club.

Blacker, C.P. (1952) *Eugenics: Galton and After.* London: Duckworth.

Branca, Patricia (1975) *Silent Sisterhood: Middle-Class Women in the Victorian Home.* London: Croom Helm.

Brand, Jeanne L. (1965) *Doctors and the State: The British Medical Profession and Government Action in Public Health, 1870–1912.* Baltimore: Johns Hopkins Press.

Bruce, Maurice (1961) *The Coming of the Welfare State.* London: Batsford.

—— (ed) (1973) *The Rise of the Welfare State.* London: Weidenfield & Nicolson.

Bulloch, William (1938) *The History of Bacteriology.* London: Oxford University Press.

Chest and Heart Association (1927) *A History of the National Association for the Prevention of Consumption and Other Forms of Tuberculosis, 1898–1926.* The National Association for the Prevention of Tuberculosis.

Chorley, Katharine (1950) *Manchester Made Them.* London: Faber & Faber.

Clark, Frederick LeGros (1948) *The Social History of the School Meals Service.* London: National Council of Social Service.

Clark, G. Kitson (1962) *The Making of Victorian England.* London: Methuen.

Craig, William S. (1946) *Child and Adolescent Life in Health and Disease.* Edinburgh: E. & S. Livingstone.

Dangerfield, George (1961) *The Strange Death of Liberal England.* New York: Capricorn Books.

Davin, Anna (1978) Imperialism and the Cult of Motherhood. *History Workshop Journal* Spring: 9–65.

Dowling, Henry F. (1977) *Fighting Infection.* Cambridge, Mass. Harvard University Press.

Dowling, W.C. (1963) *The Ladies Sanitary Association and the Origins of the Health Visiting Services.* M.A. dissertation, London School of Economics.

Dyhouse, Carol (1979) Working-Class Mothers and Infant Mortality in England, 1895–1914. *Journal of Social History* 12: 248–67.

—— (1981) *Girls Growing Up in Late Victorian and Edwardian England.* London: Routledge & Kegan Paul.

Eberson, Frederick (1948) *Microbes Militant: A Challenge to Man.* New York: Ronald Press.

Enock, Arthur Guy (1943) *This Milk Business.* London: H.K. Lewis.

Ensor, R.C.K. (1963) *England, 1870–1914*. Oxford: Clarendon Press (first published 1936).

Evans, Eric J. (ed.) (1978) *Social Policy 1830–1914: Individualism, Collectivism, and the Origins of the Welfare State*. London: Routledge & Kegan Paul.

Foster, W.D. (1970) *A History of Medical Bacteriology and Immunology*. London: Heinemann Medical.

Fraser, Derek (1981) *The Evolution of the British Welfare State*. London: Macmillan.

Freeden, Michael (1978) *The New Liberalism: An Ideology of Social Reform*. Oxford: Clarendon Press.

Gilbert, Bentley B. (1954) Sir John Eldon Gorst and the Children of the Nation. *Bulletin of the History of Medicine* 28: 243–51.

——— (1965) Health and Politics: The British Physical Deterioration Report of 1904. *Bulletin of the History of Medicine* 39: 143–53.

——— (1966) *The Evolution of National Insurance in Great Britain*. London: Michael Joseph.

——— (1970) *British Social Policy 1914–1939*. London: Batsford.

Hall, Phoebe (1976) *Reforming the Welfare*. London: Heinemann.

Hay, J.R. (1978) *The Development of the British Welfare State, 1880–1975*. London: Edward Arnold.

Hirst, J.D. (1981) 'A Failure Without Parallel': The School Medical Service and the London County Council, 1907–1912. *Medical History:* 281–300.

Hobsbawm, Eric John (1968) *Industry and Empire, An Economic History of Britain Since 1750*. London: Weidenfeld & Nicolson.

Hollis, Patricia (1979) *Women in Public, 1850–1900: Documents of the Victorian Women's Movement*. London: George Allen & Unwin.

Honigsbaum, Frank (1970) *The Struggle for the Ministry of Health*. London: Bell.

——— (1971) *The Division in British Medicine*. London: Kogan Page.

Hughes, Molly V. (1934/1980) *A London Child of the 1870s*. Oxford: Oxford University Press (originally published 1934).

——— (1946/1980) *A London Girl of the 1880s*. Oxford: Oxford University Press (originally published 1946).

——— (1940/1980) *A London Family Between the Wars*. Oxford: Oxford University Press (originally published 1940).

——— (1946/1980) *A London Home in the 1890s*. Oxford: Oxford University Press (originally published 1946).

Jones, Gareth Stedman (1971) *Outcast London*. Oxford: Clarendon Press.

Keating, Peter (ed.) (1976) *Into Unknown England, 1866–1913: Selections from Social Explorers*. Manchester: Manchester University Press.

Kopeloff, Nicholas (1930) *Man versus Microbes*. New York: Knopf.

Lechevalier, Hubert A. and Solotorovsky, Morris (1965) *Three Centuries of Microbiology*. New York: McGraw-Hill.

Lewis, Jane (1980) *The Politics of Motherhood: Child and Maternal Welfare in England, 1900–1939*. London: Croom Helm.

Lomax, Elizabeth (1972) *Advances in Pediatrics and in Infant Care in Nineteenth Century England*. Ph.D. thesis, University of California, LA.

Lowndes, G.A.N. (1960) *Margaret McMillan*. London: Museum Press.

Lubove, Roy (ed.) (1966) *Social Welfare in Transition*. Pittsburgh: University of Pittsburgh Press.

MacKenzie, Donald (1976) Eugenics in Britain. *Social Studies of Science* 6: 499–532.

—— (1981) *Statistics in Britain 1865–1930.* Edinburgh: Edinburgh University Press.

MacKenzie, Jeanne and MacKenzie, Norman (1979) *The First Fabians.* London: Quartet.

McKeown, Thomas (1965) *Medicine in Modern Society.* London: George Allen & Unwin.

—— (1976) *The Modern Rise of Population.* London: Edward Arnold.

—— (1976) *The Role of Medicine: Dream, Mirage, or Nemesis?* London: Nuffield Provincial Hospitals Trust.

Mackintosh, J.M. (1953) *Trends of Opinion about the Public Health, 1901–51.* London: Oxford University Press.

McLachlan, Gordon and McKeown, Thomas (1971) *Medical History and Medical Care.* London: Oxford University Press.

MacLeod, Roy M. (1967) The Frustration of State Medicine: 1880–1899. *Medical History* 11: 15–40.

—— (1967) Resistance to Compulsory Health Legislation: 1870–1907. *Public Law.* 107–28, 189–211.

Mansbridge, Albert (1932) *Margaret McMillan.* London: Dent.

Matthew, H.C.G. (1973) *The Liberal Imperialists: The Ideas and Politics of a Post-Gladstonian Elite.* London: Oxford University Press.

Mazumdar, Pauline (1980) The Eugenists and the Residuum: The Problem of the Urban Poor. *Bulletin of the History of Medicine* 54: 204–15.

Meacham, Standish (1977) *A Life Apart: The English Working Class, 1890–1914.* London: Thames & Hudson.

Perkin, Harold (1981) *The Origins of Modern English Society: 1780–1880* (2nd edn). London: Routledge & Kegan Paul.

Pinchbeck, Ivy and Hewitt, Margaret (1973) *Children in English Society,* 2 volumes. London: Routledge & Kegan Paul.

Prochaska, F.K. (1980) *Women and Philanthropy in Nineteenth-Century England.* Oxford: Clarendon Press.

Ravenel, Mazÿck (1921) *A Half Century of Public Health.* New York: American Public Health Association.

Roach, John (1978) *Social Reform in England 1780–1880.* London: Batsford.

Roberts, Robert (1971) *The Classic Slum.* Manchester: Manchester University Press.

Robson, William A. (1976) *A Welfare State and Welfare Society.* London: George Allen & Unwin.

Rosenkrantz, Barbara Gutmann (1972) *Public Health and the State.* Cambridge Mass.: Harvard University Press.

—— (ed.) (1977) *The Health of Women and Children.* New York: Arno Press.

Searle, Geoffrey Russell (1971) *The Quest for National Efficiency: A Study in British Politics and Thought 1899–1914.* Oxford: Blackwell.

—— (1976) *Eugenics and Politics in Britain: 1900–1914.* Leyden: Noordhoff.

Semmel, B. (1960) *Imperialism and Social Reform: English Social Imperialist Thought 1895–1914.* London: George Allen & Unwin.

Slater, Gilbert (1930) *Poverty and the State.* London: Constable.

Smith, F.B. (1979) *The People's Health, 1830–1910.* London: Croom Helm.

Sussman, George D. (1975) The Wet-Nursing Business in Nineteenth-Century

France. *French Historical Studies* 9 (2), Autumn: 304–28.

Thane, Pat (ed) (1978) *The Origins of British Social Policy*. London: Croom Helm.

—— (1978) Women and the Poor Law in Victorian and Edwardian Britain. *History Workshop* 6 (Autumn): 29–51.

—— (1982) *Foundations of the Welfare State*. London: Longman.

Thompson, Paul (1977) *The Edwardians*. St Albans: Paladin.

Thompson, Thea (1981) *Edwardian Childhoods*. London: Routledge & Kegan Paul.

Titmuss, Richard M. (1976) *Essays on 'The Welfare State'* (3rd edn). London: George Allen & Unwin (first edition 1958).

Tyler, John Ecclesfield (1938) *The Struggle for Imperial Unity, 1868–1895*. London: Longman.

Walton, R.G. (1975) *Women in Social Work*. London: Routledge & Kegan Paul.

Whitbread, Nanette (1972) *The Evolution of the Nursery-Infant School*. London: Routledge & Kegan Paul.

Williams, J.H. Harley (1932) *A Century of Public Health in Britain, 1829–1929*. London: A. & C. Black.

Winter, J.M. (n.d.) Britain's 'Lost-Generation' of the First World War. *Population Studies* 31 (3): 449–66.

—— (1977) The Impact of the First World War on Civilian Health in Britain. *Economic History Review* 30 (August): 487–503.

Archives

The Ministry of Health and Board of Education files in the Public Record Office, London, contain a wealth of useful information. See, in particular, M.H. 48 and 55, ED 50 and, less useful, 56, 101, 123.

George Newman's unpublished six-volume diary is in the Department of Health and Social Security Library, London.

Eric Pritchard's papers are in the Wellcome Institute, Contemporary Medical Archives Centre, London.

The following journals were found to be of particular interest. Signed articles have been listed by author, but the editorials and news items not individually identified are equally important.

American Journal of Diseases of Children
British Journal of Children's Diseases
British Medical Journal
Bulletin de l'Académie de Médecine
La Clinique Infantile
The Contemporary Review
Journal of Hygiene
Journal of State Medicine
Lancet
Maternity and Child Welfare
The Nineteenth Century
The Practitioner
Public Health
Revue d'Hygiene et de Médecine Infantile

BIBLIOGRAPHY

Newspapers of note:

The Daily Chronicle
Manchester Guardian
The Pall Mall Gazette
The Times

Name index

Subject index

Note: Most references are to Britain unless otherwise stated